THE ECONOMY OF IRELAND

The Economy of Ireland

NINTH EDITION

National and Sectoral Policy Issues

Edited by

John O'Hagan

and

Carol Newman

GILL & MACMILLAN

Gill & Macmillan Ltd
Hume Avenue
Park West
Dublin 12
with associated companies throughout the world
www.gillmacmillan.ie

© Editors and Contributors 2005
7171 3840 2
Index compiled by Deirdre Daly and Tara McIndoe
Print origination by TypeIT, Dublin
Printed by ColourBooks Ltd, Dublin

The paper used in this book is made from the wood pulp of
managed forests. For every tree felled, at least one tree is
planted, thereby renewing natural resources.

**A catalogue record is available for this book from the British
Library.**

Contents

Section II
PERFORMANCE AND POLICY ISSUES AT A NATIONAL LEVEL

Preface

In the ten years since the last edition but one, the Irish economy has experienced dramatic changes: the concern over large-scale unemployment has shifted to one about serious labour shortages, long-term unemployment is down from over 9 per cent in 1994 to less than 2 per cent of the labour force today and there has been an explosion in the numbers employed. The emphasis now is not on emigration but on how to respond to immigration, especially potentially large-scale immigration of people with no ethnic connection to Ireland. The huge growth in employment was accompanied by high and continuing rates of growth in labour productivity, meaning that total income in Ireland grew at an extraordinary rate. Allied to the fact that an increasing proportion of the population were of working age, this has meant that average incomes per head have soared, turning Ireland into one of the highest income countries in the world. The evidence is clear for all to see: the huge increase in the number of cars and houses and major new infrastructural projects, especially road related, have transformed the physical landscape of Ireland in a way that would have been difficult to imagine even a decade ago. There is a confidence in the country, boosted by average incomes well above those in the UK, that is palpable. For the first time in centuries perhaps there is a new and very wealthy class of Irish people, living and wanting to live in Ireland.

There have also been dramatic changes in the policy environment and emphasis of economic decision-making. Ireland is now a region of the euro zone, with the euro replacing Irish notes and coins in January 2002. As such, there are no chapters in this book on monetary policy or on balance of payments and exchange rate policy in Ireland. The policy emphasis now is almost exclusively on the competitiveness of the EU region, 'Ireland Inc.', and this is reflected in many chapters throughout the book. Competitiveness is a key determinant of our attractiveness to foreign direct investment and here there has also been an extraordinary change. The scale of US investment has been such that Ireland might be viewed, in an industrial sense, as a region of the US economy, despite the fact that in a monetary sense the country is an integral part of the euro zone.

Despite the industrial connection with the USA and the monetary and political links with the euro zone, the relationship with the UK for Ireland is still very important, for a variety of reasons. While the nature of this relationship may have altered significantly its substance has remained the same. In terms of simple geography, Ireland is a small country, an island to the west of Britain, which in turn is a somewhat larger but much more densely populated island to the west of mainland Europe: its population is over 15 times that of Ireland. Ireland and the UK have a common labour market, a common language, and huge trade and tourism flows in both directions; by and large people in both jurisdictions watch the same TV programmes and follow similar key sports and cultural events. These are inescapable facts, which, as shall be seen throughout the book, are important to an understanding of the Irish economy, past and present. The links, economic and cultural, to continental Europe though are strengthening, something the use of the euro has facilitated. Irish people are now much more familiar than they were even 20 years ago with political developments in Europe, and with European sporting and cultural events.

The island of Ireland consists of two political units, the larger portion of which forms the Republic of Ireland and the smaller portion Northern Ireland, which is part of the UK. This too has had an impact on economic, social and political life in the Republic. This book is about the economy of the Republic of Ireland, and henceforth the terms economy of Ireland and Irish economy refer to this economy, unless otherwise stated. Some reference is made to the Northern Ireland economy, but since economic policy there is largely determined in London, it is difficult to devote much attention to policy issues there without also reviewing British economic policy in general.

This book has grown out of an earlier book, first published 30 years ago. The Irish Management Institute published the first six editions, Macmillan what in effect was the seventh edition and Gill & Macmillan the eighth and current editions. The broad structure and purpose of the book have remained the same over the years, but in terms of content there have been sweeping changes, even since the last edition. For example, Chapters 3, 5, 6, 7, 8 10 and 11 have new authors. Apart from updating, major changes have also been made to the remaining four chapters.

Part I of the book focuses on the broad policy framework for the Irish economy. Chapter 1 looks at policy objectives for Ireland, especially in the light of it being a region within the euro zone. The focus is on growth in living standards and employment, with a lengthy discussion on migration in this context. It also highlights the fact that growth in material living standards need not translate into growth in human welfare; longer working and commuting hours, environmental degradation and other factors such as crime levels all have a huge bearing on human welfare but are not included in our measures of material wellbeing (a topic also discussed in Chapter 5). The chapter also examines the policy objective of equality and its relationship to growth. Price stability is also discussed and even though achievement of this objective is largely determined at EU level, the chapter explains clearly why Ireland should strongly support such a policy. Stability, be it in terms of prices, personal security (absence of crime and political violence), employment (absence of undue fear of redundancy) and the provision of social safety nets (social welfare) all play a key role in the success of a modern, democratic market economy. The chapter concludes with a lengthy discussion of competitiveness, the key policy focus for any regional economy such as Ireland's in achieving its objectives, particularly that of adjusting to eurozone determined inflation levels.

Chapter 2 examines the rationale for government intervention in an economy, exploring both efficiency and distributional considerations, and highlights the fact that the government can intervene at different levels. The increasing importance of both local and international levels of government is outlined and the advantages and potential problems with coordinating policy at these levels highlighted. Of particular importance is the pooling of sovereignty at EU level meaning that government intervention in Ireland is increasingly influenced by EU events. The discussion then turns to an examination of public expenditure policy, the central policy instrument that national government uses to fulfil its objectives. Particular attention is placed on the role of the state in investment, given the major budget items that have appeared under this heading in Ireland in recent years. Also considered is the global decline in the role of state-owned enterprises and the rationale for the global shift toward privatisation (a topic also addressed in Chapter 8). The chapter concludes with a discussion of the issue of the 'correct' size of government and the reasons for fluctuation in its actual size, both economic and political, are considered in some detail.

Chapter 3 extends the discussion in Chapter 2. A part of the chapter is concerned with taxation, the means by which state intervention is funded. It looks at the structure of the Irish tax system and then examines some key policy issues in Irish taxation. As in many areas, the chapter highlights the constraints placed on tax policy arising from belonging to the single EU market. It also assesses the role of social partnership, an institutional arrangement to which some commentators attribute much of the economic success of the last ten years. An increasingly important channel through which the state intervenes in the economy is regulation and competition policy and this is also discussed in Chapter 3. Reform in this area in the last ten years has had a profound effect on the Irish economy and on the political, institutional and legal framework of economic policy. Microeconomic policy in this area has replaced macroeconomic and monetary policy as the key focus in Ireland. Again, many of the key initiatives in this area arise at an EU level. The topic is returned to in detail in Chapter 8.

Part II of the book has three chapters and assesses policy and performance at a national level, in terms of population and employment, living standards and distribution. Chapter 4 highlights the major success story of the last decade or so, the extraordinary rise in the numbers employed. The demographic background to this is examined, as is the nature of the employment growth. The changing net migration situation in Ireland is also given considerable attention. The chapter draws attention to the fact that there are different measures of unemployment. It then goes on to assess the issues involved in adapting to new technology and trade and the need for flexibility in the labour market, and how this is affected in terms of wage setting, hiring and firing rules, taxation measures, welfare payments and active labour market policies.

Chapter 5 addresses the policy objective of growth in output and living standards. Why some countries are rich and others poor is one of the most important questions in economics. The chapter first attempts to establish the nature of the success story of the 'Celtic Tiger'. What was the actual growth in output, incomes and incomes per head? How does this compare to the experience of other countries? What do the other less general indicators of improved living standards tell us, and so on? The chapter in particular provides a fascinating 'decomposition' of Ireland's growth in GDP: namely, measurement error in GDP, growth in employment and continuing high growth in labour productivity. It then goes on to explain the last-mentioned factor in some detail, using the Solow model. The real cause of the spurt in output though was the huge increase in employment and the author, like those for Chapter 4, considers a myriad of contributing factors in the chapter, all of which appear to have come together in the last 10 years or so. The chapter concludes with a sobering assessment of whether or not the surge in living standards can be maintained.

Chapter 6 addresses one of the major concerns associated with rapid economic growth, namely its effects on the quality of life, the distribution of income and wealth, and poverty. The chapter begins by analysing the extent of inequality on a global scale highlighting not only inequalities in income but also in other dimensions such as race and gender. Various perspectives on equality and its dimensions are then outlined and overlaps that exist highlighted. The remainder of the chapter focuses on inequality in terms of economic resources, with issues relating to income, wealth and poverty examined in detail. It appears that Ireland has a more unequal distribution of income than other EU and OECD countries; only the USA has clearly a more unequal distribution of income than in Ireland. The author carries out a similar analysis in relation to wealth distribution and poverty, in the latter case highlighting the increasing emphasis on non-monetary approaches to measuring deprivation. An extensive overview of policy and equality is also provided; while the evidence suggests that the benefits of economic growth over the last number of years in Ireland have been inequitably shared, many recent policy initiatives are viewed as welcome developments in the progression of equality objectives.

Part III of the book has three chapters and is devoted to examining policy issues at the level of the three main sectors of the economy, namely the traded manufacturing and services areas, the non-traded services sector and the agricultural sector. Chapter 7 looks at trade and foreign direct investment in both the manufacturing and services sector in Ireland. Of particular note is the exceptional scale of openness in the Irish case and the link between this and the growth in inward foreign direct investment over the last number of decades. The authors begin by considering how Ireland arrived at this position by providing the historical background, reviewing the four main phases to Ireland's trade and foreign investment strategy since Independence. Following this the performance of the manufacturing sector in the 1990s and early 2000s is examined in terms of output, employment, productivity, export patterns and foreign investment. Distinctions are made between various sub-sectors such as foreign versus domestic-owned plants, high versus low-technology sectors and US versus inward investment from other countries. The chapter then turns to a discussion of an increasingly important sector of the Irish economy, the internationally traded services sector, before concluding with an extensive discussion of the future challenges facing Irish policymakers in ensuring the continued success of these sectors of the economy.

Chapter 8 highlights the increased importance of microeconomic policymaking within Ireland and focuses on the role and mechanics of competition policy and regulation, with specific application to the non-traded services sector. The chapter begins with an overview of the services sector in Ireland in terms of value added and employment emphasising its growing importance, particularly in terms of the latter. The importance of domestic policymaking for the sector is also highlighted with emphasis given to competition and regulatory policy. The chapter provides a detailed outline of the economic and legal framework for the implementation of competition policy and applies this framework to the analysis of specific competition cases arising in the non-traded services sector in Ireland in the recent past. Building on the discussion outlined in Chapter 2, the author also addresses the issue of the regulation of natural monopolies and considers various alternatives to state ownership focussing on Irish examples. The chapter concludes with an outline of future issues relating to microeconomic policymaking, specifically highlighting its increased role at international levels of governance.

Chapter 9 looks at the agricultural sector and the related issues of rural development and food safety. The agri-food sector, which includes processing, still remains a significant player in the Irish economy, accounting in 2003 for 9 per cent of output and employment. With forestry, agriculture occupies 70 per cent of the land area of the country and thus has a significant impact on the physical environment; it also remains the most substantial contributor to the economic and social viability of rural areas. Agriculture is also a sector facing major policy changes at an EU level and the implications of this for the future viability of farming in Ireland and rural development initiatives are discussed fully in the chapter. The author also addresses the growing concern about food safety and regulatory measures in this area providing excellent practical examples of issues discussed in Chapter 3.

Part IV concludes the book by critically assessing two major sectors of government intervention discussed in Chapter 2, namely health (Chapter 10) and Education (Chapter 11). Unlike many other policy areas, the provision of education and health services is largely within the remit of the Irish government, and is hugely important in determining competitiveness, growth and social cohesion. A key problem that has dominated the provision of services in these areas has been the failure to properly assess value for money and as such the focus of both chapters is on ascertaining the effectiveness of the Irish government in delivering both an efficient and equitable service. Chapter 10 pays special attention to the issue of the financing of health services and provides a detailed overview of the role of private health insurance in Ireland and how it interacts with the public system of service provision. The chapter also includes a discussion of the factors causing public health expenditure to rise over time and, given the relatively poor performance of the Irish system by international standards, emphasises the need for the government to ensure that funds are spent efficiently, costs are contained and that equal access to the system is assured.

Chapter 11 looks at the role of education in the economy and identifies two key strands to education policy in Ireland; policies aimed at fuelling economic growth and policies aimed at ensuring equal access and opportunities within the system. While the Irish education system performs well by international standards in terms of levels of education participation and attainment it does not perform well in terms of achieving an equitable system which has implications for equality of outcomes in the wider distributional sense. Education policy in Ireland will continue to address this latter issue but will also focus on initiatives aimed a promoting competitiveness, a key determinant of future economic growth.

There are many people we would like to thank who have facilitated the publication of the ninth edition of this title. We would like to thank Hubert Mahony from Gill & Macmillan for taking the initiative in this book and Marion O'Brien and Regina Barrett for their role in bringing this book to publication. We would also especially like to thank our copy-editors Tara McIndoe and Deirdre Daly and commend them on their professionalism and commitment.

The book would not of course exist without the contributed chapters. As always, it was most enjoyable work liaising with each of the contributors, at each step of the process. In particular, it was rewarding seeing chapters take shape and mesh into the overall structure of the book following comments and suggestions. We very much appreciate the input and cooperation of each and every contributor.

We would also like to thank the many lecturers and students who have used this book over the years. This has made the book both financially viable, despite the small size of the potential market, and a very satisfying experience for us. The book is also read widely outside academia and indeed these shores and we hope that this will continue to be the case.

Thirty years on with the book, and 35 years since the first of the undersigned presented the course of the same name for the first time in Trinity College, the second of the undersigned has for the past three years given all of this course. It is too interesting a course for the former to relinquish it completely when his College Bursarship job ends later in the year, but the same applies to the latter as well! So, hopefully like the new edition of the book the course will also be shared. It is the type of course that students seem to enjoy immensely and we are sure lecturers in other colleges have found this to be the case also. It does after all deal with the political economy of one of the most interesting case studies in recent decades in world economics.

John O'Hagan and Carol Newman
Trinity College Dublin
October 2004

Contributors

Chapter 1

Dermot McAleese has a B.Comm. and M.Econ.Sc. from the National University of Ireland (University College Dublin), and an M.A. and Ph.D. from The Johns Hopkins University. He is Professor Emeritus of Economics, University of Dublin (Trinity College).

Chapter 2

Philip Lane has a B.A. (Mod.) from the University of Dublin (Trinity College), and an M.A. and Ph.D. from Harvard University. His current position is Professor in International Macroeconomics and Director of the Institute for International Integration Studies CIIIS, University of Dublin (Trinity College). He is also a Research Fellow, Centre for Economic Policy Research, London.

Chapter 3

Kevin Carey has a B.A. (Mod.) from the University of Dublin (Trinity College), and a Ph.D. from Princeton University. His current position is Consultant Economist for the World Bank Institute in Washington, D.C.

Chapter 4

John O'Hagan has a B.E., B.A. and M.A. from the National University of Ireland (University College Dublin), and a Ph.D. from the University of Dublin (Trinity College). His current position is Associate Professor of Economics, and Bursar, University of Dublin (Trinity College).

Tara McIndoe is a Scholar at the University of Dublin (Trinity College). She is currently completing the final year of her B.A. (Mod.) in economics.

Chapter 5

Jonathan Haughton has a B.A. (Mod.) from the University of Dublin (Trinity College), and a Ph.D. from Harvard University. He is currently Associate Professor of Economics at Suffolk University, Boston, and Senior Economist at the Beacon Hill Institute for Public Policy.

Chapter 6

Sara Cantillon has a B.A. (Mod.) from the University of Dublin (Trinity College) and an M.Sc. from the National University of Ireland (University College Dublin). Her current position is Senior Lecturer in the Equality Studies Centre, National University of Ireland (University College Dublin).

Chapter 7

Frances Ruane has a B.A. and M.A. from the National University of Ireland (University College Dublin) and a B.Phil. and D.Phil. from the University of Oxford (Nuffield College). Her current position is Associate Professor in Economics and Chairperson of the Policy Institute, University of Dublin (Trinity College).

Ali Uğur has a B.Sc. from the Middle East Technical University, Ankara, Turkey and a Ph.D. from the University of Dublin (Trinity College). His current position is Economist in the Competitiveness and Innovation Division, Forfás, Dublin.

Chapter 8

Francis O'Toole has a B.A. (Mod.) from the University of Dublin (Trinity College), an M.Mangt.Sc. from the National University of Ireland (University College Dublin), and an M.A. and Ph.D. from Georgetown University. His current position is Lecturer in Economics, University of Dublin (Trinity College).

Chapter 9

Alan Matthews has a B.A. (Mod.) from the University of Dublin (Trinity College), and an M.S. from Cornell University. His current position is Associate Professor of Economics and Jean Monet Professor of European Agricultural Policy, University of Dublin (Trinity College).

Chapter 10

Anne Nolan has a B.A. (Mod.) and a Ph.D. from the University of Dublin (Trinity College). Her current position is Postdoctoral Research Fellow, Economic and Social Research Institute, Dublin.

Chapter 11

Carol Newman has a B.A. (Mod.) and Ph.D. from the University of Dublin (Trinity College). Her current position is Lecturer in Economics, University of Dublin (Trinity College).

SECTION I

POLICY FRAMEWORK AND IMPLEMENTATION

CHAPTER 1

Policy Objectives and Competitiveness for a Regional Economy

Dermot McAleese*

1 INTRODUCTION

The primary policy objectives of a regional economy and a national economy are very similar. Both are concerned with achieving higher living standards, a fair distribution of income, full employment and decent environmental standards. Likewise, the secondary policy objectives, meaning by this the means to achieving the primary objectives, are broadly similar. Regions and nations both want price stability. Both worry about competitiveness. And the balance of payments has implications for both the region and the nation state, though as we shall see these implications are far more transparent in the case of a nation.

The main difference between a region and a nation is *the policy context*. A region has no independent currency and no control over its monetary policy. Its trade policy is determined by outside forces and balance of payments issues have to be radically reinterpreted. It has limited discretion in the use of fiscal policy. Seen in this context, a region's approach to policy has a dual dimension. First, it has to consider how to use its limited influence on policy developments where key policy decisions are being made. In the case of the Republic of Ireland, this might be Brussels, Frankfurt or Strasbourg depending on the issue being decided; in Northern Ireland, London would figure prominently. Second, in areas where they do possess policy autonomy, regions must ensure that this degree of policy discretion is used effectively.

As Ireland becomes increasingly integrated into the European economy, the Republic is losing many of the trappings of a national economy. The completion of the single market and the establishment of economic and monetary union constitute important turning points in this respect. Hence the focus in this chapter is on the policy objectives from the perspective of a regional economy. This perspective is of special interest at present because the Irish Republic is a comparative newcomer to regional status, unlike say Northern Ireland or Scotland, and it has had to acclimatise itself rapidly to the economic limitations of regional dependence. At the same time, as a nation state, the Republic can exert more power and influence at the centre of European policymaking than many European regions of much larger size. Its approach to policy objectives has no doubt also been affected by the coincidence between the adoption of a regional economy mantle and the Celtic Tiger surge in economic growth. Thus, the Republic's policy perspectives, and to some extent its policy priorities, differ from those of European regions that have had no recent experience of political independence or booming economic conditions.

The plan of this chapter is as follows. In Section 2 we explain why growth is regarded as the primary objective of economic policy and how it is related to employment. In Section 3 the limitations of this objective are analysed by taking account of leisure and the environment. The goal of equity is considered in Section 4. In Section 5 we discuss price stability and general security as objectives of policy. Competitiveness is discussed in Section 6; the search for ways of maintaining competitiveness has become the leitmotif of economic policy in recent years. Section 7 concludes the chapter.

2 GROWTH AND EMPLOYMENT

Introduction

Rapid, sustained growth is a primary objective of economic policy. Fast economic growth means higher living standards, and is associated with an expanding and dynamic business environment. Slow or zero growth is perceived as stagnation. Confronted with the record of a slow growing economy, we instinctively ask what has gone wrong. Policymakers are always on the lookout for advice about ways of promoting economic growth. An advance in living standards is something that most people want, enjoy and expect to be delivered.

Economic growth is desired for many different reasons. Affluent countries see growth as an essential contributor to ever higher living standards, full employment and healthy government finances. They also perceive faster growth as a way of maintaining their economic and military position relative to other countries. Not long ago, Americans worried about being overtaken by the Japanese; and the Japanese in turn worry about their economic standing relative to China. By contrast, governments of developing countries see faster economic growth as a means of escaping from poverty and material want, and in particular from the vulnerability and sense of inferiority that, rightly or wrongly, attaches to low economic development. For them, 'catching up' on the living standards of the affluent countries is a key policy imperative. All countries appear to view growth as an indicator that resources are being employed efficiently, and faster growing economies are often taken as models for slower growing economies to copy and learn from.

Growth and Efficiency

Economics generally endorses the idea that efficiency and growth are related. Most fast growing economies are efficient, and most efficient economies tend to grow faster than economies of similar size and scale that are inefficient. The meaning of efficiency and growth in an economic sense is illustrated in Figure 1.1.

Imagine an economy that produces only two goods, X and Y. We set up a list of combinations of X and Y that the economy could produce if its resources were utilised in the most efficient way. In other words, for any given level of X, we find out the maximum amount of Y that can be produced in the economy. The various combinations of X and Y derived in this way are known as the *production frontier*. The production frontier is TT in Figure 1.1.

Figure 1.1

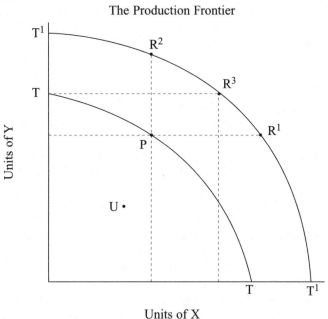

The Production Frontier

Units of X

Provided production takes place on the production frontier, where resources are fully employed, more of good X implies less of good Y. In other words, in order to produce more of X, scarce resources have to be transferred from industry Y to industry X. One can go further and define the cost of X as the amount of Y that has to be sacrificed in order to produce one extra unit of X. This is called *the opportunity cost* of X. The opportunity cost concept has many practical applications and serves as a reminder of the obvious point that 'free' education, or 'free' transport and other 'free' goods offered by the state are not costless. The resources used to supply these services could have been used to produce automobiles or holidays instead. Hence the well known maxim: in economics there is no such thing as a free lunch.

An *efficient* economy is one that operates on its production frontier (i.e. at a point such as P in Figure 1.1). At any point below the production frontier, society could have more of X and Y simply by moving to the frontier. By definition, this would not be an efficient outcome. Thus point U is not an efficient outcome. At that point, some productive resources are being either used inefficiently, or worse, not being used at all. If they were mobilised, a point P could be attained which is obviously superior. In addition to *productive* efficiency as above, one must have *allocative* efficiency. This means that the goods and services produced on the frontier represented by points such as P must be distributed between consumers in an efficient manner. Allocative efficiency is achieved when there is no feasible redistribution of the fixed bundle of goods P such that one person is better off without leaving anyone else worse off. At that stage, an economy is said to have achieved Pareto efficiency. Hence efficiency is certainly an important objective of economic policy.

Why Growth is Important

Over time, however, growth will be the main force in determining living standards. A GNP growth rate of 7 per cent maintained for ten years will result in a doubling of the original GNP level. Even a more modest 4 per cent growth rate will translate into a doubling of living standards every 17 years. Figures such as this indicate the potential gains from raising the growth rate. In terms of Figure 1.1 outward shifts in the production frontier will over time dominate the effects of movement to a given frontier from off frontier points, such as U. However, since countries that are efficient normally grow faster than those that are inefficient, the objectives of efficiency and growth are in practice complementary.

To illustrate the benefits of growth, we can depict it as a series of outward shifts in the production frontier, such as that represented by the move from TT to T^1T^1. The T^1T^1 frontier shows the expanded range of options growth provides to society. Economic growth is a 'good thing', in so far as it enables the consumers in the economy to enjoy:

- More of X and the same amount of Y – at a point such as R^1;
- More of Y and the same amount of X – at a point such as R^2;
- More of both X and Y – at a point like R^3;
- Any other desired combination of X and Y – on the expanded frontier.

Growth extends the range of consumption possibilities, and people choose between these different possibilities through the market system, supplemented by government intervention.

The production frontier can be shifted outwards by two forces: first, increases in the *quantity* of productive factors and, second, improvements in the *productivity* of these factors. Since we are primarily concerned with growth per person rather than total growth, it is common to abstract from the increase in growth that is attributable solely to the increase in the population. Growth in living standards, or GNP per person, depends on:

5

- The *amount* of productive factors at each person's disposal (the more machinery and the more hectares of land at the disposal of an employee the more will be produced per employee).
- The *productivity* of these factors of production (better machinery, better seeds and fertilisers and better technology improved productivity).
- The knowledge, skills and motivation of the workforce (see Chapter 5).

Growth and Full Employment

Full employment means that there is work available for everyone willing to seek it at prevailing pay levels. This is obviously a desirable objective of economic policy. There is a strong empirical association between full employment and economic growth and this explains why one of the major perceived benefits of faster growth is that it provides more job opportunities and reduces the unemployment rate.

Yet in strict logic there is no reason why growth should be a necessary condition for full employment. To see this, go back to Figure 1.1. Assume a situation where TT is given (i.e. zero growth). At point U, there is unemployment. As noted above, this is an inefficient point, indicating waste of resources. The solution is to implement policies such as greater labour market flexibility that address the unemployment problem. As more people are employed, we move towards a point like P on the production frontier TT.

The necessary policies might take any of the forms outlined in Chapter 4. Hence full employment can be regarded as an indicator of efficiency. In moving from U to P, there will be an increase in output and therefore some faster economic growth will be recorded. But once attained, there is no reason why full employment should not be maintained at P. Faster growth at that stage makes no difference one way or another. Hence the 'classical' conclusion: *full employment is always attainable irrespective of the level of output or of the growth of output.*

Yet intuition and empirical fact suggest that full employment is easier to attain when an economy is growing. Also when growth declines, unemployment rises. For example, Korea, long used to near zero unemployment rates, found itself facing unemployment of an unprecedented 7 per cent following the 1997-98 currency crisis. There are three main explanations why growth is positively correlated with employment. One reason is that labour productivity is increasing due to advances in technology and annual increases in efficiency. Historically the rate has been around 2 per cent per annum. If there is no growth, the implication is that fewer people could produce the same output and unemployment could result. A second reason is that pay tends to be inflexible downwards. Third, as tastes change and productivity rates vary, there is constant need for reallocation of the labour force between sectors. Such reallocation runs much more smoothly when an economy is growing than when it is static. This explains why growth is desired not just for its own sake but for the indirect benefits it provides such as helping to keep unemployment low.

Growth of GNP per Person as a Policy Objective

The focus on income per person rather than total income (GNP) as the policy objective has profoundly important implications. Suppose one had to choose between three growth profiles as follows:

Table 1.1

Growth: Illustrative Example

Growth Profile	Total GNP (%)	Population (%)	GNP per person (%)
A	5	3	2
B	4	2	2
C	3	0	3

Total GNP is increasing fastest in situation A. If total GNP were the policy objective, A would be the preferred situation. If GNP per person were the policy objective, situation C would be chosen. Ranking A and B would be more difficult. The only difference between them is that there are more people around to share a given GNP per person growth rate in A. Suppose these additional people happened to be immigrants from Africa. The economy's faster growth means that they can be accommodated without impairing average living standards of the existing population; while at the same time the immigrants' living standards are much higher in the host country than they were at home. This would suggest a preference for A over B. But there may be other effects to consider, relating to the broader social impact of immigration and effects on income distribution. An influx of unskilled immigrants, for instance, would tend to reduce earnings of native unskilled workers, but would tend to benefit the middle and upper class generally by reducing the cost of unskilled labour that these more affluent people employ (domestic help, catering staff, gardeners and so on). Clearly personal values and one's position in the income distribution ranking influence preferences between the various growth and population combinations.

In the above example, population growth is treated as if it were independent of GNP growth. A crucial question is whether and how population growth interacts with GNP and the consequential effect on living standards per person. Take, for example, a country such as Nigeria with an annual population growth of 3 per cent. Output growth of 3 per cent is needed simply to prevent living standards from falling. Many argue that population growth at that rate has a negative effect on total GNP growth and hence can depress income per person. An expanding population of young people and large family size reduces national saving and consequently limits the volume of investment. Simultaneously, a burgeoning population puts pressure on a country's natural resources. If the rate of population growth interacts negatively with GNP per person, a vicious circle of economic decline can be generated. At the other end of the spectrum, excessively low population growth can be equally problematic. The 'greying' of Europe's population for instance has led to concerns about the financial viability of pension schemes, escalating medical costs and an erosion of social dynamism and innovation. This line of reasoning reinforces the case for GNP per person, not total GNP, as the primary policy objective.

Just as affluent households tend to have smaller families than poor households, so developed countries have lower population growth than poor countries. Figures for population growth since 1980 show that higher income countries had population growth of 0.6 per cent per annum, while low income populations have been increasing by 2 per cent annually. Ireland too has experienced the same phenomenon; as Chapter 4 will show, with increasing prosperity its birth rate has declined. But have we become better off because of low birth rate, or is the birth rate low because we are more affluent? There is no definitive answer to this question, but many governments now believe that lower population growth would help to raise living standards and have introduced strong family planning programmes to encourage smaller family size. Irish governments have never gone as far in this direction as governments in developing countries such as India and China. One reason for this is that Irish people, unlike many in the present developing world, had the option of emigration.

Migration and Growth

The impact of emigration on living standards has for long been a controversial topic. Some argued that increased population would have raised living standards in Ireland. Patrick Pearse believed that the country could support a population of 30 million. With greater population would go larger domestic markets, greater economies of scale, higher productivity and, eventually, more growth. Higher living standards and a more dynamic local community would in turn induce skilled and talented Irish people to stay at home, thus reinforcing faster growth. This is a rather rosy view of what might have happened to living standards in the absence of emigration. Demographers, however, agree that if there had been no emigration since 1841, the population in the Republic would be in the region of 20 million instead of 4 million.[1] Some argued that a growing population was a good thing in itself, irrespective of its effects on material welfare. The Commission on Emigration, for example, endorsed the principle that 'a steadily increasing population should occupy a high place among the criteria by which the success of national policy should be judged'.[2]

An opposite viewpoint was that emigration acted as a welcome safety valve, enabling the amount of land and capital per person remaining in Ireland to be increased, with beneficial effects on Irish productivity. At the same time Irish emigrants would be able to find more productive employment abroad. A win-win outcome for all parties, just as predicted in John Kenneth Galbraith's famous dictum that 'emigration helps those who leave, the country they go to, and the people they leave behind'.[3] Underlying this approach was the idea that the primary focus of economic policy should be living standards of the Irish people wherever they happened to live, not just of those residing in the Irish state. Thus the policy objective should be to encourage Irish people to go to where their productivity was highest and their material rewards greatest. According to this logic, Ireland's access to the comparatively prosperous labour markets of the USA, the UK, Australia and Canada was a tremendous boon. The state's responsibility was to provide education to its citizens and equip them to adapt to and make maximum use of the opportunities open to them at home and abroad.

Which of these differing perspectives is 'correct'? Research on this question remains inconclusive. A comprehensive NESC study came to the torturous conclusion that emigration cannot be shown to have impaired the long run growth in living standards of those remaining in Ireland.[4] Recent developments have changed the focus of interest to the effects of immigration rather than emigration. Irish people continue to go abroad for work; but for the first time in centuries a lot more foreigners come each year to work in Ireland. At a broad level, this change in demographic pattern has been benign. Higher growth in GDP during the past decade has involved both significant net immigration *and* an improvement in living standards. At one level this positive correlation between total GDP growth and growth in GDP per person suggests that in Ireland's case opting for growth in GDP per person as the primary policy objective need cause no special angst.[5] At a broader societal level, however, immigration brings special problems. The burden of adjustment to unskilled immigration falls heavily on lower income groups in the host country population and it is unwise to ignore this (see later).

Optimal Growth, not Maximum Growth
While growth is a primary policy objective, it does not follow that the aim is simply to *maximise* growth. One reason for this is that growth involves a degree of intergenerational distribution. By cutting down on its consumption and investing more, any present generation can raise economic growth rates. Japan's average investment/GNP ratio during the period 1960-95 exceeded the investment ratio in the European Union and the United States by more than 10 percentage points (31 per cent as against 22 per cent and 18 per cent respectively). Not surprisingly, Japan's growth rate of 6 per cent per year was twice the rate of most industrial countries. Within Europe, the faster growing countries, such as Spain, Italy and Germany, invested more than the slower growing countries, such as Britain. By investing so much, the early post-War generation sacrificed its material welfare in the interests of future generations. But how far to go in sacrificing this generation's living standards in order to improve that of future generations? Clearly different societies place different premia on the future relative to present living standards and, by extension, to the welfare of future over present generations. Dictatorial societies like the Soviet Union under Stalin were able to record extraordinarily rapid growth, but at terrible cost to the people that had to produce the necessary saving.

Another reason for not choosing maximum growth as a policy objective relates to its undesirable spillover effects. These have become apparent in the early 2000s in Ireland. One such effect is traffic congestion. Few countries growing at a sustained rate of 7 per cent could hope to avoid this, unless the authorities are prepared to impose, and enforce, the draconian restrictions on the use of cars in urban areas that are found in cities such as Singapore. Another spillover effect is the inflow of job seekers from abroad. In the initial stages, a decline in emigration is observed and this is widely welcomed. Next comes immigration as former emigrants return to a buoyant domestic market. These immigrants help to sustain the boom by moderating pay growth and plugging vital gaps in labour supply. Generally there is no problem with immigrants of similar nationality and background to the host country. Difficulties arise, however, when unskilled immigrants of more diverse background enter the picture. Also there are income distribution effects to consider. Middle and upper income groups gain from the entry of the unskilled into the host country workforce, but those at the lower end of the income profile can easily lose out. Finally, rapid growth and escalating property prices are inseparable bedfellows. Such asset price inflation can cause much unease. Investors in property benefit, while those outside this 'charmed' circle miss out. Note that the latter do not lose absolutely, only in relative terms. Also, the charmed circle in a country such as Ireland can be quite inclusive; almost 80 per cent of households own their own home and thus gain from the rise in house prices. As in other areas of economic life, the gainers tend to make less of a fuss than the losers.

One important, intangible benefit of growth is the influence and power that it brings with it. We can learn from the growing dominance of the USA in the world economy how economic success and political and military power are closely linked. Economic growth during the past decade has dramatically shifted the balance of economic power within Ireland from the North (once the most prosperous industrial region of the island) to the Republic. There is a palpable air of self confidence and a virtual disappearance of the grievance mentality that blighted the country in the past.

All these advantages and disadvantages must be weighed in determining a country's optimum growth rate. Choosing an optimum growth path requires careful consideration of the broader sociopolitical factors mentioned above, as well as of the limitations of GNP as an indicator of welfare, a subject to which we turn next.

3 GROWTH AND HUMAN WELFARE

So far we have discussed economic growth as if growth, as measured by GNP in the numerator, were the sole objective of economic policy. Growth is taken to be desirable because it enlarges the range of consumption possibilities available to society. But it is well known that growth is an inadequate indicator of human welfare. As one critic expressed it:

> The Gross National Product does not allow for the health of our children, the quality of their education or the joy of their play. It does not include the beauty of our poetry or the strength of our marriages; the intelligence of our public

debate or the integrity of our public officials. It measures neither our wisdom nor our learning neither our compassion nor our devotion to our country; it measures everything, in short, except that which makes life worthwhile.[6]

There is no evidence that people in countries with high GNP are 'happier' or spiritually better off than those in poorer countries. GNP does not account for many of the things that make for the good life and some items are included in GNP that may worsen rather than improve human welfare. Four specific criticisms of GNP have been made on this account. First, that it puts no value on leisure and the household economy. Second, that it ignores income distribution (discussed in section 4). Third, that it takes no account of resource depletion and degradation of the environment. Fourth, that some items are recorded outputs although in reality they are inputs.

Leisure and the Household Economy
Leisure is a good like any other, so theoretically it should be included alongside other goods and services when choosing growth as a policy objective. The difficulty arises because of the way growth is measured. For various reasons, changes in leisure hours are not taken account of in the GNP statistic. Hence if GNP growth is rising but everyone is working harder and longer hours, the net improvement in human welfare may well be much lower than appears. The average American works 1,815 hours per year; the average German works 1,444 hours per year. Americans have more goods and more GNP per head, but they have miserably short vacations.

There are various manifestations of this problem. A feature of rich societies is that employees are well paid. They are well paid because they are productive and that in turn means that the opportunity cost of leisure increases as economies become more prosperous. Hence the widely observed phenomenon: people in affluent societies tend to be more harried and harassed, have less time for talk and a chat than their counterparts in poorer countries. The process of economic growth inherently tends to accentuate this problem.

To take another example, suppose that a person takes a second job. This makes large inroads into leisure time. The GNP measure includes all the output generated but ignores the welfare cost of the loss of leisure. Human welfare has presumably increased as a result of this decision – otherwise the second job would not have been taken – but the net increase in welfare will be much less than the increase in GNP indicates. The individual is likely to be more harassed and to have less time for the family.

GNP includes only transactions that involve a monetary exchange. Hence leisure is excluded. But this is not the only excluded output. Housework done by members of a household, being unpaid, is not recorded in GNP. As members of the household enter the workforce and household tasks such as repair, maintenance, care of children, are passed over to paid professionals, GNP rises. Yet all that is happening is that these functions have been shifted from the traditional realm of the household and the community to the monetised economy. Welfare has presumably increased, since the decision to work outside the home was taken voluntarily. But the increase in GNP will grossly exaggerate the increase in welfare. These examples help to explain why economic growth will bring fewer real benefits than appears.

Growth and the Environment

Conventional GNP measures do not deal satisfactorily with environmental and ecological factors. Higher GNP has implications for the environment on several levels that fail to be recorded in the statistics. Two aspects, in particular, merit attention: (1) higher levels of pollution, and (2) depletion of natural resources. Regarding the first point, higher levels of pollution can arise because higher levels of production imply more waste, including carbon emissions and other chemical waste. The adverse effect of these pollutants on welfare is not taken account of in the GNP figures.

Second, the depletion of non-renewable resources such as oil and coal is not accounted for in GNP calculations. Problems can also arise in the case of renewable resources, such as rain forests and fishery stocks, if they are being exploited in excess of the replacement rate. Other examples include soil erosion in subSaharan Africa and the decline in welfare caused by pollution of the water supply.

Inputs Recorded as Outputs

By a perverse quirk, the cost of moderating the adverse effects of pollution is sometimes included in GNP as an output (service provided) instead of as an input (a production cost to society). For example, the medical attention given to a victim of radiation will be recorded in the national accounts as addition to GNP instead of as a negative input occasioned by the damage of radiation. This is part of a more general criticism of GNP relating to inputs misclassified as outputs. For example, military spending is included as a positive contributor to GNP, even if that spending is undertaken at the behest of imprudent political leaders and with disregard of the needs of the people. Likewise the inclusion of expenditure on crime prevention as an output in GNP has been criticised. To be sure, such spending could represent improved living standards in so far as the community obtains greater security and more orderly traffic. But it could equally be a sign of diminished quality of the social environment and hence a cost of securing higher GNP (e.g. if more police were needed to maintain the same level of security and traffic movement).

GNP and Human Development Indicators

Making GNP growth a primary objective is really short hand for something much more complex. In evaluating a country's growth record, account must be taken of the quality of the lifestyle enjoyed by the population. We need to measure the quality as well as the quantity of economic growth. Imagine two countries. One has a lower GNP per person than the other, but it happens to have a healthier, more literate and less crime ridden society. In this instance, GNP is an inaccurate measure of the relative welfare of the two countries, and making GNP growth a primary policy objective may not be an appropriate response. Instead of economic growth, can we find a way of measuring human development and making it the primary policy objective?

In an effort to develop a more comprehensive socioeconomic measure than GNP, the United Nations has developed the Human Development Index (HDI). The HDI is a composite index and consists of a weighted average of data on GNP per person, income distribution, life expectancy and educational attainment of the population.

As one would expect, such exercises lead to some changes in ranking. The 2004 figures, for example, indicate a HDI ranking much higher than the GDP per person ranking for Sweden, Portugal, Greece and the UK; the opposite is the case for the USA, Singapore and South Africa.[7] Ireland is placed tenth of 177 countries in the HDI league, but it comes third in the GDP ranking (for well known reasons, GDP exaggerates Ireland's welfare). By adding to the list of indicators, and measuring them in different ways, more radical alterations in ranking can be computed. Further experimentation and analysis along these lines is continuing.

Yet, the limitations of GNP as a measure of welfare must not be exaggerated. For all its defects, a higher output per person gives society the *capacity* to achieve a better quality of life. This explains the close positive correlation between the HDI and GDP per person. Also there is a strong positive correlation between GNP growth and some important empirical measures of the quality of life. Countries with higher GNP tend to be healthier and better educated than those with lower GNP. They also tend to be better policed and are more secure in a financial and physical sense. London is safer than Lima, Manila or Sao Paolo. Affluent Tokyo is one of the safest cities in the world. While many forms of recorded crime have increased since 1945, prosperity has tended to result in a reduction in crime and disorder. During the nineteenth century, industrial nations became less crime ridden as they became more industrialised. Indeed, as pointed out in Chapter 2, these two factors are interrelated: the rule of law and good governance are essential prerequisites of a prosperous market economy.

Faster growth makes it easier to reduce unemployment, to lessen poverty, to improve education and health services and to provide all the other good things that constitute prosperity. There are, of course, negative aspects of growth, such as damage to the environment, erosion of community life, and destruction of rural values. Since the birth of the Industrial Revolution in the late eighteenth century, economic growth has had its critics, some of the most trenchant of whom have been economists. The tradition of scepticism, verging on hostility, towards growth remains active to this day.[8] Despite these downsides, governments and those who elect them evidently believe that the positive effects of growth outweigh its negative effects, and both continue to accord it a high priority.

4 EQUITY AND INCOME DISTRIBUTION

Policy Debate

GNP per person, being an arithmetic average of total output divided by total population, reveals no information about the distribution of resources within a society. It could rise, even though the majority of the population may be getting worse off. For example, if the income of the most affluent one third of a population rose by a total €50 billion, and the income of the poorest two thirds fell by a total €30 billion, GNP would increase. But does it follow that society as whole is better off?

Some argue that the long run sustainability of growth depends on income being shared on an equitable basis. Successful policymaking requires change, and such change can only be achieved if the majority of people believe that they have a stake in the economy and will benefit from its continued growth. But this still leaves open the question of what is meant by sharing income on an equitable basis? This involves complex and long debated issues concerning the welfare of society and the purpose of economic growth. Since Chapter 6 is devoted to this topic, a brief outline of the main parameters of this debate will suffice at this stage.

The value judgements underlying modern economics are derived from a philosophy of individualism and liberalism. *Individualism* means that what ultimately counts is the utility every individual attains and that the utility of each individual should be given an equal weight. *Liberalism* signifies that individuals should be free to decide what provides the greatest utility. Individual preferences are taken as given. The task of the economist, in this view, is to devise market structures that will enable individuals to satisfy their preferences, not to pass judgement on them.

Utility and income must be distinguished in this analysis. The standard assumption underlying economic reasoning is that the marginal utility of income is positive but decreases as income rises. Individuals always prefer a higher income to a lower one, but the intensity of this preference diminishes as income rises.[9] A systematic relationship thus links utility to income. On the face of it, the individualist principle of treating the utility of every person equally, coupled with the assumption of declining marginal utility for all individuals, would imply that the total utility in society is maximised when income is distributed perfectly evenly. But there are two reasons why even committed utilitarians do not push the argument to the extreme of total income equalisation.

First, different people derive different amounts of satisfaction from the same income levels. Material wealth does not matter equally to all. However, since utility cannot be objectively measured and compared among individuals, there is no way of finding out how much utility individuals derive from their income.

Second, the adverse effect of policies to achieve greater equality on incentives to work and enterprise may, after a point, lead to a fall in total income. Arthur Okun described the process of redistributing income as akin to transferring water from one barrel to another with a leaky bucket.[10] The more we try to increase equity by the redistribution of income, the more we reduce efficiency. In transferring income from the high income group to the low income group of society, the authorities levy taxes on individuals' income from employment and capital holdings. The former gives people an incentive to work less and the latter entices people to save less. Both effects lead to a reduction in the amount of income available for redistribution. The less well off in society may well lose rather than benefit from such policies in the long run.

There are nonetheless strong egalitarian tendencies in popular debate on economic issues, especially in Ireland. The assumption of decreasing marginal utility implies that when we take an amount from the rich to give to the poor, the rich will have suffered less of a utility loss than the utility gain enjoyed by the poor. A utilitarian asked to choose between a perfectly equal distribution of income and an unequal distribution *of exactly the same total income*, would favour the equal distribution. Egalitarian predispositions also emerge from other philosophies and schools of thought. Some argue that society should give the utility of the poor greater weight than the utility of the rich on grounds of need, regardless of fine points about diminishing utility. Others, such as the philosopher John Rawls, have pushed this line of judgement to the extreme, arguing that any economic change which increases inequality would be acceptable only if it serves to make the poorest better off also. This implies that the utility of the worst off individual takes precedence over all others and that a fair distribution of income is one that makes the poorest person as well of as possible after taking all costs of income transfers into account.[11]

Irish policy objectives have a Rawlsian flavour. For the past decade, governments have pursued social inclusion as a strategic objective in its own right, the primary objective being to ensure that 'the benefits of economic growth and related social improvements are shared by all sections of the Irish population'.[12] Social inclusion has been a major theme of successive agreements with the social partners (see Chapters 3 and 6).

In opposition to the egalitarian presumption, Robert Nozick argued that the idea of fairness as an outcome could not be justified. Fairness must be based on rules, not outcomes.[13] Two rules are crucial: (1) the state must enforce laws that establish and protect private property and (2) private property may be transferred from one person to another only by voluntary exchange. This has to happen in a competitive market where there exist no market or government failures. According to Nozick, the resulting distribution of income is, by definition, fair. It does not matter how unequally this income is shared provided it is generated by people each of whom voluntarily provided services in exchange for the share of income offered in compensation. The entrepreneur who accepts business risks and has succeeded deserves to be rewarded. Redistribution of these earnings is unjustified. From this perspective the key issue is equality of opportunity, not equality of outcome. Indeed given an uneven distribution of skills, motivation and willingness to work, equal opportunities will inevitably entail unequal outcomes.

So far the discussion has focused on *vertical equity*. This refers to the proposition that differently situated individuals should be treated differently. The well off, in other words, should be taxed in favour of the poor because they can afford to pay these taxes with less pain. *Horizontal equity* is also important. The underlying principle is that people with the same incomes and same circumstances should be treated in a similar fashion. For example, two different families with the same number of dependants and the same income should pay the same rate of tax. This principle is the motivating force of many income distribution policies. Regional policy, for example, is based on the idea that people in less developed regions do not enjoy the same access to infrastructure as those living in richer regions. From this, springs the justification for special state grants and incentives for industry to locate in the former. Horizontal equity considerations also underlie the case for taxing farmers in the same way as PAYE employees. This equity principle, if breached, can be a source of major grievance.

Equity and Growth
We have already referred to the debate about the relationship between economic growth and equity. The proposition is that to achieve income equality some sacrifice in growth is necessary because equality requires high taxes that can damage enterprise and investment. Some find this line of argument persuasive. Others doubt that such a trade off exists. They point to the many studies showing that countries with more evenly spread income grow faster than countries with a large gap between poor and rich. Also faster growing economies have lower unemployment rates. Since the incidence of unemployment is highest among lower income groups, these groups in particular will benefit. In Ireland's case, the virtual disappearance of unemployment has brought about a dramatic decline in levels of deprivation during the past decade. However, there is also evidence of considerable escalation of gains at the top of the income distribution. The net impact of these conflicting forces on the degree of income equality depends on the measure of inequality used. There seems to be general agreement however, that extreme income inequality is bad for growth, but not all agree on how precisely 'extreme' is to be defined.

The relationship between equity and growth depends ultimately on individual attitudes and culture. Income inequalities are more acceptable and financial work incentives valued more in some societies than in others. The combinations of growth and equity attainable in a competitive market economy full of individualistic materialists will be different from those attainable in a cooperative economy run by and for ascetic altruists! A poll conducted in 1994 showed that only 29 per cent of Americans thought it was the government's job to reduce income differentials while over 60 per cent of Germans and over 80 per cent of Italians and Austrians were of that opinion.[14] In practice governments have voted with their feet on this question. Comparison of income distribution before and after tax and state benefits in industrial countries shows massive transfers from richer to poorer income groups. Governments in these countries see no conflict between growth and redistribution. The debate about whether they are correct in this belief will, no doubt, continue.

So far, the analysis of income distribution has centred on providing all individuals with an adequate level of income. It is worth reiterating that the 'wellbeing' of an individual includes much more than income: access to public amenities, pollution free air and a crimeless environment contribute more to happiness than any monetary measure, no matter how adjusted, can adequately convey. No less important is the fact that people's definition of what constitutes an 'adequate' level of income seems to depend as much on the level of income enjoyed by their neighbour as on the absolute value of their own income (see Chapter 6).

5 PRICE STABILITY

A regional economy has a strong interest in price stability. However, a region will experience price stability only if the centre provides it. In the Republic's case the centre is Frankfurt, the headquarters of the European Central Bank, while for Northern Ireland the relevant policy centre is the Bank of England. Policy in the regional economy must therefore focus on supporting the establishment of solid financial institutions at the centre and setting clear objectives for them.

Definition and Measurement

Price stability is a relatively new phrase in the policymaker's lexicon. But it is not a new concept. In the past, inflation was so rampant and endemic that the analysis usually proceeded in terms of the costs of inflation. Over the past 35 years, for instance, prices of most Irish goods have increased on average by over a factor of ten; what cost the equivalent of €10 then cost more than €100 in 2004. After several years of price stability, inflation has emerged again as a source of concern. Since the launch of the euro in January 1999, Ireland has experienced cumulative inflation of 25 per cent.

Price stability is defined as the absence of any persistent and pronounced rise or fall in the general level of money prices. The general level of prices is measured by the Consumer Price Index (CPI). This index is defined by reference to the price of a fixed 'basket' of consumer goods. In the Republic, the selection of items for the basket is made using results of the national household budget survey (HBS). The HBS for 1999/2000 covered the spending of a sample of 7,600 households. The 985 items in the current basket include not only staple goods such as food, clothing, cars and petrol but also items such as mobile telephones, medical insurance, bank charges and child minding fees.

Three factors tend to impart an upward bias to the price increases recorded by the CPI. First, the number of goods in the sample basket is an incomplete inventory of the economy's goods. Delays in incorporating new products give rise, for technical reasons, to an upward bias (*composition bias*). Second, improvements in the quality are an important feature of new goods and services, ranging from high technology goods to medical services and drugs, and they tend to be insufficiently allowed for in CPI price data (*quality bias*). Third, the CPI may fail to take full account of people's ability to substitute low priced goods for higher priced goods or to shift purchases from high priced outlets to cheaper retail outlets when prices are rising (*substitution bias*).[15] A doubling in the price of potatoes, for example, would raise the Irish CPI by over one third of a percentage point (potatoes carry a weight in the basket of 0.36 per cent) but this takes no account of availability of close substitutes such as rice and pasta. As time goes by, people switch their buying to products which have increased less in price: but the base weights (the CPI is a Laspeyres index) take insufficient account of this switch.

The empirical importance of these measurement biases is not known with precision. Even a bias of +1 per cent is large compared with an average inflation rate of, say, 2 per cent. Because of these upward biases, the objective of price stability is not defined as a zero CPI rise, but rather as CPI increases in the range of 1 to 3 per cent. The European Central Bank (ECB) defines it as year on year increases in the CPI of the eurozone *below but close to* 2 per cent, maintained over the medium term; the Bank of England adopted a similar definition in December 2003; while the central banks of Sweden, Norway, New Zealand and Canada have opted for the wider 1-3 per cent range.

The issue of whether *asset prices*, and in particular house prices, should be included in the CPI has been much debated in recent times. The issue arises because in many countries (Ireland, the UK and Spain for example) house prices have been rising well above the CPI rate for several years. While housing costs are included in the CPI (which have a weight of 7 per cent in the Irish CPI), some believed that the index took too little account of the implications of escalating house prices on long run disposable income.

The case for not making a special adjustment is based on two arguments. First, Ireland has a high proportion of owner occupied houses, and the vast majority of them have low mortgages relative to current housing prices. Mortgage payments on average amount to only 4 per cent of total consumer expenditure. True, for the first time buyer the proportion could be as much as ten times that, but first time buyers are a small minority of the total population and the CPI strives to measure the average impact of price changes. Second, as mentioned above, while house prices are not included in the Irish CPI representative basket, like that of other EU countries, the basket does include the cost of *housing services,* (i.e. rents on rented accommodation, the cost of housing repairs, and mortgage payments on owner occupied housing). The reasoning behind the focus on housing services is that what matters for living standards is not so much the price of a house per se but the cost of owning a house (i.e. interest plus capital payments) and of renting it. Imagine the case of a house costing €100,000 when the mortgage rate is 10 per cent. If the buyer borrows the entire capital sum, mortgage interest payments will amount to €10,000 per annum, to which might be added €5,000 in capital repayments (for simplicity, assume a 20 year loan of equal annual capital repayments). Now let the mortgage rate fall to 5 per cent. Demand for houses will rise since it is now cheaper to borrow. Suppose this leads to a doubling of house prices. The price of the house rises to €200,000. Capital repayments on the house may now double also to €10,000 per annum, but the interest cost of the mortgage remains exactly the same as before, namely €10,000. Annual mortgage payments will increase by 33 per cent (€20,000 compared with €15,000). Note that this is much less than the 100 per cent increase in house prices. The house price increase will in due course also lead to a rise in rents, but these will rise in line with total mortgage repayments. The same logic applies to other assets as well as houses (e.g. shares). Thus, asset prices are by no means irrelevant to inflation, but their impact is measured indirectly rather than directly in the consumer price index.

Why Price Stability is Important

Failure to achieve price stability impacts adversely on both economic growth and income distribution. Quantifying these adverse impacts can be difficult. But the key point is to understand why deviations from price stability are bad for economic welfare. Such deviations could take the form of inflation or deflation. Of the two, inflation is the more common and persistent danger and for this reason most of the following analysis relates to the costs of inflation.

Deflation, defined as a persistent decline in the general price level, has been a rare phenomenon in recent times. In common with most developed countries, Ireland has experienced virtually no sustained deflation since 1948. The most traumatic example of deflation was that which occurred during the Great Depression of 1929 to 1933. Another case has been the deflation in Japan since the mid 1990s.[16]

Anticipated Inflation

Suppose we focus on inflation, or upward deviations from price stability. Theories of inflation distinguish between anticipated inflation and unanticipated or 'surprise' inflation. The principal welfare costs arise only when inflation is not fully anticipated. If inflation were to proceed at a steady (or otherwise predictable) rate that the public would learn to anticipate, and if institutions adapted fully to this anticipation, people could adjust their economic behaviour accordingly. There would have to be, in effect, a fully indexed economy implying, among other things, a comprehensive system of wage and salary indexation, indexing of tax brackets and allowances, taxation of real rather than nominal returns on assets, etc. In brief, all prices for goods and services, including labour services, would be perfectly adjustable. This would be an example of what has been called the 'flexprice' economy. In such an economy, the welfare cost of inflation involves only two types of costs: 'shoe leather' costs and 'menu' costs.

Cash balances yield an implicit social return by virtue of the convenience they afford in making transactions. Inflation can be regarded as a tax on cash balances: the negative yield on cash balances is equal to the rate of inflation. The higher the rate of inflation, the larger is the negative yield and the opportunity cost of holding cash. Holders of cash balances will, therefore, shift into less liquid and convenient, but income yielding, assets. This substitution involves a further loss of efficiency in so far as cash balances, which are virtually costless to produce, are economised on in favour of more frequent transactions in less liquid and intrinsically valuable assets. Anticipated inflation also imposes the so called menu cost of actually changing prices in what have been called 'customer markets' (i.e. those markets in which prices are set and, in the normal course of events, kept unchanged for some time, such as labour markets, retail and wholesale trade, pay telephones and parking meters). Both shoe leather and menu costs increase rapidly with the magnitude of the inflation rate.

Unanticipated Inflation
The costs of anticipated inflation may appear rather theoretical. Yet research shows that they are empirically important, even at relatively low rates of inflation. Far more important, however, are the costs arising from unanticipated inflation.

First, uncertainty about the inflation rate undermines the role played by money in economising on transaction costs. Fixed price orders, leases and other explicit long term contracts, fixed time schedules for price changes and the broad general commitment to continuity of offers by suppliers are important ways of assisting forward planning. Uncertainty about the future price level shortens the time horizon of such agreements, thus imposing a welfare loss on society.

Second, uncertainty about future price levels results in an arbitrary redistribution of income and wealth. A faster than expected inflation rate, for instance, will tend to discriminate against creditors in favour of debtors. It will also harm those whose incomes are fixed in nominal money terms or which are indexed only after a lapse of time (pensioners), in contrast with those whose incomes are more easily adjustable to inflation, such as unionised wage earners and owners of capital. Another effect is the redistribution of real wealth from the old (who have accumulated assets) to the young who are, in general, net borrowers. The haphazard nature of the income distribution effects can lead to social unrest and general discontent as people find it increasingly difficult to estimate the growth in their real incomes and to predict what their real earnings will be in the future. In a period of 1 per cent inflation, people who receive pay increases of 4 per cent recognise clearly that they have gained in real terms. In a world of 15 per cent inflation, those receiving pay increases of 18 per cent are likely to be much less confident about how they are faring. That loss of information is a genuine subtraction from welfare. Prices cease to fulfil their signalling function as the effects of relative shifts in prices are blurred by the general rise in the price level.

Third, although the relationship is neither direct nor simple, inflation can have adverse consequences for economic growth. Efficiency losses, though small in any one year, can accumulate over time into a significant aggregate loss. In addition, inflation has a tendency to shorten investment horizons. Investment in 'inflation hedges' such as property increases at the expense of long term investment in industry. The available evidence suggests quite significant long term losses for economic growth arising from inflation.

Inflation, Deflation and Stability
The above analysis has focused on inflation. Deflation brings similar welfare costs in its train, but for subtly different reasons. Thus, the menu costs apply in the case of anticipated deflation, with the added problem that nominal interest rates cannot be negative (the zero interest rate constraint), an inflexibility that can lead to excessively high real interest rates. At a macroeconomic level, anticipated deflation can prolong a recession by giving consumers and investors an incentive to postpone spending. Unanticipated deflation generates further costs. It benefits lenders at the expense of borrowers. It can also lead to unwarranted rises in real wages that can only be offset by a decline in nominal pay that can prove very contentious to negotiate. Like inflation, deflation tends to be self perpetuating and deflationary spirals are difficult to reverse. While deflationary episodes have been rare and short lived during the past 50 years, they were not so uncommon in the century preceding that. Several countries appeared to be on the brink of a deflationary problem in the early 2000s, among them China, Saudi Arabia, Switzerland and Germany. Their recorded CPI was rising by only 1 per cent annually which, allowing for the upward biases of the CPI was consistent with a falling underlying price level.[17]

Opinion surveys suggest that the public values price stability for its own sake, apart from the economic costs outlined in this section. One could argue that stability in general, and not just price stability, should be included among a region's policy objectives. Personal security (absence of crime), stability of employment (absence of fear of redundancy) and the provision of social safety nets (social welfare) all play a role in creating the good society. Sustained economic growth in a context of price stability brings with it the capacity to provide many of these benefits, just as they in turn make growth and stability more sustainable. Economic growth has rightly been defined as a process of cumulative and circular causation. No single policy objective can be pursued in isolation; each objective interacts with the others.

6 COMPETITIVENESS

Small regional economies are largely 'importers' of price trends abroad. Thus if the CPI is rising in continental Europe and the UK at around 2 per cent, inflation in both parts of Ireland will also approximate 2 per cent. This is a valid generalisation over the long run. But it is not universally the case and there frequently are significant short run deviations between a region's inflation rate and the national/area average. Since 1999, Irish prices have risen twice as fast as average euro area prices. By 2003, Ireland had joined Finland as the two most expensive countries in the eurozone. Theory indicates that there will be *mean reversion,* (i.e. that sooner or later the rate of price increase in Ireland will revert to the euro area average), but serious damage to the economy could be done in the interim. The Enterprise Strategy Group warned that:

> The cost of doing business in Ireland has risen significantly in recent years. It is eroding the relative competitiveness of our goods and services sectors, and reducing our attractiveness for new foreign direct investment.[18]

Why do such cost divergences occur and what can or should be done about them?

Price and Cost Divergences

One reason for the divergence in price trends stems from Ireland's rapid growth relative to the eurozone. Faster growth translates into higher pay. This is non-inflationary where productivity rises in line with pay. Thus a 5 per cent pay rise matched by a 5 per cent productivity increase leaves unit cost, and hence prices, unaffected. However, in those parts of the economy where productivity growth is relatively modest, employers will have to increase wages in line with other sectors (or else their workers will leave for better pay elsewhere). Hence unit costs and prices will tend to rise. Non-traded services are particularly prone to price inflation in such situations: restaurant meals, medical services and building and construction. Here higher pay translates into higher prices. Thus services prices in Ireland during the early 2000s increased at a rate of nearly 6 per cent compared with a CPI average of 3 per cent. The Irish experience is rather typical of any fast growing economy in this respect. A major change since monetary union, however, is that without an independent currency the inflationary effects cannot be offset by revaluation of the exchange rate.

A second source of inflationary pressure is inflation itself. In a booming economy the normal restraints on pay rises weaken. Employees, observing higher inflation, seek compensatory pay rises and hence begin a process of self defeating catch up, which generates an inflationary spiral.

Third, and for Ireland the most quantitatively important consideration, changes in the euro exchange rate have a strong effect on domestic prices.[19] A 20 per cent decline in the value of the euro has been estimated to lead to only a 1 per cent rise in the average eurozone price level. However, because of the higher proportion of the Republic's trade with countries outside the eurozone, the impact of such a depreciation of the euro on the Irish CPI is a far more serious matter. About four fifths of the Republic's merchandise imports come from outside the eurozone, compared with the eurozone average of one half. Variations in the euro-dollar or the euro-sterling rate consequently impact on Irish prices to a much greater extent than on German or French price levels. If the UK were to join the eurozone, the Republic's difficulties in this regard would of course be much diminished. For this reason, as has often been said, the Irish government has a strong interest in the UK adopting the euro.

Implications of a Loss of Cost Competitiveness

When one region's prices/costs rise relative to other regions, this is termed a loss of cost competitiveness. One immediate impact of such deterioration is a decline in exports as they become more expensive to foreigners. For the same reason, domestic goods become more expensive relative to imports and the import bill rises. The balance of payments on current account then runs into deficit.

For a country with an independent national currency the next question is the effect of the deficit on the exchange rate. If the exchange rate devalues, this offers a short run solution to the loss of competitiveness. But the resultant rise in domestic prices could set in motion an inflationary spiral, with devaluation causing domestic price increases, which lead to compensatory pay claims. This is the classic downside of devaluation as a policy response to deficits induced by cost competitiveness problems.

In the case of a small regional economy, there are no direct exchange rate implications for a loss of competitiveness. If Northern Ireland loses cost competitiveness and runs a deficit, this will not materially affect the value of sterling. Likewise the Republic's competitiveness will have no impact on the fortunes of the euro. In each case the region is too small to affect the bigger picture. Thus the region is left with its current account deficit. When a region runs a current account deficit, say because of a decline in competitiveness, this means that it is spending more on foreign goods and services than it is earning from exports. In this sense, a deficit signifies that a country is 'living beyond its means'. The deficit will have to be matched by foreign borrowing, and the corresponding capital inflow will eventually have to be financed and repaid. This will entail a future stream of current account surpluses spread over many years. The level of GDP available to future generations will thus be affected.

An adverse movement in a region's cost competitiveness cannot be indefinitely sustained. As regional prices increase, the region's cost structure will become more and more out of line with its competitors. It will begin to lose export markets and will become less attractive as a location for investment. Eventually growth will slow, labour demand will decline and pay pressures will ease. The speed of this process is an issue that is much debated in Ireland. Its price level is above the eurozone average. Like all booming regions, the hope is for a 'soft' landing, whereby rising costs will gradually erode cost competitiveness and growth will be reduced to more sustainable levels over time. Unfortunately, the historical experience of booming regions provides many examples of 'hard' landings where adjustment takes place abruptly, property markets collapse and unemployment rises. This suggests that the major concern of any region must be to influence its competitiveness in such a way as to secure optimal growth, achieving its economic potential while moderating booms and avoiding busts along the way. It must do so without two major policy instruments that a nation state might have recourse to: commercial policy and an independent exchange rate. That leaves domestic competitiveness policy as an instrument of major importance.

Definition of Competitiveness

Competitiveness has become something of a global preoccupation since the 1990s. Every region worries about it and governments everywhere feel compelled to do something to improve it. Practically every country in Europe has set up competitiveness councils. The World Competitiveness Report, and its rival, the Global Competitiveness Report, are published annually and attract worldwide publicity. Their findings are scrutinised with a fine toothcomb by development agencies and government commissions. In short, maintaining competitiveness can now be described as a key secondary policy objective, with improvements in competitiveness seen as crucial to achieving growth and full employment.

Competitiveness has been a well established theme in economic debate in Ireland. In the Republic, the National Competitiveness Council was set up in 1997. Its *Annual Competitiveness Report* is a rich source of information on competitiveness indicators. The Council's remit is to examine key competitiveness issues and to make recommendations on policy actions required to improve Ireland's competitive position. As long ago as 1993, a NESC Report identified competitiveness as the major theme for the future. In Northern Ireland, attention has also focused on competitiveness as a way of generating faster growth and more employment. The Northern Ireland Economic Council has published several reports on this topic and the UK statistical authorities produce a comprehensive set of regional competitiveness indicators.

Competitiveness can be defined in a narrow sense or in a broad sense. The narrow definition focuses on trends in pay, productivity and unit costs. These components are aggregated into a cost competitiveness index and movements in the index are tracked over time and compared with trends in competing countries. For many years, emphasis was placed on this narrow definition partly because of data limitations (information on the components of the broader definition has only recently become available) and partly because Ireland's performance on the cost competitiveness definition was poor and it has to be given priority.

The broader definition includes price and non-price factors such as product quality, reliability of supply, backup marketing services and taxation, and extends to consideration of human resource development, business services, infrastructure and public finance and administration. A country's long run competitive position can also be profoundly influenced by its policy towards research and development (R&D), and by its success in product innovation and technology. Innovation and R&D are key ingredients of a region's infrastructure (see Chapters 5 and 7). Competitiveness authorities in both parts of Ireland currently use the broader definition of competitiveness. In this they are in line with international practice. For instance, the World Economic Forum defines competitiveness as 'the ability to achieve sustained high rates of growth in GDP per capita'. Thus competitiveness measures the degree to which a nation or a region can, under free market conditions, produce goods and services that meet the test of international markets while simultaneously expanding the real income of its citizens.

Note that competitiveness is a relative concept. Success in the competitiveness league depends on how well an economy is progressing relative to others. It is possible for all countries to grow faster, to generate more employment, to export more; but by definition only some countries can become more competitive. In other words, the process of striving to be more competitive, in so far as it improves economic growth and efficiency, is a positive-sum game. But in terms of ranking in competitiveness leagues it is a zero-sum game: one region advances in the ranking order only if some other region declines. Failure to recognise this point can lead to competitiveness becoming what has been called a 'dangerous obsession' instead of a stimulus to improved performance.

Strategy to Improve Competitiveness
Policies to improve competitiveness constitute the theme of many chapters of this book. These policies change over time and according to circumstances will differ across region and nation. To date the policy objective in both parts of Ireland has focused on creating an environment that would encourage:
- The growth of export oriented firms, especially Irish-owned firms.
- The retention and attraction of foreign direct investment in knowledge based sectors and activities such as electronics, pharmaceuticals, biotechnology and software.
- The development of linkages between existing and new greenfield firms.
- A balanced location of economic activity within the island.

This ambitious programme has involved several policy dimensions and instruments, which will be analysed throughout this book.

The context of Ireland's competitiveness challenge has changed markedly in recent years. First, the Irish economy is no longer among the poorer member states of the EU. In the past Ireland has benefited significantly from the Structural and Cohesion Funds and has been an enthusiastic advocate of their development and growth. If present GDP growth rates continue, however, the Republic's status will soon change from recipient to provider of such assistance.

Second, policy measures taken at the centre (Brussels/Frankfurt/London) are becoming increasingly important. The impact of fluctuations in the euro and sterling and of changes in interest rate policy in Frankfurt and London have been touched upon already. Other areas must also be considered: fiscal policy and the Stability and Growth Pact, competition policy, state aids, taxation, and the Common Agriculture Policy. Brussels is concerned about competitiveness at the EU-wide level, and action taken to improve it will have important implications for both parts of Ireland.

Finally, the scope for regional policy initiatives, though declining, remains of crucial importance. A key fiscal incentive in the Republic is the 12.5 per cent tax rate for all corporate income from 2003 and the Brussels approved grand parenting of the 10 per cent rate up to 2010 for all companies already in operation. In addition, domestic authorities on both sides of the border have discretion in the payment of capital grants, training grants, R&D support and so on. The extension of these fiscal and financial concessions to internationally traded service industries has proved in retrospect to be a highly significant initiative, being a key factor in the development of the Irish Financial Services Centre and the attraction of major multinationals to Ireland (see Chapter 7). Provision of a good physical environment and human capital structure (education) is also an intrinsic part of a strategy for improving competitiveness (see Chapter 11).

7 CONCLUSION

Improved standards of living and rapid growth are the first priority of economic policy. In practical terms, this means that most governments' economic performance is judged by reference to changes in GNP per person. People want economic growth because of what it can do for them in terms of higher purchasing power and also because of the other good things that often accompany growth such as full employment, generous safety nets for the poor and greater security.

Growth is a primary objective, but there are limits to what it can deliver. There is no strong association between growth and happiness and none between growth and spiritual development. Growth at any price is not a sensible objective, nor is the attainment of maximum growth, particularly when this would involve a large increase in immigration. In setting medium term targets, rather than asking what is the maximum growth the economy can sustain and then working out the implications of this for policy, as is the methodology of the most medium term economic forecasts, we should instead be asking what growth we wish to obtain and work backwards from there. There is need for a more active debate in Ireland about the optimal, as distinct from the maximum, rate of growth.

GNP growth statistics have many limitations as an indicator of human welfare. GNP leaves out of account leisure, the environment, and misclassifies many inputs as outputs. Another limitation is that GNP neglects important indicators of human welfare such as education and life expectancy. Despite its many failings, however, GNP per head serves as a remarkably good proxy for more sophisticated measures of human welfare, as comparisons between rankings based on GNP per head and the United Nations' Human Development Index demonstrate.

Equity in the sense of a fair distribution of income and an adequate level of income to all individuals is an important policy objective. The issue of equity is indeed a central aspect of most economic problems. In the Irish political domain concerns with equity and income distribution often outweigh concerns with economic efficiency in discussion of policy alternatives. By providing the conditions for increasing the standard of living, policymakers have the objective of reducing the evils of social exclusion and long term unemployment. Care should be taken, however, when deciding on the degree of redistribution to avoid penalising the achievers and stifling economic growth. However, there is no consensus about the proper definition of 'equitable' or 'fair' allocations.

It is also important to consider the 'wellbeing' of the individual in the broadest sense when addressing distributional issues. As well as maximising total societal welfare from a material viewpoint, the policy objective should aim to deliver an adequate pollution free, low crime and safe society.

Price stability is a policy objective that is both desired for its own sake and as a means to the end of attaining growth. There is now more conviction among politicians of the electoral advantages of running an economy in a way that maintains price stability. As a population ages, it is likely that the constituency in favour of price stability will grow. Politicians seem increasingly content to leave monetary policy to independent central banks. This new approach is helpful for price stability and good for the overall economy, since low inflation and output growth complement one another in the medium to long run.

Has the adoption of price stability as a policy target been associated with a demonstrable improvement in economic efficiency and social stability? Many argue that it has. They would agree with Keynes that deviations from price stability, whether in the form of inflation or deflation, have inflicted great injuries; 'both evils are to be shunned'.[20] Hence the importance of ensuring that price stability, once restored, is thereafter maintained.

Maintaining equilibrium in the balance of payments was once a significant secondary policy objective for the Irish economy. This is no longer the case. In a post euro situation, with a single currency and free access to the world capital market, the direct relevance of the balance of payments to other policy objectives such as growth and inflation has declined almost to vanishing point. Participation in the common currency means that there are no longer any exchange rate implications of a change in the Irish balance of payments. Also untrammelled access to world capital markets implies the virtual disappearance of capital constraints. The balance of payments still contains useful economic information but, as a policy variable, its usefulness has been subsumed under the more general umbrella of competitiveness.

As we advance into the 2000s and beyond, we can expect competitiveness to occupy the high ground as a major secondary policy objective for the economy. Competitiveness covers a wider spectrum of economic variables. Attention of Irish policymakers used to focus on standard comparisons between cost and price indicators here and those in competitor countries. These indexes continue to be relevant. Within the space of a few years, the Republic has become a comparatively expensive location for visiting or doing business, and prices and pay rates tend to be towards the higher end of the European spectrum, so far without any obvious detrimental effect on growth. So far so good. But in the longer run, it clearly will be necessary to justify these higher earnings by higher productivity. It is here that the broader definition of competitiveness comes into play. Competitiveness in this broader sense includes R&D, education, quality improvement, marketing and physical infrastructure – the intangible and often difficult to measure aspects that are believed to impact crucially on an economy's ability to perform well.

Endnotes

* The author wishes to thank the editors for percipient and helpful comments. He has drawn on the version of this chapter (written jointly with Dominic Burke) in the eighth edition and also on Chapters 2 and 12 of D. McAleese, *Economics for Business*, Financial Times Prentice Hall, London 2004.

1 Estimated from data in National Economic and Social Council (NESC), *The Economic and Social Implications of Emigration,* Stationery Office, Dublin 1991.

2 Department of Social Welfare, *Commission on Emigration and Other Population Problems,* Stationery Office, Dublin 1954, para. 473.

3 J. Galbraith, *The Nature of Mass Poverty*, Harvard University Press, Cambridge MA 1979.

4 NESC, *The Economic and Social Implications of Emigration,* Stationery Office, Dublin 1991.

5 In the words of the Whitaker Report, 'emigration will not be checked nor will unemployment be permanently reduced until the rate of increase in national output is greatly accelerated', Department of Finance, *Programme for Economic Expansion,* Stationery Office, Dublin 1958, p. 7.

6 R. Kennedy, quoted in *Finance and Development*, Washington, December 1993, p. 20.

7 United Nations Development Programme, *Human Development Report,* Oxford University Press, New York 2004.

8 Economic texts of this genre include E. Mishan, *The Cost of Economic Growth*, Penguin, Harmondsworth 1967; S. Linder and F. Hirsch, *The Social Limits to Growth*, Routledge, London 1977; R. Doubtwaite, *The Growth Illusion*, Lilliput, Dublin 1992; R. Frank, *Luxury Fever: Why Money Fails to Satisfy in an Era of Excess,* The Free Press, New York 1999.

9 This assumption excludes extreme cases such as Ascetics, who are happiest with a minimal income, and Scrooges, for whom income becomes more important the more they have of it.

10 A. Okun, *Equality and Efficiency: The Big Trade-off,* Brookings Institution, Washington D.C. 1975.

11 J. Rawls, *A Theory of Justice*, Harvard University Press, Cambridge MA 1971.

12 NESC, *Opportunities, Challenges and Capacities for Choice,* Stationery Office, Dublin 1999, p. 51.

13 R. Nozick, *Anarchy, State and Utopia,* Basic Books, New York 1974.

14 *Economist*, 5 November 1994.

15 The upward bias in the US CPI has been estimated at 1.1 percentage points per annum, 0.5 of which is due to substitution bias. The substitution bias in the Irish CPI appears to be much smaller, 0.02 per cent, but we have no comparable Irish estimates for the other sources of bias. See also R. Somerville, 'Changes in Relative Consumer Prices and the Substitution Bias of the Laspeyres Price Index: Ireland 1985-2001', *Economic and Social Review,* Spring 2004.

16 Deflation brings with it serious problems and it is important to keep these in mind in evaluating policy options for the European Central Bank. Because it is a new institution, many feared that its urge to establish sound price stability credentials might lead it to give too much weight to the danger of inflation and pay too little attention to the dangers of deflation. The Bank asserts that this is not the case and that its commitment to price stability is symmetric: deviations on either side of its price target are equally undesirable.

17 See P. Lane, 'Ireland and the Deflation Debate', *The Irish Banking Review,* Winter 2003, and D. McAleese, *Economics for Business,* op. cit., Box 12.1.

18 Enterprise Strategy Group, *Ahead of the Curve: Ireland's Place in the Global Economy*, Forfás, Dublin 2004, p. 21.

19 P. Honohan and P. Lane, 'Divergent Inflation Rates in EMU', *Economic Policy,* Blackwell, www.blackwellpublishing.com 2003.

20 J.M. Keynes, 'Economic Consequences of the Peace', *Collected Economic Writings*, Macmillan, London 1971, p. 149.

CHAPTER 2

Role of Government: Rationale, Levels and Size

Philip Lane

1 INTRODUCTION

Chapter 1 established economic policy objectives for Ireland. The government, on the premise that it indeed cares about national welfare, is responsible for the attainment of these goals, either directly or in tandem with its international counterparts. The government's ability to achieve its policy goals is facilitated by the special powers assigned to the state, most notably its powers of compulsion. In this chapter, the role of government in pursuing these policy objectives is addressed.

The rest of the chapter is organised as follows. Section 2 reviews the theoretical basis for government intervention in the economy. The allocation of responsibilities across different levels of government is described in Section 3. In Section 4, the central role played by public expenditure policies is analysed (Chapter 3 will subsequently explore some other policy tools available to the government), while in Section 5 the role of state-owned enterprises and privatisation is discussed. Section 6 discusses the economic and political factors determining the size of the government sector. Section 7 concludes the chapter.

2 RATIONALE FOR GOVERNMENT INTERVENTION

There are a number of classic arguments that provide a rationale for government intervention in the economy. The starting point is to recognise the absurdity of a no-government economy. A central authority and a *legal system* are necessary to permit the (implicit or explicit) contracts that govern all economic activity, for example through the design of corporate and labour laws. Cross country evidence and historical examples show that anarchy and the absence of a 'rule of law' result in very poor economic performance (and the emergence of private contract enforcement systems, such as Mafia style organisations): the evidence from 'failed states' in Africa and elsewhere lends considerable support to these concerns.[1] Put another way, we can interpret economic activity as an elaborate game: as with any other game, a set of rules and a referee are required. The government is responsible for designing and enforcing the rules that determine permissible behaviour on the parts of firms and consumers: the anarchic alternative would be unstable and highly deleterious for economic performance.

A second function relates to the efficient allocation of resources. A laissez faire economy will not efficiently provide *pure public goods* (e.g. national defense). A public good is non-rival (it can be collectively consumed) and non-excludable (its benefits cannot be easily withheld from individuals): examples include the provision of national security and basic scientific research (a new mathematical formula can be used by everyone and, once published, is non-excludable). Non-excludability prevents market provision, since no one has an incentive to pay for a good if it can be freely consumed. The state must step in to provide such public goods and raise the resources required by levying taxation.

Similarly, market prices do not reflect *external effects*, with the result that activities generating positive externalities are underproduced and those generating negative externalities are overproduced. A good that produces a positive externality is similar to a public good, in that some of its benefits are non-excludable and accrue to others than just the direct consumer. However, such goods may be rivalrous and may be partially excludable, so that some private provision occurs even if the level of production is inadequate.

The road network is a good illustration of a positive externality: the gain to building an extra kilometre of motorway increases the productivity of other parts of the road network that become more accessible. An obvious example of a negative externality is environmental pollution. To promote goods that generate positive externalities, the state may engage in direct provision or offer subsidies. In contrast, it may impose quotas or taxes on goods that generate negative external effects.

Other sources of market failure include *monopoly power* and *imperfect information*. The former means that prices will be too high and output too low relative to the competitive outcome. The latter means that many credit and insurance markets are missing or incomplete, since it is impossible for private firms to adequately evaluate projects and accurately calculate default risks. Such market failures provide a *prima facie* case for some kind of government intervention, either by direct provision or through subsidisation.

However, the desirability of actual intervention is tempered by 'government failure': it is not clear that, in many cases, governments can deliver a more efficient outcome than that generated by even imperfect markets. Electoral pressures; interest group lobbying; perverse incentives in administration; corruption; restrictive practices and inflexible procedures in the public sector; and poor management skills may all lead to welfare decreasing interventions in the economy. Accordingly, the optimal degree of government intervention must balance the prospective gains against potential implementation problems. The recent planning scandals in Ireland are just one illustration of 'government intervention gone wrong'.

Even if free markets delivered a perfectly efficient outcome, *distributional considerations* would still justify government intervention. The income distribution attained by a market economy is conditional on the initial distribution of endowments (both monetary and individual characteristics such as intelligence, good health and family background). Being lucky in one's choice of parents is an important determinant of success in a market economy: for example, in Ireland and elsewhere, educational attainment levels are highly correlated with family income levels and social background (see also Chapter 11). Moreover, economic outcomes have a random element. The weather influences the success or failure of many agricultural projects and many entrepreneurs recognise the role played by fortune in creating viable new businesses.

Accordingly, voters typically demand that the government redistributes income in order to protect the poorly endowed and the unlucky. With respect to the latter motivation, an interesting empirical phenomenon is that welfare spending tends to be higher in more open economies.[2] One explanation is that the greater vulnerability of open economies to external shocks prompts the electorate to demand a more elaborate social safety net, since market based incomes depend heavily on random international events in an open economy.

However, the ability of the government to redistribute income is constrained along two dimensions. First, excessively high taxation depresses incentives, reducing the level of income and growth rates. Second, mobile factors (capital, highly skilled workers) will leave jurisdictions that impose harsh tax burdens.

3 LEVELS OF GOVERNMENT

Different levels of government can intervene in the economy. Although the traditional focus has been on national governments, local and international levels of government are increasingly important.

For some issues, international levels of government are better placed. In addition to EU membership, Ireland also participates in the World Trade Organisation, is a member of the International Monetary Fund and World Bank and subscribes to various international policy agreements.

The driving force behind international policy coordination is that the internationalisation of many economic activities enhances efficiency and is facilitated by a common set of international rules. For instance, it would be an extremely tedious procedure for each country to negotiate bilateral agreements with all its potential trading partners: the World Trade Organisation and the various regional trade agreements greatly reduce the transaction costs in ensuring trade liberalisation. Similarly, in tackling problems that are fundamentally international in character (such as preservation of the ozone layer), non-coordinated national policy responses make little sense.

Moreover, the internationalisation of economic activity also makes national policy actions less effective: for example, high tax rates or excessive regulation will prompt mobile factors to relocate to more business friendly regimes.[3] Conversely, national subsidies or tax breaks distort international location decisions, since a firm may opt to produce even in an inefficient location if it receives sufficiently high compensation from the host government. For these reasons, coordination of international policies can potentially restore the ability of governments to tax mobile factors and avoid undesirable 'subsidy auctions' in competing for footloose firms.

Membership of the EU

EU membership is the most important international commitment of the Irish government. Although a national veto still remains on some policy issues (e.g. taxation), majority voting now applies in many areas. This trend will be reinforced over the next few years, if the new EU Constitutional Treaty, which extends the scope of qualified majority voting, is ratified.

In order to create a single market, EU law guarantees intra-EU free trade and free movement of labour and capital and EU competition law also now sharply restricts national autonomy in industrial policy. For instance, EU governments can now only invest in state-owned enterprises on a commercial basis: rescuing loss making firms for non-economic reasons is no longer permitted. In addition, large public contracts must be advertised at an EU wide level, rather than directly allocated to domestic firms. In these ways, the EU can be interpreted as an international 'agency of restraint' that promotes more efficient allocations and depoliticises many economic decisions.

That said, the difficulty with international policy coordination is that there is not always consensus on the correct policy. Preferences may legitimately differ across countries on important issues such as: the appropriate level of taxation; the ideal level of social protection; and the optimal degree of risk aversion in food regulation. Since member nations bargain over many issues, some undesirable regulations may be accepted in exchange for concessions on other issues. In other cases, the level of disagreement may be so strong that coordination is not possible, with countries retaining independent national policies.

A common criticism of international policy coordination is that it leads to a 'democratic deficit', with decisions made at a level that is too far removed from ordinary voters. The EU has traditionally suffered from this objection, since policy decisions have been made at inter-governmental Council of Ministers meetings that are held in private with no review by national parliaments.

The new Constitutional Treaty seeks to redress this imbalance in several ways. First, the design of the Treaty was extensively debated in a highly participatory Constitutional Convention before the final articles were agreed. In Ireland, this debate was further widened through the activities of the National Forum on

Europe that held a large number of public meetings to improve awareness and permit debate on European policy issues. Second, the Treaty is intended to improve democratic accountability. For instance, major EU policy decisions will now be reviewed by national parliaments, in addition to the European Parliament. In addition, the European Council of Ministers will conduct more of its business in public session and it will have a 'public face' in that the President of the European Council will be elected for a two and a half year term and cannot hold any national mandate. Democratic accountability is further improved by the closer alignment of national population sizes and relative voting power in the Council of Ministers under the new Treaty.

As indicated, many decisions concerning government spending and taxation remain at the national level, providing scope for significant variation in the level and nature of government intervention across member countries. Following the earlier discussion, harmonisation of tax rates on mobile capital is advocated by some member countries. However, there is little agreement on the appropriate tax rate: a high capital tax rate may be progressive and reduce pressure on other parts of the tax base but has a negative effect on growth performance. Ireland has opted for a low tax strategy and resists pressure to harmonise rates at a higher level. Indeed, the gains to a low tax strategy have been augmented by the persistence of higher rates in other EU countries, as capital shifts to Ireland from other locations. The further widening of EU membership, with the 2004 accession of ten Central and Eastern European countries, makes it unlikely that significant further EU wide harmonisation of fiscal policies will be agreed in the near term. However, the new EU Constitutional Treaty does make provision for greater fiscal cooperation among subsets of EU member countries, even if not all members choose to participate.

Membership of the Eurozone

In 1999, a subset of eleven EU members adopted a single currency. A monetary union offers microeconomic efficiency gains and facilitates the development of a deep, liquid capital market. Moreover, a large bloc is plausibly insulated from destabilising speculative attacks on its currency, permitting lower average interest rates. Perhaps the most important advantage is that a supranational central bank may be more effectively insulated from political pressures than are national monetary authorities. The delegation of technocratic forms of government intervention, such as the conduct of monetary policy, to semi-autonomous institutions can be interpreted as a useful agency of restraint that ties the hands of political leaders that face enormous short term pressures to adopt populist policies that may damage the economy in the long term.

However, a 'one size fits all' monetary policy may itself be a source of instability for member countries with business cycles that are not highly correlated with the core of the eurozone. In the early years of EMU, Ireland fell into this category: in view of our high growth rates, interest rates were inappropriately low and excessive inflation was the result.

Other Considerations

Ireland also participates in global institutions, such as the World Trade Organisation. By agreeing on a common set of trade rules, the efficiency gains from international trade are maximised. Although trade liberalisation has deepened in recent decades, important exceptions remain, most notably in the agricultural sector. Recently, it has been argued that the development of international governance has been unbalanced: much progress has been made on cooperation in economic policy but with less effective coordination of labour or environmental regulations. However, in the absence of a directly elected 'world government', it is unlikely that much progress can be made on controversial issues that are the subject of much disagreement both within and across countries.[4]

At the other end, some policy issues are being devolved from national to local levels of government and also from international to national levels. Local government plausibly has an information advantage in designing and implementing policies that better reflect the preferences and needs of local residents. A closer relationship with the electorate may also improve the responsiveness and accountability of government. However, decentralisation also brings risks, especially if fiscal and functional responsibilities are not clearly allocated between the centre and periphery. In Ireland, local government has traditionally played a very limited role. However, with the switch towards greater local financing and autonomy in the provision of services (e.g. waste collection, water services), the trend is for greater diversity in local government in Ireland. The application of the subsidiary principle is also more evident at the EU level: there is greater recognition that the EU should focus its energies on those policy areas where cooperation is most effective, with the return of some policy issues to national governments. For instance, with the move to direct payments in subsidising the agricultural sector, it is predicted that responsibility for the agricultural sector will be shifted from Brussels to national levels of government (see Chapter 9).

Finally, in light of the improved political climate since the 1988 Good Friday Agreement, progress has been made for improved policy cooperation between the Republic of Ireland and Northern Ireland, with considerable scope for yet further integration. Significant scale economies can be achieved in areas such as tourism (e.g. with the creation of the all island Tourism Ireland marketing organisation) and network externalities can be better exploited by more efficiently integrating the transport and energy networks between the two jurisdictions. Moreover, the economic success of the Republic of Ireland has led to some reorientation of activity in Northern Ireland, with a greater focus on pursuing cross border business opportunities. Under the Good Friday Agreement, a number of inter-governmental agencies were established to facilitate enhanced policy cooperation in areas such as environment, agriculture, education, health, tourism and transport.

4 PUBLIC EXPENDITURE

There are three types of government spending: public consumption, transfers and public investment. The first category incorporates the provision of government services such as the civil service, education, health, the justice system and defense. The second includes social welfare payments, payments to the EU central budget and debt interest payments. The third refers to spending on infrastructure (e.g. the road network) and on the buildings and equipment associated with the provision of government services.

Public Consumption

Education and healthcare are the major items of public consumption. We only briefly review these sectors, since they are covered in more detail in Chapters 10 and 11. Spending on education and healthcare is in part motivated by redistributive considerations, to ensure access for all to at least a minimal level of services. At an efficiency level, private financing of education is plagued by credit problems and the healthcare sector suffers from myriad asymmetric information problems. Finally, promoting education arguably confers positive externalities and is necessary to a healthy democracy, since political participation is positively related to education levels. Although these arguments justify public financing of the education and healthcare sectors, this need not involve monopoly public provision of these services: for instance, the state could provide vouchers to parents that could be used to pay fees at private schools or pay the insurance premia to private healthcare companies.

Transfers

The welfare budget is the largest component of transfer spending. Some transfers can be justified by imperfections in insurance markets. For example, private insurance schemes are unlikely to provide fairly priced protection against the risk of unemployment. However, the stronger motivation behind transfers is redistribution: voters are unwilling to allow the incomes of unemployed, the sick or the old to fall below a minimum level. In designing a welfare system, there is a clear trade off between the level of benefits and the need to provide incentives to seek employment (in the case of unemployment benefit) or to privately save for retirement (in the case of pensions).

Producer subsidies are another kind of transfer. Although these have been declining in recent years, subsidies are still used to attract multinational corporations and support local startups. One problem with producer subsidies is that behaviour is distorted: rather than focusing on innovation and maximising profitability, entrepreneurs may divert resources to lobbying the government for subsidies. However, the worst excesses of this kind of behaviour have been sharply circumscribed by stricter EU regulations on the allocation of state aids to industry. Most notably, the European airline industry has historically been a major recipient of state subsidies but the European Commission now regularly prohibits the protection of 'national champions'. A second problem with producer subsidies is that Ireland competes with other EU countries for footloose firms: this bidding war may result in the successful country suffering a 'winner's curse', having to offer a subsidy larger than any potential benefits. With the rapid decline in unemployment, the structure of Irish producer subsidies has shifted from targeting job creation to encouraging strategic sectors with the potential for high growth.

Public Investment

Public investment has two economic functions: the provision of (1) public inputs that directly raise the productivity of the economy; and (2) public amenities that improve the quality of life and are valued by the community. Of course, the same project may contribute to both objectives. For example, an improved road network not only improves economic performance but the elimination of traffic jams is to be welcomed for its own sake in terms of reducing stress levels. Conversely, cultural projects and sports facilities not only improve the quality of leisure time but may indirectly improve economic performance by making Ireland a more attractive location for internationally mobile workers.[5]

The state plays a central role in ensuring the provision of infrastructure, such as the transport network or the planning framework for housing and urban development. Infrastructure is fundamentally characterised by external effects: the value of a network is greater than the sum of its parts. For this reason, the state plays a leading role in the planning and design of networks in transport, utilities, housing and urban development.

In addition to its planning role, the state also directly provides much infrastructure. For instance, although privately funded toll roads and bridges can make a contribution to the overall transport network, public good and equity considerations mean that much infrastructural investment is financed by the state. Direct provision also solves severe coordination problems: for instance, a laissez faire system may see wasteful duplication in those areas likely to generate the highest toll revenues.

In recent years, infrastructural investment has been extremely high in Ireland, in a bid to redress the severe infrastructural deficit that emerged from a combination of low investment during the 1980s and early 1990s and rapid economic and population growth. The National Development Plan 2000-2006 set out an ambitious programme, with the objective of both improving the physical infrastructure (new roads; LUAS; Dublin Port Tunnel; capital projects in the health and education sectors; new social housing) and the 'knowledge' infrastructure (government investment in human capital and scientific research).

However, it may have been more effective to adopt a more gradual rate of increase in public investment. The pro-cyclical timing of the acceleration in public investment led to high inflation in the construction sector, which was already under pressure due to rising private investment activity. During 1995-2002, construction inflation in Ireland rose by a cumulative 91 per cent, such that much of the increase in public investment was soaked up by inflation rather than fully translating into a larger public capital stock. The scale of the increase in public investment also ran into administrative, planning and legal bottlenecks that further reduced returns. Over the medium term, it is certainly the case that a stable level of public investment is far preferable to the 'stop-go' cycle that has characterised Irish public investment dynamics.

The healthy state of the public finances means that much of the investment has been met by tax revenues. However, some of the investment will take the form of public private partnerships (PPPs), by which a private firm is awarded a contract to build and/or operate an infastructural project. Although this is typically a more expensive source of finance (since the government can borrow at lower rates than private firms), it does enable the use of scarce private managerial talent to achieve social goals. Moreover, the PPP contract may include appropriate penalty clauses, such that the risk of cost overruns or time delays is potentially transferred to the private operator. There have been only a few PPP projects in Ireland, and the UK experience has been that the transfer of risk to the private operator has not always been successfully executed. However, the pressure to increase public investment is sufficiently large that the PPP route may become more widely used in the future.

To ensure efficient use of congested networks, particularly at a time of bottlenecks, user charges or rationing schemes may be required. In Ireland, there has been traditional resistance to charges for utilities such as the water network or waste collection. However, it is likely that such charges will have to be extended over time to include even traffic taxes to relieve pressure on limited road networks, especially in the Dublin area. Designing a scheme that retains access for low income households is a difficult challenge. Finally, the development of the Internet represents a new economic infrastructure. Although the state has played a role in supporting investment in broadband facilities, ensuring broad access to the Internet is an important new challenge for social policy.

With respect to the provision of amenities, variation in individual preferences between private goods and public amenities means that evaluation of such projects is inherently a political task: the role of the economist is just to make explicit the opportunity cost in terms of alternative uses and the overall fiscal position.

5 STATE-OWNED ENTERPRISES AND PRIVATISATION

State-owned enterprises have historically played a major role in the Irish economy, ranging from Aer Lingus to the ESB. Government ownership in the commercial sector may be explained by a number of factors. First, underdeveloped capital markets prevented private entrepreneurs from raising the finance required to build profitable firms in capital intensive sectors such as transport. Second, rather than implement regulation of monopolies (as in the USA), European countries tended to favour government ownership of utilities such as electricity production and telecommunications. Third, state ownership was seen as facilitating the pursuit of social goals such as access to cheap services and regionalisation. Finally, in many countries, state-owned enterprises have facilitated political patronage, with decisions concerning employment and investment being manipulated for electoral purposes.

In recent years, there has been a global shift towards the privatisation of such state-owned firms (see Chapter 8). The development of sophisticated capital markets now allows private entrepreneurs to efficiently finance even large scale ventures. Market liberalisation, sometimes mandated by EU law, has reduced fears of monopoly power in many sectors. Moreover, as indicated earlier in the chapter, the EU prohibition on state aid to rescue non-viable firms means that such firms can no longer be protected for political reasons. Finally, technological innovations, such as in the telecommunications sector, now make it more feasible to have multiple competitors even in 'network' industries.

Where monopoly power is likely to persist, governments typically now prefer to regulate private firms as an alternative to direct state ownership (see Chapter 8). Similarly, social goals (such as the provision of cheap postal services to remote areas) can be achieved by a combination of subsidies and regulation, without requiring actual government ownership. Finally, with accumulating evidence on the performance of privatised industries in other countries, ideological resistance to private ownership has weakened over time.

Another reason for the shift towards privatisation is that government ownership may actually be detrimental to performance. Managers and workers in a state-owned enterprise know that they need not seek to maximise profits, since there is no threat of loss of control to outside investors, and hence have a weak incentive to behave efficiently or control costs.

In addition, as indicated earlier, the government may direct state-owned enterprises to pursue non-commercial objectives, such as providing employment for supporters of the government or locating in disadvantaged areas.[6] A decline in clientilism and an improvement in the transparency of the political system have weakened the incentive of the government to manipulate the semi-state sector to achieve such non-economic goals. Even in the absence of privatisation, there are benefits to depoliticisation of these enterprises. Commercialisation of many Irish state-owned enterprises occurred in the 1980s, with significant improvements in performance. More recently, the privatisation process gained pace, with the disposal of the government interest in firms such as Eircom, ICC and ACC. Other well known state assets, such as Aer Lingus, are due to be privatised in the near future. The privatisation process may also extend to health insurance (sale of VHI) and parts of the public transport system.

In designing a privatisation process, the government faces several conflicts. To maximise revenues, the government should seek the highest issue price or permit a concentration of ownership among large shareholders but this may conflict with a social goal to broaden the shareholder base. To secure the cooperation of powerful unions, the government may feel compelled to offer sharply discounted shares to incumbent workers in the state-owned firms and insert worker protection clauses into the privatisation contract, even if this reduces the value of the firm. Of course, the privatisation process should be fully transparent, to prevent state assets being sold at artificially low prices to politically connected business interests.

Privatisation generates a one time cash windfall for the government. However, it is important to understand that the net impact on the government's balance sheet is much smaller: by transferring ownership, the government no longer receives dividends from the firm, reducing future government revenues. That said, to the extent that the firm is worth more in private hands and the buyout of incumbent workers is not too costly, the net financial gain of privatisation to the government will be positive.

Finally, the privatisation of a monopoly producer requires ancillary efforts to establish an effective regulatory regime and a vigorous competition policy (see Chapters 3 and 8). In the absence of these safeguards, the social gains to privatisation will be sharply diminished and may even turn negative.

6 SIZE OF GOVERNMENT: ECONOMIC AND POLITICAL FACTORS

In evaluating tax and expenditure policies, a fundamental question is the optimal size of government. If the size of government is too large, it makes sense to prune expenditure and cut taxation; conversely, increases in spending and taxation are required if the government is too small to achieve desired policy outcomes. Of course, determining the optimal size of government is a difficult challenge and involves both economic and political dimensions.

Trends and International Comparisons
Although the government can also exert much influence through legislation, regulation, social partnership and moral suasion, measures of public expenditure and taxation are typically employed as imperfect proxies for the size of government. Table 2.1 shows the dynamics of public expenditure over 1977-2003. The share of total government spending relative to GNP in Ireland has dramatically declined since its peak of 60.1 per cent in 1985.

However, recent years have seen some reversal in this trend: the ratio rose from 37.5 per cent in 2000 to 42.5 per cent in 2003.[7] By inspecting the composition of public expenditure, we see that a dramatic decline in debt interest payments as a share of GNP has been a major driver of the shrinkage in government size. Relative to the mid 1980s, social security expenditure has also declined, which can be attributed to the spectacular decline in unemployment over the last decade (see Chapter 4). In contrast, public investment has recently been at historically high levels and public consumption has maintained a relatively stable share of GNP. However, the low level of public investment in the late 1980s and early 1990s mean that infrastructural bottlenecks developed and the recent resurgence of public investment is intended to tackle this deficit.

Table 2.1

Composition of Public Expenditure

	Total	Consumption	Investment	Interest	Social Security
1977	46.8	17.1	4.5	5.4	11.6
1985	60.1	20.9	4.3	11.2	16.4
1995	46.7	18.5	2.6	6.0	13.3
2000	37.5	16.2	4.3	2.3	9.5
2003	42.5	19.4	4.7	1.7	11.4

Source: OECD, *OECD Economic Outlook Database*, OECD, Paris 2004.
Note: Percentages of GNP.

Table 2.2 provides some international comparisons for the evolution of total government spending as a share of GNP. This table underlines the importance of correcting for the difference between GDP and GNP in making judgments on the size of government. Measured relative to GDP, Irish public spending had descended to US levels by 2000. For Ireland, GNP is a better measure of economic scale, since the excess of GDP over GNP can largely be attributed to tax driven accounting 'tricks' by multinational firms.

Table 2.2

Total Government Spending: Cross Country Comparison

	1995	2000	2003
Ireland	41.5	32.1	34.8
Ireland (% of GNP)	46.6	37.5	42.0
EU-15	51.3	45.7	48.4
Accession			46.0
UK	44.5	36.9	42.8
France	55.2	52.7	54.7
Germany	49.6	45.7	49.1
USA	35.0	32.3	35.3

Source: European Commission's Directorate General for Economic and Financial Affairs, *AMECO database,* Europa, www,europa.eu.int 2004.
Note: Percentages of GDP, except where indicated.

However, the Irish data looks solidly European once measured relative to GNP, even if still well below the shares of France and Germany. Moreover, we should expect to see government size smaller in Ireland than in the major continental economies. First, Ireland's relatively young population means that public expenditure on pensions is naturally lower, which is reinforced by the relatively greater role played by the private sector in financing pensions in Ireland. Second, lower unemployment in Ireland means that social security payments are a smaller burden. Third, Ireland has fewer defense commitments than the major countries, such that military expenditures are lower.[8]

Causes of Variations in Size of Government
Wagner's Law
Many factors contribute to variation across countries and over time in government spending. First, across countries and over time, there is a clear positive correlation between the level of income per capita and the share of public expenditure in national income: this tendency is known as Wagner's Law. One reason is that public subsidies to health care, education and pensions may be interpreted as luxury items, with an income elasticity of demand greater than unity.

As incomes grow, voters demand more of these services, placing upward pressure on public spending. However, the damaging costs of excessive taxation place an upper bound on the sustainable level of spending on these items. The fiscal reforms attempted by many countries in recent years may in part be a result of having approached this upper bound. The increasing mobility of capital and skilled labour also places limits on the feasible size of government, by placing a cap on sustainable tax rates.

Baumol's Disease
Another driving force behind upward pressure on public spending is the so called Baumol's disease, named after the American economist who proposed the hypothesis.[9] Baumol's hypothesis is that an economy can be divided into progressive and non-progressive sectors. Productivity gains in the progressive sector drive up wages, which must be matched by the non-progressive sector if it is to attract labour. This phenomenon has clearly been operating in Ireland in recent years: strong productivity improvements in the manufacturing, software and financial services sectors has led to rapid wage growth.

Provision of education and health care services plausibly falls into the non-progressive sector, on the basis that productivity growth in such labour intensive sectors is limited. It follows that the implicit relative price of these services must rise, as wages increase without a compensating improvement in productivity. If the income elasticity of demand for these services exceeds the price elasticity of demand, the ratio of public spending to national income will increase, even if the volume of services provided is unchanged. In order to retain labour, it has been necessary to significantly raise the salaries for teachers and medical workers. For this reason, the rapid increase in education and healthcare spending in Ireland in recent years has mostly been absorbed by rising wages, with a much smaller improvement in the level of services (see Chapters 10 and 11).

It is wrong to assume, however, that productivity growth in publicly financed sectors is impossible, as another factor behind slow improvement is lack of competitive pressure to produce efficiently. Improved management, stronger cost controls and the outsourcing of some services may help in forcing more rapid productivity growth in these sectors. Moreover, recent technological change may enable new productivity gains. For example, Internet based courses and learning aids may be feasible in many education sectors. An important challenge for policymakers is to ensure such new technologies are exploited, even in the face of resistance from traditional suppliers, such as public sector unions.

Demographic Factors
Demographic factors also are important in determining the level of public spending. In the 1970s and 1980s, Ireland had an unusually large cohort of children, placing pressure on the education budget. At the other end of the life cycle, many countries now face an increase in the proportion of old people in the population, with attendant growth in healthcare and pension expenditures. Currently, Ireland enjoys an unusually favourable demographic profile, with the vast bulk of the population in the working age bracket, which allows either a decline in government spending or an improvement in the quality of services and pension levels. The problems associated with the greying of the population is not expected to significantly hit Ireland until 2010-2025 (see also Chapter 4).

Automatic Stabilisers
Welfare spending fluctuates over the economic cycle, as the numbers unemployed fall during expansions and rise during recessions. Such 'automatic stabilisers' induce a natural countercyclical pattern in government spending: however, this may be attenuated by procyclical shifts in the level of benefits: during booms, the level of benefits tends to improve.

The Public Debt
Another technical factor in determining public expenditure is the size of the public debt. Figure 2.1 shows the evolution of the Irish debt to GNP ratio, which rose rapidly between the mid 1970s and the mid 1980s but has subsequently trended downwards. As was shown earlier in Table 2.1, the debt adjustment has been a major factor in the decline in public expenditure by generating a reduction in debt servicing costs.

What explains the dynamics of public debt? Budget deficits incurred in previous years result in the commitment of funds to interest payments on that debt in the current year: in essence, deficits defer the timing of taxation. A cynical view is that accumulation of public debt can be a device whereby a government is able to constrain its successors' choices about public expenditure: if the successor faces a high interest bill, it will be constrained in its non-interest expenditure plans unless it is prepared to raise tax revenues.

It is again the case that reducing the public debt creates a virtuous cycle in that debt interest payments are also reduced in subsequent years. Debt/GNP ratio dynamics depend heavily on the gap between the interest rate and the GNP growth rate. In recent years, Ireland has benefited from the unusual good fortune of a growth rate in excess of the interest rate but, as occurred in the late 1970s, this can quickly unravel: an increase in European interest rates and a growth slowdown would sharply change the level of the primary budget surplus that is required to stabilise the debt/GNP ratio. Moreover, the asymmetry between Irish and eurozone growth patterns raises the likelihood of an increase in interest rates precisely when Irish growth is decelerating.

Figure 2.1

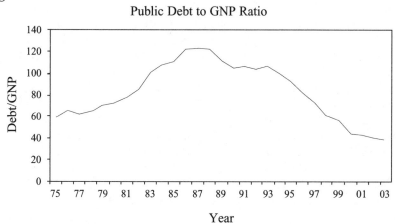

Public Debt to GNP Ratio

Source: As for Table 2.1.

Under EMU (Economic and Monetary Union), discretion over public debt dynamics is constrained by the Growth and Stability Pact. The underlying logic of the Pact is that excessive debt creation threatens monetary stability: highly indebted governments would be tempted to place pressure on the ECB (European Central Bank) to adopt an expansionary stance, with a view to reducing the real burden of the debt through inflation. As such, it is reasonable to minimise this risk by placing restrictions on excessive debt accumulation.

However, the original design of the Pact faces a number of important criticisms. First, since its primary rule is that budget deficits should not normally exceed 3 per cent of GDP, it places the focus on current year deficit rather than the level of the public debt. In this way, it does not make a distinction between a low debt country (such as Ireland) and a high debt country (such as Italy). Second, it fails to take into account that a debt financed increase in productive public capital is more sustainable than a debt financed increase in current government expenditure on consumption or transfers. Third, it does not explicitly make a distinction between the level of potential GDP and cyclical movements in GDP: a large deficit during a recession is not as problematic as a large deficit during boom times. Fourth, it ignores the 'implicit liabilities' owed by many governments – for instance, there is little difference between explicit debt and hard commitments to pay generous pensions to future generations of retirees, in that both require costly increases in future taxation. Finally, the Pact lacks credibility since its sanctions are unlikely ever to be imposed, especially if the culprit is a large country that can persuade the other member countries to exercise discretion. For these reasons, it is likely that the Pact will be redesigned in the coming years in order to take into account some of these criticisms.

A State Investment Fund

A recent innovation in Ireland has been to establish the National Pensions Reserve Fund (NPRF) in order to finance future state pension liabilities (see also Chapter 3). Rather than exclusively using budget surpluses to pay down the public debt, one per cent of GNP each year is allocated to the NPRF that invests in a portfolio of financial assets. The dividend income and capital gains on these assets can then be employed to finance pension expenditures, as a partial alternative to raising future taxation.

However, the precise design of such a fund is critically important for its success and political acceptability. A major concern is the politicisation of investment decisions. At the extreme, this might involve discriminating between domestic projects on the basis of the political connections of entrepreneurs. Less obviously, it may induce the allocation of an excessive portfolio share to domestic over foreign assets, with lobby groups pressing the state fund to support domestic firms and workers.

This is a very difficult problem. On the one side, it is desirable to minimise political interference in the operation of the fund. On the other side, in a democratic society, the operators of a state fund must be politically accountable. Much of the international debate concerning the delegation of public tasks to independent agencies, such as central banks and industry regulators, is relevant here. An important principle is that the government defines the objectives of the agency but that the agency is given wide scope in the pursuit of these objectives, subject to the issuing of regular public reports justifying any deviations from targeted outcomes.

It should be clear that the correct investment approach for a state pension fund is to overwhelmingly hold overseas assets. First, this strategy minimises the politicisation problem. Second, it is a sensible hedge. Imagine if the state pension fund held domestic assets: in the event of a domestic downturn, the public finances would be hit not only by a decline in tax revenues but also by a contraction in investment income. By holding foreign assets, in contrast, 'tax base risk' is offset. Third, the state pension fund would be large relative to the domestic market but tiny in global terms such that investing overseas improves flexibility and liquidity in portfolio management.[10]

The initial investment strategy of the NPRF has largely respected these principles. Its equity and bond holdings are overwhelmingly international, with only modest holdings of domestic securities. However, it has announced plans to play a larger role in funding domestic infrastructural investment, which increases the risk that the fund's strategy will become overly politicised.

The Political Economy of Public Spending

The preceding analysis generally assumes that the government acts to maximise social welfare. While the bulk of public expenditure may be usefully interpreted in this way, a substantial component is influenced by a more overtly political process, in which public expenditure allocations are the outcome of a struggle between interest groups, public sector workers and politicians. This process may produce outcomes that are contrary to social welfare: government failure may be as important as market failure in deviating from optimal outcomes.

Public Choice Theory

One reason why social welfare is not maximised is voter ignorance of the true costs of public expenditure. The Downs paradox (individual votes have no influence over the result of an election) suggests that it is not individually worthwhile for the electorate to learn much about the costs of different public spending programmes. In contrast, some groups have vested interests in specific areas of public expenditure (e.g. farmers and agricultural subsidies) and will act collectively to promote these specific public expenditures. In a famous book, the late Mancur Olson pointed out that such interest groups are easier to organise in a rich society and hence this problem will increase over time.[11]

The characteristics of the civil service bureaucracy can also contribute to government failure. Civil servants act as agents for the government in evaluating and monitoring the effectiveness of public spending. An influential hypothesis is that bureaucrats like to maximise the size of their departmental budgets, as this is associated with power and status. With each department seeking to promote its own expenditure programmes, the net result is to place upward pressure on the level of public spending. An exception is the Department of Finance: arguably, its focus is on holding back the overall level of spending.

The Design of the Political System

Much current research is devoted to analysing the impact of the structure of the political system on public expenditure decisions. For instance, it is suggested that governments that are coalitions of parties with significantly different political philosophies and short tenures in office are less able to control public expenditure. Each party in a coalition has a veto on reductions in its favoured areas so that a prisoners' dilemma results – it is in the collective interest to control spending but no single party has the incentive to accept unilateral spending reductions. Short tenures make it infeasible to implement spending controls as it will not have the time to enjoy the benefits before the next election.

In such circumstances, it seems that fiscal control can only occur under 'crisis' conditions, with the public debt so high that there is no alternative to reform. Often, this requires suspension of normal political rivalries and the formation of a government of national unity. Elements of this story ring true for the Irish experience during 1977-87. Once fiscal control is established, fear of a return to instability may restrain expenditure for a long period. However, memories eventually fade and the pressure for a relaxation on public spending may resume. Looking forward, it will be a challenge for the coalition based Irish political system to maintain control on fiscal spending, in the absence of binding external constraints on the budgetary position. However, the EU Growth and Stability Pact does place some limit on the potential for fiscal excess.

Another manifestation of politically driven fluctuations in public spending is the impact of the electoral cycle on public spending: in the run up to elections, there is a tendency for public spending to increase (especially on visible projects) and taxes are reduced. The timing of these fluctuations suggests such spending has little basis in terms of social welfare but rather is directed at winning favour for the incumbent government.

International evidence suggests that fiscal control is best achieved by a transparent system that places ultimate responsibility for fiscal policy on the finance minister than by a collegial and secretive system in which lines of responsibility are not clearly designated.[12] Improving transparency in the fiscal process can also help eliminate perceptions of a 'democratic deficit' in the discussion, analysis and evaluation of alternative policy proposals.

7 CONCLUSION

The central theme of this chapter is that the state is a major economic actor. A well functioning and effective government is necessary to achieve economic efficiency and redistributional objectives. The maximisation of social welfare requires that the government choose the optimal mix of policy instruments to attain its desired policy objectives.

The analysis in this chapter gives some clues as to the likely evolution of the government's role in the economy in the coming decades. One global trend is a shift from the government as provider to a greater use of private inputs to achieve social goals. Another trend is toward ever greater internationalisation of the policymaking process, as trade and financial linkages bind countries closer together. In the opposite direction, further decentralisation of some government functions to local levels of government is also likely to occur.

Public expenditure policies remain the primary method by which the state intervenes in the economy. With the economic boom, the decline in the public debt and an extremely favourable demographic structure, the government now has much more freedom in making spending decisions. Accordingly, it has never been more important that rigorous evaluation procedures are employed to ensure that the state obtains value for money and delivers public services in an efficient and equitable manner. In particular, an important priority is to ensure that the public investment programme operates in an effective manner and avoids disruptive stop-go cycles.

Finally, it should be clear that government performance is an important determinant of international competitiveness. An efficient government enhances the ability of domestic firms to compete in international markets, by reducing the taxation and other costs of attaining policy objectives, in international empirical studies, an efficient government is highly correlated with strong growth performance.[13] For this reason, and for the others discussed in this chapter, the analysis of government intervention in the Irish economy remains a primary task for those interested in maximising Ireland's national welfare.

Endnotes

1   See A. Shleifer and R. Vishny, *The Grabbing Hand: Government Pathologies and Their Cures*, MIT Press, Cambridge MA 1998.
2   See D. Rodrik, 'Openness and Government', *Journal of Political Economy*, October 1998.
3   Of course, sufficient taxes must be raised to finance required public goods.
4   See D. Rodrik, 'How Far will International Integration Go?', *Journal of Economic Perspectives*, Winter 2000.
5   J. FitzGerald, I. Kearney and E. Morgenroth, 'National Development Priorities for the Period 2000-2006', *ESRI Policy Research Series*, ESRI, Dublin 1999.
6   See Shleifer and Vishny, *op. cit.*
7   The choice between GDP and GNP as the appropriate denominator is important in the case of Ireland, since GDP is so much larger than GNP due to the high net investment income outflow. Since GNP measures national income and comprises the bulk of the tax base, we opt to measure the ratio in terms of GNP.
8   See also D. de Buitleir and P. McArdle, 'Tax and Spend: A Look to the Future with an Eye on the Past' (Kenmare Economics Conference), Justice Commission, Ireland 2003.
9   W. Baumol, 'Macroeconomics of Unbalanced Growth: The Anatomy of Urban Crisis', *American Economic Review*, June 1967.
10 In designing a state pension fund, the small and open nature of the Irish economy provides more degrees of freedom and is a great advantage compared to countries such as the USA.
11 M. Olson, *The Logic of Collective Action: Public Goods and the Theory of Groups*, Harvard University Press, Cambridge MA 1965.
12 See J. Poterba and J. von Hagen, *Fiscal Institutions and Fiscal Performance*, University of Chicago Press, Chicago 1999.
13 See R. Barro and X. Sala-i-Martin, *Economic Growth*, MIT Press, Cambridge MA 1995.

CHAPTER 3

Policy Tool Options for a Regional Government

Kevin Carey[*]

1 INTRODUCTION

This chapter will discuss the tools available to policymakers in Ireland in the light of the economy's ever increasing integration within the European Union, as explained in previous chapters. Rather than present a menu of policy tools and their use, this chapter will present three types of policy, taxation, social partnership, regulation and competition policy, within a simple analytical framework which recognises that even a single tool can have multiple uses and impacts. The framework will examine four issues: the gap between the current level of output and the full employment level of output, the gap between the full employment level of output and the competitive level of output, the distribution of income, and long term growth. For the latter two issues, the discussion will ignore any output gaps and assume that distribution and growth raise similar considerations regardless of which concept of output we are talking about.

Cyclical Fluctuations
Full employment (and its associated level of output) represents the lowest level of unemployment that the economy can attain that is consistent with normal turnover in the labour market and stable inflation. Differences between the current level and the full employment level of output, called *cyclical fluctuations*, will be attributed to changes in aggregate demand, which is the total expenditure in the economy arising from consumers, firms, the government and the rest of the world. Conventional Keynesian macroeconomics posits that output is disturbed from its full employment level because the price level and interest rates are not perfectly flexible in response to changes in aggregate demand, and that the government's own policy tools for affecting aggregate demand might be available to offset this problem. The modern Keynesian framework also incorporates the principle that the price level and interest rate adjustments that would have been instantaneous in a classical framework, and would have preserved full employment output, are

48

instead spread out over a substantial period of time, and only attain the classical levels in the 'long run'.

While the original Keynesian channel for sluggish price adjustment to affect output was via the labour market, for an open economy such as Ireland, the impact on output of the price level also arises via the real exchange rate and therefore on what is commonly referred to as the 'competitiveness' of the Irish economy. Let e denote the domestic price of a unit of foreign currency (e.g. the price in euro of a pound), P the Irish price level, and P* the foreign price level, then the real exchange rate is defined as eP*/P. The real exchange rate is a relative price: the price of a 'typical' foreign goods basket relative to that of a 'typical' Irish basket. This price is one of the major determinants of Irish exports and imports, with, other things being equal, an increase in the real exchange rate (a depreciation) making Irish goods cheaper and thus boosting exports and reducing imports.

Ireland has spent most of its history with little control over e (and of course by definition no control of P*), but nonetheless subject to substantial trade relevant movements in e whether in the sterling or EMS/Euro regimes – movements that would not necessarily be consistent with the macroeconomic requirements of the Irish economy. Therefore the ability to achieve domestic price level adjustments to ease cyclical movements in trade assumes even greater importance for Ireland than for a country with more exchange rate autonomy.

Efficiency and Distribution

The gap between the full employment level of output and the competitive level of output will reflect market distortions. By competitive, we refer to the idealised market framework of neoclassical economics in which private and social costs and benefits are equalised in all markets, and *distortion* will refer to situations where private and social incentives diverge (see also Chapter 2). It is important to keep in mind however the term distortion is used in a technical and not a derogatory sense. For instance, to cite an example to which we will return, comparative studies of developed country labour markets often note the much lower levels of labour force participation in Continental Europe than in the USA, and attribute the difference to distortions induced by the tax and retirement system. Ultimately however this difference may simply reflect a different labour leisure trade off in societal preferences, which will be manifested in the policy choices of the respective governments. Such situations, in which the apparent distortion may reflect a higher level policy goal, are discussed further under the topic of distribution below.

Of more concern are distortions induced by vested interests which benefit a relatively small group at the expense of broad sections of society. Indeed the very fact that the benefits from such distortions tend to be concentrated while the costs are diffused can make them politically difficult to challenge. The classic example of such a distortion is restrictions on entry to a particular industry; these restrictions could lie in either private control of entry, or government regulation or (more usually) a combination of the two. Therefore the government's policy instruments for tackling these distortions will be particularly important.

There is a large class of efficiency interventions which can be justified as responding to a market failure. In the classic examples, a market economy will overproduce certain outputs relative to the social optimum (e.g. pollution) and under produce others (e.g. national security). Such situations reflect the underlying problem of an economic activity with costs or benefits that do not accrue to the entity undertaking the activity. An intervention is then justified to ensure that private and social incentives are correctly aligned (e.g. a pollution tax) or, if this is not possible, regulation or collective action to correct the market failure, is justified.

Over the last thirty years, economists have broadened the notion of market failure to encompass a range of informational problems, and this work provides further theoretical basis for policy interventions. The core problem is the operation of markets under asymmetric information, i.e. when one party to a transaction has more information than the other party. The context of insurance is useful in illuminating the key issues. A driver seeking car insurance may be able to conceal relevant information from the insurance company such as his own knowledge of his driving skills, and this information gap may cause the insurance company to suspect that the person is seeking insurance precisely because he is a bad driver. This problem is called *adverse selection*. In addition, having obtained insurance, the insurance company is unable to perfectly monitor the actions of the insured driver. Yet the fact of having insurance may itself cause the driver to take riskier actions than he would in the absence of insurance. This problem is called *moral hazard*.

The existence of these problems does not of itself provide a rationale for policy intervention. Indeed, to pursue the insurance example, the insurance company has a strong private incentive to overcome adverse selection and moral hazard and has a considerable range of tools for doing so, from access to driver history to the structure of the insurance contract itself in which insurance coverage, cost, and renewal can be made conditional on driver characteristics. Nevertheless, many asymmetric information situations can be mitigated when one party to a transaction is able to send a credible signal to the other, and a policy intervention may be the best way to facilitate this. Thus we observe governments taking an active role in setting standards and facilitating the acquisition of relevant information, such as penalty points for driving offences.

In some important cases, public interventions are motivated by considerations of distributional equity rather than market efficiency, or even more broadly by a goal of national interest or cohesion, with an accompanying presumption that even an efficient market economy would fail to advance this goal if left to its own devices. At the level of economic wellbeing, economists have discussed the appropriate distribution of economic resources and the trade off between having a more equal distribution of resources versus the loss in incentives that such a distribution would imply. In practice, most economies have chosen to engage in some redistribution of resources, but well short of complete equality, while at the same time providing a safety net for those at the lowest end of the income or wealth distribution (see Chapter 6).

In particular, governments have found it impossible to leave health, education and social safety nets to market forces, because of a combination of:
- A primary goal of equality of opportunity and equal access to essential services.
- A desire to mitigate the individual or household impact of unavoidable circumstances, bad luck, or bad choices.
- Impediments to market involvement in these sectors, notably those arising from informational problems in health and insurance provision.
- A political economy goal of ensuring some minimal level of participation by everyone in society (see Chapters 10 and 11).

However, as with our hypothetical example of complete equality, distributional interventions often interact with efficiency considerations. Indeed, some interventions that may appear to be addressed as an economic inefficiency may in fact reflect a distributional concern. For instance, governments are often tempted to intervene in insurance or credit markets to ensure that specific groups (e.g. insurance for young male drivers, or credit for new businesses) are able to access these markets. It is rarely clear in practice whether such interventions are designed to correct a market imperfection or rather the market is efficiently denying access to a well identified group, creating pressure for the government to respond. If the latter is the case, then the government should not be surprised when the same problems that impeded market provision emerge in the government scheme.

Growth and Competitiveness

The fourth element of our analytical framework will be long term growth, the only source of sustained improvement in living standards. A full understanding of the sources of long term growth would take us into a vast area of ongoing research, but for Ireland as a regional economy, the key factors are the rate of technological progress at the world and supranational levels, and the country's ability to influence the location of productive activity in Ireland – which, for a small economy like Ireland, is itself a significant margin on which to expand (see Chapters 5 and 7).

So far in the discussion of this four part framework we have concentrated on output. But for a regional economy seeking to attract mobile capital, some discussion of relative prices is also essential. We have already seen the core concept here, namely the real exchange rate. The attitude to the appropriate level of the real exchange rate lies in the eye of the beholder. The traditional focus of macroeconomic policy has been to view real exchange rate depreciations as 'good' because of the associated increase in demand from the rest of the world and the improvement in the trade balance. But the counterpart to a real exchange rate depreciation is lower purchasing power over foreign goods by domestic consumers, who will feel poorer as a result. This inherent difference in perspective can be a source of disagreement and confusion about competitiveness policies.

It has been observed across countries at quite different stages of development that there can be a strong domestic constituency favouring policies that lead to low prices for imports via an appreciated real exchange rate. But the long term feasibility of these policies depends on how the real exchange rate appreciation has been achieved. It is one thing if the appreciated real exchange rate is a product of equilibrium forces, for example if a booming sector in the economy has led to a general rise in domestic wages and prices relative to other countries. More troubling is the case where the appreciated real exchange rate is related to the vested interest efficiency distortions of the type described above; rectifying this situation requires an acceptance that the high price of domestic goods will sooner or later manifest itself in a dilemma for policymakers. In addition to whatever pressure for reform may come from domestic constituencies, evidence of this problem will also be found in the current account, and adjustment will ultimately require a collective acknowledgement by society that its purchasing power over foreign goods and services may have to decline.

A very brief recent history of the Irish real exchange rate would draw attention to chronic real exchange rate appreciation in the late 1970s and 1980s, attributable to macroeconomic policy mistakes and corrected first through repeated devaluations within the EMS and then by improved conduct of macroeconomic policy in the late 1980s and 1990s. Since then, real exchange rate appreciation can be seen more as an equilibrium phenomenon, given the presence of a booming sector, and now reinforced by the global appreciation of the euro. Nevertheless, there is a legitimate concern amongst policymakers and the public that the component of Irish prices attributable to distortions has risen, or at least become more visible, in recent years (see Chapter 6). This is particularly evident in (see Chapter 8) the tourist industry, which is highly sensitive to competitiveness considerations.

Let us conclude this discussion with a brief discussion of what influences the policy choices of the government. Some of these choices will reflect fundamental preferences and the history of the society. But there are other determinants that while changing very slowly and thus seeming structural, can nonetheless be explained in terms of current circumstances and by extension allow some predictions for how these choices might change in the future. The leading example of this phenomenon in the Irish context is demography. The Republic has an unusually young age structure by European standards (see Chapter 4) and the movement of a large cohort through the age structure has exerted a considerable influence on policy priorities over the last twenty years. In the 1980s, the dominant issue for this cohort was lack of jobs, and for those who did not emigrate, unemployment benefits and further education were the key shock absorbers. Correspondingly, retirement and healthcare and infrastructure provision were less of a concern. With the employment picture since favourably transformed, attention has turned to the legacy of under provision in the latter areas. At the time, attracting an inflow of mobile foreign investment remained a central element of the growth strategy, which was able to draw on the educational base created in the 1980s, while having significant implications for corporate tax policy. We will see various manifestations of these factors below (see also Chapter 7).

2 TAXATION

Taxation refers to the raising of revenue for the financing of government activities. We follow the EU standard terminology in our typology of taxation. Some taxation is levied and collected directly from the taxpayer by the government; these are called *direct taxes* and consist mainly of personal and corporate income taxes. A second set of taxes is levied along the chain of production of goods and services and may be collected by a producer or retailer before being remitted to the government; these are called *indirect taxes* and consist mainly of the value-added tax (VAT) and excise taxes such as those on alcohol and tobacco. Finally, *social insurance* refers to a type of taxation levied on wages and salaries and used to finance pensions and other transfer schemes. In Ireland this takes the form of Pay Related Social Insurance (PRSI), a tax which has both an employee and employer share. Since there was a presumption in the design of social insurance that it would not be required by highly paid workers, PRSI is only payable on wage income below a certain threshold (it is also payable at a lower rate for public sector employees, reflecting a minimal risk of job loss). PRSI revenues in turn finance a simple fixed benefit pension system along with other social benefits (such as public healthcare provision and disability payments).[1]

Like its international counterparts, current PRSI revenues were intended to cover current PRSI outlays (i.e. it was a pay as you go system), so even though it looks like a forced savings scheme from the perspective of an individual participant, at the aggregate level it is a pure transfer programme with a specific source of financing. Because governments have tended to view the social insurance system separately from the rest of its interventions, and given the inevitable expansion of social insurance with the aging of the population, there will be an extended discussion of social insurance issues below.

User Charges and Tax Expenditures

Two additional features of the government's revenue management can be a source of ambiguity as to whether they are formally part of tax policy. The first is an increasing reliance on user fees for specific services. One type is fees for administrative services. While these do not have the formal legal compulsion of a tax, since one could choose not to avail of the associated government service, the service is often *de facto* essential (e.g. passports, vehicle registration). Thus these should be considered as a tax, broadly defined. A separate set of fees, sometimes confused with administrative fees, is that of fees for public utility services, such as water supply and waste collection. In popular rhetoric, these are also seen as taxes, but the issue of cost recovery for these services would have to be confronted regardless of whether the supplier was private or public. Even with private sector participation, utility provision raises complex issues because of its quasi-essential status, high fixed costs, and its inherent collective nature; the relevant economic issue is not taxation per se but the appropriate structure and pricing of these services. This is best seen as a regulatory issue and so we will return to it in Section 4.

Second, governments worldwide make significant use of a policy instrument that blurs the line between taxation and public expenditure and is thus commonly referred to as tax expenditure. This covers a policy which is intended to achieve a particular use of a pool of funds, but for which the government wishes to avoid a specific outlay of public funds for that purpose. The government instead provides a tax incentive to induce the private sector to undertake the desired allocation. The incentive can be either a tax credit (an offset against a tax liability) or a tax deduction or exemption (a category of income or expenditure not subject to taxation). Important examples in the Irish tax system are tax deductible pension contributions and a plethora of tax breaks for specific types of activity, such as construction of private hospitals.

The key point is that the budgetary implications of these policies are often poorly understood. The absence of an appropriation of public funds can make the policy seem low cost and shield it from accusations of being a subsidy or handout to an interest group. But there are of course costs in terms of foregone tax revenue and the higher burden on the remaining components of the tax base, and it is an open question how well the understanding of these costs seeps into popular discussion. It is not unfair to speculate that the lack of transparent costing of these policies is part of their appeal to politicians. Yet a tax expenditure can be ineffective relative to direct public expenditure for achieving a given goal. Since by design the government does not undertake the expenditure itself, there will leakage from the private funds freed up for the same purpose; money is fungible (interchangeable) and the recipient of the tax break will want to spend some of it for the actual goal of the government, but some on general unrelated purposes. To the extent that the private sector would have undertaken the preferred allocation anyway, the total impact of the tax expenditure is reduced.

International Comparisons

It is useful to present a breakdown of the government's main sources of tax revenue. Standard cross country comparisons scale tax revenue relative to the overall size of the economy, which is usually measured by Gross Domestic Product (GDP). GDP measures the market value of production within the nation's borders. Economists have drawn attention to the potentially misleading nature of GDP as a measure of the size of the Irish economy, because a significant proportion of production in Ireland generates income overseas, namely for multinational firms (see Chapter 5). A companion measure to GDP, called Gross National Product (GNP), measures income accruing to a nation's residents and is thus a more accurate measure of Irish national income than GDP would be. But GDP remains the preferred measure of international economic organisations: the GDP versus GNP divergence is small for most countries, and international income flows can be harder to track than domestic production. Furthermore, total production does provide one plausible measure of the demand for government services and the potential tax base for financing them. The correct measure of the economy's size thus probably lies somewhere between GDP and GNP. For transparency, we will present the Irish figures using the international standard, i.e. relative to GDP. But readers should bear in mind that some upward adjustment is necessary, which could be up to 20 per cent, representing the recent size of the gap between GDP and GNP.[2]

Consider first the total tax take relative to the size of the economy. In 2002, the ratio of total taxes to GDP was 29 per cent in Ireland versus 40 per cent for the European Union (whether considered in its 15 or current 25 member form). Even allowing for the full adjustment of this ratio for the GDP-GNP gap would still leave the country at the low end of the tax take within the EU, although then looking somewhat similar to the UK. However, the composition of tax revenue reveals even more striking divergences with the corresponding EU averages as seen in Table 3.1. While the personal income tax share looks typical for the EU, the indirect tax share is far higher, the share of corporate income tax is also significantly higher, while the social insurance share is about half of the EU average. The forces underlying these numbers will emerge as we evaluate tax policy along the various criteria in the following subsections.

Table 3.1
Major Components in percentages of Total Taxation in Ireland compared to EU Averages, 2002

	Ireland	EU-15	EU-25
Direct taxes	*41*	*34*	*33*
Personal income tax	25	25	24
Corporate income tax	13	6	6
Indirect taxes	*44*	*35*	*35*
VAT	25	17	17
Excise & consumption taxes	12	6	6
Social insurance	*16*	*32*	*32*

Source: European Commission (Eurostat and Directorate General for Taxation and Customs Union), *Structures of the Taxation Systems in the European Union*, European Commission, Luxembourg 2004.

Cyclical Fluctuations

As with public expenditure (Chapter 2), tax policy is accorded a relatively small role in the management of cyclical fluctuations. Nevertheless, with the complete absence of any monetary policy autonomy, its relevance cannot be ignored. First, and similar to public expenditure, the tax system can perform an automatic stabiliser role without any discretionary action by policymakers; in other words, the structure of the tax system causes the burden to relax when the economy is weakening and strengthen when the economy is booming. This ability derives from the progressive nature of the income taxation system; higher levels of income incur the higher marginal tax rate (42 per cent). Thus as the economy booms, the average income tax rate rises and it likewise declines when the economy slows down. Of some significance to the exchequer in the past was the fact that the income tax brackets, which determine marginal tax rates were not indexed, so inflation had the effect of raising average income taxes. This effect is still present in the tax system but not as visible because of the relatively low rate of inflation. However, a similar mechanism is present when wages increase because of economic growth and in fact the higher marginal tax rate (which applies above €28,000 for single or widowed taxpayers) is easily reached by workers near the average industrial wage.

While governments would normally be interested in the prospect of tax cuts as an anti-recession tool, Ireland has had to give some consideration to temporary tax increases to combat an over heating economy – but has generally come down against this use of tax instruments. Ultimately this seems to have reflected political economy concerns; in part the principle of maintaining low taxes was seen as one element of Social Partnership policies (see below); this was compounded by a more ideological view that higher taxes would ultimately lead to a larger size of government by creating pressures for higher public expenditure. If this viewpoint is valid (and there is certainly some evidence to support the idea that government spending rises to meet the resources available to finance it), then it does of course negate the case for a 'temporary' tax increase.

Efficiency and Distribution

Tax policy has been dominated by efficiency considerations. The highly stylised world of competitive equilibrium envisages lump sum taxation, i.e. taxes that can be levied with no consequences for incentives. With rare and debatable exceptions, such taxes do not exist (land taxes and poll taxes representing the closest approximations), and thus analysis of taxation must consider the impact of the tax on economic decisions. Nevertheless, the thought experiment of lump sum taxation is useful in highlighting the need to distinguish two aspects (or complaints) about the tax system: the level of taxes and the effect on decisions of taxes. Since the purpose of taxes is to finance government expenditure, then the long run determinant of the level of taxation is simply the level of public expenditure. A country where government expenditure is 50 per cent of GDP will tend towards a taxes/GDP ratio of 50 per cent, and a country where the expenditure ratio is 30 per cent will tend towards a tax ratio of 30 per cent. This will be true regardless of the efficiency with which the tax system is designed.

Distortionary Effects: Income Tax and PRSI

Economists judge the distortion caused by taxes, by the extent to which they change the decisions of firms or households from what they would have been in a world with lump sum taxes. The resulting prescription is to tax goods with very low demand or supply elasticities, precisely because of the insensitivity of the underlying decision to changes in price. However, this prescription often runs up against equity considerations, particularly when the inelasticity is associated with lower income households (e.g. patterns of smoking, or the need of poor households to work). But in addition to balancing equity and efficiency, policymakers must also confront the large uncertainty surrounding precise estimations of the distortions induced by the taxation system.

Two core issues have been debated: incentives to work, and incentives to save. As income taxation systems evolved from taxation of those with extremely high incomes or assets to embrace most of the workforce, the impact on work incentives became an increasing concern. From the perspective of tax compliance, there was a definite advantage to organising the tax system around withholding from wage and salary income. However, this ease of collection from one particular source can, and did, become an over reliance on that source, generating the widespread PAYE protests of the 1980s. Even while labour income often proved the most tempting base for taxation most tax systems, including Ireland's, seek to tax all sources of income, including income from assets. Because capital (unlike labour effort) is long lasting, taxation of capital income raises both efficiency and growth concerns, since any deterrent to capital investment arising from taxation will result in lost output both today and into the future. Leaving aside the output losses, but creating other problems, is the fact that capital income can be difficult to tax: capital is mobile, capital income can be difficult to quantify, and the arrival of capital income in accounting terms can be managed more strategically for tax purposes than labour income.

For all these reasons, a major trend in systems of taxation has been to reduce reliance on income taxes in favour of sales or consumption taxes, which in the EU case takes the form of the Value-Added Tax (VAT). However, Ireland has some divergence in structure from the typical EU VAT, notably the zero rating on children's clothes and shoes; this would become an issue in further harmonisation of VAT across the EU. The government has followed a sustained strategy of moving low paid workers out of the tax net by raising the individualised tax credit. The increased burden on the VAT can be justified: it does not directly tax work effort or savings and its administrative structure renders it more self enforcing than other taxes, because there is a necessity for a paper trail at each stage in the chain of production of goods and services. Indeed, pure efficiency considerations would lead to a preference to raise all revenue by taxation of final consumption, which could be implemented by a VAT but also by an income tax in which all saving is tax deductible. Many countries, including Ireland, have used this principle to motivate the introduction of tax advantaged pension savings accounts, although these remain subject to the general critique of all tax expenditure policies.

While a rationale of promoting saving can be offered for this particular tax expenditure, the income tax system overall is characterised by a proliferation of income tax deductions. As a general principle, such deductions should be held to an extremely high burden of justification. Deductions add to the complexity of the tax system and have an inherent tendency to be regressive because many deductions are only advantageous at high levels of income. Many deductions are characterised by lack of budget transparency in which revenue foregone is seen as 'less costly' than an equivalent outlay of public expenditure. Since deductions are designed to reward particular types of behaviour, there needs to be a case that the associated behaviour has some socially necessary purpose. This can be easy to rationalise in some cases, for instance, when a household is caring for a dependent family member at home when the burden could otherwise be passed to the state. But the Irish tax system contains substantial deductions for particular activities or sectors where the social value is, to say the least, opaque. Chief among these is property sector investments. These have become a major source of deductions for high income taxpayers and yet in a booming economy where market returns on property investments are already quite healthy, it is difficult to justify an additional incentive via the tax system. As in other countries, taxpayers have become adept at tax planning in which these deductions become a key plank of tax avoidance strategy.

From a traditional tax perspective, the structure of the PRSI system (and related levies allocated to specific social expenditure programmes) introduces two new distortions. First, because it is only levied on wage and salary income, it departs from the principal of taxing all income the same way regardless of source. Second, because it operates in parallel with income taxation of wages, PRSI can end up representing a very large proportion of the total tax burden of working poor households. Such households will typically have extremely low income tax liability but significant PRSI payments, especially when the employer share is taken into account. PRSI is thus one source of a poverty trap by creating disincentives for employment for low income households. It increases both the replacement ratio (unemployment benefits as a proportion of potential after tax wages) and the tax wedge (the gap between wages paid by the employer and received by the worker). The government is well aware of this problem and has raised the wage threshold at which the employee portion of PRSI begins; however this threshold does not apply to the employer share, so the tax wedge remains present even at very low wage levels.

Future of Social Insurance

As mentioned earlier, Ireland still has much more favourable demographic patterns for the sustainability of pay as you go transfer programmes than other developed countries, which have lower rates of both population growth and of labour force participation (see Chapter 4). From an aggregate perspective, the decisions for society regarding provision for the retired population are how much of GDP to allocate towards that group, and how to implement that allocation. In the highly stylised world of the overlapping generations models of Samuelson and Diamond, the market solution is to have the young generation work and save, with all capital income then financing their consumption when old.[3] It was clear to nineteenth century governments that in practice this laissez faire approach was resulting in high levels of deprivation amongst the older population (indeed for any households not economically active); working households lacked some or all of: sufficient surplus income to provide for retirement, access to the appropriate financial instruments, and the ability or inclination to plan for a long time horizon.

As the Samuelson and Diamond models make clear, the overlapping generations model with growth suggests a better solution: transfers from the current young to the current old, motivated by the prospect of analogous future transfers when the current young generation is retired.

The free market implementation of this solution is difficult, because it relies on the commitment of future generations, but PRSI type schemes put it on a firmer 'social contract' basis. But of course, electorates and governments can also change the basis of this contract over time, particularly if the demographic and productivity underpinnings of it become strained. Social insurance has also been criticised for reducing the incentive for private saving for retirement, and on broader political economy grounds for increasing the resources available to the government (especially when the scheme runs a surplus).

Thus while social insurance schemes have an excellent track record in reducing old age poverty, attention has returned to more market based approaches, now referred to as fully funded pension schemes. Each working generation funds its own retirement but, reflecting the concerns about a pure laissez faire approach to pensions, the government remains involved in managing the system. Savings are typically still conducted via paycheck withholding into financial instruments regulated by the government, and access to income from these instruments is severely restricted until designated retirement years. Indeed, some governments have concluded that it is inefficient to have the private financial sector maintain individual retirement accounts for the entire population and have opted for a collective fully funded approach in which a government run pension fund makes investments on behalf of the prospective beneficiaries; besides reducing transaction costs, this leaves the government some leverage for redistribution within the pension scheme. As with all tax and transfer schemes, the efficiency loss caused by departing from individualised market rates of return for every participant must be offset against the distributional gains from whatever transfers take place.

Whether managed as an individual or collective fully funded scheme, the crucial issue in social insurance reform is the transition from pay as you go to fully funded. Upon the past introduction of social insurance, there is an initial old generation that is a pure beneficiary – they receive benefits financed by the social insurance tax on the working generation, but have paid minimally into the system themselves.

It is important to note that policymakers viewed this as desirable, given the need to tackle extreme poverty amongst this generation. But the counterpart to this generation is the one paying into the system when the funding mechanism is being changed; if a switch to fully funded is introduced immediately, then the current working generation faces the double burden of having financed the current generation of retirees but now having to provide for its own retirement. The only viable solution to this problem is an injection of general tax revenue into the system to cover these transitional costs.

With this background, we can now describe some of Ireland's recent modifications to its PRSI and pension provision systems. The government has chosen a hybrid approach in which traditional PRSI will continue, but augmented by tax advantaged individual savings accounts and a collective fund for some future pensions. We have already seen a basis for concern about individual savings accounts; the net impact on national saving is smaller than the amount flowing into these accounts, and they have a tendency to be regressive. In addition, concern has surfaced about whether these accounts are well managed and there is a potential source of moral hazard if there is an implicit understanding that the government is providing a safety net for these accounts – an understanding which could be severely tested if substantial numbers of them fare poorly over the next few years.

It is therefore prudent for the government to have a third pillar to pension provision, namely the National Pension Reserve Fund (NPRF), which is a vehicle to fully fund some pension liabilities, most notably those of the public sector itself. The government has made good use of the NPRF as a way to earmark certain budgetary receipts for pension provision, no doubt aware of the expectation that large budgetary surpluses would otherwise have created pressure for tax cuts or increased public expenditure.

This political economy motivation for the NPRF should be balanced against finding the most productive use of public funds; some have argued that in fact these funds would have been better spent on domestic infrastructure rather than on the NPRF's international financial portfolio. However, policymakers have expressed legitimate concern about the political entanglements of a large domestic portfolio in the NPRF; in addition, we have already highlighted the major transition costs in the move away from PRSI as currently structured, and the NPRF will be a valuable buffer in this regard.

Taxation of Housing
One other questionable component of tax revenue: stamp duty, a tax imposed at the time of sale of houses. This is a tax that seems easiest to justify on grounds of ease of collection but, by virtue of its linkage to the housing market, is subject to considerable volatility in revenue which can cloud the government's budgetary planning. If the intended base for this tax is the value of the housing stock, then this could be better targeted through a residential property tax. Both stamp duty and capital gains tax (the latter with substantial scope for avoidance) have the flaw of only bringing housing into the tax net when there is a change of ownership, creating the anomaly of identical houses and/or residents being taxed in different ways depending on the transaction history of the houses.

Growth
While some of the efficiency considerations discussed above may have growth effects, e.g. via the taxation of capital, we will concentrate here on the role that

taxation, especially corporate taxation, has played in Ireland's growth policies (see Chapter 5 and 7). It is well understood that policymakers have seen low corporate tax rates as a key enticement for multinational corporations to locate their production in Ireland. The headline corporate tax rate of 12.5 per cent combined with the country's international tax treaties (which prevent double taxation of the same income) have made it extremely advantageous for multinational firms to concentrate their high value-added activities in Ireland – sometimes drawing the scrutiny of the US Internal Revenue Service when doing so, since the effect is to reduce the portion of profits taxed in the USA. The specifics of the corporate structure have evolved over the years, beginning as preferential tax treatment for exporters and then adapting as EU rules required a move to a low and flat corporate income tax rate for all firms. The effect of all this on corporate tax payments to the Exchequer is a nice illustration of the high elasticity of the corporate tax base; as seen in the introduction to this section, corporate tax revenue accounts for a far higher proportion of Irish tax revenue than the EU average.

The main impediment to continuing this system is the uncertain future of Ireland's tax veto in the EU, the loss of which would open the door to corporate tax harmonisation at a higher level than currently imposed by Ireland. Issues of efficient taxation provide some support for the Irish position on corporate taxes; the corporation's owners in principle pay personal income tax on dividend or capital gains from the corporation, so it is a form of double taxation to also tax it at the corporate level. One could argue on equity grounds that for a small country like Ireland, many of the owners of capital are likely to be abroad so that corporate income taxation provides a lever that would otherwise not be available. But the mobility of capital relative to labour means that the burden of what looks like taxation of capital income may be borne by labour anyway.

3 SOCIAL PARTNERSHIP

Social partnership is perhaps the most nebulous policy instrument of the government, yet one that is cited with great regularity as a vital ingredient of Ireland's economic success.[4] It has an obvious provenance in the incomes policies of the 1970s and 1980s, but whereas incomes policies had come to be seen as an ineffective tool of macroeconomic management and a recipe for poor industrial relations, social partnership has proven quite persistent and at the minimum is seen as a principle to which the social partners are expected to subscribe. The key innovation of the successful partnership era beginning in the late 1980s was the explicit bargain of economy wide wage moderation in exchange for tax cuts. In keeping with the template for evaluating the policy, we will first cast partnership within the cyclical framework, given its origins as a short term macroeconomic management policy. But its longevity also requires a discussion of its efficiency, growth and distribution aspects, to which the discussion will then turn.

Cyclical Fluctuations

The origins of social partnership lie in its potential for improved management of cyclical fluctuations. Faced with the inflationary years of the 1970s, many countries saw the need to impose some structure on wage and price increases, whether motivated by a somewhat naïve belief that the way to control inflation was via price or wage controls (even without any change in the underlying policy stance) or by a more sophisticated understanding of the strategic aspects of inflation provided by economists from the late 1970s onwards. To pursue the latter, inflation is now viewed as the outcome of two related sets of interactions: that between workers and employers, and that between the private sector as a whole and the government. This division of the economy into three sectors, which may strike the reader as somewhat corporatist, is nevertheless useful in thinking about the dynamics of inflation. Any model of economy wide price setting must be grounded in labour costs, which usually form the largest proportion of variable costs for most firms.

Modern Keynesian economics seeks to understand how the purely microeconomic setting of a real wage bargain between workers and firms gets transformed into an aggregate level of wages and prices, and the resulting implications for output. The recurring feature of these models is recognition of an important external effect: each wage price decision contributes, if only in a tiny way, to the overall price level. And since wages and prices are set in money terms, but with a view to what the purchasing power of the money will be, the price level is a factor in each individual wage price decision. Thus each decision has a small influence on the overall outcome while being influenced by the expected overall outcome. This wage setting decision must be reconciled with the economy's total planned expenditure, which the government can influence through its taxation and spending tools.

This basic setting can be appropriately tailored to see the potential for a destructive wage price spiral. Suppose that the private sector expects inflation to be high in the near future. Each individual negotiation incorporates this expectation by setting high wages and prices in money terms. In turn, the government anticipates rising prices and must decide whether to tighten policy to combat inflation, or ease policy to offset the employment losses from rising prices and thus validating the initial expectations of the private sector. If prices do rise and the exchange rate cannot adjust, then the economy suffers a loss in competitiveness through a real appreciation.

If policy remains accommodating, the economy will experience a higher built in rate of inflation. The cycle is only broken when the costs of inflation and declining competitiveness are sufficiently steep that policymakers decide to tighten policy; now output declines, and gradually the private sector adjusts money wages and prices downwards while output recovers. And of course a regional economy does not have the safety valve of the exchange rate; competitiveness is only restored by maintaining a lower inflation rate than the supranational average for some period of time.

The Social Partnership model recognises that a decentralised form of this process could involve painfully long adjustment periods in both the upward and downward movement of inflation and tries to find a way to make the policy decisions of the different sectors consistent with each other and in particular to avoid the basic expectations trap of a government faced with high incipient inflation and thus tempted towards overly expansionary macroeconomic policy. One obvious recourse is to allow wage agreements to be conditional on a government's promise to maintain a particular rate of inflation. If this promise is believed and widely incorporated, then the desired inflation rate can be achieved with minimal output fluctuations.

Clearly the Social Partnership approach deserves considerable credit for Ireland's improved management of inflation and employment since the late 1980s (see Chapter 2). Before looking at the efficiency aspects of these arrangements, note some temporary factors that may have helped jump start the process and which therefore cannot be assumed to be an ongoing basis of its success. First and foremost is the scope for continuing tax cuts to drive the government's side of the bargain. Clearly such cuts cannot be delivered indefinitely and while fiscal deficits would be the ultimate concern, it happens that concerns about the need for public spending have come onto the agenda even before the fiscal sustainability of ongoing tax cuts became an issue. It stands to reason that the private sector judges the effectiveness of government not just by the level of taxes but also by the quality of public services, especially in the social sectors and infrastructure, and it can be expected that unions will have limited tolerance for a model in which tax cuts are continued and public service provision is financed more and more by specific user fees.

A related point is that the initial scope for tax cuts contained a major one off component, reflecting the sharply reduced burden of public debt service in the late 1980s (see Chapter 2) as global interest rates fell and trended downwards throughout the 1990s with the approach of European Monetary Union. Finally, a well timed devaluation in 1986 provided some quick competitiveness gains for the social partnership arrangement to protect; of course the eurozone offers no similar room for manoeuvre in terms of aligning exchange rate and wage bargaining policy.

Efficiency and Distribution
Turning now to the efficiency aspects of Social Partnership. Here the case has to be more measured. The major concern is that, over time, the partnership approach becomes an impediment to necessary labour market adjustments and in particular that it becomes a source of persistent divergence of real wages from underlying productivity conditions. The reason is simple: the tendency of national wage bargaining will be towards similar sized wage increases for all sectors of the economy. While it is true that the wage agreements have left some discretion at the industry and firm level to vary compensation according to specific conditions, the headline wage increase from each agreement becomes in effect a minimum for all sectors. Furthermore, the common increase then locks in any pre-existing wage

differentials, which over time can become a greater source of contention. The clearest example of this phenomenon was the need for the benchmarking exercise for public sector employees; this group had seen a substantial divergence in headline wage levels versus private sector employees and demanded an equalising adjustment in public sector pay scales. The resulting 'benchmarking' agreement has been the subject of considerable criticism, with some justification.

Before implicating the specifics of the Partnership and the Benchmarking exercises in the problems, it should be noted that some fundamental economic forces are the source of a challenge. Economists have discussed the problem in terms of the Balassa-Samuelson model.[5] This is a model of an open economy with a traded and non-traded sector, with rapid productivity growth in the traded goods sector. Workers can freely move between the two sectors, so unit wages must be equalised between them. Thus more rapid productivity growth in the traded sector drives up unit labour costs in the non-traded sector, which must in turn charge a higher relative price for its output. The overall price level is higher than the trading partner, i.e. the country has an appreciated real exchange rate, or in Ireland's case, a relatively high price level within the supranational economy.

Ireland is a classic candidate for this effect because of booming productivity in the export sector. In particular, some of the country's apparently high cost of living should be understood as an equilibrium phenomenon, as the non-traded sector (whether public or private) has to match the labour costs of the traded sector. In this respect, the tensions in the partnership agreements should not be surprising. But the model also reminds us that the extent of the effect is driven by the productivity gap between the two sectors: enhancing productivity in the non-traded sector is of vital importance.[6] It is in this sense that the benchmarking exercise was most disappointing, because a specific timeline of wage adjustments was granted in return for very vague understandings about increased productivity. Analysts have pointed to a lack of transparency in how the wage adjustments were determined and the generic nature of the promised productivity improvements, which draw heavily on management terminology (results/performance orientation, monitoring indicators) but with little specifics.[7]

On the distributional side, social partnership is subject to a number of critiques. One recurring issue is the risk that the effective negotiations take place between the government, employers, and *employed* workers, to the detriment of the unemployed and non-labour force participants. This gives rise to an insider-outsider model of the labour market, where only insiders have an influence on wage determination, and use this to hold the wage above the market clearing level. While theoretical models can be constructed where this might be efficient, the outcome is damaging for the unemployed workers, especially when deterioration of skills with time outside the labour market is taken into account.

A more general concern arises from the often unquestioned focus of national wage bargaining on reaching a consensus *percentage* wage increase. As basic arithmetic reveals, an across the board percentage wage increase leads to ever widening absolute wage differentials. Thus social partnership is a poor instrument for tackling the problems of the working poor, since the additional resources accruing to them from a national wage bargain will be so modest. In the most recent partnership round (negotiated in June 2004), unions sought to include a minimum absolute wage increase of €20 regardless of previous wage levels; this proposal did not survive in the final agreement, which did however include an additional upfront 0.5 per cent wage increase for the lower paid, defined as those making up to €9 per hour.

Growth
The growth effects of Social Partnership are most difficult to pin down. It seems likely that labour market harmony plays into the location decision of multinational firms. In the discussion of cyclical factors we highlighted partnership as a tool of nominal price stability but Ireland's social partnership agreements have gone further than this and have linked wage bargaining to promised tax cuts as well as to general macroeconomic stability. The partnership agreements have been particularly effective in drawing Ireland's very fragmented unions into a single bargaining framework; in the form of unionisation in continental Europe, there tends to be a smaller number of much larger unions who are more likely to internalise the consequences of their wage negotiation strategy and for whom enforcement of wage agreements is easier. Social Partnership can help replicate this behaviour for Ireland. Of course, the Irish government shares with other EU governments an important role as an employer in its own right, via the public sector, enhancing the leverage of a centralised pay bargaining system. Thus social partnership can be seen as a pillar of labour market stability, attracting mobile capital via its general ability as a coordinating tool to limit the risk of 'leapfrogging' wage adjustments.

4 REGULATION AND COMPETITION POLICY [8]

This class of policy tool includes government interventions to correct market failures and distortions, and thus can be seen primarily as tools to enhance economic efficiency. However, not all regulatory interventions can be justified purely on grounds of efficiency, not least because the efficiency framework gives the benefit of the doubt to individual choices whereas the government has clearly decided that it can be legitimate to override individual choices in certain cases. This is starkest in the criminalisation of certain activities (e.g. drug use) but extends to the increasingly heavy regulation of smoking, for instance. Nevertheless, our main attention will be directed to the regulation of business transactions.

Cyclical Fluctuations
Regulatory policies are considered to have a very minor cyclical role. Most discussions tend to focus on the potentially dampening effect of regulatory

reforms on the economy in the short run. The idea here is that the prospect of reforms can become a source of uncertainty in which the losers from the reform are well identified while the gainers are more widely dispersed and will only become apparent over time; the net effect today is more cautious expenditure by the losers with no immediate offset. This has not been a big issue in Ireland, but has been cited as a problem in economies pursuing large and long drawn out structural reform agendas, like Germany and Japan.

Efficiency and Distribution
Product Market Distortions: Competition Policy
Regulation and competition policies are central instruments of the government to enhance economic efficiency. A standard distinction is between product and labour market regulation, although it should be obvious that, since they represent different parts of a linked chain of production, they are linked in policy terms as well. Empirical evidence suggests that product market deregulation provides strong incentives for governments and social partners to reform national labour markets, or in other words, that there is a complementarity between the two types of regulation.[9] In either market, the basic instrument of protection by vested interests will be barriers to entry and these must be the focus of competition policy. The rationale for these policies is ultimately provided by the prospect of price and quality gains to consumers, although for a highly open economy like Ireland's this is reinforced by the policy goal of competitiveness, bearing in mind that even non-traded goods and services may be used as inputs by the traded good sector (see Chapter 8).

It should be acknowledged, as mentioned before, that society may choose to embrace a broader notion of a social optimum than economic efficiency per se, within which 'quality of life' is traded off against the most competitive price. While this is conceptually straightforward, all the complications lie in the implementation; consider the common dilemma of how to evaluate the gains from an edge of town supermarket against the familiarity and local knowledge of small main street shops. There is a particular risk that 'quality of life' concerns become a Trojan Horse for incumbent interests. The country's pharmacy sector, now deregulated after years of debate, provides a good case study of the structure and rhetoric of barriers to entry (see also Chapter 8).

Two major entry restrictions existed and interacted with each other to produce some unintended consequences: pharmacies had agreed with the Department of Health to maintain minimum distances between each other, and a pharmacist qualification could only be obtained from a single college degree programme with very small capacity. Thus while a village pharmacy had in effect a captive market, a common desire of the owners to pass the pharmacy onto children was impeded by the extreme difficulty in getting the necessary qualification for them. So while the appeal of a 'know your customer' pharmacist was part of the rhetorical ammunition in defending these restrictions, the gains from restricted entry were in practice shared by the owner and a required employee, who may have no particular attachment to the locality. The public rightly questioned what they gained from this arrangement.

This example contains some recurring features of competition issues. The lack of competition reflected both collusion amongst private providers and supporting regulations from some branches of the government. This created potentially substantial rent: a return to simply being an incumbent in the industry. Entry was possible, but at high cost, much of which represented a transfer to the incumbents. The rents in turn were an obvious incentive to resist reform of the sector. The costs of the lack of competition were spread over a large group, which were difficult to organise into a countervailing interest. High profile problems may bring such barriers to the attention of policymakers (e.g. the shortage of taxis in Dublin), but some compensation for incumbents is usually a necessary part of any reform.[10] Given that tacit cooperation from the government is often a feature of these anti-competitive arrangements, we can expect to observe regulatory capture – the regulatory agency adopting similar goals to the industry or activity that it is supposed to be regulating.

For all of these reasons, governments have found it useful to be at least one step removed from competition policy. Ireland has followed the example of other countries in creating (in 1991) a specialised Competition Authority which, while functioning within the central government, is empowered and staffed to pursue vigorous enforcement of existing competition legislation while setting the agenda for any necessary legislative reforms (see also Chapter 8). As an EU member, Ireland has the additional instrument of deregulation implemented following a mandate from the very active EU competition authorities in Brussels. Indeed, it seems that throughout the EU there has been a willingness to cede significant competition powers to Brussels, unlike in other areas of policy, precisely because representative politicians recognise the resulting social gains from increased efficiency but fear the political consequences of undertaking such reforms themselves.

Substantial progress has already been made in addressing product market distortions and greater EU integration is providing an extra impetus to deal with the remaining distortions. Let us briefly highlight one sector where further effort seems to be needed. Ireland has an unusually segmented financial industry in which tax advantages have led to the rapid emergence of a large financial services sector transacting with international corporate and government clients, and thus competing with other financial centres, while the domestic retail sector has remained sheltered from international competition. The basic structure has remained unchanged for years, with four big national banks (two with foreign parents) providing the standard retail branch banking functions including the handling of cheque transactions. The need for a branch banking structure and access to the payment system seems to have acted as *de facto* barriers to entry, but information and communication technology now offers the prospect of greater reach for domestic and foreign competitors. Nevertheless, the phenomenon of Irish banks making substantial overseas investments (some of which have proven unwise) with much lower levels of inward investment in the domestic banking sector is a classic symptom of an industry using a protected home cash flow to pursue expansionist management goals, which may not be in the best interest of shareholders, let alone the average domestic consumer of retail financial services.

Labour Market Regulation

Some Competition Authority functions have labour market implications (e.g. entry into particular professions) but the primary focus of labour market regulation is the nature of employment contracts, including provisions for job loss. In this regard, Ireland has, what is by European standards a relatively deregulated labour market, much closer to the UK model than continental European counterparts (see Chapter 4). Various forms of short term contractual employment are allowed and there are mandatory notice and minimum redundancy payments for plant closure, but these are much less onerous than in other EU countries. In addition, most likely because of Ireland's fairly healthy rate of job creation, plant closures do not become embroiled in protracted protests by the affected workers.

The minimum wage is set at €7 per hour, and importantly is not indexed to inflation or growth; there is thus a tendency for its real value to erode over time in the absence of discretionary action by policymakers. From a narrow economic efficiency perspective, this would be a seen as a virtue as it makes the constraint of the minimum wage less binding over time. But there are counterarguments to this negative view of the minimum wage. First and foremost, society may decide that as part of its distributional goals it wants to place an 'esteem' value on wage rates and that the minimum wage represents such a threshold esteem level. The government may decide that outright wage subsidies would allow employers to capture too much of the associated gain and prefer the minimum wage as an instrument to concentrate the gains on the hired worker.

In addition, research in the USA and UK has found that minimum wage laws may have beneficial effects on firms' employment policies with minimal costs in terms of employment losses.[11] The explanation is that low paid jobs experience extremely high rates of turnover, with a mutually reinforcing tendency of the worker not seeing much advantage to accumulating skill for the particular job, and of the employer not seeing much advantage in providing training. With a minimum wage above the market clearing level, the calculus changes on both sides of the contract: the worker has some incentive to stay and the employer has some incentive to provide training. In the US context, it has been argued that the lower wage/higher turnover and higher wage/lower turnover models have small differences in net costs for firms (basically because the above market wage is offset by the more durable employment relationship). Thus a binding minimum wage merely tilts firms towards the latter model with very moderate employment losses.

Corporate Governance and Financial Regulation

A modern economy is characterised by a widespread separation of the ownership and control of both physical and financial assets. Families may live in houses owned by a bank through a mortgage, work for a firm which is financed by widely dispersed equity and debt holders, channel funds to insurance companies or banks to be returned back to them at some date or subject to some contingency in the future, and so on. These are simply examples of specialisation, and are the source of substantial efficiency gains for the economy. But they also can lead to divergent incentives between the owner and manager of the asset in question. The informational issues mentioned in the introduction come to the fore, because of the possibility of asymmetric information between the owner and controller of assets.

This is accentuated by another generic feature of the modern economy: limited liability. This principle restricts the financial liability of participants in an economic activity to the funds they invested in that activity; in adverse circumstances for the activity, other assets of the participants cannot be targeted by creditors. This of course is formalised in the structure of the limited liability company but extends well beyond that specific legal framework. There is an upper limit on the financial resources that can be conceivably extracted from any individual, even in cases where egregious civil or criminal misconduct can be established (and in fact, the complexity of corporate or financial litigation makes this very difficult). Modern societies sensibly dispensed with the debtor's prison, and augmented the liability shield with bankruptcy provisions. The net effect of all these forces is that many corporate and financial transactions involve someone else's money, with the ability to avoid a substantial part of the downside risk – and hence a case for regulation.

To provide a topical example of some of these issues, consider the government's wariness over the proposed management buy out of Aer Lingus. Two concerns are present. First, adverse selection: the managers may have inside information that the company's prospects are unusually good, and would like to take advantage by buying the company from parties with less information (in this case, the State). Second, moral hazard: as prospective buyers of the company but also currently in control of it, managers may take actions that hurt the company in the short term to lower its sale price.

Effective corporate governance, i.e. the definition of the responsibilities of a corporation, seeks to minimise such conflicts of interest, a challenge of course faced by policymakers worldwide, and not always successfully met, as scandals such as the collapse of Enron illustrate. There is a rough spectrum of corporate governance models: from an American model assigning the main influence to shareholders and incumbent managers, to the UK one which places more weight than the US model on creditors, through to a stylised German framework in which workers, banks and even public norms also play a substantial role.[12] For obvious reasons, the Irish model draws heavily on that of UK, but as a regional economy it is subject to the influence of all three main models. In addition, the small size of the Irish economy has given rise to a concern not fully addressed in any model: the strong likelihood of overlapping personal and professional ties between the corporate sector and the government. This is one respect in which the Celtic Tiger might run a similar risk to its East Asian namesakes, in which so called 'crony capitalism' can lead to extreme inefficiency and even crisis. While symptoms of this problem are apparent from Tribunal revelations, evidence of any efficiency impact from it is much harder to demonstrate.

Financial sector regulation is motivated by a similar set of informational problems, and is of transparent importance given the role of the sector at the nexus of saving, investment, and contingency planning decisions. While asymmetric information can always be mitigated by additional monitoring, this is a very high cost activity for the typical customer of a financial institution. Indeed, financial institutions would lose much of their scale advantage if they had excessive reporting requirements to individual customers, so a particular value of regulation attaches to its ability to define and enforce a standard monitoring framework for financial institutions to account for their allocation of clients' assets. Financial history provides abundant examples, most recently from Argentina, of the debilitating effects of loss of public confidence in financial institutions.

Regulation of the sector in Ireland was traditionally seen as a monetary policy function but is now being adapted since these functions no longer correspond to the same levels of government within the Eurozone. The government created the Irish Financial Services Regulatory Authority as an autonomous unit within the structure of the Central Bank of Ireland. While its powers are still to be fully established by additional legislation as of the time of writing, its overall mandate is extremely challenging given the complexity of the financial sector. Some general lessons from other countries that should be taken on board are: first, the necessity for significant powers of investigation and imposition of civil and criminal penalties where justified, such as those possessed by the American Securities and Exchange Commission; second, given the extremely high international mobility of financial assets, the need for vigilance so that investment flows are not attracted by dubious regulatory loopholes and third, the need for regulators to have the analytical and technical capacity to keep pace with endless innovation in financial instruments.

Telecommunications and Housing Markets
Other forms of regulation should also be noted. Ireland has a low usage of information and communication technology (ICT) despite being a huge producer of ICT equipment. This reflects a legacy of monopoly provision of telecommunications services which has proven difficult to unravel; in particular the now privatised Eircom remains the completely dominant player given its control of the telephone network and, as in other countries, government oversight will be necessary for the foreseeable future (see Chapter 8). Following UK practice, specialised sectoral regulators have been established to oversee what was previously a public monopoly. In telecoms this task is charged to the Commission for Communications Regulation which has the central function of finding a way to price access to the network for other providers of information and communication services; there is a predictable tug of war between the network owner wanting a relatively high price, while aspiring competitors (with some sympathy from the public) argue that the network cost has already been recovered

from users and taxpayers and thus should be made available at low cost. As with other forms of regulation, it appears that the EU level regulation will provide strong support for the latter position.

Perhaps the most striking gap in regulation, at least relative to its recurrence in public debate, is of the housing market. This has proven to be an extremely thorny area for policymakers, partly because the need to plan for sustained population growth is a comparatively new problem in Ireland. The issue is now entangled in subregional development policy with no decisive resolution of several conflicting forces: the developmental pull of the big cities, a preference for low density housing, the primacy of private ownership rights in land, and the poor quality of the inherited housing stock and infrastructure in rural areas.

Notably absent in Ireland is one basic principle of regulatory policy: the usefulness of creating appropriate pricing schemes when the free market is unable to do so. An efficient pricing scheme aligns the price of a service with the marginal cost of providing that service, subject to the requirement that the total cost of providing the service is also covered. For public services, the resulting prescription is for prices that contain some fixed component plus a variable component that varies with actual use (e.g. weight of garbage put out for collection, metered water rates etc). Local governments have been working towards such pricing for services they control, but with considerable controversy and uneven implementation.

The housing market highlights the consequences of this patchwork system. Rural housing relies on private wells and septic tanks but these represent classic environmental externalities because the reduction in the water table and the seepage of biotoxins into it imposes large social costs. Even where fees are imposed for construction of private water or sewerage facilities or connection to a network, most of the cost is upfront and there is still no marginal incentive to limit the damaging behaviour once this cost has been paid. The congestion and traffic hazard costs of sprawling housing development are likewise costs shifted mostly onto others. Last but not least, the lack of any specific taxation of land wealth and the preferential rate for taxation of capital gains compared to that on ordinary income has accentuated the windfall gains from the planning system and created huge incentives for rent seeking, reflected most perniciously in the findings of the Planning Tribunal. It is difficult to predict how policy in this area will evolve, but one can speculate that a significant reallocation of powers between central and local government will be necessary, with local governments gaining some taxation and pricing functions at the expense of their planning powers.

Growth
The discussion of the growth aspects of regulation and competition policy can be brief because there is significant overlap between the efficiency and growth motivations for these policies. To the extent that these policies are intended to address competitiveness, they directly pertain to the country's ability to attract internationally mobile capital and thus support a pillar of the regional growth

strategy. Sometimes the concern is expressed that an excessive focus on seeking inward investment by multinational firms can lead to a downgrading of regulatory issues, as expressed in the idea of a 'race to the bottom' promoted by increasing regional or global integration. However, Ireland displays few of the traditional symptoms of industrial policy trumping regulation, helped by (for better or worse) having skipped the smokestack era of industrial growth and having based its growth acceleration on specialisation in technological and service industries. There are pressing environmental issues, but they reside at the residential rather than industrial level, and since some of Ireland's comparative advantage in the competition for industrial location is based in perceived quality of life, there may in fact be competitiveness gains in addressing these problems sooner rather than later.

5 CONCLUSION

Let us conclude with some brief remarks about the likely direction of the three policy tools discussed in this chapter. While the chapter has offered a very broad framework for evaluating these tools, it must be acknowledged that, in practice, policy design and implementation have been driven by more proximate criteria. Tax policy reflects the goals of revenue management and encouragement of specific types of expenditure within the constraint of avoiding radical change to the existing system, social partnership reflects the desire for wage moderation, and regulatory policies reflect the pursuit of competitiveness. However, as the foundations for sustained growth in Ireland seem ever more secure, the broad framework is well placed to adapt to emerging concerns of the general public. In particular, quality of life issues can often be traced back to a failure along efficiency and distribution criteria, as illustrated in the discussion of the housing market above. However, implementation of reforms often raises tricky political issues, because even a socially valuable reform may have to take on a well entrenched vested interest. Thus social partnership can be a useful vehicle for linkage of policy reforms across different areas, encompassing changes in taxation, regulation, or public expenditure (see Chapter 2) and creating a critical mass of support for the changes. A major imponderable is the future division of authority between different levels of government, a debate which is often a reflection of thinly disguised specific policy preferences. It is important therefore to have a broad analytic framework in which changes in institutions and policies can be consistently evaluated.

Endnotes

*   I thank the editors and Des McCarthy and Noel Cahill for helpful comments and suggestions. Any views expressed are those of the author alone.

1   European Commission, *Structures of the Taxation Systems in the European Union*, Eurostat and Directorate General for Taxation and Customs Union, Luxembourg 2004.

2   The GDP-GNP gap can be calculated from the Central Statistics Office updates of the National Income and Expenditure Accounts, located on their webpage at http://www.cso.ie/principalstats/princstats.html.

3   For an accessible exposition of these issues, see R. Barro, *Macroeconomics* (Fifth Edition), MIT Press, Cambridge MA 1997.

4   See F. McCarthy, 'Social Policy and Macroeconomics: The Irish Experience' (Working Paper 2736), World Bank Development Economics, Washington D.C. 2001.

5   See P. Krugman and M. Obstfeld, *International Economics: Theory and Policy* (Sixth Edition), Addison-Wesley, Boston MA 2002.

6   The *OECD Economic Report for Ireland 2002-03*, OECD, Paris 2003, noted the strong overlap between the non-traded sector and public sector service provision.

7   The poor perception of the benchmarking round caused the influential Economic and Social Research Institute (ESRI) to question the need for a second benchmarking exercise, which is under consideration by the Government. See D. McCoy, D. Duffy, A. Bergin, and J. Cullen, *Quarterly Economic Commentary,* ESRI, Summer 2004.

8   Apart from the regulatory issues discussed here, other forms of regulation are considered in different chapters of the book: for example: regulation in relation to infrastructure (see Chapter 2), natural monopolies (Chapter 8), food safety and the environment (Chapter 9), insurance (Chapter 10) and school attendance (Chapter 11).

9   See, for example, W. Lewis, *The Power of Productivity: Wealth, Poverty and the Threat to Global Stability,* University of Chicago Press, Chicago IL 2004.

10 In the case of pharmacies, the losses to incumbents following deregulation seem to have been very mild, not least because instantaneous entry via a startup operation was not easy, so value remained to being an incumbent in the industry.

11 See A. Krueger and D. Card, *Myth and Measurement: The New Economics of the Minimum Wage*, Princeton University Press, Princeton NJ 1995.

12 On differences between the USA and the UK regarding creditors, note the higher emphasis placed by US bankruptcy law on the continued operation of a distressed firm, during which time the firm can shield assets from creditors. The differences between the US/UK model and Germany were emblematic in the 2004 prosecution of German firm Mannesmann's executives for the receipt of large bonuses upon completion of the firm's takeover by Vodafone; the bonuses drew public outrage in Germany but little notice in the UK.

PERFORMANCE AND POLICY ISSUES AT A NATIONAL LEVEL

CHAPTER 4

Population, Employment and Unemployment

John O'Hagan and Tara McIndoe

1 INTRODUCTION

In the last decade or so the area of employment and population has once again been of great importance in the Irish economy; Table 4.1 illustrates clearly the dramatic changes that have taken place since 1993. Who could have predicted the scale of the change in the intervening years? Employment in 1993 was just 130,000 higher than in 1961; the only period in which there was a significant increase in employment up to this was during the 1970s, when just over 100,000 net new jobs were created. Between 1993 and early 2000, however, over 475,000 net new jobs were created, quite a phenomenal increase in employment in such a short period. This *was* the success story of the 'Celtic tiger' years and has continued unabated into the twenty-first century as over 160,000 jobs have been created in the last four years. This extraordinary employment increase has changed the economic and physical landscape of Ireland in quite a remarkable way in just over a decade.

The increase in employment was the main force behind the extraordinary increase in output in the economy in this period. Definitionally:

(1) $$Q = (Q/E) \cdot E$$

That is, the output of an economy (Q) can be expressed as the product of the average productivity of those in employment (Q/E) and the level of employment (E). As we will see later, the level of employment in Ireland in some years increased by over 6 per cent; this alone would have pushed up Q by 6 per cent assuming no change in productivity. Thus, increases in E were the main factor explaining the exceptional growth in Q in the period 1993-2000 (especially the increase in the skilled labour supply). These continue to raise Ireland's potential growth rate above that of its neighbours; indeed, over the last forty years the main explanation for variations in the growth of Q was the variation in the growth of E.

Productivity though was also increasing during this period, hence ensuring a much faster increase in Q than in E; the causes of this growth in productivity are the subject matter of Chapter 5. The growth in productivity however in the 1990s was lower than that in the 1960s and not much higher than that in the 1970s and 1980s; productivity growth has been relatively slow in the early parts of this century with forecasts that it should pick up again after 2005 to the levels experienced in the 1990s.[1] In some senses the increase in E was feared to be a temporary phenomenon as increases in E in Ireland are constrained by the supply of suitable labour; however in the last nine years there has been an exceptional increase in labour supply (see later) which looks set to continue with the aid of net immigration.

Table 4.1

Employment: The Success Story of the Last Decade

	Employment (millions)	Unemployment rate (%)
1961	1.053	5.0
1971	1.049	5.5
1980	1.156	7.3
1986	1.095	17.1
1990[1]	1.160	12.9
1993	1.183	15.7
1996	1.329	11.9
2000	1.671	4.3
2003	1.793	4.4
2004	1.836	4.4

Source: Central Statistics Office (CSO), Dublin 2004, available at www.cso.ie.
[1]1990-2003 taken from the CSO, *QNHS: Revised Post Census 2002*, Stationery office, Dublin 2004, Table 16.

Sections 2 and 3 examine the issues of population and labour supply and emphasise the critical role that migration plays in this regard, a factor that marks Ireland apart from other OECD countries. Section 4 looks at the issue of employment, its growth and composition, and compares Ireland's performance to that of a number of other countries. Section 5 does likewise in relation to unemployment. The rest of the chapter examines the various factors that may influence the level of employment, and hence the level of unemployment, in a small open economy such as that of Ireland. Section 6 will examine three factors that impinge on job creation, namely globalisation of trade, technological change and the adaptability and employability of the labour force. The first two of these are international in origin, yet different countries have been affected by and/or responded to them in very different ways, particularly in relation to the problem of the skills mismatch that inevitably results from these factors.

A major reason perhaps for the different responses in different countries to the phenomena of technological change and the globalisation of trade relates to the flexibility of the labour market, this is the subject matter of Section 7. Issues such as the real wage and the wage setting process and the effects of employment legislation on employment creation are discussed in some detail. The effects of prolonged payment of unemployment and related benefits and the effectiveness or otherwise of active labour market policies in dealing with unemployment will also be examined in Section 7. Section 8 concludes the chapter.

2 POPULATION

Population Change and its Components

The size of the population has major emotive significance in Ireland; not surprisingly given the huge reduction in population in Ireland following the Famine. As a result, the size of the population has in a sense become an objective of policy in itself. Table 4.2 outlines the trends in population dating back to 1841. The population of the Republic of Ireland in pre-Famine days was over 6.5 million. The decline in this population size in the post-Famine period is all too obvious: a fall of over two million in 20 years despite a high birth rate. Population continued to decline up to 1926; almost 50 years later there was no increase on the 1926 level, when the population in 1971 still stood at only 2.978 million. Since then population size has increased by over one million with half of this increase occurring between 1991 and 2004, the population in 2004 topping 4 million for the first time since 1871. This for many is seen as a very positive development and reflects a reversal of a demoralising decline that had persisted for almost a century and a half.

Table 4.2

Population, Republic of Ireland, 1841 to 2004 (millions)

Years	Population	Years	Population
1841	6.529	1926	2.972
1851	5.112	1951	2.961
1861	4.402	1961	2.818
1871	4.053	1971	2.978
1881	3.870	1981	3.443
1891	3.469	1991	3.526
1901	3.222	2002	3.917
1911	3.140	2004[1]	4.043

Source: CSO, *Regional Population Projections 2001-2031*, Stationery Office, Dublin 2001, Table 1; CSO, *Statistical Yearbook 2003*, Stationery Office, Dublin 2003, Table 1.1, and CSO, *Population and Migration Estimates*, Stationery Office, Dublin 2004, Table 1.
[1]Preliminary.

The total population of a country depends on three factors: the number of births, the number of deaths and the level of net migration. The difference between the number of births and deaths is known as the natural increase and in most countries the natural increase translates directly into a population increase. This has not been the case in Ireland, where in the past the change in population has 'tracked' much more closely the trend in migration than that of the natural increase.

As seen in Table 4.3, the number of births per annum reached a peak in the 1970s and declined significantly after that; some increase again is predicted for the next ten years. As a result, from having one of the highest birth rates in Europe only twenty years ago, Ireland now has a birth rate little above the levels pertaining in Northern Europe. This means that the natural increase in the population is averaging around 23,000 per annum, down from a level of around 35,000 in the 1970s.

Table 4.3
Components of Population Change, Selected Intervals (annual average in '000s)

	Total births	Total deaths	Natural increase	Population change	Estimated net migration
1926-36	58	42	16	0	−17
1951-56	63	36	27	−12	−39
1956-61	61	34	26	−16	−42
1961-66	63	33	29	13	−16
1966-71	63	33	30	19	−11
1971-79	69	33	35	49	14
1981-86	67	33	34	19	−14
1986-91	56	32	24	−3	−27
1991-96	50	31	18	20	2
1996-02	54	31	23	49	26

Source: As for Table 4.2; CSO, *Statistical Yearbook 2003*, op. cit., Table 1.2.

Migration

While there has been a significant change in the natural increase, it is slight compared to the huge swings in net migration that can occur in Ireland: net immigration of 14,000 per annum in the 1970s, to net emigration of 40,000 per annum in some years in the 1980s, to net immigration again of 2,000 in the early 1990s and around 25,000 in the late 1990s. The picture that is emerging in the early 2000s is that on average the natural increase will be lower than in the past, but, because of the reality of significant net immigration, a sizeable increase in the population is likely in the next ten years.

Table 4.4 illustrates the migration trends of Irish nationals in the last eight years. Historically Ireland has experienced huge outflows of emigrants during periods of economic depressions; less often have these turned to inflows during economic booms, although the late 1990s and early 2000s certainly represent one such period. The numbers of Irish emigrants has slowed over the time period examined, from 31,200 in 1996 to just 18,500 in 2004 (though there was an increase between 1997 and 1999); immigration on the other hand increased from already high levels of 17,700 in 1996 to 27,000 in 2002, though as evidenced by the 2003 and 2004 figures this trend does not look set to continue. The last column of Table 4.4 shows a steady decline in the proportion of immigrants of Irish nationality despite the increase in the absolute numbers, up to 2002, of returning Irish immigrants. In 2001 and 2002 more Irish nationals returned home than went abroad.

Table 4.4
Estimated Migration of Irish Nationals 1996-2003 ('000s)

| | Emigrants | Immigrants | |
	Irish	Irish	% of total
1996	31.2	17.7	45.2
1997	25.3	20.8	46.7
1998	28.6	24.3	52.8
1999	31.5	26.7	54.6
2000	26.6	24.8	47.1
2001	26.2	26.3	44.6
2002	25.6	27.0	40.4
2003[1]	20.7	17.5	34.7
2004[1]	18.5	16.9	33.7

Source: CSO, *Population and Migration Estimates,* op. cit., Tables 5 and 7.
[1]Preliminary.

Immigration, on the other hand (as seen in Table 4.5), increased steadily until 2002 with a growing proportion of the immigrants originating beyond European or US borders; almost 30 per cent of immigrants in 2004 were nationals from

Table 4.5
Estimated Immigration Classified by Nationality, 1996-2003 ('000s)

	Irish	UK	Rest of EU	USA	Rest of World	Total
1996	17.7	8.3	5.0	4.0	4.2	39.2
1997	20.8	8.4	5.5	4.2	5.5	44.5
1998	24.3	8.6	6.1	2.3	4.7	46.0
1999	26.7	8.2	6.9	2.5	4.5	48.9
2000	24.8	8.4	8.2	2.5	8.6	52.6
2001	26.3	9.0	6.5	3.7	13.6	59.0
2002	27.0	7.4	8.1	2.7	21.7	66.9
2003[1]	17.5	6.9	6.9	1.6	17.7[2]	50.5
2004[1]	16.9	5.9	10.6	1.8	14.9	50.1

Source: As for Table 4.4.
[1]Preliminary.
[2]While at the overall level the population estimates cover persons resident in private and non-private households (i.e. institutions) the breakdowns provided are based solely on the QNHS, which covers private households only. The number of migrants accommodated in institutions is estimated to be in the region of about 4,500 in the year to April 2003.

outside the EU or USA. In the last 20 years immigration has increased from all areas with a slight decrease between 1993 and 1996 across the board and another decline between 2002 and 2004. The CSO estimates that in 2003 seven per cent of immigrants were nationals from African countries predominantly Nigeria and South Africa, a similar proportion originated from Asia.[2] This is the most obvious change in Irish society over the past five years, i.e. the increasing number of non-Irish nationals who currently make up the country's population.

3 LABOUR SUPPLY

Labour supply in any country depends on three factors: the total size of the population, the proportion of that population of working age, and the proportion of the working age population seeking or in work. This is illustrated by the identity:

$$(2) \qquad L = (P) . (Pa /P) . (L/Pa)$$

where L is the size of the labour force, P the size of the population, and Pa the size of population of working age. The labour force, in turn, consists of those in employment (E) and those unemployed (UE). Hence:

$$(3) \qquad L = E + UE$$

Two further identities of interest to this discussion are the following:

$$(4) \qquad Q/P = (Q/E) . (E/P)$$

$$(5) \qquad \text{where} \quad E/P = (E/L) . (L/Pa) . (Pa/P)$$

Equation (4) links the demographic factors back to (1). It states that output per person employed and the proportion of the population employed determine output per head of population. We saw in Equation (1) that increases in E was the most important factor allowing for record increases in Q in Ireland in the last ten years; E/P has also increased at a record rate, thereby pushing up Q/P (our measure of living standards, as seen in Chapter 1) to record levels. E/P (the proportion of the population in employment) as can be seen from Equation (5) is influenced by three factors, all of which have been increasing in the last decade; E/L (the proportion of the labour force in employment) has increased as unemployment decreased, Pa/P as shall be seen later has increased because of demographic factors and L/Pa has increased principally because of increased participation by married females in the labour force. These very favourable demographic trends, in terms of their impact on living standards, have become known as Ireland's 'demographic dividend' in the 1990s.[3]

Working Age Population

As a result of the fall in the number of births in the last two decades, there has been a large fall in the population aged 15 and under. However, because of the high birth rate prior to this, there has been a large increase in the population aged 15 to 64, and especially in the prime working age population, 25-64. The decline in the population aged under 15 clearly has had major implications for the economy in, for example, the area of education, but what is of most interest here is the increase in the prime working age population in Ireland. The number of people aged 25 to 64 rose from 2.183 million in 1991 to over 2.340 million by the year 2002;[4] this is a very large increase in such a short period and had a marked effect on Ireland's age dependency ratios.

Table 4.6 highlights these changes in the composition of the population. In 1981, those aged less than 15 years accounted for 51.4 per cent of those aged 15 to 64, but in just over twenty years this had dropped by almost 21 percentage points. At the same time, the population aged 65 and over, expressed as a proportion of the 15-64 population, also declined, albeit slightly. As Table 4.6 illustrates, these favourable demographic trends have now run their course; importantly though there will be no worsening of the demographic situation until after 2011, when the percentage classified as 'old' begins to rise significantly.

Table 4.6

Age Dependency Ratios,[1] 1981 to 2021

Year	Young	Old	Total
1981	51.4%	18.2%	69.6%
1991	43.4%	18.5%	61.9%
1996	36.5%	17.6%	54.1%
2002	29.3%	16.4%	45.7%
2011[2]	33.0%	17.9%	50.9%
2021[2]	32.2%	22.9%	55.1%

Sources: NESC, *Opportunities, Challenges and Capacities for Choice*, Stationery Office, Dublin 1999, Table 1.5, and CSO, *Population and Labour Force Projections 2001-2031*, op. cit., and CSO, *Census 2002 – Principal Demographic Results,* Stationery Office, Dublin 2003, Table 5A.
[1]The ratios in the first two columns are obtained by dividing the populations aged 0-14 and 65 years and over by the population aged 15-64. The final column is the sum of these two.
[2]Forecasts.

Participation in Labour Force

An important factor when examining the employment situation in any country is the proportion of the working population that actually seeks work. This is known as the labour force participation rate.

Table 4.7 provides data for Ireland, a number of other small EU countries, two countries of particular interest to Ireland (namely the UK and USA) and the OECD group; where possible these will also be used as the comparator countries in the other tables in this chapter. As may be seen in Table 4.7, the labour force participation rate for males in Ireland is below that for most other countries listed; that for females is considerably less. The figure for females for Ireland is 57.6 per cent, compared to a figure of 51.0 per cent in Greece (the lowest country), 69.2 per cent in the UK and 75.9 per cent in Norway.

Table 4.7
Labour Force Participation Rates[1] in Selected OECD Countries, 1990 and 2003

| | Males | | Females | |
	1990	2003	1990	2003
Belgium	71.3%	72.6%	46.1%	55.8%
Denmark	87.1%	84.0%	77.6%	74.8%
Greece	76.8%	77.0%	42.6%	51.0%
Ireland	*77.5%*	*78.3%*	*42.6%*	*57.6%*
Netherlands	79.7%	84.2%	52.4%	68.4%
Norway	83.4%	82.9%	70.7%	75.9%
OECD	82.6%	80.2%	56.4%	59.6%
UK	88.3%	83.9%	67.3%	69.2%
USA	85.6%	82.2%	67.8%	69.7%

Source: OECD, *Employment Outlook*, OECD, Paris 2004, Table B.
[1]Ratios refer to persons aged 15 to 64 years who are in the labour force divided by the total population aged 15 to 64.

The female participation rate in Ireland increased considerably in the 1980s and 1990s, thereby closing the gap with other countries in this regard. It is difficult to predict how much further this participation rate will grow in Ireland, but with the much lower birth rate, and improved employment prospects, it could increase to the UK level if not to those in Denmark and Norway. If this happened, it would lead to a large increase in the labour force arising from this factor alone. The increase in the female participation rate is primarily due to the increase in the participation rate of married females. The dramatic changes in this regard can be seen in Table 4.8.

Table 4.8
Labour Force Participation Rates, Married Females by Age Group, 1986-2011

Age group	1986	1996	2001[1]	2006[1]	2011[1]
30-34	33.1	59.8	65.0	70.0	75.0
35-39	26.7	55.4	63.0	67.0	72.0
40-44	27.3	49.9	60.0	65.0	70.0
45-49	26.6	41.8	53.0	60.0	65.0

Source: CSO, *Population and Labour Force Projections 2001-2031*, op. cit., Table A6.
[1]Forecasts.

There have been huge changes in the participation rate for all of the age groups shown and it is predicted that these increases will continue for the next decade, bringing Ireland into line with other EU countries in this regard: by 2006 for example, it is expected that over 65 per cent of all married women aged between 30 and 50 years will be in the labour force, a figure that will be up from under 30 per cent less than twenty years ago.

A further potential concern could be a relatively low participation rate for foreign immigrants in the labour force and concentration in certain sectors, i.e. blue collar work. In Europe the greater vulnerability of foreign workers to unemployment and their lower degree of employability suggests that they face difficulties in integrating into the labour market. These may be attributable partly to: a need for a period of adaptation; qualifications and experience, which do not always match the needs of the labour market; and employment discrimination compounded by a weak grasp of the host country's language.[5] As the number of foreign immigrants in Ireland increases the above could emerge as a significant issue.

Conclusion

A consideration of migration trends is central to any discussion of labour supply in Ireland. It, more than any other factor, determines changes in population increase and the growth of the labour force. As seen from Table 4.3, more than half of the 49,000 people added to the Irish population on an annual average basis between 1996 and 2002 were as a result of net inward migration. The decline in the birth rate and the rise in the labour force participation of females aged 25 to 64 may have been dwarfed by the changes in net migration, but in themselves they are very significant changes which, after the effects of net migration are removed, will have a marked bearing on the growth of the labour force in years to come.

4 EMPLOYMENT: GROWTH AND COMPOSITION

Overall Employment

The first point worth noting from Table 4.9 is the tiny size of the workforce in Ireland: 1.8 million in 2002, as opposed to 7.1 million in the Netherlands, 27.9 million in the UK and 136.5 million in the USA. Given that there is an effective common labour market between Ireland and the UK, it is very important for labour policy purposes to bear in mind the relative sizes of the two labour markets.

The most striking fact in relation to employment in Ireland has been its growth relative to other countries. In the ten years to 2001, employment grew on average by 4.2 per cent per annum in Ireland compared to less than 1 per cent growth in many countries; only the Netherlands, at 2 per cent had a comparable rate of growth to that in Ireland. This is remarkable given that employment in Ireland had actually declined in the 1980-86 period and had not managed to rise significantly over the entire decade spanning the years 1980-1990 (see Table 4.1).

Table 4.9

Employment and Employment Growth in Selected OECD Countries

	2002 millions	1991-2001	2002	2004[1]	2005[1]	E/Pa % (2003)
		annual percentage change				
Belgium	4.186	0.7	- 0.3	0.3	1.0	59.3
Denmark	2.733	0.3	0.4	0.0	0.4	75.1
Greece	3.925	0.8	0.1	1.7	1.4	58.0
Ireland	*1.765*	*4.2*	*1.4*	*1.4*	*1.6*	*65.0*
Netherlands	7.141	2.0	1.1	- 0.9	1.2	73.6
Norway	2.286	1.3	0.4	0.5	1.0	75.9
OECD	486.034	0.9	0.1	0.8	1.3	65.0
UK	27.865	0.6	0.7	0.8	0.7	72.9
USA	136.487	1.5	- 0.3	1.0	1.7	71.2

Source: OECD, *Employment Outlook*, op. cit., Table 1.2 and Table B.
[1]Forecasts.

The growth of employment since 2002 has continued to outpace many of the countries listed in Table 4.9. This means that for nearly 15 years Ireland has managed to outperform both the smaller European countries as well as the UK and the USA in the employment growth stakes. In general the Irish employment growth rate has been converging towards those of our European and OECD counterparts in recent years; yet the projections for 2005 still clearly show Ireland with a 1.6 per cent growth increase, second only to the USA (1.7 per cent).

Ireland of course had a much greater increase in potential labour supply than any of the other countries and hence unemployment would have remained at a very high level and the position of net immigration may have been translated into substantial net emigration without this growth in employment. Much of the immigration after all was the return of people who had had to emigrate in the depressed labour market conditions of the 1980s.

These points are well borne out by the last column in Table 4.9; this shows the ratio of total employment to population size aged 15-64 years for each of the countries listed. Despite the rapid growth of employment in Ireland, just 65 per cent of the population aged 15-64 were in employment in 2002, similar to that experienced by the entire OECD in the same year; the figure for the USA was 71.2 per cent, the UK 72.9 per cent and that for Norway as high as 75.9 per cent. These figures reflect what was seen earlier in Table 4.7: the relatively low labour participation rate for men and the very low figure for females. The low figure for females is explained wholly by the low employment rates for females with children: for women with two or more children, the employment rate in 2000 was 40.8 per cent for Ireland, compared to a figure of 65.8 per cent for Irish women without children and an OECD average of 61.9 per cent for women with two or more children, a truly dramatic difference.[6]

It could be argued therefore that the employment increase in Ireland in the last 10 years is strongly associated with a huge increase in the labour force, an increase that is simply bringing Ireland up to the international norm in terms of the proportion of the total working age population in employment.

Part Time and Temporary Employment

An important issue relating to the growth of employment in some countries, including Ireland, since the late 1980s is the extent to which it consisted of part time employment. The available data suggest (Table 4.10) that the level of part time employment as a proportion of total employment is low throughout the countries examined. In this regard Ireland is not out of line with its OECD counterparts. Similarly there appears to have been no significant increase in part time employment, especially amongst males, in recent years.

There is a marked gender difference in relation to part time employment, as may be seen in Table 4.10. Only 8.1 per cent of total male employment in Ireland is part time, whereas 34.7 per cent of female employment is part time. These percentages vary considerably from country to country, but on balance the position in Ireland is not unusual. Some countries have a much higher and others a very much lower proportion of part time to total employment for females. The figures for males are much closer for the countries shown, with the Netherlands having the highest share of total male employment in part time employment, at 14.8 per cent, well below the figure though for female employment.

Table 4.10
Incidence and Composition of Part time Employment in Selected OECD Countries,[1] 2003

| | Part time employment as a proportion of total employment | | | Share in part time employment |
	Men	Women	Total	Women
Belgium	5.9	33.4	17.7	81.0
Denmark	10.5	21.9	15.8	64.2
Greece	2.9	9.9	5.6	67.9
Ireland	*8.1*	*34.7*	*18.1*	*72.1*
Netherlands	14.8	59.6	34.5	76.0
Norway	9.9	33.4	21.0	75.2
OECD	7.2	24.8	14.8	72.3
UK	9.6	40.1	23.3	77.3
USA	8.0	18.8	13.2	68.8

Source: As for Table 4.7, op. cit., Table E.
[1]Part time is usual hours of work less than 30 hours per week.

Even more striking, as evidenced by the figures in the last column of Table 4.10, is the very high share in total part time employment accounted for by females. In Ireland this is approaching the OECD average, yet it is still above that for Denmark, Greece and the USA. It is interesting to note, that in 2003, women accounted for 81 per cent of part time employment in Belgium.

What is more important perhaps is the extent to which part time employment is involuntary, i.e. chosen by the individual only because they could not get full time work. The evidence suggests that involuntary part time employment has not grown significantly as a proportion of total employment in the countries for which data exist.

There is little evidence therefore that the increase in employment in Ireland and other countries was not 'real', in the sense that it took place in involuntary part time employment. In other words, where the increase in employment was due to an increase in part time employment, this reflected a desire for such employment, largely it seems from female employees entering the labour force and with a preference for part time work as it fits better with family and other commitments.

A different but related issue is the extent to which the increase in employment was in temporary work. This is a much debated topic in labour market economics as some economists believe that an increasing proportion of jobs will have to be temporary if labour markets, especially in Europe, are to be sufficiently flexible to cope with an employment/unemployment crisis, a topic that will be returned to later.

Temporary work is where a worker is employed by a firm under a fixed term contract. The conditions under which someone can be employed as a temporary worker vary enormously across Europe, with Ireland having one of the least restrictive regimes in this regard. Recent growth in this area of employment has raised concerns that temporary jobs may be crowding out more stable forms of employment, becoming an additional source of insecurity for workers. As can be seen from Table 4.11, the share that temporary jobs have contributed to overall employment growth in various European and OECD countries has varied considerably; in half of the cases examined temporary employment had a negative effect on employment growth in the ten years from 1990-2000. However in the Netherlands 9.9 per cent of the 25.1 per cent increase in employment during this

Table 4.11
Contributions of Temporary and Permanent Jobs to Total Employment Growth in Selected OECD Countries, 1990-2000

	Cumulative growth of total employment	Percentage point contribution of employment	
		Temporary	Permanent
Belgium	17.7	5.3	12.4
Denmark	4.8	−0.1	5.0
Greece	18.5	−1.0	19.5
Ireland	*47.4*	*−1.6*	*48.9*
Netherlands	25.1	9.9	15.2
Norway (1996-2000)	8.0	−2.8	10.8
OECD	11.6	4.2	7.4
UK	6.5	1.9	4.6
USA (1995-2001)	9.3	−0.5	9.8

Source: OECD, *Employment Outlook,* OECD, Paris 2002, Table 3.2.

time period was due to temporary employment. In Ireland as can be seen, the cumulative growth in total employment was 47.4 per cent, whereas the increase in permanent employment exceeded this (48.9 per cent) implying a *decline* in temporary employment. Part time work is more likely to be temporary than permanent, thus the decrease in temporary employment in Ireland may suggest that part time employment has not increased in the last decade. Although experiences across the OECD vary, it does appear that younger and less educated workers disproportionately fill temporary jobs. On the other hand temporary workers are a diverse group who work in a wide range of occupations and sectors.

Other characteristics of temporary employment include the tendency for temporary jobs to pay less than permanent ones as well as sometimes offering less access to paid vacations, sick leave, unemployment insurance and other fringe benefits including less access to training. Temporary workers are generally less satisfied with their jobs and more often report inflexible work schedules and monotonous work tasks than their permanent employment counterparts.[7]

Sectoral Composition of Employment

Table 4.12 outlines the composition of employment in Ireland over the last ten years; while the data are not strictly comparable, the table shows some broad trends in this composition in the period 1994 to end 2004.

Table 4.12

Employment by Sector: Ireland

	('000s)		%	
	1994	1998	2004 (Q1)	2004 (Q1)
Agriculture, Forestry and Fishing	*147.0*	*135.9*	*119.0*	*6.5%*
Industry	*343.3*	*428.1*	*499.7*	*27.2%*
of which:				
Other production services	251.8	302.0	297.4	16.2%
Construction	91.5	126.1	202.3	11.0%
Services	*730.2*	*929.1*	*1,217.1*	*66.3%*
of which:				
Wholesale and retail trade	169.2	211.1	263.4	14.3%
Hotels and restaurants	68.4	97.8	113.1	6.2%
Transport, storage and communication	55.9	87.0	113.3	6.2%
Financial and other business services	114.3	171.0	234.4	12.8%
Public administration and defence	66.4	70.9	89.9	4.9%
Education	80.5	93.3	119.4	6.5%
Health	101.0	113.9	177.2	9.7%
Other	74.5	84.1	106.4	5.8%
TOTAL	*1,220.6*	*1,494.0*	*1,835.9*	

Sources: CSO, *Labour Force Survey*, Stationery Office, Dublin 1994, and CSO, *QNHS*, Stationery Office, Dublin 1998, Quarter 2, Dublin 2004, Quarter 1.

Note: The data given in the first column and the later columns are not exactly comparable as there was a discontinuity in the data between April 1997 and Q1 1998 due to the introduction of the *Quarterly National Household Survey*. The broad trends shown though are likely to hold.

One very striking feature is the relatively small size of the agricultural sector; there are many more people now, for example, employed in education and health (see Chapter 5, 10 and 11), financial and business services or the wholesale and retail trade than in agriculture.

The once mighty position of the agriculture sector has truly diminished. In the not too distant future there will be more people employed in hotels and restaurants than in the total agricultural sector, reflecting the increased importance of tourism to the Irish economy. The services sector as a whole is now over twice the size of the industrial sector and three times that of the manufacturing sector. The growth areas have clearly been the wholesale and retail trade, hotels and restaurants, transport and financial and other business services.

Table 4.13

Employment by Sector: International Comparison

| | Proportion in total employment | | | |
	1992	1996	2000	2003
Agriculture				
Belgium	3.0	2.8	2.5	2.2
Denmark	5.2	4.4	3.6	3.3
Ireland	13.6	11.2	7.7	6.5
UK	1.4	1.2	1.2	0.9
EU-15	5.6	4.8	4.3	4.0
Industry				
Belgium	26.0	24.0	22.4	22.2
Denmark	24.2	24.4	23.1	22.2
Ireland	28.1	27.7	29.0	27.7
UK	23.6	22.1	20.6	18.7
EU-15	29.1	27.1	25.8	24.6
Services				
Belgium	71.0	73.2	75.1	75.6
Denmark	70.6	71.3	73.3	74.5
Ireland	58.3	61.1	63.3	65.8
UK	75.0	76.7	78.3	80.4
EU-15	65.3	68.1	69.9	71.4

Source: Eurostat, *Long term Indicators*, www.europa.eu.int 2004.
Note: Due to data constraints a different set of countries was used in this comparison than in the other tables in this chapter.

Although data constraints meant only Belgium, Denmark, the UK and the average EU-15 could be used for comparison with Ireland, in Table 4.13 some interesting conclusions can be drawn. First, Ireland's share of employment in the agricultural sector although declining steadily is far above our EU counterparts;

in 1992, 13.6 per cent of the Irish workforce was involved in agricultural activities more than nine times that in the UK. This had dropped to 6.5 per cent in 2003, still more than seven times that in the UK. Ireland again consistently displayed the highest proportion of employment in industry of all the countries examined and in the period 1996-2000 had actually increased this proportion from 27.7 to 29.0 per cent, though decreasing to 1996 levels by 2003. Last, and as a corollary, the share of total employment in services in Ireland is well below the EU-15 average (65.8 compared to 71.4 per cent in 2003). The gap between Ireland and the three countries shown though, is much larger, with the UK having over 80 per cent of total employment in the services sector in 2003.

Using the same four countries as in Table 4.13 as well as an average figure for the EU-15, Table 4.14 provides further subsectoral comparisons in relation to the services sector. In 2002, employment in the Irish services sector was at least 6 percentage points lower than in Belgium, Denmark and the UK as well as over 2 points lower than the EU-15 average. This was due mainly to relatively low employment shares in the education (6.4 per cent in Ireland compared with 8.2 per cent in the UK) and health (9.9 per cent in Ireland compared with 18.4 per cent in Denmark) sectors. Though it must be noted that the Irish health and education figures are close to the EU-15 average. Public administration and defence also displayed lower than average employment in Ireland compared with the other countries examined. However, the share in employment in hotels and restaurants was significantly higher in Ireland than in any of the other countries examined and financial and other business services displayed higher employment shares in Ireland (13.3 per cent) than in Belgium (12.6 per cent) and Denmark (12.7 per cent), though lower than the 16.0 per cent observed in the UK.

Table 4.14

Employment in the Services Sector: International Comparison 2002

| | Proportion of total employment | | | | |
	Belgium	Denmark	*Ireland*	UK	EU-15
Overall	72.4	73.4	*65.7*	74.4	67.9
Wholesale and retail trade	14.3	14.6	*14.2*	14.9	14.6
Hotels and restaurants	3.3	2.3	*6.1*	4.5	4.2
Transport, storage and communication	8.1	7.3	*6.9*	7.4	6.5
Financial and other business services	12.6	12.7	*13.3*	16.0	12.7
Public administration and defence	9.6	5.8	*5.2*	6.7	7.7
Education	8.1	7.8	*6.4*	8.2	6.9
Health	12.4	18.4	*9.1*	11.1	9.8
Other	4.1	4.7	*4.7*	5.2	4.7

Source: European Commission, *Employment in Europe 2003*, Office for Official Publications of the European Communities, Luxembourg 2003, Table 11.

5 UNEMPLOYMENT: EXTENT AND FEATURES

International Comparisons

Table 4.15 provides the key information on recorded unemployment rates in Ireland and selected OECD countries, including, as mentioned earlier, some small EU countries, since 1990. The unemployment rate is given by $E/(E + UE)$ and the picture is fairly clear. In 1990 Ireland had an unemployment rate that was almost double the rate applying in all of the countries listed. By 1995 the unemployment situation in Ireland had improved only marginally; whereas for all of the other countries shown it had deteriorated, in Belgium by as much as three percentage points.

Between 1995 and 2000, all countries bar Greece experienced significant declines in unemployment. The most dramatic decline of course was for Ireland, down from 12.3 per cent in 1995 to 4.3 per cent in 2000. The unemployment rate increased again in most countries between 2000 and 2003, up from 6.3 to 7.1 per cent in the OECD as a whole. The figure for Ireland, 4.6 per cent, in 2003 was higher than the rates applying in the Netherlands and Norway; though it was well below the figures for several other countries shown, plus those for the large EU countries of France, Germany, Italy and Spain who all faced over nine per cent unemployment rates in 2003.

Table 4.15
Standardised Unemployment Rates in Selected OECD Countries[1]

| | As a percentage of the labour force | | | |
	1990	1995	2000	2003
Belgium	6.6	9.7	6.9	8.1
Denmark	7.2	6.8	4.4	5.6
Greece	6.3	9.1	11.0	10.0[2]
Ireland	*13.4*	*12.3*	*4.3*	*4.6[3]*
Netherlands	5.9	6.6	2.9	3.8
Norway	5.8	5.5	3.4	4.5
OECD	6.1	7.3	6.3	7.1
UK	6.9	8.5	5.4	5.0
USA	5.6	5.6	4.0	6.0

Source: As for Table 4.7, op. cit., Table A.
[1]All series are benchmarked to labour force survey based estimates and have been adjusted to ensure comparability over time.
[2]Figure for 2002.
[3]Figure differs from that in Table 4.1 where the CSO was the data source.

Comparison/Measurement Problems

The discussion above is based on the assumption that the data can be used for valid comparison both across countries and over time. Is this the case? There are three main issues of concern here. The first is whether or not all countries are using the same methods of defining and compiling data on unemployment; the second is whether or not over time there is a consistent series for Ireland; the last is whether or not there are certain categories of persons that are not, and perhaps cannot be, included by any country but which should be included in any discussion of labour market slack (i.e. where labour demand is less than labour supply) in an economy.

International comparison of unemployment rates is fraught with difficulty despite the best efforts of the OECD and the EU. Nonetheless, there are reasonably reliable comparative data for the EU member states, if not for most of the OECD countries, and these are the data that inform comparative studies and international policy debate.

In relation to Ireland, there are two main sources of data on unemployment: the Quarterly National Household Survey (QNHS) and the Live Register.[8] The QNHS gives two measures of unemployment: the International Labour Office (ILO) measure and the Principal Economic Status (PES) measure. The first of these is the internationally recognised measure of unemployment and defines somebody as 'unemployed' if their response in the survey makes clear that they did not work even for one hour for payments or profit in the previous week, actively sought work in the previous four weeks, and are available to start work within two weeks. These criteria are strict. The QNHS also asks people to choose, from a list of eight supplied options, what is their 'usual status as regards employment', three of which leads to their principal economic status being considered as one of unemployment. This is a less strict measure of unemployment, but not nearly so as the Live Register measure. The latter counts each month all those in receipt of unemployment benefit or unemployment assistance, plus those who, though entitled to no payment, wish to have social insurance contributions 'credited' to them; in addition casual and part-time workers who work for not more than three days in the week may be entitled to register on account of the days they do not work. There is little doubt therefore that it gives an overstatement of the number unemployed in the normal sense of the term.

The trends given by these sources have diverged since 1997: by 2004, the ILO measure of unemployment was showing 84,200 unemployed in Ireland compared to 175,800 using the Live Register measure, with the PES measure giving 112,600 unemployed. These clearly are not trivial differences; the gaps are very large and widened between the ILO and Live Register measure between 1997 and 2004 (see last column in Table 4.16).

It is the ILO data though that are used for international comparison, as the methods used in arriving at these data are considered to give the more accurate indicator of the underlying level of unemployment in a country. These data are also used in this chapter, unless indicated otherwise. It is important to remember that the ILO definition is quite a restrictive measure of unemployment and gives the most favourable picture of the unemployment problem in a country. It excludes, for example, many who are in involuntary part time work and also those described as discouraged and marginalised workers. Evidence suggests that if involuntary part time and marginalised workers are taken into account that it would add, in 2004, only 0.4 percentage points to the unemployment rate of 4.4 per cent; on the other hand, if marginalised workers (i.e. those seeking work but not meeting all of the ILO criteria) are taken into account it would add a further 2.6 percentage points. These additions would appear to suggest then that the Live Register may provide a more accurate indicator of the true level of unemployment.

Table 4.16
The Level of Unemployment ('000s) Using Different Unemployment Measures/Definitions

	(1) Live register	(2) Principal economic status	(3) International labour organisation (ILO)	(1)/(3)
1997	254.4	171.3	159.0	1.60
2000[1]	155.4	109.3	74.5	2.09
2004	175.8	112.6	84.2	2.09

Source: CSO, *QNHS Revised Series Post Census 2002*, Stationery Office, Dublin 2004, Tables 16 and 21; CSO, *Statistical Yearbook 2002*, Stationery Office, Dublin 2003, Table 2.16, and CSO, *Live Register Analysis*, Stationery Office, Dublin 2004, Table 1a.
[1]QNHS Q2 data used as this is the most comparable to the pre 1998 Labour Force Survey data.

There are also many people unable to work through invalidity or disability; the proportion of the working age group in this category has grown significantly in some EU countries in recent years, with some commentators suggesting that some of the decrease in unemployment, in the Netherlands and the UK in particular, could be linked to this development.

Helping disabled people find and keep jobs is a major challenge for all OECD countries including Ireland especially given that the potential personal, social and financial benefits are huge. An OECD report in 2003 found that in most countries once a person entered a disabilities related programme they remain a beneficiary until retirement; on average only 1 per cent of benefit recipients find a job each year. Although it is costly to leave disabled people outside the labour force, no country has so far been successful in crafting policies that will help disabled people return to work. The OECD suggests various broad areas for improvement including: individual benefit packages with job search support, rehabilitation and vocational training; new obligations for disabled people including, for those who are capable, a requirement to look for work; involving employers and trade unions in reintegration efforts; and more flexible cash benefits, depending on job capabilities and changes in an individual's disability over time.[9]

Long-term Unemployment
Apart from the level of unemployment, its composition is also of considerable interest to economists, for reasons alluded to already. The most important

consideration in this regard relates to its composition between short-term (less than 12 months) and long-term (12 months or more) unemployment.

Table 4.17

Long-term Unemployment in Ireland, 1994-2004

	Number ('000s)	Rate	Share of total unemployment
1994	128.2	9.0%	60.8%
1998	63.6	3.9%	50.3%
2000	27.7	1.6%	37.2%
2004	26.3	1.4%	31.2%

Source: CSO, *QNHS Revised Series Post Census 2002*, op. cit., Table 16 and CSO, *QNHS*, Stationary office, Dublin September 2004.

Long-term unemployment (LTU) in Ireland rose significantly between 1980 and 1994. The long-term unemployment rate was only 2.8 per cent of the labour force in 1980, this figure rising to 8.3 per cent of the labour force in 1988 and rising again in the early 1990s to 9.0 per cent of the labour force. Table 4.17 shows the marked decline that has taken place in LTU since 1994. The reductions on all three counts are remarkable; the numbers in absolute terms are down to nearly a fifth their level in 1994, the drop in the LTU rate is even more dramatic and the share of LTU in total unemployment dropped from over 60 per cent in 1994 to around 31 per cent by early 2004. As a result, the LTU rate (1.4 per cent) in 2004 was below the level pertaining in 1980.

What has brought about these reductions? There were probably three factors at work: very favourable aggregate demand conditions, the effects of special labour market programmes (in particular the Community Employment Programme and Back to Work and Back to Education Allowance Scheme) and the effect of tighter social welfare control measures (see later).

6 ADAPTING TO NEW TECHNOLOGY AND OTHER GLOBAL FACTORS

Introduction

The increase in unemployment in the 1980s and early 1990s was not unique to Ireland, but affected almost every country in Europe, including as seen earlier the Nordic countries. What caused the rise in unemployment in Europe? More specifically why have high unemployment rates persisted into the 2000s in most of Europe, especially in France, Germany and Italy? A number of causes have been suggested. First, there are arguments relating to global factors such as increased competition in international trade and technological change, factors that would have affected every country in Europe, but some to a greater extent than others. How each country fared depended largely on the adaptability and employability of their labour forces in the new circumstances. These issues will be discussed in this section. Second, there are structural arguments relating to such issues as the role of unions and wage bargaining/setting, employment protection legislation and the taxation and social welfare systems. All of these issues will be discussed in Section 7.

Trade and Technological Change
Given the extent of Ireland's trade, factor and corporate links with the world economy; it is inevitable that the increasing globalisation of economic activity has, and will have, a major effect on economic activity and employment in Ireland (see Chapter 7).

It is generally believed by economists that an increasing intensity of trade will lead to higher incomes, but that it will also lead to the displacement of labour in some activities and the expansion of labour in other activities. The net impact on employment should be negligible as long as labour and product markets function well and wages are reasonably flexible. Thus, if decreased overall employment should result from increased trade intensity it is not trade per se that is causing the problem but the functioning of the labour and product markets, a topic that will be returned to in a later section. The evidence, according to the OECD, supports such an argument. This indeed is the reason why Ireland has adopted such a pro-trade liberalisation stance in the last 30 years.

Increasing international trade may also have an impact on innovation and the absorption of technological change. It is argued by some that labour saving technologies are, at least in part, introduced in anticipation of and/or in response to the increased competition both on domestic and foreign markets that arises from the increased globalisation of trade. As such, the effect of increased international trade and technological change are difficult to separate in practice.

Technology is central to the process of growth (see Chapters 5 and 7): it allows increases in productivity and thereby real incomes. But does it destroy jobs and in the process create unemployment? Is it the cause of the so called 'jobless growth' experienced in most of Europe in the last 20 years?

Fears about widespread job losses associated with the emergence of new technology are not new and are in the aggregate largely unfounded. It is true that technological change involves a process of job destruction in some older occupations, firms and industries, but it also involves a parallel process of job creation in new and emerging sectors and occupations. There are many historical examples of predictions of large scale technological unemployment being followed in fact by large net expansions of jobs. For example, just after World War II it was predicted in the USA that the invention of the computer would create technological unemployment that would make 'the Great Depression look like a picnic', yet in the following fifty years there was a massive increase in employment in the USA and almost no increase in the unemployment rate (see earlier).

The argument is made, though, that the *nature* of the new technologies being introduced in the last twenty years is very different to anything experienced previously. The wave of new technologies in electronics, computers, telecommunications, industrial materials and biotechnology are applicable not just to manufacturing and agriculture, like past developments, but across the whole economy, even into areas such as banking, accountancy, retail trading and health care.

It is also argued that not only the nature, but also the *pace* of the technological change is new. The central point here relates to the earlier discussion on the increasing globalisation of world trade. This increase in world trade has put pressure on industries everywhere to innovate and absorb new technology in order to survive. Thus the globalisation of trade and changing technology are interlinked and, as mentioned already, their effects hard to differentiate.

Ireland clearly could not and cannot escape the effects of these technological changes. Ireland is in the fortunate position in that much of the growth in the last decade came from technology based industry. The IDA has had success in marketing Ireland as a technology hub, with many companies from the USA locating their European bases here. As a result, in 1999 Ireland was the second largest exporter of software, supplying around two-thirds of the European software market. The country is also host to two-fifths of US share-service, call and technical support centres located in Europe. Moreover, in recent years offshoots from this high technology foreign investment have sprung up in the form of small, Irish-owned IT companies (see Chapter 7 for a further discussion of these issues).

There are four key technology areas that influence a country's success in IT: infrastructure, competitive market conditions, education and training and access. It has been, and will be, the country's ability to take appropriate action on all four fronts that will allow us to absorb and adapt to the new technology: our ability to do this in turn will be the key to employment, not only in manufacturing but more important perhaps, given its scale, in the services sector as well.

Adaptability and Employability

Over the last 20 years the structure of work in the industrialised world has, for the reasons mentioned above, been changing. There has been a shift in demand away from low skilled, low wage jobs towards high skilled, high wage jobs. The change in the nature of work arises not only from the transformation of jobs by technology and international trade but also from the 'natural' sectoral changes that have occurred with regard to employment (see Table 4.12).

The skills required in services are different to those needed for industry and hence the declining industrial workforce cannot be automatically transplanted into services jobs. The new wave of employment creation leads, as mentioned earlier, to a transformation of the competencies required from the workforce. Not only do they need different qualifications and skills but the continuously changing nature of work also requires them to have a high degree of flexibility that was not necessary in the past when permanent, stable positions were the norm.

The skills of the labour force then have to be altered to take account of the changing environment and nature of work that accompany this. In the absence of this adjustment, mismatch can, and may have, become a serious problem in the labour market in Ireland. Evidence for this is reflected in repeated statements of serious skills shortages in the Irish economy.

It is for these reasons that the EU has placed special emphasis on upgrading the skills and competencies of the labour force, as part of the search for a solution to the unemployment problem. Not all persons have acquired adequate initial education and training before they enter the labour market and these are the people most likely to experience long-term unemployment in Ireland and elsewhere in Europe. The first priority then must be to reduce through preventive and remedial measures the number of young people who leave school without some qualification.

The next concern is to ensure that those who have acquired satisfactory initial qualifications make the transition to employment and this may be assisted by a more employer led approach to education, particularly vocational education. Last, and of most relevance perhaps in relation to the issues discussed in this section, is the need to emphasise continuing education and training (see Chapter 11), as individuals need the opportunity to upgrade their knowledge and competencies to prepare themselves for the changes brought about by increasing international trade and technological change.

For similar reasons the Irish government has altered its policy on work permits and visas slightly for immigrants seeking work, i.e. it actively recruits suitably qualified people intended for designated sectors where skills shortages are particularly acute. In addition, FÁS proactively deals with skills shortages via its skills training for the unemployed and redundant.[10]

7 FLEXIBILITY IN LABOUR MARKET

It has been mentioned already that structural rigidities in labour markets, especially in those of many countries in Europe, may largely explain why unemployment is still at such high levels in these countries. Putting it more positively, it is argued that it is the countries with flexible labour markets that have experienced the lowest rates of unemployment in the 2000s. There are several dimensions to the structural rigidity and labour market flexibility arguments and some of the key ones will be looked at here.

First, wage and price adjustments are examined, with the main attention devoted to industrial relations. Second, quantity adjustments (which refer to barriers facing the movement of people in and out of jobs) are analysed. Policies to enhance quantity adjustment include reforms of employment protection legislation and active labour market policies. Last, the effect of the tax and social welfare systems on the working of the labour market will be looked at briefly.

Wage Adjustments

Price formation in the labour market is, by necessity different from that in other markets. This is because wages are not simply a price of one type of product among others, but 'determine to a large extent the well being of the majority of citizens in modern society. Societies' concern about social justice and the distribution of income therefore becomes integrally linked to wage-setting'.[11] Because of this, distinct social arrangements and institutions intervene in every country in the market clearing role of wage adjustments. However, even if the operation of the price system for labour is different than for that of products, the effects of prices being too high are the same: i.e. wages above market clearing levels will result in excess supply and therefore lower levels of employment than would otherwise be the case.

Industrial Relations and Competition in Product Markets

As mentioned previously, the response of wages to market conditions has to be seen against the background of the institutional arrangements, particularly those relating to industrial relations and the role of trade unions, in the labour market in each particular country. These arrangements have been partly designed to encourage stable employment relationships and to avert the income insecurity that can accompany rapid price adjustments in the market for labour, as happened in the USA in the 1980s. However, in so doing these arrangements may encourage anti-competitive behaviour in the labour market and, as in all markets, this will result in lower demand because prices are not set at their clearing rate. This of course must be set against the advantages for employees of the protective industrial relations arrangements and the potential advantages for employers, in that these arrangements may strengthen cooperation by workers and prevent the harmful behaviour that may be inherent in a more atomistic wage setting environment (see Chapter 3 for a further discussion of this issue).

Imperfect competition in the product market can also affect the wage level and thereby the level of employment and unemployment. If there is an absence of competition in the product market, firms have an option of choosing 'supranormal' profits ahead of increased employment. They also have the option of retaining the entire surplus for themselves or sharing it with existing employees. The latter will happen if the workers have bargaining strength or the rents may be willingly shared with workers to encourage efficiency and to boost work motivation, i.e. the employers may be prepared to pay what are called 'efficiency wages'. Whatever the rationale for rent sharing with workers, such arrangements favour the 'insiders' at the expense of the 'outsiders' and create a united lobby between unions and employers to oppose the removal of the imperfect competition in the product market that is giving rise to the rent. The solution to reducing the distortionary effects of imperfect product market competition on labour market outcomes is clearly to remove the opportunity for producers to earn rent and this calls for a strict and tough competition regime, a topic that is covered at some length in Chapters 3 and 8.

Irish Experience
It is generally recognised that income restraint is essential to employment creation in Ireland and that there *is* a trade off between pay and employment. In the multinational high tech sector of the economy pay moderation can lead to more employment in the medium to longer term, through increased profitability and its effect on investment location decisions. In the more traditional labour intensive parts of the traded sector there is likely to be a substantial trade off between pay and employment, as in many cases pay moderation is essential in this sector, simply to retain existing jobs. In the sheltered private sector, pay moderation is necessary to underpin the competitiveness of the traded sector and also to generate increased employment in this sector. Last, in the public sector, given a fixed budget, there is a very direct and almost immediate trade off between pay and employment.

A broad measure of competitiveness is unit wage costs in the economy overall. The picture again, using this measure, is that of a gain in competitiveness, although the most recent data appear to suggest a change in this situation. In 2002 Ireland had the second lowest increase in the OECD in unit wage costs; in fact Ireland along with five other OECD countries experienced unit wage cost reductions between 2001 and 2002; but by 2003 Ireland had slipped to twenty-third, although this is set to improve in the next two years.[12] In general though, the wage setting process in Ireland appears to have been a key factor in benefiting Irish competitiveness, and thereby employment, since 1987.

While the unionisation rate in Ireland fell in the 1990s, in line with many other countries, the rate in Ireland was still above that in the UK and way above that in the USA, although well below the Scandinavian countries.[13] In relation to the wage bargaining process, there is a degree of corporatism in the Irish labour market with a large proportion of wages being determined by national wage agreements (see Chapter 3). Ireland therefore appears to have adopted in recent years the preferable system of wage bargaining (i.e. centralised) where participants are more likely to take wider economic interests into account.

A national minimum wage (NMW) was introduced in Ireland in 2000 (see also Chapter 3). Although the ESRI predicted that this would decrease employment and increase unemployment and inflation, 95 per cent of firms surveyed a year later viewed the NMW as having had no impact on the numbers of employees they had subsequently hired. Those paid less than the NMW are concentrated in sales and personal services, which reflects a wider concern that younger female and non-national workers are most likely to experience low pay.[14] The Department of Enterprise, Trade and Employment estimated in 2001 that 5 per cent of all employees benefited as a direct result of the introduction of the NMW.

Employment Protection Legislation
Employment protection relates to the 'firing' and 'hiring' rules governing unfair dismissal, lay-off for economic reasons, severance payments, minimum notice periods, administrative authorisation for dismissals and prior discussion with

labour representatives. A number of benefits are alleged to justify employment protection legislation: encouraging increased investment in firm specific capital, reducing contracting costs by setting general rules and standards, and early notification of job loss to allow job search prior to being laid off. As against this, employment protection legislation imposes constraints on firms' behaviour that can raise labour costs and adversely affect hiring decisions. It may also provide strong incentives for employers to use forms of employment (e.g. short-term contracts) that do not involve high firing costs. Labour security legislation does not only affect the actions of employers, it also influences the bargaining power and, hence, strategy of the insiders (see earlier). With the legislation in place, workers' fear of job loss will be greatly diminished and they will push for higher real wages. This will then have an impact on labour demand. Labour security legislation therefore could cause labour demand to be inflexible both directly (i.e. through employers' immediate decisions) and indirectly (i.e. through its promotion of higher real wages). In fact, employment protection laws are thought by many to be a key factor in generating labour market inflexibility.

It appears though that a certain level of employment protection is justified to protect workers from arbitrary or discriminatory dismissals. However, the OECD believes that dismissals that are required on economic grounds must be allowed and that the provision of more explicit, long-term commitments to job security should not be imposed on all firms but decided on a firm by firm basis. Whether and to what extent reform is required clearly depends on the country specific circumstances. A related issue is that the emphasis is now increasingly on employment security rather than job security, that is on guaranteed employment rather than employment in a specific job. The best way to ensure this is to increase adaptability and employability, as discussed earlier.

Attempts have been made to construct various summary indicators to describe the 'strictness' of employment protection in each country, including Ireland. Given the complexity of constructing such indicators, they are inevitably somewhat arbitrary, but nonetheless are indicative. An OECD study ranking EU countries according to 'strictness' of protection in the areas of individual dismissals of regular workers, fixed term contracts and employment through temporary employment agencies, using objective methods and surveys of employers, showed in 2003 that employment protection was ranked relatively low as a problem in Ireland.[15] Compared to other European countries, there does not appear to be excessive employment protection legislation here. Ireland was ranked fifth in the OECD, the USA first followed by the UK and Canada; Portugal was ranked last with an almost identical score to Turkey. It is noteworthy, though, that in relation to the most relevant other European labour market from Ireland's point of view, namely that of the UK, Ireland is ranked higher in terms of strictness of employment protection legislation. It is also the case that employment protection legislation in Europe in general is much stricter than in Canada and the USA.

Taxation
Payroll taxes, such as employers' social security contributions, raise the costs of employing labour over and above the wage paid. Income taxes and employees' social security contributions reduce the return to working. These taxes therefore are important because they directly affect the rate of return from decisions to enter the labour market and thereby affect the supply of labour (see Chapter 3). They may also influence the choice between working in the black economy and declared paid employment. These taxes may have an even greater impact on employment and unemployment through their influence on wage determination and therefore on the demand for labour. In a perfectly competitive labour market these effects would be minimal, but as seen earlier most labour markets are far from perfectly competitive. Hence, cuts in real wages through the imposition of increased personal income taxes or social security contributions may be resisted by workers and compensated for by higher nominal wages – but at the cost of higher unemployment. Likewise, an increase in employers' social security contributions can also result in unemployment when workers resist offsetting wage cuts.

Marginal and average tax rates have fallen significantly in the last decade in Ireland and are now among the lowest in the OECD. Reductions in average tax rates at low levels of earnings are clearly an important way of increasing the income differential between being in and out of work, for the groups for which this is the most serious problem. It appears that particular attention needs to be devoted to social security contributions in this regard, not just to the level of these contributions but also their structure: employers' taxation not only influences the amount of people that are employed but may also influence the type of worker that is hired.

The rate at which social benefits are withdrawn, as seen in Chapter 3, is also another important aspect of the problem. A feature of many tax and benefit systems, including that in Ireland, is that they embody very high marginal tax rates for those on low incomes, especially those with large families, as benefits are reduced and earnings are taxed. There have been some successful attempts to address this problem in Ireland in the last decade.

Unemployment Payments
The rationale for unemployment insurance payments is 'to relieve people who have lost a job through no fault of their own from immediate financial concerns, and thus allow efficient job search. Insurance benefits, therefore, have an economic efficiency as well as a social equity objective'.[16] In relation to unemployment assistance payments, which apply in Ireland after twelve months and effectively for an indefinite period, the social or equity role, in reducing poverty among unemployed people and cushioning the adverse effects of high and rising unemployment, becomes paramount. As a result of the above, there would be strong political objections to resist any cuts in unemployment benefits or assistance and this clearly 'flavours' any debate on the causal connection between

unemployment benefit/assistance and unemployment. However, the possibility of such a causal connection, and its extent, must be addressed, especially in countries such as France, Germany and Italy, where unemployment has persisted, at high levels, and has led to a build up of large scale, long-term unemployment and 'handout' dependency.

Few economists question the fact that there *is* a link between the benefit system and unemployment. At the simplest level, unemployment payments may create an option of leisure and low income, which some people might choose in preference to full-time work and a higher income. However, such payments could affect employment in many other ways. First, receipt of such payments may prolong intervals of job search, even for those who want to work. Second, because unemployment payments reduce the cost of becoming unemployed, employed people may take a tougher stance in industrial relations disputes or in collective bargaining over wages (see earlier), thereby exacerbating the high real wage problem. Last, payments may increase employment in high turnover and seasonal industries, by subsidising these industries relative to those which provide long-term contract jobs.

The adverse effects of unemployment payments may, however, result not so much from the existence and level of these payments, but more from the entitlement conditions, the administration of the system and other institutional background factors. For example, payment of unemployment benefits is conditional upon the claimant being available for, and willing to take, full-time work. If this condition is not effectively implemented, people *not* in the labour force (i.e. not available for or not seeking work) may register as unemployed simply to collect unemployment payments. If this condition is strictly enforced and payments stopped if it is not met, then many of the distortionary effects of unemployment payments could be substantially reduced. This problem has been tackled with some success in Ireland due to the 2002 Irish National Action Plan; although strictly speaking decreases in the numbers claiming unemployment benefit does not necessarily translate one for one into reductions in the numbers unemployed according to the ILO definition. A related issue is that the employment agency must not only enforce this condition but must also facilitate effective job search (see later).

In terms of replacement rates (i.e. benefit entitlement before tax as a percentage of previous earnings before tax),[17] in 1999 Ireland belonged to the upper range countries of Europe, with an overall average of 29 per cent (as measured by the OECD). This compared to figures of 52 per cent in Denmark, 43 per cent in Belgium, 37 per cent in France, 33 per cent in Spain and 28 per cent in Germany. The figure for the UK, the country with which Ireland has the closest labour market links was only 18 per cent, and those for Japan and the USA only 8 per cent and 11 per cent respectively. The low figures in the last two countries arose from relatively low replacement rates in the first year of unemployment and, more importantly, the effective withdrawal of benefit in subsequent years.

Active Labour Market Policies

The OECD is unequivocal concerning the changes that need to be effected in benefit administration. They suggest, for example, much more in-depth verification of eligibility, much better matching of workers to job vacancies, and fieldwork investigation of concealed earnings and related fraud. A more fundamental problem they claim is making unemployment payment, especially to the long-term unemployed, effectively conditional on availability for existing vacancies. In particular, they stress that the long-term unemployed should be expected to take, and unemployment payments made conditional on taking, even low status jobs. Since already employed people will not move into these jobs, the danger is that there may be a steady tendency for these jobs to disappear altogether, resulting in the progressive erosion of total employment. As the OECD notes, 'much may depend upon achieving a social, political and analytical consensus on this, rejecting the opposite idea that modern economies should be able to afford to make work optional'.[18] The real concern here is that if people are allowed to drift into long-term unemployment, as happened in Ireland in the 1980s and in the early 1990s, that the problem becomes more difficult to overcome. At an individual level long-term unemployment may lead to significant deskilling and demotivation. At a macroeconomic level, and partly as a result of this, the long-term unemployed may not be regarded as 'employable' and in a sense may cease to be part of the labour market.

What is being suggested above is effectively a much more active approach to labour market policy on behalf of the employment service in each country. The purpose of active labour market policies is threefold: first to mobilise labour supply, second to improve the quality of the labour force, and third to strengthen the search process in the labour market. They are particularly appropriate for those experiencing long-term unemployment, because as mentioned many of them are effectively not participating in the labour force. Because of the deskilling and demotivation that has taken place, they need assistance with education and training, and because of demotivation and the indefinite nature of unemployment and related payments the search for jobs may not be as active as might be desired.

Active labour market policies can be classified into four categories: first, there are state employment services (e.g. placement and counselling); second, there is labour market training (i.e. for unemployed and employed adults); third, there are youth measures (e.g. remedial education, training or work experience for disadvantaged young people); and last, subsidised employment (i.e. subsidies to increase employment in the private sector, support for the unemployed persons starting their own enterprises and direct job creation in either the public or non-profit sector). All OECD countries have had a mixture of such policies for many years, but there is very considerable variation in the proportion of GDP devoted by each country to such active labour market policies.

There have been significant moves in Ireland, since 1995 in particular, in relation to active labour market policies and there is reason to believe that the

103

large reduction in the numbers in long-term unemployment since then was in large part explained by such a policy change. By the end of the 1990s 1.5 per cent of GDP was being spent on active labour market initiatives in Ireland.

Throughout the EU, as previously mentioned, many of the large economies are currently facing high unemployment figures that they seem unable or unwilling to tackle with any effectiveness. It does, however, appear that Germany has embraced various active labour market policies as it aims to reduce its high structural unemployment problem; these include polices aimed at increasing the efficiency of the federal employment service as well as reforms of the unemployment benefit system.[19]

8 CONCLUSION

The outstanding economic policy failure in the last 25 years in Ireland was the inability to increase employment in the 1980s, despite the huge increase in the potential labour force in this period. The result of this failure was a dramatic increase in the unemployment rate and emigration of almost 200,000 people. More seriously, perhaps, the sustained failure to increase employment meant not only that the high level of unemployment persisted into the mid 1990s, but also that an increasing proportion of that total start drifting into long-term unemployment and, in many cases therefore, effectively out of the labour market.

The outstanding policy success of the last 25 years, indeed of the whole post-Independence era, in contrast was the increase in employment between 1993 and 2004, and the corresponding huge reductions in unemployment and the dramatic switch from large scale emigration to significant immigration. In a very short period the disastrous failures of the 1980s had been turned around into one of the most remarkable success stories in terms of employment growth in the Western world. A variety of explanations for this have been looked at in this chapter, with further insights to follow in Chapter 5. There are no simple explanations though. The policy of attracting foreign investment, much of it in the high tech sectors, allowed Ireland cope with the trade and technological effects of globalisation (see Chapter 7). The positive policy stance to trade in general, and the EU and the euro in particular, may have helped in this regard (see Chapter 5). The advent of the 'borderless' economy meant that Ireland's peripheral location mattered much less than before (see Chapter 7). The increased emphasis on competition in the non-traded sector of the economy added to Ireland's competitiveness (Chapters 3 and 8), while the centralised wage bargaining process appears to have delivered on competitive wage setting and a good industrial relations climate (Chapter 3). Past policies on education also appear to have been a factor (see Chapter 11) and the relatively flexible employment protection environment that was in place would have assisted in the huge employment increase that the above facilitated. Ireland also appears to have a relatively 'entrepreneur friendly' climate, as measured by relative cost and length of time, and minimum charter capital required, to form a private limited liability company.[20] Finally, changes in taxation and the increased emphasis on active labour market policies made inroads into the most intractable unemployment problem that Ireland faced in the mid 1990s, namely that of long-term unemployment.

Ireland's success on the employment front in the last decade though must be set in context. It followed decades of failure to provide jobs for Irish people, the result being large scale emigration in the 1950s and again in the 1980s. This resulted also in extraordinarily high unemployment levels in the decade 1985 to 1995. Potential labour supply had been increasing rapidly in Ireland since 1980 and a large employment increase was required to absorb this growth in supply; without it there was initially, and would continued to have been, large scale emigration and high levels of unemployment. The country, in other words, for the first time in its history provided employment to those who needed it. This has been the norm in other small European countries such as Denmark, the Netherlands and Norway for decades. Indeed, the unemployment rate in Ireland is still higher than in two of these three countries and the proportion of those of working age in employment in Ireland lags well behind that for these countries. Much progress has been made, but more has to be achieved and the failures of the past on the employment front must not be repeated.

Endnotes

1   M. Cassidy, 'Productivity in Ireland: Trends and Issues', *Quarterly Bulletin*, Central Bank, Dublin Spring 2004.
2   CSO, *Population and Migration Estimates*, Stationery Office, Dublin 2003.
3   See D. Duffy, J. Fitz Gerald, I. Kearney and D. Smyth, *Medium-Term Review 1999- 2005*, ESRI, Dublin 1999, Chapter 2, for a discussion of how these various factors have contributed to the growth in living standards in Ireland in the last 40 years. See also B. Walsh, 'The Transformation of the Irish Labour Market: 1980-2003' (presented to the Statistical and Social Inquiry Society of Ireland), Dublin 2004, p. 10.
4   CSO, *Census 2002 – Principal Demographic Results*, Stationery Office, Dublin 2003.
5   OECD, *Employment Outlook*, OECD, Paris 2001, Chapter 5.
6   OECD, *Employment Outlook*, OECD, Paris 2002, Table 2.4.
7   OECD, 'Taking the Measure of Temporary Employment', *Employment Outlook*, OECD, Paris 2002.
8   This discussion draws on NESC, *Opportunities, Challenges and Capacities for Choice*, Stationery Office, Dublin 1999.
9   OECD, *Annual Report 2004*, OECD, Paris 2004, p. 35.
10 Department of Enterprise, Trade and Employment, *National Employment Action Plan 2003-2005*, Stationery Office, Dublin 2003, Chapter 3.
11 OECD, *Jobs Study, Part II*, OECD, Paris 1994, p. 1.
12 OECD, *Employment Outlook*, OECD, Paris 2004, Table 1.4.
13 *Ibid*, Table 3.3.
14 NESC, *An Investment in Quality: Services, Inclusion and Enterprise*, Stationery Office, Dublin 2003, Chapter 8.
15 OECD, *Employment Outlook*, 2004, op. cit., Chart 2.1.

16 OECD, *Jobs Study: Part II*, op. cit., p.171.
17 The higher the replacement rate the less incentive to seek work.
18 OECD, *Jobs Study: Part II,* op. cit., p. 213.
19 CESifo, *Forum,* IFO Institute for Economic Resrearch, Munich Summer 2004, p. 35.
20 'EU Aims for More Entrepreneurship', *Financial Times*, 23 March 2000.

CHAPTER 5

Growth in Output and Living Standards

Jonathan Haughton

1 THE CELTIC TIGER

According to the World Bank, Irish Gross Domestic Product (GDP) per capita overtook that of the USA in 2002.[1] By this measure, Ireland is the fourth richest country in the world, after Luxembourg, Norway and Switzerland. A decade ago, nobody would have predicted this outcome; Ireland then was one of the poorer members of the European Union, perceived at home and abroad as something of an economic laggard.

The dramatic Irish growth spurt of the 1990s – although it has now run its course – has attracted the attention of researchers and would be emulators, especially among the new EU members of Eastern Europe. How did Ireland become so rich? What were the keys to the recent success of the Celtic Tiger?

We address these questions here, beginning with the numbers. To anticipate the argument: Ireland's recent economic growth is real and impressive. It is indeed a rich country, but not quite as affluent as the GDP per capita numbers imply. Taking a long view, most of Ireland's recent growth may be thought of as an overdue catch up; but there remains the suspicion that Irish economic performance has now gone beyond what would be expected, so there is something exceptional to explain.

Why is Ireland rich? And what underlies the growth that propelled Ireland to the ranks of the most affluent nations? It is helpful to address these questions in two steps. First, we use the Solow growth model to identify the proximate determinants of growth and living standards: how much is due to high levels of investment, long hours of work, or more technology. This then guides us in our search for the more fundamental explanations, which are likely rooted in policy decisions, demographic changes, and the evolution of the world context.

It is argued that Ireland's growth spurt in the late 1990s was due to a fortunate confluence of events – the opening of the economy and society to trade and the flow of ideas, the arrival of the EU single market that made Ireland an attractive platform for US investors, a boom in the US economy that provided a supply of investment, an improvement in the educational level of the Irish labour force, transfers from the EU, a highly credible macroeconomic stance, fiscal discipline, improved labour relations, and relatively modest taxes. This created a virtuous circle: as jobs were created, well educated and experienced workers immigrated (or did not leave); an entrepreneurial 'can do' attitude took root; financing remained available.

Now that Ireland has caught up, there are signs of complacency. The boom was extended by an unsustainable rise in public sector hiring; minimum wage legislation limits the creation of entry level jobs; recent wage settlements have been more generous than productivity gains would justify; yet productive public services, most notably infrastructure, do not match those of many western European nations. Maintaining and consolidating the new found affluence will be a challenge over the coming decade.

2 IS IRELAND REALLY SO AFFLUENT?

Output, Income and Consumption

The commonest measure of affluence is GDP per capita. It measures the money value of goods and services produced and marketed in the economy in a year, and represents the value added by economic activity. Table 5.1 shows that real GDP rose by over 4 per cent annually for most of the period from 1960 to 1994, the exception being a spell of slow growth between 1979 and 1986. Then came the growth spurt, as real GDP rose by 9.0 per cent annually between 1994 and 2002. Irish per capita GDP in 2004 was 5.8 times larger than in 1960.

Not all of the goods and services produced in Ireland accrue to Irish citizens or residents; for instance, profit that is repatriated does not contribute to local incomes. A more satisfactory measure of the output that stays in Ireland is Gross National Income (GNI), which starts with GDP and adds net factor income from abroad (NFIA) as well as net transfer payments from abroad (NTPA). In 2003 these amounts, in billions of euros, were as follows:

GNI	=	GDP	+	NFIA	+	NTPA
104.7	=	129.3	-	25.9	+	1.3

The most striking feature of these numbers is the exceptionally large value of transfer payments out of Ireland, mainly the repatriation of profits by foreign firms operating in Ireland.

An unknown, although no doubt significant, part of this profit may be attributable to transfer pricing, as some corporations overstate their exports and understate their imports in order to book their profits in low tax Ireland. As a result of this measurement error, reported GDP may overstate 'true' GDP by as much as 10 per cent.

Table 5.1

Measures of Recent Performance

	1960-73	1973-79	1979-86	1986-94	1994-02
	(annual growth rates, %)				
Real GDP	4.4	4.2	1.8	4.7	9.0
Real GDP/capita	3.7	3.3	1.5	4.6	7.7
Real GNI/capita	3.5	2.6	0.4	4.5	6.1
Real GDP/worker	4.3	3.5	2.9	3.5	5.0
Real GNI/worker	4.2	2.8	1.8	3.4	3.4
Real consumption/capita	3.2	2.7	-0.1	3.5	5.3
	(levels at end of period)				
Employment (millions)	1.06	1.15	1.09	1.20	1.61
Population (millions)	3.07	3.37	3.54	3.57	3.92
Unemployment rate	5.9	7.1	17.4	15.6	4.2

Sources: Central Bank of Ireland, *Bulletin*, Central Bank, Dublin, various issues; Department of Finance, *Economic Review and Outlook*, Department of Finance, Dublin, various issues; World Bank, *World Development Indicators*, www.worldbank.org 2003.

In 1960, GNI was 6 per cent higher than GDP; by 2002 it was 19 per cent lower. Table 5.1 shows that GNI has consistently grown more slowly than GDP; the exceptional growth of GDP in the late 1990s is highly attenuated in the GNI figures (and there was no acceleration in the growth of GNI *per worker* in the late 1990s). Nonetheless, by 2002 Irish GNI per capita was exceeded by only five countries;[2] by this measure Ireland is indeed rich.

The GNI numbers in turn probably overstate the growth in *living standards*. It is standard practice to decompose GDP into the amounts spent on private consumption (C), investment (I), government purchases of goods and services (G) and exports (X), adjusted for imports (IM). Again using 2003 data we have, in billions of euro:

$$\begin{array}{ccccccccccc}
\text{GDP} & = & \text{C} & + & \text{I} & + & \text{G} & + & \text{X} & - & \text{IM} \\
129.3 & = & 60.1 & + & 28.7 & + & 17.6 & + & 121.5 & - & 97.0
\end{array}$$

The most unusual feature of this breakdown, when compared with other developed countries, is the low proportion (46 per cent) of GDP that is represented by private consumption spending, although it represents a more substantial 59 per cent of GNI.

For a typical household, what matters most to its material living standards is presumably 'full consumption' (C+G): this is the private consumption of goods and services, plus publicly provided goods and services such as education, some health care, and security. Figure 5.1 tracks the evolution of per capita GDP and full consumption over time. The two were very close until about 1980, after which they diverged.

Between 1960 and 2002, real full consumption per capita rose almost four fold. This is a big increase; Ireland has become rich because consumption (and GNI and GDP) per person has risen rapidly, if not always steadily, for over forty years. The sprightly Irish tortoise has even overtaken the Japanese hare.

Figure 5.1

GDP, GNI and Consumption per capita, 1960-2004

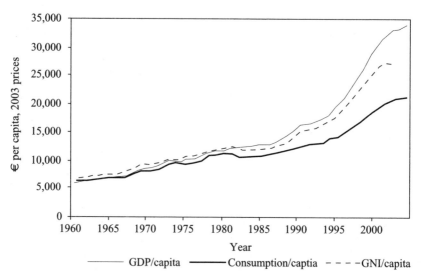

Source: OECD, *OECD in Figures 2003,* OECD, Paris 2003; US Census Bureau, *Statistical Abstract of the United States 2003,* www.census.gov 2004; Department of Finance, *Budgetary and Economic Statistics*, Department of Finance, Dublin 2004; World Bank, *World Development Indicators*, www.worldbank.org 2003; UNDP, *Human Development Indicators 2004*, www.undp.org 2004.

An unsurprising consequence of the increase in real incomes and consumption has been a drop in poverty, particularly over the past decade. Using a poverty line set at 60 per cent of average income in 1987, the proportion of the population in poverty was then 16 per cent, falling to 15 per cent by 1994, 8 per cent by 1998 and 5 per cent by 2001 (see Chapter 6). Those most likely to be poor are parents living alone (24 per cent), the unemployed (18 per cent), and children (7 per cent).

Employment and Population
An economy's success could also be measured by its ability to provide employment for those who want it, and to sustain a larger population. Between 1960 and 1986 the rise in employment was negligible, from 1.05 to 1.09 million. Then came a remarkable, and historically unprecedented, burst of job creation, pushing employment up to 1.61 million by 2002 (see Chapter 4). Between 1986 and 2002, employment rose from 31 per cent to 41 per cent of the total population.

Migration flows mirrored the changes in employment, albeit with a lag of a few years. There was immigration in the 1970s, when Irish economic growth was higher than elsewhere in Europe. Emigration resumed in the early 1980s, peaking at 44,000 (1.3 per cent of the population) in 1989. In due course the pendulum swung back, and about 100,000 people migrated into Ireland in the course of the 1990s. The population reached its lowest point in about 1961 (2.8 million), but in 2004 it just topped 4.0 million, with particularly rapid increases in the 1970s and late 1990s, as Figure 5.2 shows clearly.

Figure 5.2

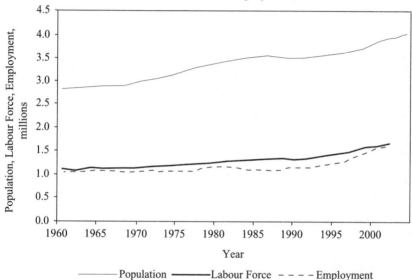

Population, Labour Force and Employment, 1960-2004

Source: As For Figure 5.1.

The unemployment rate, 5 per cent in 1960 and 7 per cent in 1980, surged to 17 per cent by 1986, remaining in double digits for a decade before falling very rapidly in the late 1990s to a low of 3.7 per cent in 2001, after which it edged up again slightly. The high unemployment rate of the 1980s was a consequence of slow economic growth, coming at a time of diminished employment opportunities abroad (particularly in the UK), a rapid increase in the working age population, and a system of taxes and subsidies that made working unremunerative for many low skilled workers.

One consequence of Ireland's poor track record in creating employment prior to the early 1990s was to keep many women out of the labour force completely. As recently as 1994 the labour force participation rate for women was 40 per cent, one of the lowest in the OECD countries, although by 2002 it had risen to 55 per cent, just marginally below the average of 56 per cent in the EU-15 countries.[3]

111

Economic Performance in International Context

In order to judge Ireland's economic performance, it helps to put it in an international context. A problem arises immediately: how is one to compare GDP across countries, given differences in currencies and in the cost of living. A euro in Ireland barely buys a cup of coffee; converted into rupees and spent in India, it would buy a whole meal. So if the exchange rate were used to convert India's GDP into euro, it would understate the true purchasing power of India's GDP.

Figure 5.3

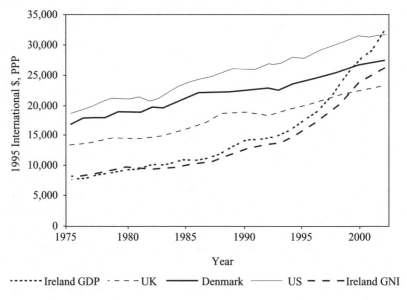

Irish GDP and GNI per capita Compared, 1975-2002

Source: As for Figure 5.1.

The standard solution is to recompute every country's GDP using a common set of 'international' prices, giving a measure of purchasing power parity (PPP) GDP that is reasonably comparable across countries. Figure 5.3 graphs Ireland's per capita GDP since 1975, in 1995 PPP US dollars, and compares it with the USA, Denmark and the UK. Denmark is included here because it is, like Ireland, a small open economy, and has often been held up as a role model for Ireland to emulate. Until 1994, Irish growth was in line with (or slightly above) that of these comparator countries. Then there was a decade of clear acceleration, as Ireland overtook the UK (in 1998), Denmark (in 2000) and the USA (in 2002).

For the UK, Denmark and the USA, GNI is almost identical to GDP; only in Ireland is there a large difference. Figure 5.3 shows that Irish GNI per capita has passed the UK level and is approaching (but has not exceeded) the Danish level;

it is still somewhat below the level in the USA. This is probably a more appropriate comparison of income levels, given that Irish GDP is somewhat inflated by transfer pricing.

Other Measures of Living Standards

While Ireland's GDP (or GNI) per capita is undisputedly one of the five highest in the world, other indicators of living standards still lag those of many of its EU peers, despite showing real improvement since 1960. Several indicators related to the quality of life are shown in Table 5.2, with comparative information for the EU-15 group and the USA.

Table 5.2

Indicators of the Quality of Life

	Ireland					EU-15	USA	EU-15 Max
	1960	1970	1980	1990	2002	2002	2001	2002
Health								
Infant mortality rate	31	20	12	8	5.8	4.8	6.9	5.9
Life expectancy, F	72	74	75	77	79.8	81.6	79.5	82.9
Life expectancy, M	68	69	70	72	74.1	75.5	74.1	78.3
Crime								
Crimes/1,000	..	..	..	..	21	65	41	131
Prisoners/100,000	..	..	..	..	72	87	682	131
Homicides/millions	..	..	..	6	15	17	56	113
Environment								
CO2/capita, t	4	6	7	9	11.2	9.5	19.8	19.0
Waste, kg/cap	..	..	..	..	626	535	760	665
Smoke, μg/m3	..	..	211	269	41	..	..	..
Connectivity								
% hh, Internet	..	..	..		36	39	60	56
Airline pass, m	..	1.5	1.8	4.8	19.7	..	..	..
Mainlines/1000	..	..	142	281	502	565	886	797
Cellphones/1000	0	0	0	7	763	832	488	1,061
Assets								
New houses, '000	..	..	26.8	19.5	57.7	..	..	..
Cars/1000	..	..	216	227	370	410[1]	482	..

Sources: As for Figure 5.1.
[1]1998.
Note: Figures for 2002 are sometimes for 2001. Smoke figures are for Dublin only. EU-15 numbers show unweighted means.

While Ireland's life expectancy continues to rise, and is in line with the US experience, it is one of the lowest in the European Union. The infant mortality rate

– defined as the number of deaths of infants up to six months old per 1,000 population – is very low by historical standards, but remains one of the highest in the EU. These measures, considered to be good indicators of health outcomes, show that Ireland is something of a laggard by the standards of Western Europe (see also Chapter 10).

GDP (or GNI) represents an annual flow of final goods and services; even when GDP rises, it can take time to build up a good stock of assets – cars, houses, and fine roads. This helps explain why Irish visitors to France, for instance, are often struck by the high quality of the infrastructure, in a country whose consumption per capita is now lower than that of Ireland. However, Table 5.2 shows evidence of catch up: car ownership per capita rose by 63 per cent between 1990 and 2002 (which explains the rising congestion on Irish road); and house building has accelerated, averaging an impressive 49,000 annual completions in 1996-2003, well above the annual level of 22,000 seen in 1988-95.

Ireland is also connecting fast. The stock of telecommunications assets has risen remarkably, with a tripling in the number of mainline phones between 1980 and 2002; there is high cell phone penetration, although home use of the Internet, at 36 per cent, is below the EU-15 average and well below the 56 per cent rate seen in Denmark. There has also been an explosion in airline traffic.

By European and US standards, Ireland has a low level of reported crime, although recently the homicide rate has risen to close to the EU-15 norm. The incarceration rate remains relatively modest.

Tourism operators boast of Ireland's wild beauty – the woodlands were cleared by the sixteenth century! – and its clean air and water. While water is relatively clean, and smoke levels in Dublin have fallen dramatically since 1990, emissions of CO_2, the main 'greenhouse gas', now exceed the EU-15 average.

There is another interesting way to evaluate Irish levels of affluence. The United Nations Development Program annually constructs its *Human Development Index*, which combines measures of life expectancy, educational achievement (literacy and school enrolment rates), and GDP per capita into a single index. The most recent figures refer to 2002, and rank Ireland tenth in the world with a score of 0.936 (out of a maximum possible 1.000). Ireland scores well on GDP per capita and education, but these are offset by the comparatively low life expectancy. Ireland's Human Development Index has risen rapidly since 1975, when it was first measured, as Table 5.3 shows.

Table 5.3

Human Development Index for Ireland

1975	1980	1985	1990	1995	2000	2002
0.810	0.825	0.844	0.869	0.893	0.926	0.936

Source: United Nations Development Project, *Human Development Report 2003*, http://hdr.undp.org/reports/global/2003.

An Obsession with Output per Capita?
It is clear that most measures of living standards are correlated, if not perfectly, with GDP per capita. That is one of the reasons why economists and others tend to use GDP per capita as their primary measure of welfare.[4]

Is this an unhealthy obsession? In an oft-quoted speech (see also Chapter 1), Robert Kennedy in 1968 said, 'we will find neither national purpose nor personal satisfaction in an endless amassing of worldly goods ... the gross national product measures neither our wit nor our courage, neither our wisdom nor our learning, neither our compassion nor our devotion to country. It measures everything, in short, except that which makes life worthwhile.'

Perhaps the only way to respond to Kennedy's challenge is to ask people how satisfied they are with their lives, and then to determine whether these subjective evaluations are linked to GDP per capita. In a recent study in which a sample of adults were asked whether they felt excluded from society, 10 per cent of Irish respondents answered 'yes', slightly below the 12 per cent response for the EU-15 countries. Fully 92 per cent of Irish households reported that they were 'fairly' or 'very' satisfied with their lives, somewhat above the EU-15 average of 88 per cent; this lies below the level in Denmark (97 per cent) but well above the level in Greece (71 per cent). Commenting on the findings, Jens Alber and Tony Fahey write, 'the comparisons of countries across Europe ... [show that] the level of GDP per capita in the country in which the individual lives turns out to be the best predictor of individual life-satisfaction'.[5] In short, Robert Kennedy overstates the case: GDP may not measure personal satisfaction, but it is closely correlated with it, in which case it is indeed a useful guide to happiness!

We are left with the conclusion that Ireland is indeed a rich country; not as affluent as the GDP/capita figures would have one believe, perhaps, but few would disagree that by any reasonable measure it ranks in the ten most affluent countries in the world. The interesting question, to which we now turn, then is: how did it get there?

3 DETERMINANTS OF GROWTH IN OUTPUT PER WORKER

The Production Function
The immediate cause of the increase in the output of the Irish, or any other, economy is a rise in the inputs – the factors of production – used to generate output. The relationship between output (Q) and inputs of labour (L), capital (K) and 'human capital' (H) may be summarised as a *production function* of the form

$$(1) \qquad Q = A.F (L, K, H)$$

where the function F(.) is increasing in its arguments. The constant A is usually taken to represent 'technology', but this should be interpreted broadly to include everything that enhances the productivity of inputs, including such things as better managerial techniques or regulatory changes that spur competition. Economic historian Douglas North won a Nobel Prize largely on the strength of his work emphasising the importance of institutional change – such as the development of private property rights, or patent law – in enhancing economic growth over time.

If inputs are doubled, it is reasonable to suppose that output would also double; more generally, this implies that equation (1) is linearly homogeneous in labour, capital and human capital. So we may write

$$\text{(2)} \qquad \frac{Q}{L} = A.F\left(1, \frac{K}{L}, \frac{H}{L}\right)$$

or

$$\text{(3)} \qquad q = A.f(k, h)$$

Used creatively, Equation (3) can be illuminating. It implies that output per worker (q) will rise if:

– the capital stock rises – via investment, mainly financed by savings – since this boosts k. Note that by investment is meant the acquisition of more physical capital such as machinery, buildings or infrastructure, and not financial 'investment' which merely amounts to a transfer of ownership of existing wealth.
– workers acquire education, training and experience, and enjoy good health, since this raises h;
– technical advance, innovation and institutional change occur, since these increase A.

These are useful, if rather obvious, conclusions. However it is possible to make the analysis much more interesting.

Solow Growth model
The workhorse for understanding the role played by investment and other factors of production in economic growth is the model developed by MIT professor and Nobel laureate Robert Solow. Here we develop the model graphically and apply it to the Irish case.

The production function in (3) may be graphed as the curve 0-q in Figure 5.4. It curves because of the 'law' of diminishing marginal returns: as the amount of capital per worker (k) rises, output per worker (q) also rises, but less and less quickly.

Now assume that a constant fraction, s, of output is invested. This gives the investment supply curve 0-s.q, which has the same shape as the production function but is only s per cent as high.

To complete the story we may add a line that reflects the investment that would be necessary to prevent k (and therefore q) from falling. Simply to maintain the capital stock per worker, we need to:

- Invest enough to replace the wear and tear ('depreciation') of the capital stock; represented by δ, this is of the order of 5 per cent per annum in most economies.
- Invest enough to equip newcomers to the labour force; otherwise their arrival would dilute the capital stock and capital per worker (k) would fall. An n per cent rise in the labour force thus requires n per cent more capital for this purpose.

Taken together, 'necessary' investment per worker thus represents $(n+\delta).k$, and is shown by the straight line in Figure 5.4.

Figure 5.4

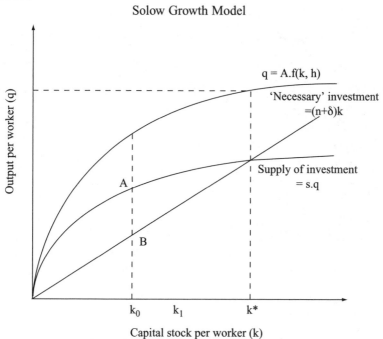

Solow Growth Model

A poor country will have a low stock of capital per worker, such as k_0. At this point, the supply of investment (s.q) exceeds necessary investment $((n+\delta).k)$, leaving an investment surplus that will serve to deepen the stock of capital. Thus by the next year, the stock of capital will rise to k_1, and so on.

There is an important implication. Poor countries should be able to grow faster than rich ones, because their investment 'surpluses' are larger relative to GDP.

Note that the process stops at k^*! In other words, investment alone can raise k to k^*, and therefore output per worker to q^*, but then growth stops – unless, of course, other influences can be brought to bear.

This has an immediate and interesting implication: economies should experience (conditional) convergence. For a given savings rate (s), technology (A.f(.)), employment growth rate (n) and depreciation rate (δ), all countries should converge on the same k* and hence the same level of output per worker. It is worth emphasising that the relevant variable here is output per worker, not per capita; to move from one to the other one needs to take into account the employment rate and demographic factors, a point to which we return below.

Has Ireland Converged?
It is natural to ask whether recent Irish economic growth follows the predictions of the Solow model, in effect causing the Irish economy to converge to those of the rest of the EU.

Figure 5.5

Initial Income and Subsequent Growth: OECD, 1960-2002

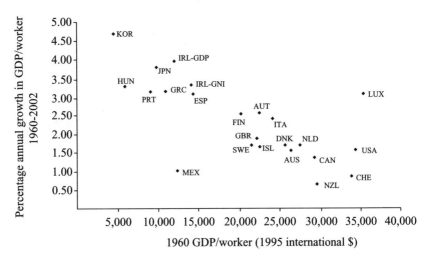

Source: As for Figure 5.1.

This question may be addressed with the help of two graphs. Figure 5.5 shows GDP per worker in 1960 (in 1995 international PPP US dollars) on the horizontal axis and the annual percentage growth rate of GDP per worker from 1960 to 2002 on the vertical axis. Each point represents one OECD country;[6] for Ireland, the graph shows points both for GDP per worker and GNI per worker, since it is possible that GDP per worker is too high due to measurement error (induced by transfer pricing). In 1960 Ireland was relatively poor, grouped with Greece, Spain, Japan and Mexico. The Solow model predicts that poorer countries should grow faster than richer ones, until they have caught up: thus South Korea (initially poor) should grow faster than Switzerland (initially rich). It follows that we would expect the observations in Figure 5.5 to fall along a line that slopes downwards to the right. And indeed this is what was seen; the correlation coefficient between the two series is –0.71. Viewed this way, it would appear that Irish economic growth was no more than one would have expected. Taking the 1960-2002 period as a whole, it makes sense to use the Solow model to try to identify the proximate causes of Irish growth (in output per worker).

Figure 5.6

Initial Income and Subsequent Growth: OECD, 1980-2002

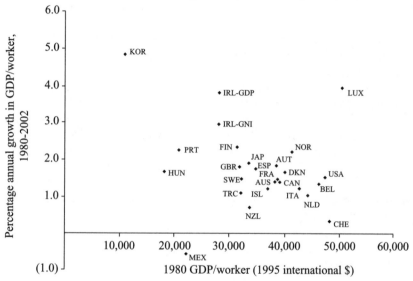

Source: As for Figure 5.1.

Figure 5.6 is similar to Figure 5.5 except that it takes 1980 instead of 1960 as the starting point. It is difficult to see any clear pattern in these observations; now Ireland – whether one uses GDP or GNI – along with Luxembourg and South Korea, stands out from the other observations, suggesting that growth in these countries was higher than would have been predicted by Solow type conditional convergence. The correlation in this case is –0.25, not significantly different from zero. The exceptional nature of Irish economic performance is even clearer if a larger sample of countries is used; most countries poorer than Ireland have not grown as rapidly as Ireland did over the past two, or four, decades.

In short, Ireland appears to have gone beyond convergence in terms of growth in output per worker. This calls for an explanation.

Beyond Solow: Endogenous Growth Theory

The Solow model assumes diminishing marginal returns to capital. Not all economists accept this premise. The endogenous growth school argues that there are likely to be important *external economies of scale*: for instance, the investments made by a computer software firm may also help other nearby firms, by training workers who move from firm to firm, by contributing to a local community of programmers who exchange ideas frequently, and so on.

Formally, the production function might now look like a straight line instead of being concave downwards as in the Solow model (see Figure 5.4). Now there is no limit to the capital/output ratio (k); and a rise in the investment rate (s) or fall in the growth of the labour force (n) would increase the amount of 'surplus' investment relative to GDP and boost economic growth indefinitely. There is no presumption of convergence in this case.

There is some wisdom to this view, but it should not be pushed too far. Ireland probably has enjoyed external economies of scale in the high technology and pharmaceutical industries that have developed over the past two decades; for instance, many who started as employees in foreign corporations have gone on to found their own businesses, some of them highly successful. But as countries become rich it has always been observed that economic growth slows down; it is hard to imagine that Chinese real GDP per capita will continue to grow at 7.7 per cent – the average between 1975 and 2002, for the next 75 years, by which time its real per capita GDP would exceed a million US dollars (in 1995 prices)! In short, the Solow model, with its assumption of diminishing marginal returns, is still the most useful starting point for a discussion of economic growth, provided it is not applied too rigidly.

4 OUTPUT PER HEAD: EXPLAINING THE GROWTH SPURT OF 1994-2002

We now use the Solow model to help identify the immediate (proximate) causes of the rapid economic growth of the late 1990s. Between 1994 and 2002, GDP *per worker* grew by 5.0 per cent annually, or significantly faster than in any other recent period (see Table 5.1). Why?

Investment

In the Solow model, a higher savings rate (s), by allowing more investment, would cause an acceleration of economic growth in the short run, and allow growth to continue longer *but not indefinitely*. In other words, even if Ireland were to invest a higher proportion of its GDP, it would not permanently grow faster than other countries.

In 2002, Ireland invested 22.1 per cent of GDP, higher than the EU-15 average of 19.4 per cent, but below the rates of 25 per cent or more seen in Spain and Portugal. Table 5.4 shows that the Irish investment rate was particularly high in the 1970s and early 1980s, falling sharply for almost a decade before recovering somewhat after 1994. The growth spurt of 1994-2002 was not accompanied by an unusually high level of investment, and so an explanation of the rapid growth must lie elsewhere.

Table 5.4

Gross Investment and Economic Performance, 1960-2002

	1960-73	1973-79	1979-86	1986-94	1994-02
			(average for period)		
Investment as % of GDP	20.1	25.0	23.0	16.7	20.9
			(annual growth rates, %)		
Real GDP/worker[1]	4.3	3.5	2.9	3.5	5.0

Source: World Bank, *World Development Indicators*, www.worldbank.org 2003.
[1]From Table 5.1.

Labour Force Growth

The Solow model implies that slower growth in the labour force (n), by reducing the number of new workers who need to be equipped with capital, will delay, again not indefinitely, the time when economic growth per worker stops. Formally, when n falls, the line $0-(n+\delta).k$ swivels down, and k^* moves to the right (see Figure 5.4). However, the increase in employment would contribute to faster growth of GDP (as distinct from GDP per worker).

Between 1994 and 2003, the period of most rapid growth, employment in Ireland grew by a remarkable 3.4 per cent annually, significantly faster than the 1.0 per cent annual rise in the population over the same period (see Chapter 4). The rapid rise in employment was due to a large inflow of young people into the labour market, a resumption of immigration, and a substantial rise in the proportion of adults employed (with an associated dramatic fall in the unemployment rate). By 2003, 65 per cent of the working age population – defined as those aged from 15 to 64 – were employed, up from 52 per cent in 1994, and slightly higher than the EU-15 mean of 64 per cent, as Table 5.5 shows. The male employment rate peaked in 2001, while the female employment rate is still rising.

Table 5.5

Employment Rates, 1994-2003

	Ireland		EU-15	Denmark[1]
	1994	2003	2002	2002
% of population 15-64 employed	*52.2*	*65.0*	*64.2*	*76.4*
Male employment rate (%)	64.6	74.5	72.9	80.2
Female employment rate (%)	39.6	55.4	55.5	72.6

Source: CSO, *Measuring Ireland's Progress*, Stationery Office, Dublin 2003.
[1]The Danish figures are shown here because they were the highest in the EU-15.

The rapid growth in employment helped raise Ireland's total GDP (and GNI), but the new workers had to be equipped with capital, which one would expect to restrain the growth of GDP (or GNI) per capita (q). Yet the growth of GDP per worker was over a percentage point faster in 1994-2002 (5.0 per cent p.a.) than in earlier periods (3.5 per cent p.a. in 1986-94, 2.9 per cent p.a. in 1979-86), as Table 5.1 shows; and even the growth of GNI/capita remained steady at 3.4 per cent per year from 1986 onwards.

This is a remarkable case of the dog that did not bark. Employment grew by 1.2 per cent annually between 1986 and 1994, and 3.8 per cent annually in the period 1994-2002. This represents an increase in employment creation of 2.6 per cent per year. Equipping just these additional workers would typically require investment equivalent to 8 per cent of GDP, or over a third of total investment; normally this would have lowered the growth of GDP (or GNI) per capita by a third, yet this did not happen.[7]

In other words, the growth in GDP (or GNI) per worker was maintained in the late 1990s despite an unusually rapid increase in employment. This requires an explanation. One possibility, still within the framework of the Solow model, is that there was an improvement in human capital.

Human Capital
Education, training, experience and good health make workers more productive, and more employable. Thus increases in 'human capital' can boost economic growth. There are likely to be diminishing returns to additional human capital, which means that the effect, at the margin, on economic growth will eventually become negligible. Formally, an increase in human capital (h) will shift the curves 0-q and 0-s.q in Figure 5.4 upwards, pushing the steady state capital-labour ratio (k*) to the right.

Universal secondary education was only introduced in Ireland in 1968, and older workers are not particularly well educated by Western European standards (see Chapter 11). However, the recent expansion of higher education has created a well educated cohort of young people; 35 per cent of those aged 25-34 had some third-level education in 2002, up from 28 per cent in 1999, and well above the EU-15 rate of 26 per cent. In passing it is worth noting that women are substantially more likely than men to get tertiary education in Ireland, as in all other countries of the EU except Germany and the Czech Republic.

The improvement in the quantity of higher education does coincide substantially with the growth spurt of the late 1990s, and undoubtedly played a significant role, although Ireland is by no means the European leader in this area. In 2001 Ireland produced locally 6 PhDs in mathematics, science and technology per million of population, in line with the EU-15 average (also 6), but well below the levels of Sweden (14) and Italy (12).

On average, the Irish educational system provides a solid base. A standardised test administered to 15 year olds in OECD countries in 2000 found that Irish students scored 527 in reading literacy, 503 in mathematics, and 513 in science, compared to an OECD average of 500. Only Finland performed consistently better, although several countries showed better scores in mathematics.

Technological and Institutional Change
Logically, within the framework of the Solow model, the only potentially persistent source of growth is technological change, including institutional

progress. Formally, this raises the A parameter year after year, which shifts upwards the 0-q curve (see Figure 5.4) and hence also the 0-s.q curve. That technological change is the only durable source of economic growth is not surprising; 'modern' economic growth, with its concomitant rise in popular living standards, only began with the industrial revolution in the late eighteenth century.[8]

Technology may be created or acquired. A narrow view of technology would focus on the creation and application of technology through spending on research and development (R&D). The numbers in Table 5.6 show that Irish spending on R&D, as a proportion of GDP, is low by EU standards, and has levelled off after a rise in the early 1990s.

Table 5.6
Research and Development Spending as a Proportion of GDP, 1991-2001

		Ireland		EU maximum: Sweden	EU minimum: Greece
	1991	1996	2001	2001	2001
R&D / GDP (%)	0.93	1.32	1.17	4.27	0.67

Source: As for Table 5.5.

This level of spending is too low to explain much of Ireland's economic growth. But until recently, Ireland was a 'follower' country that, like China, could still acquire technology that had been created elsewhere.

The acquisition of technology is helped if a society and economy is highly open – to trade (making it easy to import goods, including investment goods, that incorporate improved technology), to ideas (so managerial, organisational and institutional changes can be learned and copied), to foreign direct investment (so that international firms can bring best practice technology and skills), to allowing labour market flexibility (so resistance to technological change is low), and to competition (forcing firms to stay on their toes).

By such measures, Ireland has become a truly open society. Exports in 2002 were equivalent to 94 per cent of GDP, well above the EU-15 average (in 2001) of 36 per cent. In 2002, inflows of foreign investment amounted to 20 per cent of GDP; the next highest rate in the EU-15 group, excluding the anomalous case of Luxembourg, was the Netherlands where the inflows were 6 per cent of GDP (see Chapter 7). Home based access to the Internet is less impressive (see Table 5.2), at 36 per cent of all households in 2003, slightly below the EU-15 level of 39 per cent (in 2002), and well below the level of Denmark (56 per cent in 2002).

Ireland's march towards openness is not new. It began in earnest in the 1960s with the Anglo-Irish Free Trade Agreement, and was boosted by EU membership (1973) and the advent of the European single market (1992). The Irish growth spurt of the late 1990s may have required such openness, but Ireland was not unique among European countries – including those that grew far less quickly – in this respect.

The contribution of technological change may be measured as the growth in output per unit of input, or total factor productivity (TFP); for instance, if inputs (labour, capital, land) each rise by 2 per cent and output rises by 5 per cent, then total factor productivity – which we conventionally attribute to 'technology' – rises by about 3 per cent.

Some recent figures on the growth of Irish total factor productivity are displayed in Table 5.7. The pattern they show is quite remarkable, although exaggerated because they are based on GDP figures that are subject to measurement error. That said, the figures show that between 1975 and 2001, Irish TFP rose by a total of 98 per cent, far outstripping the EU-15 mean of 39 per cent, and well above the total TFP growth of 32 per cent seen in the USA and Japan over the same period. There is nothing pre-ordained about TFP growth: since 1975 it also rose rapidly in Finland and Portugal, but hardly changed in Greece.

Table 5.7

Total Factor Productivity Growth, 1975-2001

	1975-85	1985-90	1990-95	1995-01	1975-01
	(annual growth rates, %)				(total % rise)
Ireland	*1.8*	*2.9*	*2.6*	*4.0*	*98*
EU-15	1.4	1.5	1.1	1.0	39
USA	1.0	0.9	0.9	1.5	32
Japan	1.4	2.8	-0.3	0.2	32
Finland	1.5	2.0	1.8	3.3	70
Portugal	1.9	3.6	1.3	1.8	71
Greece	-0.2	-0.1	0.1	1.9	10

Source: Spring Singapore, www.spring.gov.sg, July 2004.

From Output per Worker (q) to Output per Capita

To recapitulate, we have argued that Ireland's high level of output per worker, and its surprising but real continued rapid growth in the late 1990s, is due to a combination of moderately high investment rates, solid educational advance, and especially the absorption of technological and institutional change as the country continued to look outwards.

But the relevant variable in the Solow model – GDP per worker (or perhaps GDP per hour worked) – is not the same as GDP per capita. The following identity breaks down GDP per capita into its component parts, and also shows the *total* (log) percentage growth rate of each component between 1994 and 2002 and the contribution of each component to the growth spurt.

$$\frac{GDP}{population} = \frac{GDP}{GNI} \cdot \frac{GNI}{hour} \cdot \frac{hour}{worker} \cdot \frac{worker}{labour\ force} \cdot \frac{labour\ force}{adults} \cdot \frac{adults}{population}$$

$\frac{GDP}{population}$	$\frac{GDP}{GNI}$	$\frac{GNI}{hour}$	$\frac{hour}{worker}$	$\frac{worker}{labour\ force}$	$\frac{labour\ force}{adults}$	$\frac{adults}{population}$
59.4	12.4	32.8	-6.1	11.7	4.1	4.5
100%	21%	55%	-10%	20%	7%	8%

A case can be made that as much as a fifth of the rise in GDP per capita during this period – the part represented by the rise in GDP relative to GNI – is measurement error, largely due to transfer pricing. To the extent that this is so, then GNI may come closer to measuring 'true' output than GDP. Even admitting this, the remaining economic growth was real, and 55 per cent of the increase in GDP per capita is attributable to the increase in output (here measured by GNI) per hour worked, which is the part of economic growth that the Solow model is designed to explain.

This decomposition shows that the growth in Irish GDP per capita was significantly helped by an increase in the proportion of adults in the population (whose output was therefore not diluted as much by the presence of children); a rising share of adults in the labour force; and a large increase in the proportion of the labour force that was actually working (which is the mirror image of the unemployment rate). These unusually favourable factors are sometimes referred to as the 'demographic dividend', although in earlier years the need to create jobs was seen as a demographic drag! Together they accounted for a third of the rise in GDP per capita during Ireland's growth spurt: and around 4.5 per cent of the growth in GNI per capita. The important point is that these factors are not expected to contribute substantially to growth in the years ahead; other things being equal, this alone will cut Ireland's growth rate by a third to two fifths compared to the recent past.

5 GROWTH SPURT OF 1994-2002: HISTORICAL CONSIDERATIONS

Introduction

To recap, we have argued that the rapid growth in measured GDP during 1994-2002 was due to three factors: first, employment rose at an historically unprecedented rate of 3.8 per cent annually; second, output per worker continued to grow rapidly, which is remarkable given the very rapid increase in employment; and third, GDP growth may be overstated by as much as a fifth due to measurement error. In addition, the growth in GDP *per capita* was boosted by an increase in the proportion of adults in the population.

The application of the Solow growth model in Section 4 helped identify the sources of the growth in output per worker, but is most notable for not producing a 'smoking gun'. Ireland's growth spurt was exceptional, but the Solow framework does not indicate exceptional causes: investment rates were solid, not remarkable; educational levels improved, but this occurred elsewhere too; the economy opened up, but so did Greece and Belgium, yet neither experienced comparable economic growth.

In our search for some additional ingredients – particularly to explain the extraordinary growth in employment – it is helpful to provide a more thorough historical context, to see what brought Ireland to the threshold of rapid growth.[9] We will then be in a better position to examine the fundamental causes of the growth spurt of the late 1990s.

A century ago, Irish incomes were on a par with those of most of the countries of Western Europe, with the exception of Britain, which was twice as affluent. In 1951, GDP per capita was still 75 per cent of the EU-15 average, but this proportion fell to 60 per cent by 1958, as Ireland missed the train during the first part of Western Europe's economic 'golden age'. In the 1950s, half a million people emigrated; by 1961, when the population reached its nadir, more Irish born people lived outside the country than at home.

In an influential report entitled *Economic Development*, published in 1958, then secretary of the Department of Finance T.K. Whitaker wrote, 'the mood of despondency was palpable'. He argued, among other things, for a reorientation of government investment towards more 'productive' uses and away from a primary emphasis on 'social' investment (such as housing); this was an early recognition of the importance of the quality, as opposed to just the quantity, of investment. Perhaps most importantly, he proposed that tariffs be dismantled unless a clear infant industry case existed – an adaptation that would require a major change from a highly protected economy to one that was oriented outwards. The report favoured incentives to stimulate private industrial investment, and warned against the dampening effects of high taxes (see Chapter 7).

1960-1973: From Protection to Free Trade

Between 1960 and 1973 real output increased at 4.4 per cent per annum, the highest rate sustained until then. Immigration began. Per capita incomes rose by three fifths, kept up with income growth elsewhere in Europe, and significantly outpaced growth in Britain or Northern Ireland.

This first wave of substantial economic growth has been largely attributed to the strategy of export led growth that the government, heeding the recommendations of *Economic Development*, pursued; less publicised, but important nonetheless, were a notable improvement in the terms of trade (39 per cent better in 1973 than in 1957), expansionary fiscal policy, the boom in the nearby European economy, and the fact that solid institutional foundations had been laid in the 1950s.

The policy of export led growth stood on two legs – trade liberalisation, and the attraction of foreign direct investment (see Chapter 7). Trade liberalisation called for reducing tariffs; these, by making inputs dearer and by drawing resources away from other sectors of the economy had worked to inhibit exports. Foreign investment, it was hoped, would bring new skills to the country, and help raise the overall investment, and hence the growth rate.

Trade liberalisation was begun in the 1960s as Ireland unilaterally cut tariffs in 1963 and 1964, negotiated the Anglo Irish Free Trade Area Agreement in 1965 and subscribed to the General Agreement on Tariffs and Trade (GATT) in 1967. These moves also prepared for eventual membership of the European Economic Community (EEC as it was called then).

With a panoply of tax breaks and subsidies, Ireland successfully, although at considerable expense, induced foreign companies to set up branches in Ireland,

and by 1974 new industry accounted for over 60 per cent of industrial output. The 10 per cent tax on profits in manufacturing also made the country something of a tax haven, although it did require at least a fig leaf of manufacturing presence.

The final thrust of government policy was wage restraint, viewed as necessary, especially with a fixed exchange rate, to help keep industrial costs at a competitive level. In the 1960s government efforts amounted to exhortation. In the 1970s wage bargaining was centralised, under the National Wage Agreements. Given the option of emigration, the scope for manoeuvre here was small. If real wages were pushed below the British level they would simply stimulate faster emigration, and so could not be sustained.

Into Europe: Trade, Investment, and Subsidies

In 1973 Ireland, along with the UK and Denmark, joined the European Economic Community (EEC, but refered to here as EU).

Membership immediately led to a reduction in trade barriers. The EU was founded as a customs union, with low internal barriers to trade and a common set of external barriers. By joining, Ireland was committed to trading freely with the other member countries, and by 1977 all tariff barriers had been removed. Many of the remaining, less obvious, restraints on trade within the European Union were dismantled as part of the effort to create a Single European Market. Officially these changes came into effect in 1992, although the full elimination of barriers remains a work in progress.

With lower trade barriers, it was recognised that some of Ireland's industry would wither under the competition, but it was also expected that Ireland would become a good platform from which companies from outside the European Community could serve the European market.

These expectations were met. While Irish exports amounted to 34 per cent of GDP in 1963, and 38 per cent in 1973, the proportion had risen to 94 per cent by 2002, one of the highest in the world (see Chapter 7). This burst of exports paralleled a similar increase in intra-EU trade that took place in the 1960s, and shows how even small reductions in the cost of trading can have a large impact on the volume of trade.

Membership of the EU also led to a net inflow under the Common Agricultural Policy (CAP), which subsidises farm prices. Higher farm prices help farmers at the expense of consumers, but as a net exporter of farm produce, Ireland was a net beneficiary (see Chapter 9).

Although about two thirds of EU transfers to Ireland are farm related, the remaining third consists mainly of transfers from the 'structural funds,' including the Regional Development, Social, and Cohesion funds. In principle these funds might have added to investment and thereby boosted economic growth, but in practice they mainly appeared to have substituted for projects that the government would otherwise have had to finance; they thus made a more important contribution to living standards than to growth. Net receipts from the EU peaked at 6.5 per cent of GDP in 1991, and stood at 1.1 per cent of GDP in 2003.

1979-1986: Growth Interrupted

Between 1979 and 1986, per capita consumption in Ireland actually fell slightly (see Table 5.1), and GDP rose very slowly. What went wrong?

Membership of the EU coincided with a fourfold increase in the price of oil (from $3 to $12 per barrel) that resulted from the first oil shock in late 1973; a sharp worldwide recession followed.

The government's response was thoroughly Keynesian. The higher price of oil meant that spending was diverted towards imports, thereby depressing aggregate demand for Irish goods and services. The solution adopted was to boost government current spending, and as a consequence the current budget deficit rose from 0.4 per cent of GDP in 1973 to 6.8 per cent by 1975. For a while the policy worked: despite a difficult international situation, GDP growth during the first six years of EU membership was robust.

Then came the mistake, the source of the failure of the fiscal experiment: successive governments were unwilling to reduce the budget deficit, and continued to borrow heavily, so the ratio of government debt to GDP rose from 52 per cent in 1973 to 129 per cent by 1987, by then easily the highest in the European Union. By 1986 the cost of servicing this debt took up 94 per cent of all revenue from personal income tax (see Chapter 2). Although efforts were made to solve the problem by raising tax rates, especially in 1981 and 1983, these changes hardly increased tax revenue, suggesting that the country was close to its revenue maximising tax rates. Much of the additional spending went to buy imports, and the current account deficit widened to an untenable 15 per cent by 1981. Partly as a result, the Irish pound was devalued four times within the European Monetary System in the early 1980s. In 1986 an estimated IR£1,000 million of private capital left the country, anticipating a devaluation; the smart money was right, and the pound was devalued by 8 per cent in August.

In 1987 the Fianna Fáil government introduced a very tight budget, cutting the current budget deficit to 1.7 per cent of GDP through reductions in real government spending that made Margaret Thatcher's efforts look anaemic. Capital spending was also sharply cut, and by 1992 the ratio of debt to GDP had fallen below 100 per cent.

The 1987 reform worked. Economic growth resumed, as confidence (and investors) returned, and exports boomed, thanks in part to the devaluation of 1986 and to continued wage restraint. But the lessons of the failed fiscal experiment are important and have been internalised: fiscal rectitude is important for long-term growth, and taxes cannot be pushed too high.

1979-1999: From Sterling to EMS to Euro

In 1979, in a move which was hailed at the time as foresighted, Ireland broke the link with sterling (which dated back to 1826) and joined the European Monetary System (EMS). The reasoning was straightforward. Ireland had experienced inflation averaging 15 per cent between 1973 and 1979, necessarily the same rate as in Britain, and it was believed that the key to reducing the inflation rate was to uncouple the Irish pound from high inflation sterling and attach it to the low inflation EMS, which was dominated by the deutschmark. Some also argued – correctly as it turned out – that sterling would appreciate with the development of North Sea oil, and that this would hurt Irish exports. Although over 40 per cent of exports still went to the UK in 1979, about a quarter went to the other EU countries and so a change in exchange regime was considered feasible.

The adjustment to the EMS was slow and rocky. In the early 1980s inflation actually fell faster in the UK, which stayed out of the EMS, than in Ireland. The slow reduction in Irish inflation towards German levels meant that the Irish pound became overvalued, and had to be devalued within the EMS. The standard explanation is that wage demands – which often respond to recent inflation – were slow to change, so wage increases continued to be too large to be consistent with very low inflation. The lesson here was clear: economic growth and macroeconomic stability can all too easily be undermined if wage increases get out of line.

By about 1990 Ireland could boast of low inflation, a tight budget, and a falling ratio of government debt to GDP, and it looked as if, after a decade of relative economic stagnation, the decision to join the EMS was finally paying off. Then in late 1992 the EMS fell apart. High interest rates in Germany, resulting from that country's need to finance reunification, caused the deutschmark to appreciate. Sterling devalued, and the Irish pound ultimately followed, because 32 per cent of Irish exports still went to the UK, and in the absence of a devaluation, Irish competitiveness in the important British market would be too severely compromised.

After the collapse of the EMS, it became clear that a regime of 'fixed but flexible' exchange rates is an oxymoron. Without a viable middle way between floating exchange rates and a single currency, the European Union opted for the latter. The schedule was set out in the Treaty of Maastricht, signed in 1992 and ratified the following year. Ireland easily met the criteria for graduating to the euro, and the exchange rate was locked at €0.787564 per Irish pound on January 1, 1999. Ireland, like the states of the USA, no longer has the option of an independent monetary policy. This is not a radical break from the past; an independent monetary policy was not possible when the Irish pound was linked with sterling, and was severely circumscribed during the period of the European Monetary System.

6 GROWTH IN OUTPUT: A SYNTHESIS

Let us now return to the central puzzle of this chapter: what accounts for Ireland's growth spurt of the late 1990s – a puzzle that is all the greater because, as we have just seen, Ireland in the 1990s had almost no scope for changing fiscal, monetary or exchange rate policy.

As noted above, we can dismiss a number of non-explanations. The growth spurt was not associated with a significant rise in the investment rate; the economy did not suddenly become more open; EU subventions, if anything, fell; macroeconomic stability was re-established after 1987, but in this respect Ireland differs little from most of the rest of western Europe.

There are however four areas where Ireland, wittingly or not, has espoused pro-growth strategies, or has been just lucky – in the role of the state, attitudinal changes, social protections, and the US factor.

Role of the State

Like the USA, UK and Japan, but unlike most of the EU-15 countries, the government sector in Ireland is relatively small (see Chapter 2). The most obvious measure of this is the share of tax revenue relative to GDP, which stands at 31 per cent in Ireland compared with 42 per cent for the EU-15 group and 30 per cent for the USA. Or one could look at government expenditure relative to GDP, 34 per cent in Ireland and 47 per cent in the EU-15 countries as a whole.[10] The low tax burden helps limit distortions to the choices that households make about work, consumption and investment. More specifically, Ireland's regime of low tax rates on corporate income makes the country attractive to foreign investors: the effective marginal tax rate on the profits generated by foreign investments in Ireland is estimated at 13 per cent, well below the OECD mean of 21 per cent.[11] Ireland also has the lowest restrictions on inflows of foreign direct investment of any OECD country.[12]

The relatively light weight of the state sector is possible in part because of low military costs (0.7 per cent of GDP, compared to 1.8 per cent in the EU-15 countries and 3.4 per cent in the USA, in 2002), and health and educational systems that are inexpensive relative to their outputs. But one might point to 1987 as the turning point: in national discussions, the government promised to lower taxes if wages were restrained and labour peace restored. Thus began a dynamic that has been maintained since, and differs sharply from the European norm where governments typically promised more welfare payments, rather than lower taxes, in return for wage restraint. The comparatively modest size of the public sector has also kept in check the proportion of the public with a vested interest in raising taxes.

Some argue that much of the credit for the rise in employment in the 1990s should go to national wage agreements that kept labour costs low and bought labour peace; they point to a reduction in strikes since 1987 as evidence of the success of these efforts. However, this argument is not entirely compelling: labour unrest abated in most of Western Europe at the same time, without a corresponding rise in employment; and in practice, actual wage increases bore little relation to the rates negotiated in national agreements – hardly surprising given that Ireland's labour market is integrated with that of the UK.

One may also measure the weight of government by the extent of rules and regulations. Like the UK and USA, but in contrast with most of continental Europe, Irish rules protecting employment and product markets are relatively light, again a feature that endears the country to investors (see Chapter 4).[13] The 1990s also saw a new government commitment to fostering competition (see Chapter 3 and 8), with changes that were particularly successful in the airline industry but have yet to affect some expensive and cosseted groups, such as lawyers.

Attitudes

Although it is hard to quantify, there appears to have been a change in attitudes over the past three decades, a change that favours economic growth. In the 1970s, college students tended to aspire to jobs in the Foreign Service, or as employees in well established firms. Now they are more likely to want to be entrepreneurs. There is no better metaphor for the transformation than the relative decline of staid, state-owned Aer Lingus and the rise of tough, profitable, private and entrepreneurial Ryanair. By the 1990s Ireland's fertility rate, once the highest in Western Europe, had fallen to the same level as a number of other EU countries, again a symptom of changing attitudes, including an increasing disregard for some of the teachings of the Catholic Church.

It is difficult to account for the change in attitudes, but a case can be made that in the 1980s Ireland's best and brightest found it difficult to emigrate; forced to stay at home, but unable to find wage paying work, they began to improvise, learned to like the change, and began to succeed. With greater opportunities for success, attitudinal change was strengthened. At the same time Ireland became better informed about, and more closely attuned to, attitudes prevalent in continental Europe.

Social Protection

The comparatively small government sector has a price too – less social protection, including relatively modest spending on health, education and pensions, and fewer national cultural institutions. Government pensions and transfers (such as unemployment assistance) do reduce income disparities in Ireland, but less markedly than in almost any other EU-15 country.

On the other hand, this relatively hard nosed attitude towards social protection has probably helped economic growth. A decade ago, the structure of taxes and subsidies was such that, for low skilled workers, it did not pay to go to work. This structure has now been rationalised, unblocking a serious barrier to employment; equivalent changes have been much slower to arrive in countries such as France and Germany, although such changes are now underway.

US Factor

If the USA did not exist, Ireland would not have experienced a growth spurt. In recent years, four-fifths of foreign direct investment has originated in the USA, and US firms now account for a quarter of manufacturing employment and about a half of manufacturing output and exports (see Chapter 7). The high tech wave that lifted the US economy in the 1990s washed over Ireland too, but not over most of the rest of Europe. The point is not that US investors raised the Irish investment rate, but rather that the investments that they made, and the associated learning and external economies of scale, had a large and immediate effect on output, and employment.

It may now be more realistic to think of the Irish economy not as a region of Europe, but as an outpost of the USA attached to the edge of the EU.

We still need to ask why US investors steered so much of their investment to Ireland rather than, say, Scotland or Greece or Portugal or India. In part the answer is because Ireland made them welcome, with low taxes and other benefits. But Ireland has historically had close links with the USA; there are strong cultural similarities between the two countries; and they share a common language.

By 2001, foreign investors owned assets in Ireland equivalent to $36,016 per capita, six times the level in the EU-15 countries ($6,099). Irish companies have begun to return the favour, and in the same year they held assets internationally to the tune of $8,791 per capita, above the EU-15 mean of $8,002 and higher even than the US level of $8,061.

The Combination
In a nutshell, the Irish growth spurt occurred because all the economic planets came into alignment at the same time. The key elements: a booming US economy providing firms there with the profits to invest abroad; a 10 per cent tax on manufacturing profits to attract them to Ireland, coupled with relatively light regulation of labour and product markets; the lure of a pool of well educated and English speaking workers; the creation of a Single European Market that could be served efficiently from Ireland; a credible and conservative macroeconomic stance; wage restraint due to the inertia built into early rounds of National Agreements; and a new found attitude favourable to entrepreneurial activity (see also Chapter 4 where a similar conclusion is reached).

Once the boom began, it led to a virtuous circle, raising the demand for housing and other construction, as well as for a wide array of services such as restaurants, banks and accountants.

In a recent book on spatial economics, Fujita, Krugman and Venables present a model of 'punctuated equilibria' that matches the Irish case rather well.[14] Consider a region that exports some good. Part of the export earnings are spent and respent locally; the computer exporter pays local workers, who buy restaurant meals from chefs, who spend their money buying haircuts, and so on. Now suppose that as the region grows, the proportion of export spending that goes into local purchases rises, which is plausible. Then it can be shown that as exports rise, local income will rise too, at first fairly slowly, then increasingly quickly, and then it will suddenly jump from one equilibrium path to another, before resuming a slower and steadier rise. Ireland has just jumped.

7 WILL GROWTH CONTINUE?

It is natural to ask whether rapid economic growth will resume in Ireland, or whether the growth spurt has completely passed. Sweden, once one of the most affluent countries in Europe, has in recent years slipped in the rankings. So has

Japan, still struggling for an encore after its spectacular growth prior to 1989. Can Ireland expect the same?

'Forecasting is difficult' wrote Nobelist Neils Bohr, 'especially about the future.' Even so, some things are clear.

On the positive side, an interesting feature of the Fujita, Krugman and Venables model is that if exports fall, the economy will not decline as quickly as it grew. Having reached a higher plateau, the economy will be able to remain there relatively easily. This helps explain why the OECD expects Irish economic growth to exceed the OECD average over the next few years.[15] Moreover, corporate income tax rates remain low, entrepreneurialism is alive and well, and anticipated improvements in infrastructure and the regulatory environment are likely to help sustain growth.

Nonetheless, the growth spurt is over, for several reasons:

First, the decomposition of Section 4 indicates that Ireland's growth in GDP *per capita* will fall. This is because it will be difficult substantially to increase the proportion of the population at work, thanks to a low unemployment rate, a rising proportion of old people, and a taste for shorter working hours.

Second, the Solow framework predicts that the growth in GDP (or GNI) *per worker*, will eventually fall, although continued external economies and ongoing improvements in human capital and technology suggest that this need not happen for some time yet. A high proportion of the investment during the growth spurt was directly productive and had a rapid payoff; this will be harder to maintain as Ireland seeks to catch up on infrastructural investments that have a slow payback.

Third, some of the economic planets discussed in Section 5 are going out of alignment: the US economic recovery is anaemic; wage restraint is not in evidence; the government sector has been expanding; and a number of eastern European countries, particularly new EU members, are quite explicitly trying to emulate the 'Irish model', and now provide cheap entry points to the EU market, much as Ireland did a decade ago.

And fourth, Ireland has become a victim of its own success. It is now a high cost destination for investors. This is to be expected; with a tighter labour market, wages have risen; and with rising incomes, the demand for housing and land has increased, pushing up their prices. Here we have a textbook case of a boom running its course.

Even staying near the top of the GDP per capita ranking will be challenging. Irish education is good, not extraordinary; the investment rate is solid, not spectacular; government regulatory policies are fairly light, but the public sector is not universally honest, transparent or efficient (as the OECD points out in a recent report).[16] The World Economic Forum ranks Ireland twenty-second worldwide in 'business competitiveness' and thirtieth in 'growth competitiveness', and the World Competitiveness Yearbook ranks it tenth; whatever one may think of rankings of this nature, these do not point to overwhelming international confidence in the growth prospects of the Irish economy.[17]

Moreover, if investment and jobs can flow rapidly into Ireland, they can leave quickly too. In 2003, there were 227,000 jobs in industry; yet since 1970 an estimated 274,000 industrial jobs have been lost![18] Given the rapidity of turnover of industrial jobs, the sector could shrink rapidly.

The biggest danger to growth is complacency. The government sector could expand too quickly – it increased its employment by 19 per cent between 2000 and 2003. Individuals could lose their work ethic; in Norway, the average worker is absent from work for an average of 4.8 weeks per year (not counting regular holidays).[19]

But one person's complacency is another's relaxation. If economic growth increases congestion, stress, and the pace of life, is it worth it? Why not sit back, like the Romans in the waning days of their empire, and enjoy the new affluence?

Endnotes

1   World Bank, *World Development Indicators*, www.worldbank.org 2003. The OECD figures are somewhat different, with the GDP per capita in 2002 PPP US dollars as follows: Luxembourg: 48,400; USA: 36,200; Norway: 35,500; Ireland: 32,600.

2   Denmark, Luxembourg, Norway, Switzerland, and USA. *Source:* World Bank, *World Development Indicators*, op. cit.

3   The EU-15 countries are the member countries of the European Union prior to the EU expansion of 1 May 2004, that added ten new members.

4   In measuring living standards, it might make more sense to use gross national income (GNI) rather than gross domestic product (GDP). However, for most countries, GNI and GDP are very similar; and GDP data are published more quickly than GNI figures (which require measures of international flows of factor payments and transfers).

5   J. Alber and T. Fahey, *Perceptions of Living Conditions in an Enlarged Europe*, European Foundation for the Improvement of Living and Working Conditions, and European Commission, Luxembourg 2004, p. 51.

6   The members of the Organisation for Economic Cooperation and Development (OECD) are mainly the world's rich countries.

7   This assumes a capital output ratio of three.

8   The term 'modern economic growth' was coined by Nobel Laureate Simon Kuznets, whose magnum opus traced the growth of the UK and USA over the past two centuries.

9   For a fuller treatment of the historical context, see J. Haughton, 'The Historical Background', in J.. O'Hagan (editor), *The Economy of Ireland: Policy and Performance of a European Region*, Gill and Macmillan, Dublin 2000.

10   The Irish government sector still looks relatively small if revenue is expressed as a proportion of GNI (38 per cent); the comparable figure for expenditure is 42 per cent (see Chapter 3).

11   K. Yoo, 'Corporate Taxation of Foreign Direct Investment Income 1991-2001' (OECD working paper UnECO/WKP(2003)19), Paris 2003.

12   S. Golub, 'Measures of Restrictions on Inward Foreign Direct Investment for OECD Countries' (OECD working paper ECO/WKP(2003)11), Paris 2003.

13   Nicoletti et al., 1999, as reported in O. Blanchard, 'European Growth over the Coming Decade' (unpublished), September 2003.

14   M. Fujita, P. Krugman and A. Venables, *The Spatial Economy*, MIT Press, Cambridge MA 1999.

15   OECD, *Economic Outlook*, OECD, Paris 2004, Preliminary Edition.

16   OECD, *Economic Surveys: Ireland*, OECD, Paris 2003.

17   World Economic Forum, *The Global Competitiveness Report 2003-2004*, www.weforum.org 2004, and IMD, *World Competitiveness Yearbook*, Lausanne, Switzerland 2004.

18 Based on information from the Department of Enterprise, Trade and Employment, as reported in Ireland, Department of Finance, *Budgetary and Economic Statistics*, Dublin 2004. The lost jobs refer to notified redundancies.

19 L. Alvarez, 'In Norway, a Nation Calls in Sick: Oil Money Affecting Work Ethic', *New York Times*, 25 July 2004.

CHAPTER 6

Equality in Economic and Other Dimensions

*Sara Cantillon**

1 INTRODUCTION

The persistence of poverty in rich countries, the increase in inequality in income and wealth within many industrialised countries and the widening gap between developed and developing countries has sparked renewed interest by academics and policymakers in the issues of distribution and equality. There is also a growing recognition of the economic costs of inequality in terms of ill health, crime, educational underachievement and social exclusion. In addition, the relationship between good economic performance and high incomes on the one hand and quality of life and individual and societal well being, on the other, is an issue of increasing concern in public policy.[1] It is against this background that this chapter addresses the issues of equality and distribution in Ireland focusing in particular on income, wealth and poverty.

Section 2 gives a brief overview of the scale and the patterns of existing inequalities in Irish society and globally. It is a relatively easy job to demonstrate inequality, it is much more difficult to specify what we mean by equality, both itself and in the distribution of economic resources, and much harder again to put any agreed consensus on an equality objective into practice.

Notwithstanding these difficulties, Section 3 provides a framework for thinking about equality in economic and other dimensions. It outlines three equality perspectives, basic, liberal and radical; identifies four generative dimensions of equality including political, cultural/social, affective and economic, and indicates the key equality issues that arise within each dimension. Clearly, a central area is inequality in economic resources, both in its own right, and in terms of its implications for the other dimensions of equality discussed and it is the focus for much of this chapter. This section also describes the type of equality outcome desired in the economic dimension under liberal and radical views of equality.

Sections 4 and 5 address key inequalities in economic resources by looking at the distribution of income, wealth and poverty. They provide an overview of the conceptual and measurement issues raised in relation to income, wealth and poverty; examine recent trends, some of the factors underlying those and some international comparisons. Section 6 examines the extent to which some of the equality objectives outlined in Section 3 are incorporated into government economic policy focusing in particular on efforts in relation to poverty but also addressing other distribution issues such as social deprivation indicators and the changes in 'quality of life' in Ireland. Section 7 concludes the chapter.

2 THE EXTENT OF INEQUALITY

The annual reports from the UN and the World Bank illustrate the stark contrast in the life prospects of the rich and the poor.[2] Figures for the Human Development Report, for 2004, show that life expectancy ranges from 34 years in Sierra Leone to 89 years in Sweden. Of every 1,000 children born in sub Saharan Africa, 174 die before their fifth birthday, compared to 14 in the OECD countries. It is estimated that there are about 1.2 billion people who have no access to safe drinking water. These statistics are stark reminders of global inequality, but even within countries the better off have longer and healthier lives than the worse off. 'Unskilled' workers in the UK are three times as likely to die from heart disease and four times as likely to die from lung cancer as professionals. African Americans are eight times as likely as whites to die from homicide. These differences in how people's lives turn out reflect a range of inequalities in their circumstances – in the conditions of their lives. One of the most researched inequalities of condition is those to do with income and other economic resources. Global income inequality is reflected in the widening gap in average incomes between the richest and the poorest countries. In 1960 per capita GDP in the richest countries was 18 times that in the poorest. By 1998 this gap had widened to 37 times. This sharp increase in income inequality between countries has been reflected within the majority of industrialised countries from the mid 1980s. The increase in income inequality was most conspicuous in the UK and the USA from the mid 1980s to the mid 1990s.

Income inequality has several recognisable patterns. The most obvious is that income reflects social class. The wealthiest belong to a class whose income is derived almost entirely from investment. Within paid employment there is a marked difference between the incomes of executives and workers. In the USA post tax average income for chief executives was 12 times that of average workers in 1960. By 1980 the average CEO was making 84 times as much as the average worker and by 1999 it had increased by a factor of 400. There is also a difference between the income of men and women. Even in the more egalitarian countries, like Denmark and Sweden, women's share of incomes is estimated at 72 and 83 per cent, respectively, of men's. Another common pattern of income inequality is its connection to 'race' and ethnicity. In the USA, African American families receive, on average, less than two-thirds the income of non-Hispanic white families. Income inequality also reflects disability. The incomes of severely disabled people in Britain are only about half of average incomes. Further, within the paid workforce, women, disabled people, ethnic minorities and other marginalised groups are disproportionately represented among casualised workers. While the proportion of women in professional jobs has increased, women are still disproportionately represented among part time and low paid workers. This trend is particularly evident in Ireland, where 23 per cent of all women employees work part time compared with 5 per cent of men.

As this short overview indicates, inequality has some clear patterns: social class is a major factor in determining the shape of inequalities with higher socioeconomic groups having more resources, higher status, better working conditions and greater access to education. Gender is another pervasive feature of inequality. Women are, on the whole, worse off in terms of resources, status, power, work and education than men although of course within any particular social group there will be men who are worse off. 'Race' and ethnicity are strongly implicated in how inequalities are patterned in most societies. One example, is the situation of Irish Travellers, an ethnic minority of about 30,000 people – approximately 1 per cent of the Irish population. The needs of Travellers have been marginalised in Irish economic and social policy, resulting in exceptionally high levels of poverty, severe popular prejudice, high levels of unemployment and low levels of formal education.[3] Although anti-Traveller racism is distinct from the forms of racism most familiar in the UK, USA and other developed countries because of the absence of a 'colour line', it shares many of the same features and results in similar deprivations. At any rate, traditional racism 'along colour lines' is now becoming a feature of contemporary Irish society.[4] These social divisions do not exhaust the range of factors on which inequalities have been and continue to be erected. Age plays an important role in structuring inequality in every society. Differences between indigenous and settler populations are important in nearly all ex-colonial societies. Some of the factors that typically mark ethnic difference, such as language, nationality and religion, can be independently important. Other specific groups that suffer from inequality include prisoners and ex-prisoners, people with mental illnesses, refugees and asylum seekers and economic migrants. Some of the issues affecting these, and other social groups, are referred to in what follows.

3 EQUALITY PERSPECTIVES

Idea of Equality

Over the past century, there have been many attempts to define equality and highlighted here are some aspects that have concerned theorists across different disciplines. Very generally, equality can be described as a relationship between two or more people regarding some aspect of their lives.[5] What this relationship is, who it is about and what aspect of their lives it concerns is far from straightforward, which helps explain the many different conceptions of equality.

A key question, raised by Amaryta Sen, is: equality of what? What is it that should be distributed equally? For example, is the concern overall well being or 'welfare'? Or are the aims more tangible, like equality of income and wealth? Should the focus be on outcomes such as educational attainment, or on the opportunities people have for achieving these? Needless to say economists and political theorists interested in egalitarianism give different answers to this distribution question – Rawls talks about primary social goods, Sen talks about the distribution of capabilities to achieve valued functionings while Atkinson focuses on the right to a minimum level of resources.[6] Whichever particular one is focused on, they all overlap in their aim and particularly in their overall effect.

Another key issue, raised by Iris Marion Young, is whether to apply the idea of equality to individuals or to groups. In other words, equality between whom? When the Universal Declaration of Human Rights, Article 1, states that 'All human beings are born free and equal in dignity and rights', it is referring to each and every individual person. But equality also matters in terms of groups, such as women or ethnic minorities. An important factor determining individuals' lives is the way social structures work to privilege the members of some groups over others. For example, there are inequalities structured around religion, race, gender, etc. In addition, there are many different and overlapping groups, even in relatively homogeneous societies. Equality between men and women, for example, does not necessarily involve equality between social classes, or equality between disabled and non-disabled people.

Equality then, can be defined in terms of both individuals and a wide variety of groups, it can relate to many different dimensions of people's lives and it can refer to many different types of relationship, with all of these differences having some kind of basis in the idea of treating people as equals. It follows that far from being a single idea, equality refers to countless ideas, which may have very different implications and in particular may conflict. The conflict between equality and other societal objectives, and in particular the relationships between equality and economic growth and equality and efficiency, is an area that has generated a vast literature within economics.

Perspectives on Equality[7]
Basic equality is the idea that all human beings have equal worth and deserve some basic level of concern and respect. It is a fairly minimalist conception of equality and poses little challenge to the widespread inequalities in people' s living standards, life chances and opportunities. Nonetheless in the context of some of the inequalities described earlier and especially in relation to inequalities between North and South where access to water, sanitation, basic health care and other basic necessities is severely lacking, basic equality is a fundamental first step in any move towards greater equality.

Liberal equality can be interpreted in many different ways, all of them embracing basic equality but varying quite a lot in terms of the other levels of equality they believe in. For some liberals, the minimum to which all should be entitled barely differs from basic equality. Others have a more generous idea of the minimum, for example by using an expanded idea of what counts as a basic need or by defining poverty in relation to the normal activities of a particular society. Perhaps, the most ambitious liberal principle is Rawls' 'difference principle', which states that 'social and economic inequalities' should work 'to the greatest benefit of the least advantaged' member of society. Liberal equality of opportunity means that people should in some sense have an equal chance to compete for social advantages. This principle has two major interpretations. The first, non-discrimination or 'formal' equal opportunity, is classically expressed in the French Declaration of the Rights of Man (1789) as the principle that all citizens 'are equally eligible for all positions, posts and public employments in accordance with their abilities' (Article 6). One form of equal opportunity insists that people should not be advantaged or hampered by their social background and that their prospects in life should depend entirely on their own effort and abilities. Rawls calls this principle 'fair equal opportunity'. A very different perspective on what could be considered 'fair' is offered by Robert Nozick who argues that if the current state of distribution of ownership of assets and of income was derived by fair means (i.e. generated through the voluntary provision of labour in exchange for compensation or through inheritance rather than theft) then by definition the outcome is just. Further, he argues that no attempt should be made to redistribute this outcome, as that would be unjust.

The *radical equality* perspective is much more ambitious. Its objective, equality of condition, aims to eliminate major inequalities altogether, or at least substantively to reduce the current scale of inequality. The key difference is the view that inequality is created, and continually reproduced in social structures, and particularly in structures of domination and oppression and that these are far from inevitable. This is what differentiates it from the liberal view which is based on the assumption that many major inequalities are inevitable in a market based economy and that the task is to dampen their impact.

Dimensions of Equality
Table 6.1 identifies some of the key factors that affect well being or quality of life. These are identified as four core contexts in which the generative causes of inequality may emerge, namely: the economic, the political, the cultural and the affective, all of which impact on each other. These dimensions do not necessarily pick out every aspect of equality and inequality that may be of economic, sociological or political interest, but the categories are sufficiently broad to cover most of the contemporary equality issues. The equality framework set out in Table 6.1 is open enough to allow for different interpretations and perspectives and is designed to be relatively á la carte: to allow for someone to have a liberal view in one respect, while believing in the more radical perspective in another.

Table 6.1

An Equality Framework

Dimensions of equality		Perspectives on equality	
	Basic	Liberal	Radical
		Key Issues	
Economic		Distribution of resources	
Social/cultural		Recognition and respect	
Political		Representation/power relations	
Affective		Love, care and solidarity	

The economic sphere is concerned with the production, distribution and exchange of goods and services; the social/cultural sphere is concerned with the production, transmission and legitimisation of cultural practices and products, including various forms of symbolic representation and communication; the political sphere refers to all activities where power is enacted, including decision making procedures within all types of organisations and institutions, policymaking procedures, and decision making within political life generally; the affective domain connotes those activities involved in developing bonds of solidarity, care and love between human beings. It refers to the socio-emotional relations that give people a sense of value and belonging, of being appreciated, loved and cared for in their personal, community, associational and working lives. The focus of this chapter is on the issues of inequality that arise in the economic sphere and below the liberal and radical perspectives on issues of distribution are outlined. First, however, a brief overview of the types of inequality that arise in each of the other dimensions is provided.

The social/cultural sphere raises issues of inequality rooted in patterns of representation, interpretation and communication. They take the form of cultural domination, symbolic misrepresentation or non-recognition all leading to a lack of respect. Promoting socio-cultural equality is concerned fundamentally therefore with the status systems that exist in a given society. The core concern is with the mutual respect and recognition that is due to all members of society independent of their race, gender, age, marital or family status, sexual orientation, physical or mental capacities, ethnicity, social origin, or political or religious affiliations. Because a person's status is both a function of personal characteristics and group affiliations, equality of recognition relates to both individuals and groups.

The political sphere is concerned with where power is enacted, for example, in the realms of decision making, including policymaking, and in power structures generally. It may take the form of political exclusion, marginalisation, trivialisation or political misrepresentation. Equality of power is about eliminating relations of dominance and subordination in social life. It refers to all types of political equality, including the protection of civil and political rights and the democratisation of decision making procedures in public and private institutions.

As shown, equality is usually discussed in terms of an equitable distribution of benefits and burdens, be that in terms of economic, political and status considerations. The individuals involved are assumed to be free and equally autonomous agents. Human beings, however, are not simply rational actors in social life; they are also affective, emotional actors, engaged with others at various levels of intimacy and care throughout their existence. One of the defining features of being human is being interdependent, and, at various times in life, dependence such as childhood, old age, impairment or illness. Both dependence and interdependence therefore need to be integrated into our conceptions of equality.

Inequalities in people's access to relations of love, care and solidarity are hard to quantify, but they are perfectly familiar. The most striking inequalities of this type are found where the normal expectation of love and care is replaced by its opposite, as in the abuse of children by their parents or by those who have institutional control over them. Inequalities also arise in the doing of dependency work; for example, when the work itself is not recognised for what it is and consequently given neither the status nor the income that necessitate its continuance. Second, it arises when this important, but unrecognised, work is unequally distributed, for example between genders and social classes.

The focus of the framework is on identifying the major contexts for generating inequality in the first instance, the key inequalities relating to these contexts and the different equality interpretations or perspectives on them. It is important to keep in mind that each dimension overlaps and that the key inequalities identified as correlating with a particular dimension are present in each. For example, in the political system, there are certainly inequalities of power, but there are also inequalities of politically relevant resources, of respect and recognition, of income, wealth and other material resources, and of prospects for solidarity. Furthermore, the contexts that generate inequality vary for different groups. While the economic context may be the principal one generating inequality among those groups whose most defining status is an economic one (the homeless, low income workers or those who are welfare dependent) other groups may experience economic inequality or poverty as a derivative of either socio-cultural and/or political factors. So, for example, while the primary generative cause of inequality for gays, lesbians and bisexuals may be generally defined as socio-cultural, arising from the lack of recognition and respect for sexual difference, the implications of this extend beyond the socio-cultural sphere. For example, those who are gay or lesbian may feel vulnerable in educational, health and other employments that are controlled by religious organisations that regard same sex partnerships as immoral.

Although the Employment Equality Act provides them with greater protection, it remains to be seen how Section 37 of the Act will be interpreted in allowing employers to treat gay people as being a threat to the ethos of the organisation in which they work. Not only does the lack of recognition impact on employment opportunities in particular areas, it also affects such issues as pension entitlements, taxation issues (e.g. transferring of standard allowance), and property rights (e.g. inheritance).

Equality and Economic Resources

The first dimension, identified in Table 6.1, is economic which concerns the distribution of resources. The most obvious resources are income and wealth, and these are the resources that economists typically concentrate on. A wider view of economic resources, however, would also include non-financial conditions relating to their access to goods and services, such as their right to public services and their right not to be excluded from privately provided goods and services by discriminatory treatment, as well as environmental factors such as a safe and healthy environment, the geographical arrangement of cities, the accessibility of buildings and so on. Time, particularly leisure time, is another important resource. Also to be included in a broader view of economic resources is what Pierre Bourdieu calls, social and cultural capital. Social capital consists of the durable networks of social relationships to which people have access, while cultural capital includes both people's embodied knowledge and abilities and their educational credentials.[8]

Liberal Perspective on Economic Resources

Assuming that significant inequality in the distribution of resources is inevitable, liberal egalitarians aim to regulate this inequality by combining a minimum floor or safety net with a principle of equal opportunity. The minimum floor is a logical extension of the basic human needs approach and is an intrinsic part of the modern welfare state. Quite where the floor should be and how it should be defined are continuing issues, as will be illustrated later in the chapter, when looking at the debates about whether poverty is 'absolute' or 'relative' and whether it can be defined entirely in terms of income or should include other resources. The key point is that, for the most part, a liberal equality objective is primarily concerned with eliminating poverty rather than promoting equality of resources. Because liberal egalitarians take inequality of resources to be inevitable, they are concerned with ensuring that the competition for advantage is as fair as possible and that it is governed by equal opportunity. One of the most difficult problems for liberal egalitarians is that this appears a forlorn hope. Major social and economic inequalities inevitably undermine all but the thinnest forms of equal opportunity. For example, the introduction of free fees at third level in Ireland has not, in itself, produced a significant change in the socioeconomic profile of those attending university with about 20 per cent of children with fathers in 'unskilled manual' occupations entering third level compared with 80 per cent of children with fathers in 'higher professional' occupations (see also Chapter 11).

Radical Perspective on Resources

In contrast to the liberal equality view, radical egalitarians aim at what can best be described as equality of resources. While the radical perspective recognises income and wealth as key resources it is also concerned with the wider idea of resources which includes other products (goods and services) that people need to achieve their aims in life as described above. The radical view of equality accepts the urgency of satisfying basic needs and providing a safety net against poverty, but its wider understanding of resources helps us to recognise a wider range of needs than some liberal egalitarians are inclined to attend to and to take a less market oriented view of how these needs should be satisfied. For example, people with physical impairments may not only need higher incomes than those without these impairments, but also may need changes in the physical environment that promote their inclusion into the activities that others take for granted.

Beyond the level of need, the objective of equality of condition aims for a world in which people's overall resources are much more equal than they are now, so that people's prospects for a 'good' life are roughly similar. Because of the multifaceted and disputable nature of well being and the complicated relationship between resources and prospects for well being, one cannot hope to provide a precise account of equality of resources. It certainly cannot be equated with the idea that everyone should have the same income and wealth, because people make different choices in relation to work, have different needs and because there are other important resources to consider. However, if differences in need, or choosing to work harder or longer, were the only reasons that justified inequality in income then it should follow that people who have similar needs and who work in similarly demanding occupations for similar amounts of time should have similar levels of income. This implies, for example, that there should be no significant differences in income between manual workers and office workers, between men and women, between people of colour and whites or between migrant workers and Irish workers. As the empirical evidence for Ireland, and elsewhere, confirms this is not the case. Radical equality would involve a dramatic change in the distribution of poverty, income and, in the longer run, wealth.

4 INCOME AND WEALTH

The concept of income is complex. Perhaps the simplest way to think of income, is as a flow deriving from a stock of wealth which, on an individual basis, can arise broadly in three forms: physical wealth such as houses, cars, paintings and other consumer durables; financial wealth such as stocks and shares, government bonds and bank deposits and human wealth which is primarily embodied in individuals as a result of education and training (i.e. human capital) but which can also arise from 'natural talent.' Each of these forms of wealth produces money and non-money income. Money income being easier to quantify receives most attention but equally deserving are non-money income flows from the different forms of wealth. This includes such intangibles as job satisfaction (or dissatisfaction), enjoyment of leisure, and non-money income in the form of your own production such as housework, childcare and other caring functions. Non-market does not mean non-work and this area features prominently in feminist economics, an important contribution of which has been to explore the interface between feminist theory and political economy with particular emphasis on caring and other forms of non-market work.[9]

Income
Income Measurement
The income of individuals or households is not easy to measure. Usually it is derived at an individual level through tax and social security records and at a household level through household surveys. While surveys are the main data source used in Ireland these can be problematic because of issues of coverage and accuracy. Household income surveys collect data on income from the following sources: employee earnings, self-employment, farming, secondary jobs, casual employment, state training or work schemes, social welfare transfers, child benefit, the renting of land or property, interest or dividends, retirement pensions, pensions from abroad, annuities, covenants or trusts, sick pay, maintenance from outside the household and educational grants. Not all income, however, is included in the data collected. For example, it does not cover imputed rents, capital gains, fringe benefits or the value of publicly provided goods and services. This latter omission is particularly relevant when making cross-country comparisons where, for example, comparisons in income distribution between the USA and the UK fail to take into account the availability of free education and health in the latter. The reliability of responses, especially in relation to self-employment and income from property, also raises difficulties, as does the very low response rate of people at the top of the income range.

Other measurement issues that arise include the definition of income used; the time period chosen; the recipient unit and the use of equivalence scales. Three types of income are separated for analysis: direct or market income; gross income which includes both market income and social welfare transfers and disposable income, i.e. after income tax and social insurance contributions are deducted. The definition of income must be clarified based on what you want to evaluate and disposable income is the one most used in welfare analysis. The time period chosen is also of importance, while income is a flow on a weekly, monthly, or annual basis people cannot freely borrow on the basis of future or expected income.

If income did not fluctuate or if you could borrow and lend freely on the basis of expected income then it would not matter which time period was chosen for comparison purposes. As financial markets do not perfectly accommodate smoothing of incomes, weekly income is usually used for poverty analysis, annual income for income distribution and lifetime income for differences in age groups.

The recipient unit refers to whose income is being measured which raises questions as to how it should be defined, whether on a household or individual basis, and how different size units should be compared. Using individual income would greatly distort the actual welfare of women working in the home and of children who have no independent income. On the other hand, any household based comparison between, say, a single person and a couple with children needs to takes account of the differences. What is at issue is not income per se but what it means in terms of welfare or living standards – how far does an income have to be stretched within a family or household unit. While we can easily calculate income on a per capita basis this does not take into account different needs within households or economies of scale which implies the costs for two people living together is expected to be less than two living singly, e.g. heating in a room or bulk buying. So instead of dividing the total income by each individual, equivalence scales are used for each adult dependent and child.

The scales range considerably, which obviously implies that there will be difference across measuring. What is referred to as the OECD scale gives the first adult a value of 1, each additional adult a value of 0.7 and each child 0.5. The difference in needs between various household members is thus identified by the difference in the value of the equivalence scales used for adults and children but this principle is not extended to other types of need, for example disability or caring for an elderly person at home. This is a key issue from an equality perspective.

A final point to consider in relation to the recipient unit is the implicit assumption that income, and other resources, are shared equally within it. This is an area to which increasing attention is being paid and which on the evidence to date suggests that the processes of intra-household resource allocation should be studied rather than assumed *a priori*. For example, a number of studies show that resources are not shared equally and that there may be hidden poverty within non-poor households or that some members of poor households may be worse off than others. As a result the risk of poverty for certain household members, in particular women and children, may be underestimated. If living standards within households are not equivalent this has serious implications for income support policies aimed at eliminating poverty.[10]

Income Distribution
Having collected the data at household level, the most common form of summarising and presenting the data is by ranking households from lowest income to highest. Decile shares identify what share of total income is held by each decile so that the percentage share of total income of the bottom 10 per cent and up to the top 10 percent can be analysed. This can be illustrated graphically by what is called the Lorenz curve which shows the share going to the bottom 10 per cent, 20 per cent etc. (Figure 6.1). The position of the Lorenz curve gives an indication of the extent of inequality in a given distribution of income.

The Lorenz curve is constructed by plotting the percentages of the national income received by different percentages of the population when the latter are cumulated from the bottom. That is, it plots the percentage of income received by the bottom 20 per cent, the percentage received by the bottom 40 per cent, the bottom 60 per cent and so on. If there were full equality – such that the bottom 60 per cent received 60 per cent of total national income, or the top 20 per cent received 20 percent – then the Lorenz curve would lie along the diagonal of the diagram. So, the further that the curve is from the diagonal, the further is the distribution from full equality and therefore the greater the inequality.

Figure 6.1

Lorenz Curve

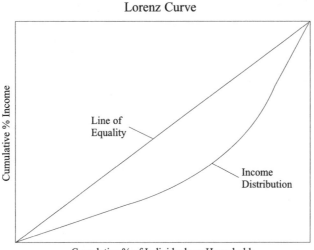

A summary measure of the amount of inequality implicit in a Lorenz curve can be obtained by use of the Gini coefficient. This is calculated by dividing the area between the Lorenz curve and the diagonal by the area of the triangle formed by the diagonal and the axes. As the Lorenz curve moves further from the diagonal, the Gini coefficient approaches 1, indicating greater inequality. As the Lorenz curve moves closer to the diagonal the Gini coefficient approaches zero, indicating greater equality. Another summary measure often used is to calculate the decile (semi-decile or quintile) ratio which compares the average income of someone in the top 10 per cent of incomes to the corresponding average for the lowest 10 per cent.

One has to be careful in interpreting numbers such as these as summary measures because they conceal distributional judgements. For example, it is not apparent from the Gini coefficient what the welfare of different groups are. Lorenz curves allow you to unambiguously rank distributions provided they do not intersect which seldom occurs in practice. If they do cross, however, then the ranking will depend on which part of the income distribution you focus on. So if one is very poor then country X might rank higher than country Y whereas if you were in the middle-income bracket it may be the other way around.

Income Inequality in Ireland 1973-1998

Table 6.2 shows the distribution of disposable income among households from 1973 to 1998. Overall, it shows a considerable degree of consistency over the twenty-five year period with the top 10 per cent having over 25 per cent of income and the bottom 10 per cent having around 2 per cent of income. However, within this there are changes in the shares of the decile groups. Between 1973 and 1994 there was an increase in the proportion going to the bottom decile but since 1994 there has been a decrease in this proportion. These reversing trends are also evidenced in the Gini coefficient, which showed a decrease in inequality between 1973 and 1987, and an increase thereafter.

Table 6.2

Decile Shares and Summary Inequality Measures

	Percentage share in total disposable income						
Decile	1973 HBS[1]	1983 HBS	1987 HBS	1994 HBS	1994 LII[2]	1997 LII	1998 LII
Bottom	1.7	1.7	2.2	2.1	2.3	2.1	1.8
2	3.3	3.5	3.7	3.5	3.3	3.3	3.0
3	5.0	5.1	5.0	4.8	4.6	4.5	4.4
4	6.5	6.6	6.3	6.0	6.0	6.0	6.0
5	7.8	7.9	7.6	7.6	7.5	7.7	7.7
6	9.2	9.3	9.2	9.2	9.1	9.5	9.5
7	10.9	11.0	11.0	11.3	11.1	11.2	11.3
8	13.0	13.0	13.4	13.6	13.5	13.4	13.5
9	16.2	16.2	16.6	16.7	16.5	16.5	16.7
Top	26.4	25.7	25.0	25.1	26.4	25.8	26.1
Gini	*0.367*	*0.360*	*0.352*	*0.362*	*0.377*	*0.373*	*0.386*

Source: B. Maitre, B. Nolan, D. O'Neill and O. Sweetman, *The Distribution of Income in Ireland*, Combat Poverty Agency, Dublin 2000.
[1]Household Budget Survey.
[2]Living in Ireland Survey.

Earnings are the main determinant of welfare in Ireland, and inequality in earnings increased in the late 1990s and early 2000s, particularly in the top half of the earnings distribution, reflecting increasing returns from higher levels of education and increased demand for skilled labour. There was a widening of the gap between low and high earners, with an increase in earnings in the top 2 quintiles of over 61 per cent while earnings of the bottom 2 quintiles rose by only 37 per cent. In terms of average weekly disposable income the ratio of highest to lowest quintile rose from 11:1 in 1994/95 to 13:1 in 1999/2000. While in absolute terms the situation has improved for all, in relative terms it has worsened for the poor. Another factor underlying the distribution of income is the interaction of the tax and social welfare system (see Chapter 3). As will be seen later in relation to trends in poverty, social welfare payments increased faster than average incomes in the 1980s and early 1990s, while from 1994 onwards, social welfare increases, while in excess of inflation, lagged well behind increases in average income.

Section 2 indicated the sharp increase in income inequality between developed and developing countries but also within most industrialised countries and especially in the UK and the USA. Ireland fits into the general pattern of increase in income inequality but fares badly in comparative terms. On the basis of the Luxembourg Income Study of the 1980s income inequality in Ireland was very high vis-à-vis other OECD countries with only the USA having a higher Gini coefficient. The European Community Household Panel Survey undertaken in 1994 re-iterated Ireland's inequality status although it was lower than Portugal and in the same cluster of countries as the UK, Spain and Greece. The OECD provides a more recent comparative picture in 2000.[11] It shows Ireland having about the same level of income inequality as the UK in the mid 1990s with the level of inequality in the latter having risen dramatically since the mid 1980s. Outside the EU it showed Ireland having a higher level of inequality than Canada or Australia but still managing to be more equal than the USA.

Wealth
Wealth is a measure of your 'net worth', the sum of your physical, financial and human capital assets. The distribution of wealth is much more unequal than the distribution of income. Like income, its measurement is based on data drawn from household surveys of assets, from taxation (wealth and estate tax records) and from investment data. The limitations of the data in relation to income also apply to wealth but the issues of coverage and accuracy are even more pronounced. In particular, the collection of data on wealth suffers from severe under representation and under reporting.

Household surveys are a main source of information on the distribution of wealth in the USA, Canada, Japan and other countries but they are problematic. Wealth is more concentrated than income and because of the low participation of respondents at the top end, as well as under reporting by those who do respond, it is unlikely that the survey will provide a very accurate picture of the distribution of wealth. Some corrections can be made to improve data such as over sampling the very rich or using additional information that is external to the survey. Estate tax records provide another source of data on wealth, for example the capital acquisitions tax (CAT) in Ireland. These are derived from the size of the estates of people dying each year, adjusted to reflect the proportion of adults of each age and gender in the total adult population (referred to as the estate multiplier method). While these are a good source of information on the very wealthy they are also problematic because: small estates are omitted (there is a wealth threshold for taxation purposes); some joint property (e.g. houses) are omitted; and because there are tax incentives to hide or reduce wealth. Nevertheless the picture this data provides is useful not least in illustrating that the form that people hold their assets in changes with wealth level. Studies in the UK show that the proportion of gross wealth held as interest bearing assets and household goods falls as wealth grows. Residential property, as well as financial assets, forms a significant part of the middle wealth owners while for the very wealthy, shares and assets like land are more important. The importance of housing as a component of wealth for middle wealth groups is particularly relevant in Ireland in the context of the economic boom of the 1990s and early twenty-first century and the subsequent huge rise in house prices.

Distribution of Wealth in Ireland

To date, only two studies appear to have been undertaken on wealth inequality in Ireland.[12] A study, by Lyons in 1972, based on 1966 estate tax records showed that 66 per cent of the population had a net wealth of zero. The top 5 per cent of adults held 60 per cent of wealth and the top 1 per cent of adults held 33 per cent of wealth. The second study, undertaken by the ESRI, was based on data from a 1987 household survey. The data are not comparable as the results of the former are based on individual adults while the latter refers to wealth concentration among households. The ESRI study found that 90 per cent of the population had some form of wealth; about 10 per cent held 50 per cent of wealth and the top 1 per cent held 20 per cent of wealth.

There are no data available on the current distribution of wealth in Ireland. Against the background of sustained economic growth since the mid 1990s, there have been a number of significant developments in asset holdings and values. The most obvious example being the rise in property values, but other factors include the increase in share ownership, the increase in profits and in employee profit share schemes and the transfer of public sector housing into tenant purchase. What this translates to in terms of the overall distribution of wealth is difficult to estimate. On the one hand, the massive rise in the value of property is likely to contribute to a more equal distribution of total wealth with the major caveat that there is now a much wider wealth gap between those with and those without property. Against this trend towards greater wealth equality is the enormous increase in capital income which one suspects will ensure a greater concentration in the distribution of wealth.

5 POVERTY

Definition and Relationship to Equality

Possibly the first thing that can be said about the meaning of poverty is that it is controversial and there is no politically neutral standpoint. There is debate about its definition, its measurement, its extent and its relationship with other forms of disadvantage or discrimination. Thus we can argue about absolute or relative conceptions of poverty; which poverty measurement is best or gives the most complete picture; the relationship between poverty and inequality or the relationship between poverty and income, material deprivation, class, education;

issues of social exclusion and multiple disadvantage and finally we can debate the causes and/or consequences of poverty.

At a very broad level two main debates dominate – absolute versus relative poverty and poverty versus inequality. Poverty and inequality while related are quite distinct concepts. The concepts are usually separated by the notion that poverty refers to living standards whereas inequality relates to the distribution of resources between individuals. The theoretical distinction between the two is clear in that even if there is no poverty, in the sense that no one would be so far below the general standard of living so as to be excluded from participation in the ordinary life of that society, there could still be substantial inequality in the distribution of income between the wealthy and the rest of society. However, an extreme view sees poverty as synonymous with inequality, especially when using the relative poverty line approach, and would lead simply to the identification of bottom groups in the income distribution, for example the bottom 20 per cent, as the 'poor'. In this case the proportion of the population in poverty cannot rise or fall whereas with the relative poverty line set at, say 50 per cent of mean income, relative poverty can rise, fall or be totally eradicated. In Ireland the emphasis over the last two decades has been on the reduction of poverty rather than on explicitly addressing inequality and while the rationale for this has been based, to some extent, on pragmatism in terms of inducing a more concrete policy response it is also on the basis that at, an analytical level, poverty is a phenomenon distinct from inequality, that the extent and especially the experience of it matters in and of itself and, further, that it is not confined to poor countries.[13]

Another debate at the conceptual level is whether an absolute or relative approach to defining poverty is used, but the relative approach is, and always has been, the one adopted in practice. The basic question is whether poverty is seen as absolute deprivation or as socially defined (relative) deprivation.[14] Regarding poverty as an absolute concept stems from the time when it was natural to think in subsistence terms but today in the developed world people, for the most part, live above the subsistence level and the concept of deprivation is more relevantly applied to emotional and cultural standards as well as physical ones. The core of the debate between absolute and relative definitions is whether standards are to be fixed over time or change with the standard of living. Townsend's definition when income is so below average that people are in effect excluded from the normal living patterns of the society to which they belong, makes the relative concept explicit and is probably the most widely adopted definition of poverty. It was the model used for the National Anti-Poverty Strategy's (NAPS) definition of poverty launched in 1997 following the UN Social Summit in Copenhagen and it underpins most research on poverty in EU countries. Sen dissents somewhat arguing 'that ultimately poverty must be seen to be primarily an "absolute notion" while Piachaud, in a sense, concedes to both views in his definition which allows that at subsistence level there is some absolute minimum necessary for survival, but beyond this any poverty standard must be relative, i.e. it must reflect prevailing social standards.'[15]

Despite the terminology used the relative view represents actual practice. Rowntree's study of poverty in York in 1899 is classified under the absolute standard approach based on his compilation of food items deemed necessary for survival. And yet, as has been observed, tea with little or no nutritional value is included because eating habits are profoundly influenced by social conventions. Further, items included such as newspapers and presents are difficult to justify on an absolute subsistence definition. Sen argues it is in the notion of shame that the core concept of poverty is to be found which echoes back to Adam Smith's view on linen shirts being a necessity of life in England so much so that 'the poorest creditable person would be ashamed to appear in public without them'.

Measuring Poverty

A number of standard quantitative approaches to measuring poverty in industrialised countries can be identified. While all of them employ income to distinguish the poor, they use a variety of methods to establish the income cut-off point including reference to budget standards (classified under absolute measures but as indicated above only 'relatively absolute'); to income supports offered by the social welfare system (also referred to as official poverty lines); to subjective views on minimum income needs (consensual poverty lines); to average or median income itself. A less explicitly income oriented approach is to focus directly on deprivation based on the use of non-monetary deprivation indicators which measure exclusion from normal living patterns. In this chapter we focus on the two approaches, namely relative income lines and non-monetary deprivation indicators, which underlie most of the research on poverty in Ireland since 1987 and which have also been applied in numerous EU countries.

Relative poverty lines are framed in terms of relative income. Lines are generally set at a particular percentage of mean or median income, for example 50 per cent, and then adjusted for household size and composition using equivalence scales. The choice of cut off is entirely arbitrary and there is no firm basis for the selection of any particular ratio to serve as the poverty line. For this reason research on poverty undertaken by the ESRI has tended to use more than one cut-off (at 40, 50 and 60 per cent of mean, or more recently at 70 per cent of median, income) in order to examine the sensitivity of the results to the choice of cut-off. The rationale behind relative poverty lines is that those falling more than a certain distance below 'normal' income levels in society are unlikely to be able to participate fully in the life of that society. The main advantage of this approach is the ease with which results can be understood and applied in cross-country comparisons. The main disadvantage of adopting a purely relative approach is the anomaly highlighted by Sen – any improvement in the living standards of low-income groups, which are shared by the rest of the population, are discounted while a general decline in prosperity will not show up as an increase in poverty if the relative picture has not changed. We return to this point later when reviewing trends in Ireland over the last ten years.

Non-monetary deprivation indicators focus directly on exclusivity from normal living patterns. Townsend pioneered this approach in the late 1970s in his research on Britain. It measures exclusion directly – by examining what you do without either by choice, because it is not needed; or because it cannot be afforded. Examples of the items in Townsend's deprivation list include certain items of clothing, visits to the doctor, heating, shoes and a television. Table 6.3 shows the full set of 23 non-monetary indicators used in the Living in Ireland Surveys. The difference between this approach and consensual poverty lines is that this reflects, at least to some extent, social consensus on necessities or actual pattern of possession. The selection of deprivation indicators and the role of choice and differences in tastes is one of the major criticisms of this approach. It has also been argued that the aggregation of deprivation indicators into a single index assumes that poverty is one-dimensional which may not be an accurate reflection of reality. If poverty is multidimensional, for example households can

Table 6.3

Indicators of Basic Style of Living Requirements

Basic Life Style Requirement
New not second hand clothes
A meal with meat, fish or chicken every second day
A warm waterproof overcoat
Two pairs of strong shoes
A roast or its equivalent once a week
Had day in last two weeks without substantial meal
Had to go without heating during last year through lack of money
Experienced debt problems arising from ordinary living expenses or availed of charity
Secondary Life Style Requirements
Telephone
Car
Washing machine
Refrigerator
Colour television
Was not able to afford an afternoon or evening out in previous two weeks
Housing Requirements
Central heating
Bath or shower
Indoor toilet
A dry-damp free dwelling
Other Requirements
A week's annual holiday away from home
To be able to save some of one's income regularly
A daily newspaper
A hobby or leisure activity
Presents for friends or family once a year

Source: B. Gannon, R. Layte, B. Maitre, B. Nolan, D. Watson, C. Whelan and J. Williams, 'Monitoring Poverty Trends in Ireland', *Policy Research Series*, ESRI, Dublin 2003.

be 'food poor' but not 'house poor', etc. then it is difficult to bring these different facets to serve as a basis for a cut-off between poor and non-poor. Notwithstanding these criticisms, which have partly been met by more sophisticated approaches to measuring deprivation, explicit analysis of living standards and deprivation gives a greater insight into what it means to be poor and the nature of poverty. Combining indicators of deprivation with income lines produces a very different perspective on trends in poverty than using income poverty lines alone, as demonstrated in the next section.

Trends in Poverty

Table 6.4 shows the percentage of households below average relative income poverty lines between 1994 and 2001. There has been a considerable increase in those households below the 40 and 50 per cent income lines especially in the mid 1990s, with the percentage remaining more stable between 1998 and 2001.[16]

Table 6.4

Percentage of Households Below Mean Relative Income Poverty Lines

	1994	1997	1998	2000	2001
40%	4.9	6.3	9.5	10.6	9.8
50%	18.6	22.4	23.8	23.7	23.8
60%	34.2	34.3	32.2	32.0	32.2

Source: As for Table 6.3.

By using three different points of 40, 50 and 60 per cent of mean/median income the ESRI in their research on poverty, in the 1987 Household Survey and in the subsequent Living in Ireland Surveys, 1994-2001, produced findings on characteristics of households that were seen to hold across the range of poverty lines. For example, in 1994 those where the household was headed by an unemployed person made up a substantial proportion of the poor or were at high risk of being in poverty while elderly or retired head of households were a small element among the poor and had lower than average risk of being poor. By 2000, however, households headed by a retired person were at significantly higher risk, 34 per cent compared to 8 per cent in 1994.

What is more revealing perhaps than the overall head count is what is called the poverty gap which refers to how far below the poverty income line households fall.[17] It is a depth of poverty measure and to some extent reflects policy response to the interaction of factors which underlie poverty such as employment and unemployment and social welfare rates increases. For example, if we compare what is happening between 1987 and 1994, between 1994 and 1997, and 1997 to 2001 we get quite different stories. The 1987 poverty figures showed unemployment to be the single most important cause of poverty. Perhaps in response, between 1987 and 1994 priority was given to raising the lowest social welfare rates. Means tested unemployment assistance increased more rapidly than incomes while support rates for other groups (for example the elderly) rose less rapidly, though still ahead of inflation. Not surprisingly, between 1987 and 1994 the poverty gap, using per capita income gap and weighted gap measures, decreased across all three relative income lines even though the numbers below the lines were rising. Between 1994 and 1997 the poverty gap widened. Even though unemployment was falling, other groups dependent on social income support did not fare so well in terms of relative income poverty lines. Between 1994 and 1997 inflation increased by around 6 per cent; social welfare rates by 12 per cent but average income rose by 20 per cent. The poverty gap has continued to widen since 1998 and what this shows is that those falling behind relative income thresholds are falling further and further behind the middle of the income distribution.

As discussed, one of the difficulties of focusing exclusively on relative income poverty lines, especially in a period of rapid growth in average incomes is that it can give a misleading picture, with the improvement in living standards being discounted. This is where the non-monetary deprivation approach to measuring poverty can provide a particularly useful complement to relative income lines. An approach developed at the ESRI combining income lines and deprivation indicators (see Table 6.3) gives a measure of what is termed 'consistently poor' and the trend in these figures shows a steady decline. Using households which are deprived of one or more items on the index and the 60 per cent of mean income the consistent poverty measures shows a decline from 15.1 per cent in 1994 to 8.0 per cent in 1998 to 5.2 per cent in 2001. Using 70 per cent of median income as the income element of the measure shows a very similar picture down from 14.5 per cent in 1994 to 7.7 per cent in 1998 to 4.9 per cent in 2001. Using Eurostat's standardised statistics we can compare Ireland's poverty figures, based on median income lines, with other European countries. For 1999, the percentage of households below 60 per cent of median income in Ireland at 22 per cent was very similar to that in Spain, Italy and the UK and lower than that in Portugal and Greece. About 11 percent of households were below the 50 per cent median income line in Ireland in 1999 with the comparable figure for the EU ranging from 6 to 14 per cent.

6 POLICY AND EQUALITY

There have been several important policy and legislative changes to progress equality over the last number of years. These include the adoption of equality legislation, namely the Employment Equality Act, 1998, and the Equal Status Act, 2000, and the establishment of equality institutions, namely the Equality Authority and the Office of the Director of Equality Investigations. Further, the establishment of the Disability Authority and the Human Rights Commission are all developments with potential to contribute to reducing poverty, inequality and discrimination.

In the affective domain there have been a number of legislative provisions addressing the regulation of the care of children in particular (such as the Parental Leave Act 1998, or the Education (Welfare) Act, 2000). The development of increased maternity and parental leave also signifies a growing recognition of the importance of care for infant children. However, the overall lack of support for childcare, the inadequate support for home carers of adults and dependent disabled persons suggest that affective relations generally are not a political priority to date. There has also been an attempt to promote greater equality of power through the social partnership system, although the extent to which the system has achieved substantive, as opposed to symbolic, gains has been called into question. Some authors have suggested that 'Irish policy objectives have a Rawlsian flavour' and that 'there are strong egalitarian tendencies in debate on economic issues', but the evidence would suggest otherwise. While the partnership agreements do have the potential to promote greater equality in the distribution of economic resources (see Chapter 3) this has not been an explicit objective and the result has been aptly described as 'solidarity without equality'.[18]

Focusing on economic policy, and in particular on the issues of poverty, income inequality and 'quality of life', it is quite difficult to assess the present state and direction of the economy from the different equality perspectives discussed in Section 2. As the recent NESC strategy commented there are very 'different perceptions as to whether Ireland has become a fairer and more just society with its improved economic circumstances'.[19] The stable environment of rapid economic growth since 1994 has ensured that the majority of people in Ireland have higher standards of living and higher real incomes than a decade ago, although new pockets of inequality are being created, especially among migrant workers, asylum seekers and refugees. On the one hand, the unemployment and 'consistent' poverty figures are testament to the general economic improvement, with the unemployment rate currently around 4 per cent and with those living in consistent poverty reduced to 5 per cent, both of which meet the revised targets for 2004 set by the National Anti-Poverty Strategy. On the other hand these do not seem to be translating into improved quality of life as inadequate childcare supports and over-stretched public services, most notably in health, demonstrate.

With the launch of the National Anti-Poverty Strategy (NAPS) in 1997 Ireland became the first European Union member to adopt a national poverty reduction target. From an equality perspective, this represented a significant step forward in terms of: political acceptance of a definition of poverty; explicit recognition of the responsibility of government for reducing the extent of poverty; and the need for a systematic, institutionally based strategy to combating poverty. In assessing what has been happening to poverty in Ireland since the adoption of the NAPS, we can see a number of different issues arising. Section 5 showed that different patterns emerge depending on whether the measure used is based on income alone or one based on income and direct measures of deprivation. Using the income and deprivation measure combined shows there was a considerable reduction in the numbers of 'consistently poor', which fell from 15 per cent in 1994 to 5 per cent in 2001. Focusing on median income poverty lines there have been increases in the number of persons across all the different income cut offs but particularly below the lower poverty lines, with the number below the 50 per cent median income line more than doubling from 6 to 13 per cent between 1994 and 2001. Of particular concern is the fact that income poverty gaps have risen substantially over the same period indicating that those falling below the income thresholds are falling further and further behind the middle of the income distribution. The gap between the poor and the non-poor is consistently and substantially widening.

There is also a growing degree of income inequality in Irish society as detailed in Section 4. Better off households have gained from the economic boom to a greater extent than those who were less well off. Overall income inequality increased during the 1990s. In 1998 the bottom 10 per cent of households, adjusted for size and composition, had 3.4 per cent of disposable income compared with 25 per cent held by the top decile. One of the most significant findings of research on income distribution was a shift in the disposable income distribution away from the bottom 30 per cent of households. The share going to the bottom 30 per cent declined by over 1 per cent of total income between 1994 and 1998, which represents a substantial shift in a short period. In international comparisons Ireland is shown to be one of the most unequal countries in the EU.

The discussion of income inequality and poverty has not differentiated between any given group within the economically disadvantaged. However we know that various forms of social marginalisation tend to be coterminous. Thus those who are unemployed, elderly, lone parents, Travellers, children or disabled are more likely to be poor than those who are adult, middle class, settled, in dual parent households or without impairments. Given both that income inequality has increased and the gap between the poor and non-poor widened, it seems likely that the relative position of these groups has also worsened. In relation to women, for example, the evidence shows that there has been a significant feminisation of poverty in Ireland throughout the 1990s. Data from the 1994 LII surveys showed a substantial increase in the risk of poverty experienced by households headed by women since 1987 and a reversal of the trend found between 1973 and 1987. By 2000 the gender gap had widened further with 23 per cent of women at risk of falling below the 60 per cent poverty line compared to 19 per cent of men.[20] Further, the poverty statistics examined are based on household surveys and therefore do not include homeless people, many Traveller families, people living in institutions such as hospitals, nursing homes, convents or prisons and others not in private households.

In summary, the economic boom, the increase in real incomes standards and the fall in deprivation levels has not meant that everyone is now able to participate fully in society. Rather as the average standard of living rises in Ireland, so the cost of participation also increases. Our examination of trends in poverty and income inequality, and the examination of taxation and social expenditure in other chapters, illustrates how inequitably the benefits of economic growth are being shared with those who have benefited least. This picture of a wealthier, but more unequal, Ireland is itself part of a much broader question that is increasingly occupying a central position in public policy, that is the relationship between economic growth and 'quality of life', or well being. Ireland's outstanding economic performance during the 1990s and into the twenty-first century provides a case in point for the renewed interest, internationally, in examining this relationship. The OECD recommenced the publication of social indicators in 2001 on the basis of the need for 'quantitative evidence as to whether our societies are getting more or less unequal, healthy, dependent and cohesive' and a number of countries have been making attempts to assess social progress including Germany's system of social accounts, New Zealand's social report and the annual report on the social situation in Europe. Alternative, broader, measures of economic growth and development such as the Human Development Index (HDI), which try to incorporate a summary measure of well being rank Ireland tenth out of the 175 UN member countries a lower ranking than that based on GDP alone (see Chapter 5). When the focus is specifically on human and income poverty, HPI-2, Ireland ranks sixteenth out of the 17 selected OECD countries with only the USA in a worse position. When gender equality is introduced as a component of economic and social development and as an indicator of societal well being Ireland ranks fourteenth. While there has been criticism of the validity of the statistics used to compile the UN rankings for the 2004 Human Development Report, the rankings provide a clear example of the difference in focusing on income alone as a measure of economic and social progress or looking at broader measures such as those that incorporate a poverty or gender dimension (see also Chapter 1 and 5).

While Ireland does not yet have a social report the CSO has announced its intention of doing so in 2005.[21] The acceptance of the idea that an informed assessment of how overall societal well being is developing, and whether implicit and explicit social and equality goals are being met, is necessary in addition to, and part of, ongoing economic indicators, which themselves have a strong social import, seems an important step in linking some of the economic and equality issues raised in this chapter.

7 CONCLUSIONS

This chapter provided a framework for thinking about equality in economic and other dimensions. It showed first that equality is a complex concept, that people have different conceptions of what it means and more crucially how any agreed equality objective is to be applied. It outlined three equality perspectives, basic liberal and radical, which encompass most of the viewpoints on the idea of equality and identified four key generative dimensions of equality including the political the cultural/social sphere, the affective and the economic sphere. In relation to the latter it discussed the central equality issues that arise and looked at the difference in the liberal and radical perspectives on equality in economic resources. An examination of the trends in poverty and income inequality indicated that a fairly minimalist equality outcome was being achieved. Ireland is one of the most unequal of industrialised countries in terms of income distribution and while the poverty levels of the poorest have risen, the gap between the poor and the non-poor is consistently and substantially widening.

While the institutional developments in relation to equality must be seen as welcome progress, it is too early to evaluate the long-term implications of their equality objectives or to assess the effectiveness of the various legislative initiatives. Again, what can be noted however, is that the majority of the changes which have occurred relate to the more minimalist conception of equality rather than dealing substantively with equality of outcome.

Endnotes

* Many thanks to the editors, John O'Hagan and Carol Newman, for their helpful comments.

1 For example, see A. Glyn and D. Miliband, *Paying for Inequality – The Economic Cost of Social Injustice,* Rivers Oram Press, London 1994; R. Wilkinson, *Unhealthy Societies: The Afflictions of Inequalities,* Routledge, London 1996; OECD, *Society at a Glance: OECD Social Indicators,* Paris 2002.

2 The statistics presented in this section are taken from recent World Bank and United Nations Development Programme reports; from B. Sutcliffe, *100 Ways of Seeing An Unequal World,* Zed Books, London 2001, and from the OECD website www.oecd.org.

3 See M. McCann, S. O'Siocháin and J. Ruane (editors), *Irish Travellers: Culture and Identity,* Queen's University, Belfast 1994; J. McLaughlin, *Travellers and Ireland: Whose Country, Whose History?,* Cork University Press, Cork 1995; Government of Ireland, *Report of the Task Force on the Travelling Community,* Stationery Office, Dublin 1995.

4 In 2003, the Equality Authority received requests for assistance under the Employment Equality Act in 166 cases on the grounds of 'race' and 9 in relation to membership of the Travelling Community. Under the Equal Status Act they received requests for assistance in 80 cases in relation to 'race' and 327 in relation to membership of the Travelling Community. Additional figures for racist incidents and racist violence can be obtained from the Gárda Pulse system and from the National Consultative Committee on Racism and Interculturalsim (NCCRI) Racist Incidents Reporting System.

5 The chapter draws on the framework of equality developed by the Equality Studies Centre in UCD and, in particular, on work undertaken for J. Baker, K. Lynch, S. Cantillon and J. Walsh, *Equality: From Theory to Action*, Palgrave Macmillan, Basingstoke 2004.

6 For those interested in pursuing this literature some useful starting reference points are: A. Sen, *On Ethics and Economics,* Basil Blackwell, Oxford 1988; J. Rawls, *Justice as Fairness: A Restatement,* Belknap Press, London 2001; I. Young, *Justice and the Politics of Difference,* Princeton University Press, Chichester 1990; R. Nozick, *Anarchy, State and Utopia*, Basic Books, New York 1974.

7 See also Chapter 1.

8 P. Bordieu, 'The Forms of Capital', in J. Richardson (editor), *Handbook of Theory and Research for the Sociology of Education*, Greenwood Press, Connecticut 1986

9 See for example, N. Folbre, *The Economics of the Family,* Edward Elgar, NewYork 1996.

10 There is a substantial international literature in this area. For a good theoretical overview, see T. Bergstrom, *A Survey of Theories of the Family,* Elsevier, New York 1997. For some empirical results for Ireland, see D. Rottman, *Income Distribution Within Irish Households,* Combat Poverty

Agency, Dublin 1994; and S. Cantillon and B. Nolan, 'Are Married Women more Deprived than their Husbands?', *Journal of Social Policy,* 1998, pp. 151–71.

11 M. Foster, 'Trends and Driving Factors in Income Distribution in the OECD Area' (Occasional Papers No. 42), Labour Market and Social Policy, OECD, Paris 2000.

12 See P. Lyons, 'The Distribution of Personal Wealth in Ireland', in J. Bristow and A. Tait (editors), *Ireland: Some Problems of a Developing Economy*, Gill and Macmillan, Dublin 1972; B. Nolan, *The Wealth of Irish Households*, Combat Poverty Agency, Dublin 1991.

13 See, for example, B. Nolan, 'Economic and Sociological Perspectives on Poverty and Poverty Research' (Paper to the Annual Conference of the Swedish Sociological Association), Swedish Sociological Association, Stockholm 2004.

14 While a discussion of this debate features in all the poverty literature one of the best sources for a clear overview of both the meaning of, and the various approaches to measuring, poverty remains Chapters 1 and 2 of T. Callan, S. Creighton, D. Hannan, B. Nolan and B. Whelan, 'Poverty, Income and Welfare in Ireland', *GRS Papers*, ESRI, Dublin 1989.

15 A. Sen, 'Poor, Relatively Speaking', *Oxford Economic Papers,* Oxford University Press, Oxford 1983; D. Piachaud 'Problems in the Definition and Measurement of Poverty', *Journal of Social Policy*, 1987, pp. 147-64.

16 The percentage of households below median relative income poverty lines show similar trends but with no levelling off of the increase in the later years. For full details, see B. Gannon, R. Layte, B. Maitre, B. Nolan, D. Watson, C. Whelan and J. Williams, 'Monitoring Poverty Trends in Ireland', *Policy Research Series*, ESRI, Dublin 2003.

17 A number of measures have been developed to measure the poverty gap; see for example J. Foster, J. Greer and E. Thorbecke 'A Class of Decomposable Poverty', *Econometricia*, May 1984.

18 See for example D. Mc Aleese and D. Burke, 'Policy Objectives for a Regional Economy', in J. O'Hagan (editor), *The Economy of Ireland,* Gill & Macmillan, Dublin 2000; S. Ó Rian and P. O'Connell, 'The Role of the State in Growth and Welfare', in B. Nolan, P. O'Connell and C. Whelan (editors), *Bust to Boom?: The Irish Experience of Growth and Equality,* Institute of Public Administration, Dublin 2000.

19 National Economic Social Council, *An Investment in Quality: Services, Inclusion and Enterprise,* NESC, Dublin 2002.

20 Combat Poverty Agency, *Poverty In Ireland: The Facts*, Dublin 2002.

21 The CSO has published a first and preliminary national progress indicators report, *Measuring Ireland's Progress*, Stationery Office, Dublin 2003.

PERFORMANCE AND POLICY ISSUES IN THE PRIVATE SECTOR

CHAPTER 7

Trade and Foreign Direct Investment in Manufacturing and Services

Frances Ruane and Ali Uğur

1 INTRODUCTION

Trade, Investment and Growth

In the past two decades, the importance of international trade and investment to economic growth has received increased attention in both developed and developing countries. From a policy perspective, both the widening scope of the World Trade Organisation (WTO) and the increase in its membership, most importantly China in recent times, have ensured that facilitating trade and foreign investment flows are major policy issues in most countries. While the costs and benefits of globalisation are still hotly debated, and especially their distributive impact on groups within developing countries, there are few if any economists who would advance the case for reduced global trade and investment flows. From a theoretical perspective, it has been argued and demonstrated empirically that export expansion is one of the key determinants of growth and that international investment can enhance the productivity of recipient economies.[1] Ireland has been long recognised as an economy that has benefited from this dual strategy, and much of its recent exceptional growth rates have been attributed to it.[2]

The consequences of increasing openness are that any loss in Ireland's economic competitiveness is immediately evident, *inter alia*, in a loss of international and domestic market shares and a decline in the activities of foreign companies that have located in Ireland. That loss in competitiveness can be driven by external factors (other countries become relatively more competitive) or internal factors (costs rise because economy is not well managed). The Lisbon Strategy, published in 2000, recognises that increasing productivity is now an EU wide challenge and identifies actions that EU economies, including Ireland, should pursue. Ireland's productivity must continue to increase if it is to remain

162

internationally competitive at rising income levels in the context of EU enlargement and expanding global trade and investment. Building on the Single European Market (SEM) policies of the early 1990s, the Lisbon strategy sets targets for improving the science and technology (S&T) infrastructure in the EU, as well as reducing the inefficiency of government, and increasing labour market flexibility. These targets are part of the context in which Ireland's current trade and investment strategy will operate. Further contextual elements of importance to Ireland include the increased monitoring of state aids in Europe, and the environmental targets set at Kyoto.

International Trade and Investment: Some International Comparisons
Ireland's international stance, in terms of openness to trade and international investment, is clear from trends in comparative data for a selected group of economies. To look at international trade, Table 7.1 shows the ratio of merchandise trade, measured as the average of imports and exports, to GDP at ten year intervals for the period 1970-2000. To set Ireland in context, the countries included are the original six members of the European Community, the second group of three members (which included Ireland), and the USA, which is the most important international economy in terms of Ireland's manufacturing sector.

Table 7.1
Trade Openness: Ratio of average Merchandise Exports and Imports to GDP, 1970-2000 (%)

Country	1970	1980	1990	2000
Belgium-Luxembourg	45.5	56.9	60.9	66.2[1]
France	13.0	18.9	18.9	23.0
Germany	17.4	23.5	25.1	28.0
Italy	13.1	19.9	16.1	22.1
Netherlands	42.8	50.4	45.5	55.7
Denmark	24.0	26.6	25.3	28.7
Ireland	*33.8*	*48.7*	*48.8*	*67.8*
UK	16.7	21.0	21.0	21.8
USA	4.2	8.9	8.2	10.3

Source: Derived from F. Ruane and J. Sutherland, 'Globalization, Europeanization and Trade in the 1990s: Export Responses to of Foreign and Indigenous Companies', in H. Kierzkowski (editor), *Europe and Globalization*, Palgrave Macmillan, New York 2002.
[1]Figure for Belgium-Luxembourg refers to 1997 due to data limitations.

Several patterns emerge. First, while trade openness is generally greater for smaller rather than larger countries, the scale of openness in Ireland is exceptional. The only countries with ratios that appear close to Ireland are Belgium-Luxembourg and the Netherlands; however, these countries host the key entry freight ports in mainland Europe and hence their trade ratios overstate their degree of openness. Second, there has been an upward trend in the degree of trade openness in the EU since 1970, though for several countries the ratio fell in the 1980s. This increased openness is regarded as a direct product of: the reductions in non-tariff barriers to trade within the EU; the lowering of tariff and non-tariff barriers under the General Agreements on Tariffs and Trade (GATT) and more recently by the WTO; the decrease in transportation costs per unit trade; the rise in the share of 'weightless products' in consumption; and the growth in the EU market. Note that the ratio for the USA is much lower than those for the individual European countries, reflecting both the scale of the US market and the increasing economic integration within Europe.[3]

Paralleling the focus on merchandise trade in Table 7.1, Table 7.2 shows trends in foreign direct investment (FDI) in the merchandise goods sector between 1970 and 2000 for the same set of countries.[4] There are wide variations in the ratios of the average of inward and outward FDI to GDP in different EU countries for the six sub periods. As with the trade data, the ratios are generally higher in the EU countries than in the USA, and have risen very steeply in the six year period to 2000. The higher ratios in the EU in the 1990s are generally attributed to the SEM effect, and in the USA to the unprecedented boom in that period. The relatively low ratio for Ireland may seem surprising, but it reflects the fact that historically Ireland has had virtually no outward FDI so that the ratio reflects inward FDI only until the last decade. There is a strong link between Ireland's position in Tables 7.1 and 7.2, as most investment in merchandise goods leads to production for export markets, and many of the inputs used in this production have to be imported.

Table 7.2

Investment Openness: Ratio of average Inflows and Outflows of FDI in Merchandise Goods to GDP per period, 1970-2000 (%)

Country	70-74	75-79	80-84	85-89	90-94	95-00	70-00
Belgium-Luxembourg	2.2	2.1	1.5	4.4	7.4	22.8	6.7
France	0.7	0.8	0.9	1.8	3.5	6.3	2.3
Germany	1.2[1]	0.8	0.7	1.3	1.3	5.0	1.7[2]
Italy	0.6	0.4	0.6	0.7	0.9	1.4	0.8
Netherlands	5.2	3.7	4.3	5.6	7.5	18.3	7.4
Denmark	0.9	0.3	0.4	1.3	3.0	10.8	2.8
Ireland[3]	*0.7*	*2.0*	*1.1*	*0.3*	*2.8*	*8.1*	*2.5*
UK	3.2	3.4	3.0	6.0	4.1	12.0	5.3
USA	0.7	1.0	0.9	1.6	1.6	3.2	1.5

Source: As for Table 7.1.
[1]Refers to 1971-74.
[2]Refers to 1971-2000.
[3]Inflow and outflow data for Ireland from 1998 onwards have been amended to take account of changes in the methodology and coverage.

Outline of the Chapter

The layout of this chapter is as follows. Having established Ireland's particularly open economic position in Tables 7.1 and 7.2, Section 2 looks at how Ireland has arrived at being such an open economy with a high ratio of inward FDI. This section looks at the historical background, covering the period up to the end of the 1980s. Section 3 examines the performance of the manufacturing sector over the decade 1991-2001; this sector has been the main driver of trade openness and the main recipient of inward FDI. This section looks at how the sectoral pattern within manufacturing has changed over the period and then focuses on productivity growth, distinguishing between the performances of foreign-owned (foreign) and Irish-owned ('Irish') companies. Section 4 examines the export focus of the Irish manufacturing sector in terms of who is exporting and to where. A distinction is drawn between Irish companies and those that are owned by EU and non-EU investors. Section 5 considers briefly a new area where Ireland is developing a stronger international presence, namely, internationally traded services. In this sector, there is a growing presence of foreign and Irish companies that are exporting financial, software/computing and other professional services. While the sector is small compared with manufacturing, it is growing rapidly and is seen as a vital sector for generating high quality employment in Ireland. Finally, Section 6 looks at some of the issues that face Ireland in seeking to develop its present strategy. These include: strengthening the relationship between foreign and Irish companies, assessing increasing the technological base of Irish industry, diversifying the export markets of Irish companies, the potential role for FDI, and the increasing EU/WTO restrictions on state aids. The Section concludes with a discussion of some of the key issues in the Enterprise Strategy Group Report published in 2004.

2 HISTORICAL BACKGROUND

The main focus of analysis in this chapter is on the period since 1990, when Ireland began to move into its present, higher growth phase. This section presents some background on the period up to 1990, while later sections discuss the period since then in much more detail. This brief historical review (see also Chapter 5) is structured around the four phases to Ireland's trade and foreign investment strategy since Independence in 1922.

In the first phase up to 1932, Ireland continued to have a regional relationship with the UK rather similar to what existed prior to Independence. Goods moved freely between the two countries in both directions, with primarily agricultural output moving east and manufactured goods moving west. With the exchange rate fixed to the pound sterling, capital also moved freely between the two areas. Political Independence did not give much immediate economic benefit as growth was slow in the 1920s and the economy remained heavily dependent on agricultural exports to the UK market. In that decade, well over 50 per cent of employment was in the agricultural sector, over 85 per cent of exports were based on agricultural output, and over 90 per cent of exports went to the UK market.

Protectionism

In the early 1930s Ireland moved into the second phase, which was characterised by protectionism and economic nationalism. This change, which came with the election of a new government in 1932, was driven by several factors including: Ireland's perceived over dependence on the UK as a source of manufacturing imports and as a market for agricultural exports; the growth in worldwide protectionism following the Wall Street Crash in 1929; and a dispute with the UK over land annuities, which had been part of the 1922 Independence settlement. The policy change envisaged Ireland's becoming more self sufficient and this required the production of manufactured goods to replace those being imported. In introducing this policy, the politicians of the time were influenced by the famous 'infant industry doctrine', which argued in favour of protection from international trade as a means of helping the establishment of a new manufacturing sector.

Protectionism took the form of high tariffs being levied on all imports, and import quotas also being set for certain products; these ensured that Irish producers did not have to compete with imports on equal terms.

Economic nationalism (under the banner of self sufficiency) was manifest, both in the protection of Irish production from international competition, and in a ban being placed on investment by foreigners in Irish manufacturing. This restriction on investment from abroad further reduced the degree of competition on the Irish market for manufactured goods.

Several of the key arguments for protection disappeared relatively soon after it was introduced. For example, there was a reduction in global tariffs towards the end of the 1930s, the economic war with the UK over land annuities was sorted out in 1937, and the infant industry arguments were naturally time limited. However, the intervention of World War II and a fear that reducing tariffs would lead to a rapid increase in imports with consequent balance of payments problems, led to a retention of the tariffs into the mid 1960s. How should the success of policies during this second phase be ranked? By 1960 industry certainly had increased its share of employment (from 13 per cent to 23 per cent), with agriculture reducing to around 35 per cent. Dependence on agricultural based exports also fell (down to 65 per cent), as did dependence on the UK market (down to 75 per cent). Economic growth during the period averaged 2 per cent per annum.

Export Led Growth

The third phase began very slowly in the 1950s and evolved throughout the 1960s, with the key regime change being Ireland's entry into the European Community (EU)[5] in 1973.[6] This phase is usually referred to as the Export Led Growth and FDI Promotion phase. It comprised several key elements:

- A gradual shift to free trade in manufactured goods, with the phased reduction of the high tariffs to zero for countries within the European Community (EC) and to the EC's Common External Tariff Rate for countries outside;
- Identification of certain sectors as target sectors for foreign investment; specifically noted for development were electronics, pharmaceuticals and medical devices;
- Corporate tax relief for companies on the profits which they generated on export sales, with sales on the domestic market being subject to the standard rate of corporate tax;
- Financial supports, by way of capital grants on investment, to both Irish-owned or foreign-owned companies, which were producing manufactured goods for export;
- Financial assistance to Irish companies which were prepared to restructure in a major way to compete with imports following the introduction of free trade;
- Additional assistance for companies which were located in areas of the country in which rates of unemployment and emigration were high.

Key early landmarks in this strategy were the establishment of a Customs Free Industrial Zone established at Shannon Airport in 1947, the Industrial Development Authority (IDA) in 1949 and the Export Promotion Agency (CTT) in 1951. These institutions provided financial aid to Irish and foreign manufacturing companies that were engaged in export trade. Furthermore, and of more importance in financial terms, these export companies also benefited from the introduction of a holiday from taxation of corporate profits generated by export sales taxes from 1956. The introduction of these generous incentives coincided with the phased dismantling of the 1930s legislation that had prohibited foreign ownership of new manufacturing plants. The reduction in tariffs/quotas began with the Anglo-Irish Free Trade Area Agreement in 1966, which involved the bilateral phasing out of import quotas/tariffs and culminated in the full adjustment to EC tariffs in 1978. These reduced tariffs enhanced the attractiveness of Ireland as a base for foreign companies. For EC companies from higher cost countries, especially Germany, Ireland became a low cost production base within the EC. For non-EC companies, Ireland was an attractive investment option as an English speaking country within the EC that had a long tradition of welcoming foreign investors.

During this period, some important features of the Irish approach to policy were established. First, and in contrast to most other countries, policy was very consistent and evolved slowly and steadily. This had the effect of increasing the confidence of investors in Ireland, especially foreign investors. Second, all companies were eligible for the tax holiday on exports, and this incentive was attractive to high profit companies as it had the effect of enhancing their net profits. Third, the scale of financial aid given to companies was increasingly determined on the basis of the quality of the project from an Irish perspective – in particular the scale of grant given reflected the number and quality of jobs being generated by the project. Finally, the financial package for companies was implemented in a flexible way to match their needs and the needs of the location in Ireland where they were locating. This type of project based approach was unique to Ireland in the 1970s.[7]

By 1980 many of the key objectives of 1960s policy had been achieved. GDP grew on average by over 4 per cent per annum over the two decades. By 1980 agriculture's share of employment was down to 15 per cent, with industry's share just under 30 per cent. Exports expanded rapidly and export dependency fell in both geographic and sector terms – to 43 per cent on the UK market and to 27 per cent on agriculture based products. The policy of attracting foreign investment had led to over 30 per cent of manufacturing jobs being in foreign-owned companies, and many of these companies exported all of their output. There was one further change of great economic and political significance – the Irish population began to increase from 1961 onwards for the first time in a century and by 1979 it topped three million.

However, despite the obvious success of policy, there was general agreement that there were no grounds for complacency. Concerns were widespread that Irish companies were still selling most of their output on the domestic market and were encountering increased competition with imports from less developed countries. It was also recognised that some foreign-owned companies in the Irish high tech sectors were under pressure from increased competition in global markets and the constant flow of new products and processes, while in more traditional sectors, some of the foreign-owned companies were beginning to look to new and cheaper locations for production. From 1982, the government also had to change its export tax incentive, as its export bias was in breach of the Treaty of Rome. This change meant that the corporate tax rate had to be the same for all manufactured goods (independently of whether they were exports, imports or not traded at all) and this meant that for many companies the corporate tax rate would soon rise from 0 to 10 per cent. Such were the concerns of government at the end of the 1970s that they instituted a major review of industrial policy (the Telesis Report), which was published in 1982.[8] This report pointed to the vulnerability of large sections of the manufacturing sector to increased competition and to ways in which policy to support investment in manufacturing could be operated more efficiently. In effect, it laid the basis for the fourth phase of Ireland's development strategy.

Value-Added Growth

This fourth phase, building on what had been developed in Phase 3, has continued to evolve since the early 1980s. It can best be described as the Value-Added Growth phase, and central to its focus is the objective of increasing productivity in Ireland. It involves:

– Extending the range of target development sectors to include internationally traded services, which are seen to have high productivity potential;
– Promotion, using discretionary grant support, of investment in niche products which command high global prices;
– Promotion, by way of specific grants and tax relief, of more research and

168

development (R&D) intensive production, both by attracting foreign-owned, R&D intensive companies and by encouraging existing companies to expand the scale of their R&D activities;

– Financial supports to build up the capability of Irish companies to develop more sophisticated products and wider product markets, through labour training, technology transfer, etc.;

– Enhancing the operational environment for companies doing business in Ireland by improving infrastructure, reducing taxes, rationalisation of regulations, etc.

There have been several key landmark events in this fourth phase of strategy. The first, and arguably most important, has been the neutralising of sectoral biases in the corporate tax system; first by giving import substitutes the same low tax rates as exports (1982), and subsequently by moving, on a gradual basis, all businesses in Ireland to a low corporate tax rate of 12.5 per cent (2003). A second key landmark was the establishment of the Irish Financial Services Centre in 1987; it has created significant service sector employment and has raised very substantial tax revenue for the Irish Exchequer. A third event was Ireland's success in winning two crucial investment projects – Intel and Microsoft. Not only were these projects important in terms of direct employment and tax revenue, they also signalled to the electronics and software sectors worldwide that Ireland was an attractive investment base for this sector in the EU.[9] A consequence of this was that the electronics sector expanded hugely in terms of output, employment and exports.

In terms of policy, the Culliton Report in 1992 was a highly significant event; building on the Telesis recommendations, it recommended the refocusing of policy from direct aids to manufacturing in favour of using Exchequer funds to create a better operating environment for business, e.g. lower personal tax rates, greater domestic competition, and reduced charges for key services (electricity, phones, transport, etc.). In addition, it reconfigured the present pattern of policy and implementing agencies, creating separate agencies to support foreign investment (IDA Ireland) and Irish investment (Enterprise Ireland).[10] The focus given to Enterprise Ireland was to improve the innovative capacity of Irish companies by, for example, building their management and R&D capability and forging links between Irish companies, foreign companies and universities. As part of this process, Enterprise Ireland began to provide a component of aid in the form of equity participation rather than grants and to support the creation of venture capital companies in Ireland which would help to increase the equity base of small Irish companies.

The early and mid 1980s were very difficult years for Ireland and the expanding share of foreign companies in manufacturing sector employment reflected a very significant decline in employment in Irish companies. The share of employment in agricultural based activities continued to fall, reaching 9 per cent in 1990, at which time industrial employment had stabilised at 35 per cent of total employment. The rapid growth in electronics and pharmaceuticals contributed to the reduction in the dependence on agricultural based exports (from

37 to 15 per cent) and the UK market (from 43 to 34 per cent) over the decade. The decade ended with the commitment of significant EU structural funding for Ireland and this funding provided the support for further development of manufacturing and internationally traded services in the 1990s. The next three sections examine in more detail how these sectors have developed in the 1990s.

3 MANUFACTURING: EMPLOYMENT AND LABOUR PRODUCTIVITY [11]

Employment and Output

As noted in Section 2, for many decades employment creation has been the priority for industrial policy in Ireland. This objective stemmed from the combination of high unemployment and emigration and the perceived need to restructure the economy, primarily out of agriculture and the older manufacturing sectors and into the newer, higher value sectors. Table 7.3 shows that over the period 1991-2001 employment levels in Irish manufacturing industry grew by 27 per cent. Growth in employment levels in foreign companies accounted for over 67 per cent of the overall growth.

Table 7.3
Employment and Net Output in Irish Manufacturing Industry, 1991-2001

	Employment ('000s)			Net output (€ bn, 1995 prices)		
	1991	2001	% Change	1991	2001	% Change
Total	196	250	27	13.5	47.0	249
Irish	110	127	16	4.3	6.2	46
Foreign	86	123	42	9.2	40.8	342
EU	33	36	10	2.2	4.1	84
Non-EU	53	87	62	7.0	36.6	425
High Tech	36	74	104	3.0	13.5	346
Medium Tech	63	75	19	4.1	17.9	332
Low Tech	97	101	4	6.3	15.6	147

Source: CSO, *Census of Industrial Production,* Stationery Office, Dublin 1991 and 2001. Note: The data in this table relate to 2001, which is the latest year for which these data are available at this level of disaggregation. The data classification used to designate sectors as High/Medium/Low Tech is taken from OECD, 'European Innovation Scoreboard 2003' (OECD Innovation/SMEs Programme Technical Paper No: 4), OECD, Paris 2003.

While the growth in employment in Irish companies appears modest by comparison, it should be seen in the context of a very significant decline in employment in Irish manufacturing companies throughout the 1980s and the negligible growth in manufacturing in the EU countries during the 1990s. Non-EU companies (mainly US) account for 90 per cent of the growth in employment levels in foreign companies over the 1990s, and in 2001 these companies accounted for almost 35 per cent of total manufacturing employment in Ireland. Sectoral adjustment within manufacturing is evident in the shift in employment from low tech to high tech sectors. In 1991, high tech sectors accounted for only 18 per cent of total employment in manufacturing; employment doubled in these sectors over the decade, increasing this share to 30 per cent in 2001. While the share of low tech employment fell by 10 percentage points over the period, employment in the sector actually grew, albeit modestly.

The growth in real net output has been much higher than the growth observed in employment. Over the decade net output increased by nearly 250 per cent with foreign companies accounting for 88 per cent of this change; in 2001 their share of total net output was 87 per cent. Paralleling the growth in employment levels, non-EU companies accounted for over 95 per cent of net output growth observed in foreign companies. Net output figures also show that high tech sectors increased their share in total manufacturing over the period, from 22 per cent in 1991 to 29 per cent in 2001.

These aggregate figures indicate the extent of sectoral change and the important role that investment from outside the EU has played in reshaping the Irish manufacturing sector. Table 7.4 examines in more detail the extent of sectoral

Table 7.4

Significance of Foreign Companies in Irish Manufacturing Employment, 1991 and 2001

	Sector as % of total employment		Employment in foreign companies as % of sectoral employment	
	1991	2001	1991	2001
Food, beverages and tobacco	23	20	28	25
Textiles and leather	11	4	44	58
Wood and wood products	2	2	11	18
Paper and paper products	2	2	26	28
Printing and publishing	6	8	18	30
Chemicals	7	10	77	80
Rubber and plastics	4	4	54	40
Non-metallic minerals	5	4	18	17
Basic and fabricated metals	7	6	28	23
Machinery and equipment	6	6	57	47
Office machinery and computers	4	8	84	89
Electrical machinery	5	5	76	67
Radio, television and communication	2	5	84	86
Medical, precision and optical	5	8	92	87
Transport equipment	5	4	18	58
Other manufacturing industries	5	4	39	31
Total manufacturing	100	100	44	49

Source: As for Table 7.3.

Note: The data in this table relate to 2001, which is the latest year for which these data are available.

adjustment in employment at the two digit level. The two largest sectors in terms of employment in 1991 were Food, Beverages & Tobacco and Textiles & Leather. These key traditional sectors lost greatest employment share over the decade, giving way to the key sectors which had been promoted by policy throughout the 1970s and 1980s. These sectors are: Chemicals (including Pharmaceuticals); Office Machinery & Computers; Radio, Television & Communications; and Medical, Precision & Optical.

The second pair of columns in Table 7.4 shows that the relative importance of foreign companies varies widely across individual two digit manufacturing subsectors, varying between 11 and 92 per cent in 1991. Overall, foreign companies increased their share of total employment from 44 per cent in 1991 to 49 per cent in 2001.

In all of the key technology sectors, they accounted for over 75 per cent of employment and by 2001, the lowest share of foreign employment in these sectors was Chemicals at 80 per cent. The continuing high presence of foreign companies in the traditional sectors reflects both the longstanding presence of foreign companies in Ireland and significant recent investments in high value-added niche areas in these sectors.

Labour Productivity: 1991 to 1999
As the Irish economy has moved closer to full employment in the 1990s, there has been a shift of emphasis from employment towards labour productivity, where labour productivity is defined as the ratio of net output to numbers of employees. Increasing productivity is widely regarded as the key to sustaining competitiveness levels and raising living standards. Increases in productivity can occur through sectoral restructuring, e.g. as high productivity sectors expand; or through increases in productivity within existing plants, e.g. as changes within established plants make them more productive. Most studies examining productivity growth at plant level conclude that plant productivity performance is heterogeneous and the net productivity changes observed in aggregate data are marked by large increases in some plants and decreases in others within the same sector.

The first panel of Table 7.5 shows the growth in labour productivity and the sources of this growth at plant level for the period 1991-1999, distinguishing both Irish and foreign owned plants. Table 7.5 also identifies three potential sources of productivity growth: improved productivity of *continuing* plants, the *entry* of above average productivity plants, and the *exit* of below average productivity plants.

Between 1991 and 1999, overall labour productivity grew by 158 per cent, a combination of very high productivity growth in foreign plants (185 per cent) and much lower growth in Irish plants (37 per cent). In effect, foreign companies drove productivity growth in Irish manufacturing during this period. Analysis of the sources of this productivity growth indicates that for both foreign and Irish manufacturing, continuing plants made twice the contribution of new plants with above average productivity.

Table 7.5

Labour Productivity Growth and its Components

	Labour Productivity growth (%)	Continuing	Entry	Exit
1991-1999				
All	*158*	*69*	*29*	*-2*
Irish	37	71	32	3
Foreign	185	70	28	-2
1991-1995				
All	*40*	*101*	*0*	*1*
Irish	8	103	-7	-4
Foreign	46	101	0	1
1995-1999				
All	*84*	*65*	*29*	*-6*
Irish	27	57	38	-5
Foreign	95	68	24	-8

Source: Derived from tables in F. Ruane and A. Uğur, 'Labour Productivity and Foreign Direct Investment in Irish Manufacturing Industry: A Decomposition Analysis' (Discussion Paper Series No. 27), Institute for International Integration Studies, Trinity College, Dublin 2004.

Note: The decomposition sources sum to 100. A negative value for *Exit* indicates a positive contribution to productivity growth.

Published data show that the growth in output and particularly in employment in Irish manufacturing has been much higher in the second half of the 1990s than in the first half. Comparison of the productivity growth for the two periods in Table 7.5 reveals that overall labour productivity growth after 1995, when Ireland earned its reputation as a Celtic Tiger, was over twice that in the early 1990s. This productivity increase is no mean achievement given the rapid increase in employment during that latter period compared with virtually no change in employment during the earlier period. Particularly noteworthy is the much better productivity performance of Irish companies after 1995.

The contrast between the sources of productivity growth in the two periods is striking. In the early period, it came entirely from continuing plants, in fact entering plants actually lowered the average productivity of Irish plants. (This suggests that many of these new entrants were operating below minimum efficient scale). In the later period almost 40 per cent of productivity growth in Irish plants was due to new entrants, while for foreign plants it was under 25 per cent. During this same period, the exit of below average productivity plants made a small positive contribution to productivity growth of both Irish and foreign plants.

Labour Productivity: High and Low Technology Sectors

As outlined above, the industrial restructuring during the 1990s saw the high tech sectors becoming a more important part of the manufacturing sector. Table 7.6 shows the productivity growth patterns and the sources of this growth for the high tech and low tech subsectors. Somewhat surprisingly, perhaps, overall productivity growth was higher in low tech sectors than in the high tech sectors. This is mainly due to the exceptionally high productivity growth of foreign plants (180 per cent) in the low tech sectors, while Irish productivity was just 35 per cent. In the high tech sectors by comparison, Irish plants almost matched the productivity growth of their foreign counterparts. An important difference between the sectors is the contribution of the continuing plants and entrants. In the high tech sectors very high levels of productivity growth come from the entry of plants that are above average industry productivity, especially in Irish plants. This can be interpreted as affirming the success of policy emphasis in these sectors. On the other hand, in the low tech sectors the opposite trend is observed, with virtually all of the productivity growth coming from continuing plants.

Table 7.6
Labour Productivity Decompositions by OECD Sectoral Classification,
1991-1999

	Labour productivity growth	Continuing	Entry	Exit
High tech				
All	*98*	*60*	*38*	*-2*
Irish	89	34	66	0
Foreign	101	57	39	-4
Low tech				
All	*109*	*91*	*10*	*1*
Irish	35	91	14	5
Foreign	180	98	1	-1

Source: As for Table 7.5.
Note: The sectors in the high tech category are Pharmaceuticals, Office Machinery & Computers and Radio, Television & Communications. The sectors in the low tech category are Food, Beverages & Tobacco, Textiles, Wood & Wood Products, Paper & Paper Products and Printing & Publishing.

This analysis demonstrates that labour productivity growth in Irish-owned plants continues to lag behind that in foreign-owned plants but the relative gap between them narrowed during the period of rapid growth in the late 1990s. Over the period productivity growth in both Irish and foreign plants has mainly come from improvements within the continuing plants, especially in the recent period and in the low tech sectors. In the high tech sectors, and particularly in the second half of the 1990s, entering Irish plants have played an important role in improving aggregate productivity levels.[12]

4 MANUFACTURING: FOREIGN INVESTMENT AND INTERNATIONAL TRADE

Since the beginning of the 1960s, there has been a commitment in Ireland to expanding industrial exports, as it entered its export led growth phase of development. As noted in Section 2, this has involved two strands: attracting to Ireland foreign companies which would produce for export markets, and encouraging Irish companies to sell into export markets, and in particular, beyond the UK market.

Foreign Direct Investment
The type of foreign direct investment attracted into Irish manufacturing is typically referred to as *export platform foreign direct investment* (EPFDI). It is characterised by foreign companies that use the host country as a base from which they export their output. For this type of investment, the local market does not significantly influence the company's location decision, although in the Irish case the regional market (i.e. the EU) clearly does. The increasing global importance of EPFDI in the 1980s and 1990s reflects two distinct phenomena – the international fragmentation of production associated with globalisation/new technologies and the promotion of this type of investment by countries such as Ireland. International fragmentation is important for products that have a high market value-added relative to weight, such as pharmaceuticals and electronic products. For these products transportation costs are low relative to output values, and thus it is efficient to make production global in order to avail of the cost advantages offered by different locations. ·

The promotion of EPFDI makes a lot of sense for economies, like Ireland, that have small domestic markets and require access to international technology. Ireland has become recognised as a world leader in this area over the past thirty years, as it sought the type of FDI that would make sense in an island environment. As Table 7.7 illustrates, since 1996 Ireland has attracted an exceptional amount of US FDI going into Europe, relative to the size of the economy. This is especially marked in electronics in all years with the exception of 2001, the year in which global stock markets collapsed. The volatility in shares reflects primarily the timing of large projects, such as the creation of a new Intel Fab plant at Leixlip, rather than volatility in the numbers of foreign projects.

Table 7.7
The Irish share of US Manufacturing FDI coming into Europe, 1994-2003

	1994	1995	1996	1997	1998	1999	2000	2001	2002	2003
Total	8	3	11	14	12	8	13	6	24	16
Electronics	8	5	18	40	54	13	11	-2	93	36

Source: US Department of Commerce, Bureau of Economic Analysis, 'U.S. Direct Investment Abroad: Balance of Payments and Direct Investment Position Data', data available from http://www.bea.doc.gov/.
Note: The figure for 2001 is negative because in that year the *net flow* in electronics FDI was negative.

Trade Growth and Diversification
Ireland has been very successful in attracting EPFDI, when one considers that 50 per cent of manufacturing employment is now in foreign-owned companies.

However, it has been much less successful in developing successful Irish exporters; this is evident in the contrast between the patterns of export ratios of foreign and Irish sections of manufacturing for 1991 and 2001 presented in Table 7.8.

A striking feature of this table, and consistent with the small size of the Irish market, is that more than 50 per cent of all manufacturing companies are exporters. The fall in the share of Irish companies exporting by 10 percentage points over the decade is likely to be due to the number of new Irish companies that were created in the 1990s, as well as to the increased value of the fast growing Irish market for Irish producers. The vast majority of foreign companies (circa 90 per cent) are exporters, and the slightly higher ratios for non-EU companies is consistent with their continuing use of Ireland as a base for exporting into the EU. The minor reduction in the share of EU companies exporting may also reflect the buoyancy of the Irish economy over the decade.

Table 7.8

Percentage of Companies Exporting and Export Intensity in Irish Manufacturing Industry, 1991-2001

	Proportion of companies exporting		Export intensity	
	1991	2001	1991	2001
All	*63*	*54*	*72*	*87*
Irish	59	49	49	49
Foreign	90	88	88	94
EU	86	82	64	78
Non-EU	93	94	96	97

Source: As for Table 7.3.
Note: Export intensity is equivalent to exports/gross output.

The proportion of gross output of Irish manufacturing exported rose from 72 to 87 per cent over the decade. This increase is entirely driven by the higher export propensities of foreign companies based in Ireland, which rose from 88 to 94 per cent. The unchanged export propensity of Irish companies (49 per cent) can be interpreted in a number of ways. It may be further evidence that Irish companies have not yet broken into foreign markets, despite policies supporting this strategy going back four decades. It may also represent the growth of demand for the output of Irish companies by foreign companies in Ireland, as linkages based on outsourcing became more significant in the 1990s, especially in the electronics sector. The constant export propensity combined with the reduced share of companies that are exporting suggests that those companies now exporting sell a larger share of their output on the international market.

Recent research on Irish manufacturing exporters indicates that Irish companies still export mainly to the UK and, increasingly, to the EU.[13] Those Irish companies that export typically have higher productivity prior to exporting than their non-exporting counterparts; in effect, higher productivity companies are more likely to start exporting. Furthermore, the companies that export beyond the UK, e.g. to the EU or USA for example, have yet higher productivity per worker. This suggests that it may be the case that many Irish companies simply are not strong enough to enter the international market. This problem continues despite the fact that Ireland has had an agency promoting exporting in manufacturing for over 50 years.[14]

Table 7.9 demonstrates that, even in the 1990s when exports of Irish manufacturing companies increased by over 33 per cent, Irish companies did not succeed in reducing their dependency on the UK market.

The only significant change in that period was the switch in export shares of Irish companies between the USA and the rest of the world. Foreign-owned companies dominate the growth of manufacturing exports, with the result that Irish companies' share of exports fell from over 25 per cent to less than 10 per cent in the decade. EU-owned companies in Ireland more than doubled their export sales in the same period and increased the share of their exports sales going to the USA. Non-EU companies, primarily US companies, more than quintupled their export sales, and, reflecting plant and location specialisation patterns, their share of output going to the fast growing US market rose. This suggests that in the recent period of globalization, foreign companies based in Ireland are using Ireland as a global and not just an EU export platform.

Table 7.9
Manufactured Exports by Nationality of Ownership and Market Destination
Shares, 1991 and 2001

Nationality of ownership	Total exports (€bn)	Market shares			
		UK %	Other EU %	USA %	Other[1] %
Total 1991	*18.1*	*27*	*46*	*8*	*19*
Irish	4.7	42	28	8	22
EU	2.5	30	53	6	11
Non-EU	10.9	20	52	8	20
Total 2001	*67.0*	*17*	*48*	*17*	*18*
Irish	6.3	44	28	14	14
EU	6.1	18	44	31	7
Non-EU	54.6	14	51	15	20

Source: As for Table 7.3.
Note: Value figures are in 1995 prices, adjusted using producer price indices.
[1]Other is the residual for all countries not otherwise identified.

Ireland's strategy of promoting international investment has been exceptionally successful, particularly from the US. However, what has been less successful has been the strategy of getting Irish companies to export more of their output and to more diversified markets. We return to this issue in Section 6.

THE ECONOMY OF IRELAND

5 INTERNATIONALLY TRADED SERVICES

As noted in Section 2, the present phase of promoting value added growth has naturally led to investment in internationally traded services. This section looks at just how much growth there has been in these services over the past decade and what is happening to gross sales per employee[15] and exports in these sectors.

International statistics show that services globally have an increasing share of total output. This reflects changes in production patterns, as outsourcing by manufacturers means that some activities, which had previously been described as manufacturing, are now defined as services. It also reflects the change in global production patterns where fragmented production requires increased use of services (IT, logistics, insurance, legal services, etc.) in order to function successfully. Data on the service sector are limited in most countries and Ireland has only recently begun to collect these data systematically; consequently it is not possible to analyse trends using these data.

However, because Ireland has promoted international trade and investment in certain services, there are some data available on three important parts of this sector that have received state assistance. These subsectors are: international financial services (IFS), software/computing services (S/CS) and other services (primarily call centres, education services, general engineering, and construction). Table 7.10 shows how employment in these three subsectors has grown by over 300 per cent over the decade, compared with growth of 27 per cent in manufacturing employment in the same period. Employment in these sectors reached over 75,000 in 2001, which is equivalent to over 30 per cent of employment in manufacturing.

Table 7.10

Employment in International Services, 1991-2001

	All	Domestic	Foreign
Financial Services			
1991	1,187	323	864
2001	11,162	2,179	8,983
% change	840	575	940
Software/Computer			
1991	9,434	2,812	6,622
2001	38,515	16,137	22,378
% change	308	474	238
Other			
1991	7,172	5,331	2,381
2001	26,009	11,829	14,180
% change	237	122	496

Source: Forfás data bank, www.forfas.ie/ncc/framework html

The highest growth in employment was in the IFS sector, based in the Irish Financial Services Centre in Dublin; over 80 per cent of IFS employment is in foreign financial institutions. The S/CS sector is much larger and here Irish companies have expanded employment at a more rapid pace than foreign companies, albeit from a very low base.

This sector has been hugely successful from a policy point of view, benefiting from the reputation of the electronics sector in manufacturing and from government investment in education. The 'Other' sector has also grown rapidly, and mainly reflects Ireland's success in attracting 'call centres' of large US multinationals as well as increasing the number of foreign students studying in Ireland. The growth also reflects the internationalisation of some of the Irish engineering and construction companies.

Table 7.11
Sales in International Services (€bn current values), 1991-1999

	Software / Computer			Other		
	1991	1999	% change	1991	1999	% change
All	*1.9*	*13.5*	*610*	*0.6*	*1.8*	*200*
Irish	0.2	0.8	300	0.3	1.0	233
Foreign	1.7	12.7	647	0.3	0.8	166

Source: As for Table 7.10.
Note: There is no deflator for these sectors.

Data on the activities of the IFS sector are limited, and of course there are no data on their sales or exports.[16] The data available on the sales and exports of the S/CS and Other sectors (in nominal values) are presented in Tables 7.11 and 7.12. Foreign companies dominate the growth in S/SC sales, whereas in the Other sector, the growth has been more evenly spread across foreign and Irish companies. Comparing this table with Table 7.10 shows contrasting patterns in the crude indicator of labour productivity, namely, gross sales per employee. In S/CS, sales per employee of Irish companies actually fell while it more than doubled in foreign companies, while in the Other sector, sales per employee rose in Irish companies by 50 per cent, but fell by 50 per cent in foreign companies. These data have to be interpreted carefully both because they are a crude indicator of productivity and because of the heterogeneity of activities especially in the Other sector.

Exports from the S/CS rose much more quickly than exports from the Other sector over the decade. In both sectors, the export growth was dominated by the foreign companies, especially in the Other sector, where they now account for almost 70 per cent of exports. The growth in S/CS exports by Irish companies looks strong at 400 per cent, but they still account for only a tiny portion (4 per cent) of total exports from that sector. The data in Tables 7.11 and 7.12 allow the export intensity, i.e. exports as a percentage of total sales, of the S/CS sector to be examined and compared with that of manufacturing industry in Section 4. Overall export intensity increased from 79 per cent to 92 per cent over the period in the S/CS sector. This high ratio is mainly driven by the exports coming from foreign companies, which export 94 per cent of their sales, whereas exports only account for 62 per cent of sales in Irish companies in 1999. However a comparison of the export intensities in Irish companies in S/CS and manufacturing sectors show that Irish companies were able to increase their export intensity in the former from 50 per cent in 1991 to 62 per cent in 1999 whereas in the latter the ratio remained unchanged at 49 per cent over the 1990s. This shows that, although having a disadvantage in terms of the size of the sector, Irish companies in S/CS were more successful in increasing their exports in total output than in Irish companies in manufacturing industry.

Table 7.12
Exports of International Services, 1991-1999 (€bn current values)

	Software / Computer			Other		
	1991	1999	% change	1991	1999	% change
All	*1.5*	*12.4*	*726*	*0.2*	*0.7*	*250*
Irish	0.1	0.5	400	0.1	0.2	100
Foreign	1.4	11.9	750	0.1	0.5	400

Source: As for Table 7.10.
Note: There is no deflator available for these sectors.

6 FUTURE POLICY CHALLENGES

Dependence, Dualism and Linkages

One of the questions that naturally arises after four decades of promoting export platform development is whether Ireland could be seen as having become excessively dependent on EPFDI, and consequently whether this is becoming a high risk economic strategy. There is also a question of whether, being close to full employment, foreign enterprises may now be crowding out Irish enterprises. (This was never an issue prior to the late 1990s when levels of unemployment and emigration were high.) It is clear from Table 7.4, that Ireland has a significant number of sectors that are largely foreign-owned and Forfás, the industrial policy agency, has noted that these foreign companies have fewer linkages with the economy than equivalent Irish companies.[17] This suggests a kind of dualism that may undermine economic sustainability in the medium to long term. It may be expected that such dualism would be reflected in differences in the types of sectors in which the foreign and Irish companies operate, and, where they coexist in the same sector, that they are engaged in different activities. For example, do foreign and Irish companies in the same sector have similar export ratios, the same patterns of labour productivity, or the same patterns of wages? And regarding any such differences, do they persist or diminish over time?

Recent research has examined the question of dualism.[18] It found high levels of sectoral concentration in Irish and foreign companies, with the difference between them narrowing over the 1980s and 1990s. It also revealed that the export patterns of foreign and Irish companies are very similar across sectors; in other words, Irish companies are tending to be high exporters in the sectors where foreign companies are high exporters. In all sectors it was found that, the productivity of foreign companies was on average 60 per cent higher than that of Irish companies, and that these differences are not showing any sign of reducing.[19] Not surprisingly with such differences in labour productivity, average wages are also higher, but not to the same extent; they are typically 10 per cent higher in foreign than in Irish companies. However, in terms of dualism, it is noteworthy that this gap actually widened over the 1990s.

While Ireland has strongly encouraged supply linkages between Irish and foreign companies for almost two decades, there has been no policy to promote joint venture investments between Irish and foreign companies. In most countries which have pursued inward FDI strategies, such joint venture investments have been common, mostly driven by government insistence that there be some Irish involvement in large companies, especially when the domestic market is significant. In the Irish case, the domestic market is typically not significant, so the idea of a compulsory joint venture strategy would never have made sense and was, wisely, not pursued. However, the idea of voluntary joint venture investments is different and lack of support for their development may represent a lost opportunity. The absence of joint ventures certainly will have contributed to the dualism in the economy as well as reducing the likelihood of technology transfers and spillovers. In effect, after forty years of the present strategy Ireland's foreign enterprises are almost 100 per cent foreign-owned (i.e. with zero equity participation by domestic investors), which contributes to explaining the large productivity differences between foreign and Irish companies in Ireland. Given the continuum of investment arrangements now developing globally (including joint ventures, outsourcing contracts, licensing and joint sales partnerships) Ireland may be missing out strategically on a range of inter-company relationships that might have emerged from more interactive links between Irish and foreign companies. Arguably the present structure of having IDA Ireland and Enterprise Ireland as two separate agencies is an impediment to this development.

Research and Development

While there is some evidence of linkages in certain sectors, especially electronics, it is not evident that Ireland has gained as much from the presence of some of the world's top enterprises as it might. Part of the explanation for this is that the activities in high tech sectors are not necessarily high tech activities themselves; in other words, the parts of the production processes being undertaken in Ireland are not at the high value-added end of the spectrum. Concern about the low R&D content in Irish manufacturing grew over the late 1990s, as increases in the ratio of business expenditure on R&D to GNP were not sustained; they continue to hover around 1 per cent, which is approximately three quarters of the EU average, and just over half of the OECD average. This poor performance is at variance with the objectives of the Lisbon Strategy, one of whose targets is to increase this ratio to 3 per cent by 2010. Furthermore, in two key sectors, Electrical & Electronic Equipment and Pharmaceuticals, business expenditure on R&D as a percentage of output is less than 15 and 6 per cent respectively of the levels pertaining in the lead country in the OECD.[20] Towards the end of the 1990s, the government followed the European example of undertaking a technology foresight exercise, to examine which technologies were likely to be crucial for Ireland in the future and how the country might position itself to engage more with these. This exercise concluded that biotechnology (Biotech) and information and communications technology (ICT) were likely to be key drivers of economic growth and that Ireland needed to develop a world class research capability in selected niches of these two enabling technologies.

This conclusion led to the establishment of Science Foundation Ireland (SFI) in 2003 as a statutory body supporting the development of strategic science and technological expertise (see also Chapter 11). Where previously support for enhancing the quality of Irish manufacturing had been at the level of the individual company, primarily through grant support, SFI's role is to build the infrastructure required to strengthen Ireland's scientific base in Biotech and ICT. It has begun to do so by providing funds for basic research in Irish universities and institutes. It has also established major Centres for Science, Engineering and Technology (CSETs), which directly link academic researchers to industry partners in Ireland in high level (rather than applied) research. The scale of this endeavour is much greater than any previous policies supporting industry/academic links and it is intended to ensure that Ireland develops an indigenous research base that can prosper in a knowledge based global environment. This strategy will make Ireland a more attractive base for foreign companies and may help Ireland meet the targets of the Kyoto protocol, since many of the high tech industries are less energy intensive than traditional manufacturing. It will also, if successful, increase productivity within Irish companies and hence reduce Ireland's dependence on foreign companies for productivity growth. The impact of these endeavours will be more long than short term but they are likely to be reflected in the share of national expenditure on research and development rising towards the Lisbon Strategy's target.

Potential for Outward FDI

Another area where Ireland has potential to develop strategy is in the promotion of investment abroad by Irish-owned companies. Such investment now makes sense for three reasons. First, Ireland is no longer competitive as a base for those parts of the production process that use relatively unskilled labour; consequently, sourcing through subsidiaries in lower cost countries would make sense. Second, there are Irish producers who will need increasing amounts of workers if they are to expand production and, as Ireland is now close to full employment and has skill shortages in certain areas, it could make sense for these companies to expand outside rather than inside Ireland. Third, such outward investment would help counterbalance the strong presence of foreign-owned companies in Ireland. There are several Irish companies at this point with foreign subsidiaries and branches, but these have been developed outside of government policy for the most part. As yet, there has been little discussion of the potential role, if any, for the state in supporting this development, perhaps because it gives rise to the historically and politically unpalatable idea of 'exporting jobs'. However, as production processes and structures become more complex and fragmented, the need to develop a strategy in this area gains importance. The justification for government having a role in this area derives from the fact that market information costs, associated with developing these opportunities, are high, uncertain and mostly 'sunk'.

Restrictions on State Aids

The potential for government intervention in internationally traded sectors is increasingly restricted by both EU and WTO rules, which are committed to ensuring a more level playing field in both European and global markets. Consequently, any assistance given to private sector companies, as Ireland has done for decades, is now subject to increasing scrutiny in Brussels, lest it be seen as undermining the EU's internal market.

Ireland continues to argue in the EU that its low corporate tax rate does not infringe the spirit of internal competition. However, Ireland will have to argue its case more strongly in the fact of increasing opposition from the larger EU countries, especially Germany. Increasing pressure for change in Europe is growing because several of the new EU entrants are following a corporate tax strategy similar to Ireland's.

In recent years, the areas where support can be granted have narrowed considerably and R&D is one area where assistance is allowable because of the EU wide commitment in the Lisbon Strategy of strengthening Europe's innovating capacity. Thus it is not surprising that the Irish government has become more keen on supporting R&D in recent years and that in 2003 it introduced tax credits for R&D for the first time. These credits are intended both to encourage indigenous companies to invest and foreign companies to locate their R&D functions in Ireland. One of the anomalies of the low corporate tax rate is that it makes Ireland a relatively unfavourable environment for R&D, because international companies prefer to undertake R&D investment in high tax companies where the value of the tax write off is larger.

The climate of controlling state aids has had two further effects. First, because aids can no longer be used to compensate companies trading internationally for domestic inefficiencies, it has led to increased focus on competition in the non-internationally traded parts of the economy (see Chapter 3 and 8). Second, it has reopened the regional focus of Irish industrial policy, as investments in the less developed Border-Midland-West region are eligible for grants and grant rates that cannot be given in the more developed South & East region.

New Policy Perspective: Enterprise Strategy Group Report

The intention of the Culliton Report (see earlier) was that enterprise strategy in Ireland would continue to strengthen with the creation of a specific policy agency for industrial development, Forfás. Under the auspices of Forfás, several permanent consulate groups were established in the late 1990s: the expert skills group, to coordinate the needs of industry with developments in education; the Science, Technology and Innovation (STI) committee, to ensure that the STI needs of the knowledge economy were met; and the National Competitiveness Council (NCC), to monitor all the elements of Ireland's competitiveness position in global terms. Despite the existence of Forfás and these three consultative groups, the government considered that it was necessary, in the context of changed global circumstances, to establish the Enterprise Strategy Group (ESG) in July 2003 to advise on Ireland's strategic needs in this area.[21]

While the report claims to take a new strategic direction, its key message, namely that indigenous industry has yet to reach a sustainable development path, is an old message. It was clearly stated (albeit in different language) in the Telesis Report (see earlier) and remains relevant despite a series of policies that have been implemented over the years to promote the development of Irish small and medium sized enterprises (SMEs). In effect, large numbers of Irish SMEs are not likely to survive as globalisation continues, unless they develop higher value-added products at competitive prices. This requires increasing productivity and diversifying exports as discussed in Sections 3 and 4.

Enhancing Productivity
Regarding productivity, the ESG report emphasises the need to increase R&D and innovation within business and for state support for building a science and technology (S&T) infrastructure to support this. The difficulty is that R&D expenditure is essentially a sunk cost for an SME, in the sense that, were the investment not to succeed, the expenditure on it must be totally written off. Thus the SME faces a deterrent in investing in R&D. This means that it is efficient for government to provide an R&D incentive, as long as it can be targeted, and that certain types of R&D expenditure should be eligible for grant support. Regarding the S&T environment, further sustained investment in research expertise in colleges and institutes is needed to take account of the historical under investment. To complete the policy, it is proposed that links between businesses and colleges should be further strengthened.

With regard to innovation, the recommendation is that geographic based innovation networks should be established in Ireland. This follows an approach adopted in Denmark, and currently being considered in countries such as the UK, New Zealand, Canada and the USA. The underlying argument is that natural information failures can be overcome by enterprises learning from each other through networking. It is argued that the government has a role in establishing these networks.[22] What seems to be new on this topic, compared with earlier documents, is that Ireland would be trying to follow a model that appears to be working successfully elsewhere.

Enhancing Export Performances

In the report, the narrow base of Ireland's export market is attributed to the producer rather than consumer focus of indigenous entrepreneurs. The ESG report usefully identifies some additional niche markets suited to Ireland, such as education and bloodstock services, and manufacturing of ethical pharmaceuticals and food ingredients. Regarding a more consumer focus, it recommends joint public private funding of marketing executives to help connect SMEs with international consumer markets.

Not surprisingly the report notes the importance of physical infrastructure and education to sustained development. It recommends greater emphasis in anticipating infrastructure needs, in order to avoid bottlenecks. Sensibly, it does not propose infrastructure driven development – an error made in so many developing countries and in less developed areas in Europe. Its analysis of education is somewhat disappointing – lacking the long term vision of what globalisation might mean for the Irish educational system, and making proposals that seem at best superficial, e.g. teaching entrepreneurship at second level. It does, however, connect the crucial importance of education to Ireland's winning foreign investment projects, which are seen as vital for future growth.

As with earlier reports, much of the analysis relates to policy implementation rather than formulation. The need to develop foreign markets and R&D within enterprises, and the connections between foreign and indigenous enterprises, raise questions as to whether the Culliton recommendations for the structure of agencies were correct. The ESG report suggests increased cooperation between the agencies as a solution, but does not make clear why the present structure, which was designed following Culliton to achieve this, has not worked in practice and why the new proposal will be better. Some scepticism might also be sensible regarding the recommendation that there should be twice yearly discussions of enterprise strategy by the Cabinet. The real benefits of such discussions are not immediately obvious given the developed institutional structure currently in place.

Ireland's recent economic success owes much to the performance of the internationally traded enterprises in manufacturing and services, and unquestionably policy has contributed to this success. However, the success patterns of recent years cannot be presumed to continue as the global environment in which these sectors operate is constantly changing. Of immediate relevance to Ireland is the increased competition that will be generated in the market for FDI projects by the ten new entrants into the EU in 2004, and the phenomenal success of China in competing on global markets. Ireland cannot change the external environment, what it must concentrate on, is ensuring that enterprises in internally traded sectors continue to increase their productivity and hence remain competitive.

Endnotes

1   For a review see J. Bhagawati, 'Export-promoting Trade Strategies: Issues and Evidence', *The World Bank Research Observer,* Oxford 1988, and A. Krueger, 'Trade Policy and Economic Development: How We Learn', *American Economic Review,* Spring 1997.

2   See F. Barry, and J. Bradley, 'FDI and Trade: the Irish Host-Country Experience', *Economic Journal,* 1997, pp. 1798-1811; A. Gray (editor), *International Perspectives on the Irish Economy,* Indecon, Dublin 1998, and F. Barry (editor), *Understanding Ireland's Economic Growth,* Macmillan, London 1999.

3   The EU Commission has estimated that over 50 per cent of total EU trade is now intra-EU trade. There is no corresponding figure available for intra-US trade which would allow one to complete the comparison.

4   Annual averages over five year periods (six years in the case of 1995-2000) are used in order to take account of the large inter-year variations in the flows.

5   The Treaty on European Union was signed in Maastricht on 7 February 1992 and entered into force on 1 November 1993; this was the beginning of the European Union (EU), see www.eu.int. From now on the EC etc will be referred to as the EU in all instances.

6   For an interesting overview of the first three phases by a policy insider, see T. Whitaker, *Interests,* Institute of Public Administration, Dublin 1983, Chapter 3.

7   For an overview of the third and fourth pages, see A. Murphy, and F. Ruane, 'Foreign Direct Investment in Ireland: An Updated Assessment', *Central Bank of Ireland Annual Report,* Dublin 2004.

8   For a discussion of the implications of the Telesis Report, see K. Kennedy, F. Ruane and P. White, 'Symposium on Industrial Policy in Ireland', *Journal of the Statistical and Social Inquiry Society of Ireland,* 1982-3, pp. 33-51.and S. Nolan, 'The Telesis Report – A Review Essay', *Economic and Social Review,* Dublin 1983, pp. 281-289.

9   See the paper by P. Krugman, in Gray, *op cit.*

10   Originally the two agencies were IDA Ireland and Forbairt. The latter was built by combining the domestic divisions of IDA with an agency called Eolas, which had been responsible for supporting industrial R&D. In the late 1990s Forbairt merged with An Bord Tráctála, which had been responsible for promoting exports by domestic companies to form Enterprise Ireland. IDA Ireland and Enterprise Ireland are often referred to as the development agencies.

11   Because of transfer pricing issues related to FDI companies, it is common with Irish data to use employment rather than net output to measure the relative importance of the FDI sector.

12   Given the importance of foreign plants in these sectors, this could be due to spillover effects arising from the activities of foreign companies, which could have an effect on the productivity levels of domestic companies.

13   See F. Ruane and J. Sutherland, 'Exporting and Enterprise Performance: Exploration of Further Issues using Irish Manufacturing Data' (Discussion Paper No. 32), Institute for International Integration Studies, Trinity College, Dublin 2004.

14   Ireland has had an export promotion agency since 1951, which has operated under three different titles: CTT, ABT and, most recently, it has been part of Enterprise Ireland.

15   The concept of sales per unit of labour is the only indicator available relating output to labour in the services sector. Ideally profit per employee would be used, which is closer to the labour productivity measure in manufacturing (value-added per employee). Unfortunately such a measure is not available.

16   There has been some analysis undertaken in recent times as data have become available. See P. Lane, G. Milesi-Ferretti, 'International Investment Patterns' (Discussion Paper No. 24), Institute for International Integration Studies, Trinity College, Dublin 2004.

17   The term linkage is used to define the process of inter-company relationships in production – they may be forward linkages (the foreign company's output is an input to another domestic company) or backward (the foreign companies buys inputs from a domestic company).

18   See F. Ruane and A. Uğur, 'Export Platform FDI and Dualistic Development' (Discussion Paper No. 28), Institute for International Integration Studies, Trinity College, Dublin 2004.

19 These differences in part reflect the effect of transfer pricing, whereby the accounts of international companies report maximum value-added in the Irish production stage in order to maximise the value of the low Irish corporate tax rate.

20 See Forfás, *Business Expenditure on Research and Development (BERD)*, Forfás, Dublin 2001, Table 2.4, available on the Forfás website at: www.forfas.ie/.

21 This was reported in July 2004 with the publication of: Forfás, *Ahead of the Curve*, Enterprise Strategy Group, Dublin 2004, available on the Forfás website at www.forfas.ie/.

22 The details are set out in a companion document: Forfás, *Innovation Networks,* The National Policy and Advisory Board for Enterprise, Trade, Science, Technology and Innovation, Dublin 2004, available on the Forfás website: www.forfas.ie/

CHAPTER 8

Competition Policy, Regulation and Non-Internationally Traded Services

Francis O'Toole*

1 INTRODUCTION

There is growing awareness of the increased importance of microeconomic policymaking within Ireland. This is partly because of the recognition that the scope for an activist approach to macroeconomic policy has been reduced by the increased role of the EU in monetary and fiscal policies (e.g. the adoption of a single currency and the Growth and Stability Pact). However, it is also the case that there has been an increased realisation that microeconomic policy decisions can have significant macroeconomic effects on the Irish economy. For example, positions adopted by the Competition Authority and details of corporation tax policy can impact significantly upon both the structure of the economy and its evolution. The Competition Authority's very likely negative stance towards any proposed merger of AIB and Bank of Ireland, the two largest banking entities in the state, provides a specific example of the former, while the relatively low corporation tax rate imposed on the Irish manufacturing sector in recent decades provides a specific example of the latter.

This Chapter focuses attention on two related policy issues: (i) the importance of competition policy and regulation, with the consideration of regulation being restricted to the relatively narrow context of economic markets in which issues of market power arise (e.g. monopolies), as opposed to any broader context, for example, equal rights, or minimum wage, legislation; and (ii) the importance of the non-internationally traded services sector of the economy. The importance of competition policy and regulation is felt throughout all sectors of the economy. Within the agriculture, forestry and fishing sector, for example, the Competition Authority (Authority) have been involved in recent court proceedings in order to facilitate the importation of grain and have also in the past restricted Coillte's (the Irish forestry company) ability to vertically integrate, via a proposed acquisition, within the forestry industry. Within the manufacturing sector, Microsoft, one of the larger companies based in Ireland, appears to be in never ending legal conflicts with international competition policy authorities. However, this Chapter highlights the particular importance of competition policy within the services sector, and, in particular, in the non-internationally traded services sector of the Irish economy, as may be witnessed by the Authority's ongoing investigations or studies into many providers of professional services (e.g. solicitors and barristers) and various insurance and banking markets (e.g. services provided to current account holders and to small companies).[1]

Products encompass both goods and services. While economic goods are characterised as providing utility (i.e. happiness or satisfaction) to the consumer, as well as being transferable (between consumers) and storable (by consumers), services are characterised by their non-transferable and non-storable nature. In particular, the consumption of services occurs simultaneously with their production; the service provided by a hair stylist provides an obvious example. A policy distinction is sometimes made between internationally traded services and non-internationally traded services, as significant levels of international trade may appear to negate, to at least some extent, the need for an activist approach to competition policy or regulation. Financial services and tourism provide two important examples of internationally traded services, e.g. the Irish Financial Services Centre (IFSC), while the services provided by wholesalers and retailers, as well as the advice and other services provided by doctors, hair stylists, dentists, pharmacists, solicitors, bankers, lecturers, etc. to consumers in Ireland constitute, in general, non-internationally traded services. While the process of globalisation implies that some non-internationally traded services may become internationally traded over time, e.g. internet or mail order pharmacy, the increased ability of Irish students to study abroad or the purchasing of health services abroad by, or for, Irish clients, it is also essential to note that some aspects of what may appear to be internationally traded services may be non-internationally traded, e.g. certain banking services and short holiday breaks within Ireland. More generally, it is also important to note a distinction between exports and imports in this regard. Irish exporters may be forced by the presence of international competitors to be competitive in foreign markets, but it is the reality, or at least the credible threat, of a substantial level of imports from abroad that may force Irish based firms to be competitive in Irish markets. In summary, it is not the reality of international trade in itself, but a substantial level of imports that may negate to some extent the need for an activist competition policy in Ireland. It is also important to note the dependence of the internationally traded sectors on the non-internationally-traded services sector; for example, although tourism is to some extent an internationally traded service, its success or otherwise is highly influenced by the performance of the non-internationally traded services sector (e.g. hotels and restaurants). More generally, Irish consumers depend on wholesalers (i.e. distributors) and retailers for access to almost all internationally traded products, e.g. petroleum products.

189

Particularly within the non-internationally traded services sector, there has been an additional distinction drawn between services provided by the private sector, often referred to as market services, and services provided by the public sector, often referred to as non-market services. Retailing provides an example of the former, while the provision of health and education services provide standard examples of the latter (see Chapters 10 and 11). However, the increasing importance of private health insurance, various examples of private education services, as well as the increased usage of various forms of contracting out by the public sector (e.g. administration of the National Car Test (NCT), operation of toll bridges or, more generally, public private partnerships (PPPs) in Ireland) has blurred this distinction. In addition, some of these so called non-market services have become at least somewhat internationally traded, e.g. public health patients being treated abroad.

The contents of this Chapter have links with much of the rest of the material in this book. Non-internationally traded services should be considered in the context of the material on health and education and against the backdrop of the sectoral material on manufacturing, internationally traded services and the food industry. In addition, at a policy framework level, competition policy and regulation should be considered in the context of the material on policy objectives and options for the government of a small regional economy, while specific examples of the application of competition policy and regulation can have significant effects with respect to employment, unemployment and even economic growth and distribution. The recent, and on going, transformation of the Irish telecommunications sector provides an example of the latter point.

Section 2 provides an introduction to, and overview of, the services, and in particular, the non-internationally traded services, sector of the Irish economy. Section 3 reviews the economic principles that should underlie competition policy and provides a brief overview of EU and Irish competition law, while Section 4 addresses the specific issue of the regulation of natural monopoly, at both a theoretical and policy level. Section 5 provides some salient examples of the application of competition and regulatory policy in Ireland, particularly in the non-internationally traded services sector, and attempts to place many of these examples in a more appropriate broader political economy context. Section 6, by way of conclusion, considers some of the ongoing and emerging competition and regulatory policy debates.

2 THE SERVICES SECTOR

As previously indicated economic services are characterised by their non-tradable (between consumers) and non-storable (by consumers) nature. From an economic perspective, however, the importance of services, as opposed to goods, should not be underestimated.

190

Value-Added and Employment

Table 8.1 highlights the importance of the services sector to the economy in terms of the proportional value of total output produced within Ireland, while Table 8.2 focuses attention on the specific importance of the services sector for employment within Ireland. In terms of the total value of output produced in the economy, the importance of the services sector has remained fairly constant since 1991 at approximately 55 per cent, with reduced activity, in a relative sense, in the agriculture, forestry and fishing sector (down by over 5 percentage points to a little over 3 per cent) being offset by increased activity in the industrial and building sector (up by almost 6 percentage points to 41 per cent). In absolute terms and at current prices, the services sector accounted for approximately €64 billion of the total gross value of Irish output at factor cost in 2002, up from approximately €19 billion in 1991.

Table 8.1

Gross Value Added at Factor Cost by Sector of Origin (per cent)

	1991	2002[1]
Agriculture, forestry and fishing	8.5	3.3
Industry (including building)	35.2	41.1
Services	56.3	55.5

Source: CSO, *National Income and Expenditure*, Stationery Office, Dublin, various years.
[1]Preliminary.

In terms of total employment, the relative importance of the industrial and building sector has remained fairly constant since 1991 at approximately 27 per cent, with the reduced role of the agriculture, forestry and fishing sector (down by over 7 percentage points to 6.5 per cent) being more than offset by the increased importance of the services sector (up by over 8 percentage points to over 66 per cent). In absolute terms, the numbers employed in the services sector have increased from approximately 675,000 in 1991 to almost 1.25 million by 2004.

Table 8.2

Persons at Work in the Main Branches of Economic Activity (per cent)

	1991	2004
Agriculture, forestry and fishing	13.8	6.5
Industry (including building)	28.1	27.2
Services	58.1	66.2

Source: CSO, *Labour Force Survey*, Stationery Office, Dublin, various years.

In summary, the declining relative importance of the agricultural sector in terms of the value of economic output produced has been more than offset by the industrial and building sector, while the declining relative importance of the agricultural sector in terms of employment has been more than offset by the services sector.

Of the total of almost 1.25 million employed within the services sector in Ireland, the most important services subsectors (in terms of employment) are education and health (294,700), wholesale and retail trade (263,400), financial and other business services (235,700), hotels and restaurants (117,200) and transport, storage and communication (114,400). Table 8.3 attempts to facilitate readers who may wish to distinguish between the public services sector and the private services sector, with approximately 325,000 or 25 per cent of the services workforce being employed in the former.

Table 8.3

Public Sector Employment 2004 (000s)[1]

Public service	*279,641*
Civil service	37,243
Guards	12,688
Defence	11,600
Education	76,989
Non-commercial state-sponsored bodies	11,476
Health services	95,800
Local authorities	33,845
Commercial state-sponsored bodies	*44,989*
Public sector	*324,630*

Source: Department of Finance.
[1]Estimates.

In general, the output of the public sector is not priced, particularly if general taxation and rationing mechanisms (e.g. hospital beds in A&E units) are ignored, and is often referred to as non-market services, while the output of the private sector, which is priced, is often referred to as market services. The boundaries of this overly neat distinction are increasingly blurred by service charges (e.g. bin charges by public bodies) and by increased contracting out by the public sector (e.g. public health services being provided by private health providers or abroad). As such, distinctions between the public and private sectors are probably becoming somewhat less important. However, the issue of non-marketed, non-priced and non-measured services should also be considered. For example, housework and childcare that takes place outside the domain of the standard market place (either formally/legally or informally/illegally, e.g. within partnerships or within the so called shadow economy) contributes greatly to the well being of society and suggests that the contribution of services to the Irish economy are being significantly underreported. Indeed, some of the measured increases in output and employment in recent years in Ireland is accounted for by many of these services becoming increasingly marketed, e.g. the location of childcare and care, more generally, has to some extent moved from within the (in general, non-priced) household to (priced) crèches and private nursing homes.

Role

Historically, the three standard sectors of the economy, agriculture, industry and services, have been regarded, and treated, very differently. The agricultural and industrial sectors were perceived of as producing something tangible, being productive and hence important, while the output of the services sector was seen as being somewhat frivolous, non-productive and hence relatively unimportant. While it is no longer particularly fashionable to distinguish between the intrinsic values of the outputs of the three sectors, the industrial sector is still often viewed as being particularly dynamic (e.g. the pharmaceutical or chemical subsectors), while the services sector is still sometimes viewed as being somewhat of a burden in Ireland, particularly in the context of a discussion of the relative merits of imports and exports. From an international trade perspective (see, for example, Table 8.4), the industrial sector is seen as 'contributing' very significantly to a very large merchandise surplus (with over 95 per cent of the value of merchandise exports being accounted for by industrial, as opposed to agricultural, products), while the services sector is seen as being responsible for a significant trading deficit.

Table 8.4
Balance of International Payments Current Account Balances (€m) 2002

	Exports	Imports	Surplus (Deficit)
Merchandise	91,236	54,222	37,014
Services	29,922	42,792	(12,871)

Source: CSO, *Balance of International Payments*, Stationery Office, Dublin 2003.

In Ireland, from the 1960s until very recently, this somewhat anti-services perspective, and, in particular, the importance attached to exports, manifested itself in differential tax treatment. For example, the manufacturing sector (as well as the internationally traded services sector) benefited from a 10 per cent corporation tax rate, while the non-internationally traded services sector was taxed at rates of well over 30 per cent for many of these years. The process of increasing European integration has, however, forced Irish policymakers to impose a uniform tax rate (currently set at 12.5 per cent) on both sectors. Grant aid reinforced this discrimination against the services sector with the availability of state aid often being linked to the recipient's likely ability to generate a significant growth in sales, i.e. in practice, implying the need for foreign sales, although it should be noted that state aid was also often granted against the backdrop of attempting to attract foreign investment to Ireland. However, it has become increasingly clear to many policymakers that the role of the non-internationally traded sector, and, in particular, the non-internationally traded services sector, is vital for the performance of the economy, as well as for the performance of the internationally traded sector itself. Irish based producers in the internationally traded sector depend on the Irish non-internationally traded services sector for many of their inputs, e.g. energy and distribution/transport services; inefficiencies in the non-internationally traded services sector create inefficiencies in the internationally traded sector. Given that the non-internationally traded sector is directly and heavily influenced by the decisions of Irish policymakers, arguably the non-internationally traded sector is even more important from a policy perspective. In addition, producers in the non-internationally traded sector may well be operating in less than competitive environments where inefficiencies can be tolerated. As such, domestic policymaking should be particularly focused in the non-internationally traded sector of the economy, where decisions can have significant effects.

A recent report by PricewaterhouseCoopers (PwC) for Forfás, which examined recent trends in Irish inflation, provides an illustrative example of the importance and influence of the non-internationally-traded services sector.[2] Within the eurozone area, which consists of 12 countries, Ireland was found to have the seventh highest index of prices for consumer goods/services in 1995 but the second highest, just behind Finland, by 2002. For the three year period up to the end of January 2003, annualised inflation rates for the internationally traded, and non-internationally traded, sectors were 3 per cent and 7 per cent, respectively. For the twelve month period to the end of January 2003, the following services were found to be major contributors to Irish inflation, i.e. their inflation rates were significantly above the average inflation rate: financial services; water, refuse and related services; pubs & restaurants; catering services; insurance (in particular, health insurance); third, second and primary level education; cultural services (in particular, television services) and hospital services.

Notwithstanding the merits or otherwise of distinctions drawn between the various sectors of the economy, it is clear that the role of domestic policymaking is extremely important. In particular, the role of competition and regulatory policy in the non-internationally traded sector of the economy as well as in parts of the internationally traded sector deserves special consideration.

3 MARKET STRUCTURE AND COMPETITION POLICY

Given the particular importance of competition policy and regulation for the non-internationally traded services sector of the economy, it is essential to have a consistent policy framework in place for competition and regulation. The most important economic concept in this policy area is market power and, in particular, significant market power. The presence of significant market power indicates the ability to raise prices substantially above cost. In contrast, the absence of significant market power indicates the presence of a competitive market. As such, the role of a suitably designed competition policy should be to discourage the conditions that give rise to the presence of significant market power. Where such conditions are inevitable, the role of a suitably designed regulatory policy should be to simulate, to the greatest extent possible, the outcomes associated with a competitive market.

Perfect Competition v. Monopoly v. Contestable Markets

Perfectly competitive markets have the important economic characteristic of being allocatively efficient, as firms are forced by the pursuit of their own self interests to price at marginal cost, i.e. $P = MC$. This equality, between price and marginal cost, is generally regarded as being highly desirable by economists, as price represents the economic value placed by society on the marginal or last unit of the product produced, while marginal cost represents the economic cost to society of producing that marginal unit. In contrast, inequality, through either price being greater or less than marginal cost, would signify inefficiency, as there would exist unexploited gains from trade. Indeed, the primary disadvantage of a (profit maximising) monopoly is that the monopolist produces a level of output at which price is greater than marginal cost (i.e. $P > MC$), i.e. the monopolist produces too little when viewed from society's perspective.

Perfectly competitive markets are also characterised as being productively efficient, as, in the long run, no firm could survive without producing at the lowest point on its average cost curve. In comparison, monopolists tend to produce at a higher average cost, as they respond to the incentive to restrict output below the technically most efficient level in order to raise price. In addition, it is often claimed that the monopolist's costs are higher than the equivalent competitive firm's costs, simply because the monopolist can afford to be at least somewhat inefficient; the 'technical' term used is X-inefficiency.[3] Finally, it is claimed that the monopolist's excess (i.e. above normal) profits do not simply represent a simple transfer from consumer (surplus) to producer (surplus), as profit seeking (or, rent seeking, as it is generally referred to as) dissipates these profits over time. In particular, prior to the creation of the monopoly (e.g. markets for various mobile telephony or broadcasting services), firms will involve themselves in socially unproductive activities in order to increase their chances of being the chosen monopolist, while once the monopoly is created, the incumbent will involve itself in unproductive activities, when viewed from society's perspective, in order to sustain its monopoly position.[4]

Although the state is seldom given a stark choice between choosing a perfectly competitive structure or a monopolistic structure for a particular market, the state can attempt to facilitate the conditions or characteristics that encourage the outcomes associated with perfectly competitive markets, i.e. the state can encourage the competitive process. The competitive process, although difficult to define precisely, is facilitated by the presence of effective competition and/or potential competition. Effective competition focuses particular attention on a number of issues including the degree of interbrand, and intrabrand, competition between firms within a particular market. Inter-brand competition refers to competition between sellers of different brands within a given market (e.g. different brands of beer), while intrabrand competition refers to competition between sellers of the same brand (e.g. Guinness stout). Potential competition focuses particular attention on the ability of potential entrants to dissuade incumbent firms from attempting to take too much advantage of, or abusing, their market position. In the extreme case, of perfectly contestable markets, potential competition can simulate perfectly the process of perfect competition, even in a monopoly. The incumbent firm, a monopolist, is forced to price at marginal cost, as any divergence between marginal cost and price would allow an equally efficient entrant to invoke a hit and run strategy, i.e. enter with a price below the incumbent's price but above marginal cost and exit if/when the incumbent reduces its price to marginal cost. Perfectly contestable markets are, however, in practice almost as nebulous as perfectly competitive markets, as their presence requires two extreme assumptions. First, the market must be characterised by the complete absence of sunk costs, i.e. the entrant must not have to incur any non-recoverable fixed costs in order to enter the market. It is sometimes claimed that competing on a specific airline route provides such an example, as the entrant's plane and other investments can be withdrawn and used elsewhere at little additional cost. In contrast, it would be difficult for an entrant to withdraw, without incurring substantial sunk costs, after attempting to compete with respect to the provision of a rail network. Second, the entrant must be able to enter and trade before the incumbent can react by lowering price, i.e. the entry lag must be shorter than the price lag.

Market Power and Competition Policy: Economic Issues
The presence of market power threatens the process of competition. An individual firm is said to have market power when it has the ability to price above marginal cost. A perfectly competitive firm does not have market power, as it cannot (profitably) price above marginal cost; a monopolist has market power as it can (profitably) price above marginal cost. In practice, however, almost all firms have some degree of market power, at least in the short run. As such, it is generally accepted that the process of competition is only threatened when a firm (or a small number of firms acting collectively) has substantial market power, i.e. the firm has the ability to price substantially, or significantly, above marginal cost.

Ideally, the existence, or otherwise, of substantial market power could be identified by a close inspection of data on a firm's own price elasticity of demand. A firm's own price elasticity of demand measures the percentage decrease (increase) in demand that would follow from a percentage increase (decrease) in the price of the firm's product. A low own price elasticity (in absolute terms) signals the possession of substantial market power as the firm has the ability to significantly increase price without losing significant market share. However, a high own price elasticity of demand (in absolute terms) does not necessarily imply the absence of substantial market power. Such a result would show that the firm is not able to profitably increase price beyond the present price – it does not, in itself, show that the firm has not already increased price substantially above the cost of production. As such, the firm's own price elasticity of demand would not generally provide useful evidence with respect to market power. In addition, the general non-availability of detailed data on own price elasticity of demand for different points on the demand curve, tends to lead to the need for indirect indicators of the existence, or otherwise, of substantial market power.

Typical indicators of market power for competition authorities include data and information on market shares, market concentration, entry barriers and the competitive environment within the market. Initially, the various competition authorities were probably guilty of rather thoughtlessly following the so called structure, conduct, performance (SCP) model of, or approach to, industrial economics, in which engineering or technical factors (e.g. minimum efficient, or viable, scale of production) would dictate the numbers of firms in a market, which, in turn, would dictate the economic behaviour of the firms, which, in turn, would dictate the economic performance of the market, i.e. a simple one way chain of causation was assumed. Since the early 1980s, and in tandem with the arrival of the so called new industrial economics (with its insights being gleaned from the application of game theory to the subject matter) and empirical industrial organisation (with its insights being gleaned from the application of econometrics to the subject matter), it was widely recognised that the standard SCP approach was too simplistic. In particular, it ignored the importance of potential competition and underestimated the likelihood of various feedback effects, e.g. fierce rivalry at the conduct stage could, in itself, dissuade potential entrants and particularly efficient firms could, and perhaps should, be rewarded with at least temporary monopolies, i.e. efficiencies that would be an offence under the naïve SCP approach as they would lead to the existence of a monopoly, would not be discouraged under an appropriately enhanced approach. Under what might be regarded as a structure, conduct, performance approach, but one that is enhanced or informed by the insights offered by the new industrial economics and empirical industrial organisation literatures, the previously mentioned indicators attempt to identify the presence, or otherwise, of substantial market power in the context of a previously well defined market. The first step, therefore, in general is the defining of the relevant market.

Market Definition and Market Power
The relevant market, for competition policy purposes, is thought of as representing the minimum set of products over which a (hypothetical) firm would have to have monopoly control before it could be sure of exercising a given degree of market power. In practice, this 'given degree of market power' is perceived of as the ability to profitably raise prices, above competitive levels, by 5 per cent for a significant period of time (say, a year). Profits would fall if the price increase resulted in a large fall in volume demand.[5] The European Commission has, in the past, adopted the following somewhat more descriptive approach to market definition and market power. A market is said to be composed of those products

that are regarded as interchangeable or substitutable by the consumer, by reason of the products' characteristics and their intended use. Market power, in turn, is defined as a position of economic strength enjoyed by a firm that enables it to hinder the maintenance of effective competition on the relevant market by allowing it to behave to an appreciable extent independently of competitors and ultimately of consumers.

Market Power and Market Concentration
Once the market has been established the market shares of the market participants and overall market concentration should be estimated. Competition authorities have commonly adopted two alternative approaches for this purpose, concentration ratios and the Herfindahl Hirschman Index (HHI). A concentration ratio measures the total market share of a given number of the largest firms. For example, the C_4 ratio measures the total market share of the four largest firms in a market. The HHI is defined as the sum of the squared percentage shares of all firms of the relevant variable (e.g. volume or value of sales) in the market. As such, the HHI varies between 0 (corresponding to a market with an infinite number of infinitesimally small firms) and 10,000 (corresponding to a market with a single firm, i.e. a pure monopoly). For example, a market consisting of only two equally sized firms would have a HHI of 5,000 ($= 50^2 + 50^2$) whereas a market consisting of five equally sized firms would have a HHI of 2,000. A market with a HHI below 1,000 is generally regarded as a non-concentrated market and as a market in which market power issues are unlikely to arise. In contrast, a market with a HHI above 1,800 is generally regarded as a concentrated market and as a market in which market power issues may arise.[6]

Market Power and Barriers to Entry
It is clear from the insights offered by the new industrial economics and empirical industrial organisation approaches that necessary conditions for the existence of substantial market power are the existence of both high market concentration and high entry barriers. Without entry barriers, any attempt by an incumbent firm or incumbent firms to abuse an apparent position of market power will attract entry by other firms. The definition of entry barriers, however, provoked a great deal of disharmony between protagonists of the so called Chicago and Harvard Schools approaches to antitrust economics, the term given to the study of the economics of competition policy in the USA. The Chicago School viewed entry barriers as being restricted to '…costs that must be borne by an entrant that were not incurred by established firms.' In the extreme, so called Chicago economists only accepted restrictive licensing schemes as valid examples of entry barriers. In contrast, the Harvard School had a much broader definition of entry barriers in mind, '… factors that enable established firms to earn supra-competitive profits without threat of entry.'[7] Economies of scale, excess capacity, lower average costs as a result of experience (i.e. learning by doing), brand proliferation, restrictive distributional agreements and product differentiation (perhaps as a result of

excessive advertising) represented some of the major examples of entry barriers, as justified by this broader definition.

In practice, competition authorities and courts appear to feel most comfortable with the approach of the so called Chicago School towards the formal definition of a barrier to entry, but with the approach of the so called Harvard School in terms of actually deciding whether or not a specific market feature represents a barrier to entry. In addition, competition authorities and courts appear to distinguish between exogenous or natural barriers to entry (e.g. economics of scale), which tend to arise as a result of the incumbent firm attempting to lower its own costs of production, and endogenous or strategic barriers to entry (e.g. some exclusivity agreements), which tend to arise as a result of the incumbent firm attempting to increase potential entrants' costs.

Market Power and Competitive Environment
As previously indicated, the overly mechanical reliance on summary statistics on market concentration is fraught with some danger. In particular, the existence or otherwise of a competitive environment within a market must also be considered. Economists often distinguish between unilateral (price) effects, which can arise particularly in differentiated product markets perhaps as a result of a merger or acquisition, and coordinated (price) effects, which can arise particularly in homogeneous products markets. Unilateral effects arise where it is in the joint interests of two firms to increase their prices, even if their competitors' prices remained constant, i.e. the firms produce relatively close substitutes. Coordinated effects arise where conditions exist that tend to dampen price competition between all competitors. Market conditions that would facilitate tacit or implicit price coordination between competitors signify the presence of a non-competitive environment. When reviewing the competitive environment within a market, the relevant competition authority examines the market for the presence, or absence, of the following features (whose presence would tend to be supportive of tacit collusion): symmetry in market shares; stability in market shares; homogeneity of product; transparency with respect to trading conditions (and, in particular, transparency with respect to prices), low price elasticity of demand; the non-existence of maverick firms; the non-existence of strong buyers; and, the non-existence of excess capacity.

An Example of Market Power
Notwithstanding the previously mentioned general shortage of suitable data for the purposes of ascertaining directly whether or not market power exists, competition authorities have recently encouraged the appropriate interrogation of the data that may be available, in case obvious conclusions, either positive or negative, can be drawn with respect to the appropriate market definition and the presence, or absence, of market power. The most cited case in this regard is the proposed merger of Staples and Office Depot (USA, 1997), where the crucial issue was whether or not, from a competition policy perspective the three largest

office supplies superstores (Staples, Office Depot and OfficeMax) were in a different product market from the very many remaining relatively small office supplies stores.[8] On the basis of a detailed examination of prices and other data across different geographical locations in which different numbers of office supplies stores were present, the USA Federal Trade Commission was satisfied, as ultimately was the relevant court, that the three office supplies superstores were in a distinct office supplies (superstores) market from the much smaller office supplies stores. In particular, the Federal Trade Commission demonstrated that product prices were significantly higher (all other factors held constant) in geographical locations in which less than the three largest office supplies stores were present, but were not influenced by the presence, or absence, of the remaining, and much smaller, office supplies stores. As such, econometric interrogation of the available data facilitated the drawing of two strong conclusions: (i) the appropriate product market consisted of various services provided by office supplies superstores; and (ii) a decrease in the number of superstores from three to two would significantly increase prices. It should be emphasised, however, that the data interrogation exercise facilitated, as opposed to negated the need for, the examination of market concentration, barriers to entry and the competitive environment.

Market Power and Competition Policy: Legal Issues
From an economics perspective, a suitably drafted competition law should address a number of potential concerns. The anti-competitive creation of a position of market power, or what is formally referred to as a dominant position, as well as the abuse of any previously existing market power (e.g. excessively high or low pricing) should be curtailed. Competition law should also contain a suitable proactive approach to proposed mergers, acquisitions or takeovers, as a reactive approach would in certain circumstances require the equivalent of an unscrambling of eggs.

In addition, anti-competitive agreements between firms (e.g. price fixing or market sharing agreements), either formal or informal, should be addressed. In this regard, economists generally distinguish between horizontal agreements (i.e. agreements between firms at the same level of the production and distribution chain) and vertical agreements (i.e. agreements between firms at different levels of the production and distribution chain). Horizontal agreements are, and as such, should generally be discouraged, as the effect of such agreements is to dampen competition at the almost inevitable expense of customers. Horizontal agreements can be between suppliers of inputs (e.g. farmers), between manufacturers, between distributors or between retailers; in each case, a suitably designed competition policy should generally frown upon the agreements, although some allowance should be made for at least considering certain classes of potentially beneficial, or pro-competitive, agreements (e.g. research and development joint ventures). In contrast, vertical agreements tend to be treated on a case by case basis, as an agreement between, say, a manufacturer and a retailer that enhances the efficiency of their relationship and does not necessarily come at the expense of consumers. In the standard terminology, as the product moves through the production and distribution chain, it is said to move from the upstream level, with manufacturing representing the standard example, to the downstream level, with retailing representing the standard example. In practice, competition authorities tend to be rather dismissive of vertical agreements that focus on price restraints, e.g. the manufacturer imposes a minimum resale price restraint on the retailer, but supportive of limited exclusivity agreements, e.g. service stations being restricted to supplying only one brand of motor fuel to its customers. The latter provides an example of the standard underlying considerations with respect to vertical agreements, the service station and its customers are restricted with respect to choice, but the manufacturer will have to offer suitable inducements to the retailer that may compensate, e.g. a lower wholesale price and/or support for improved facilities at the service station, both of which would likely benefit final consumers.

EU and Irish Competition Law
EU competition policy has two main aims: the promotion of competition and the promotion of the integration of member states. Where there is a conflict, Community competition law takes precedent over national law, provided that there is a significant actual or potential effect on inter-state trade. Article 81 of the EC Treaty prohibits anti-competitive agreements while Article 82 prohibits abuse of a dominant position. Article 86 limits the freedom of member states to intervene in the process of competition, through the actions of public undertakings (e.g. state-owned bodies) or private undertakings granted exclusive rights by member states. Under Articles 87-89, member states are prohibited from granting state aid that would distort competition. In addition, various EU public procurement rules regulate the awarding of contracts by public authorities. Since 1989, mergers with a sufficient 'Community Dimension' have been dealt with under the EEC Merger Regulation.

The European Commission enforces EU competition rules; DGIV is the Directorate of the Commission specifically responsible for competition policy. The Court of First Instance hears appeals against Commission competition decisions and the Court of Justice hears appeals on points of law. The above system of prohibition in the EU is supported by the imposition of fines by the Commission. An individual firm can be fined up to 10 per cent of its previous year's worldwide turnover on all its products. However, unlike in the USA, structural break ups are not available as a remedy for violations of Articles 81 and 82 in the EU. The European Commission acts for all EU member states; as such, individual member states cannot be represented separately in European Commission proceedings. This is in contrast to the USA where individual states can be represented separately in proceedings: for example, the USA Department of Justice, 20 States and the District of Columbia sued Microsoft. In pursuit of a policy of increased subsidiarity, the EU is in favour of, where feasible, allowing national courts and member states' competition authorities administer Articles 81 and 82. Arguably, the EU competition policy institutions have reached a stage in their development where they can afford to delegate responsibility to the national authorities; the increased similarity between national competition laws and Community competition law is at least partly responsible for this shift.

Legislation to prohibit restrictive business practices in Ireland was first enacted in 1953 with the Restrictive Trade Practices Act that established the Fair Trade Commission (FTC). The FTC could issue Fair Trading Rules; however, these rules or guidelines had no legal force. In addition, the Minister (Industry and Commerce), on the advice of the FTC, could issue a Restrictive Practice Order to cover a particular trade. The legislation was based on the 'control of abuse' principle with restrictive practices considered on a case by case basis. A failing of competition policy in Ireland was that it was reactive; for sectors of the economy not covered by an Order, it remained legal to engage in price fixing and market sharing agreements. Repeated enquiries were carried out into the behaviour of several trades as new anti-competitive practices emerged. Policy towards mergers and monopolies was dictated by a separate piece of legislation – the Mergers, Take overs and Monopolies (Control) Act 1978 – by which, the Minister of Enterprise, Trade and Employment had sole jurisdiction over acquisitions and mergers. Although this Act could have also been used to impose severe sanctions on monopolies, no such sanctions were imposed.

The Competition Act 1991 introduced a prohibition based system of competition law to Ireland, although the Groceries Order (1987) has been, to date, retained. Anti-competitive agreements between undertakings (firms) and restrictive trade practices are prohibited under Section 4 and the abuse of a dominant position is prohibited under Section 5. The Competition Authority was established under the Act to play a supportive and advisory role; it had no enforcement powers. However, the passing into legislation of the Competition (Amendment) Bill 1996 represented a significant change in emphasis. The primary aim of this legislation was to provide more effective enforcement of competition policy. It became a criminal offence not to comply with the conditions of a licence granted by the Authority. This Act also criminalised anti-competitive behaviour and allowed for prison sentences of up to two years and fines of up to 10 per cent of a firm's worldwide turnover. New powers of search and greater rights of discovery, including the right to conduct a 'dawn raid', were granted to the Director of Competition Enforcement (a member of the Competition Authority) and the ability to initiate prosecutions, both civil and criminal, was granted to the Authority. Furthermore, it could now carry out studies without being requested to do so by the Minister. More recently, the Competition Act 2002 transferred responsibility for mergers to the Authority, increased the search powers of the Authority and increased the penalties for business executives in hardcore anti-competitive (e.g. cartel) cases.

Summary

This Section has outlined a consistent economic and legal framework for the implementation of competition policy. This framework can also be used for the subsequent analysis of specific competition cases. The most important economic concept is significant market power. In order to establish the existence, or otherwise, of significant market power, it is necessary to be guided by the standard four step procedure, which consists of defining the relevant market (from both a product and geographical perspective), measuring market concentration, addressing the issue of barriers to entry and establishing the existence, or otherwise, of a competitive environment. Section 5 utilises this standard procedure for the purpose of examining a number of Irish cases.

4 REGULATION OF NATURAL MONOPOLY

Competition policy complements the process of competition as it attempts to facilitate the market conditions, both in factor markets and product markets, that give rise to market outcomes associated with perfectly competitive markets. For example, competition policy attempts to facilitate ease of entry into, and exit from, markets and attempts to create the conditions generally associated with a competitive environment. Competition policy does not replace, or substitute itself for, the process of competition; for example, competition policy does not directly dictate the number of firms within markets, nor the price or output that individual firms must charge or produce. In contrast, regulatory policy, in the context of economic markets in which issues of market power arise, often replaces, or substitutes itself for, at least part of the process of competition. Regulation tends to dictate the number of firms within a market and/or the price (output) that individual firms can charge (produce). Cable TV, electricity, gas, telecommunications, transportation, postal services and domestic waste services represent just some examples of the many markets that are, or have been, regulated in this sense in many countries, including Ireland.

Regulation and Natural Monopoly: Theory
From an economics perspective, the major justification for the use of regulatory policy, as opposed to competition policy, is the existence of so called natural monopolies. A market is said to be a natural monopoly if its total output can be produced more cheaply by a single firm than by two or more firms. Technically, a natural monopoly exists if

$$C(Q) = C(Q_1 + ... + Q_N) < C(Q_1) + ... + C(Q_N)$$

where Q represents total output, $C(Q)$ represents the total cost of producing Q and N represents the relevant number of firms. In addition, the breadth (or scope) of a natural monopoly may be determined by the existence, and degree of, so called economies of scope. Technically, economies of scope arise if,

$$C(Q_A, Q_B) < C(Q_A, 0) + C(0, Q_B)$$

where A and B represent different products; economies of scope arise where it is cheaper for one firm to produce two different products than it is for two firms to each produce one of the two products; wool and mutton offers an obvious example. The provision of a national electricity or natural gas grid, the provision of a railway network and the provision of a broadband network represent just some of the standard examples of natural monopolies. A natural monopoly exists if there are very significant economies of scale. In such a case, an individual firm's marginal cost (MC) and average cost (AC) curves decline continuously and the firm's marginal cost (MC) curve will be below its average cost (AC) curve. From an economics perspective, the existence of a natural monopoly gives rise to some concerns. As in the case of the standard, i.e. non-natural, monopoly, the natural monopolist has an incentive to maximise profits by producing a level of output at which price is greater than marginal cost, i.e. resources are allocated inefficiently. However, the application of competition policy, in terms of attempting to increase the number of competitors, would be inefficient and ineffective. Assuming that the number of firms increased, the average cost of production would also increase, perhaps dramatically. In addition, it is not clear that firms would enter the market, given the underlying cost conditions. Given the obvious difficulties associated with applying the principles of competition policy in the environment of natural monopolies, various more direct regulatory approaches have been utilised.

Marginal Cost Pricing
Regulators can apparently achieve allocative efficiency by insisting that the natural monopolist produces a level of output at which price is equal to marginal cost. There are, however, at least two problems with this proposed solution. First, the regulator may not have enough information to be able to determine the output level at which price would be equal to marginal cost and it may not be in the natural monopolist's interest to facilitate the regulator in this regard. Second, if the natural monopolist produces the allocatively efficient level of output, it will sustain losses; pricing at marginal cost implies pricing below average cost as the marginal cost curve lies below the average cost curve in a natural monopoly. One possible solution to this latter problem is for the regulator to provide the natural monopolist with a subsidy to offset the losses associated with achieving allocative efficiency. However, these subsidies must be financed by increased taxation elsewhere, which, in turn, lead to other inefficiencies. It may also be difficult politically to be seen to provide a monopolist with a subsidy.

Average Cost Pricing
The problems associated with implementing marginal cost pricing have tended to lead regulators towards the adoption of some form of average cost pricing. Setting price at average cost, where the natural monopolist makes neither excess profits nor losses, avoids the problem of having to subsidise the natural monopolist, but

at the expense of sacrificing allocative efficiency. More sophisticated versions of regulation allow the firm to engage in two part pricing, where a fixed fee is used to finance the almost inevitably present large fixed cost element within the market (e.g. creation or upkeep of the network itself), while an additional per unit user fee is kept relatively close to marginal cost. Average cost pricing regulation, however, suffers from the problem of dampening cost reducing incentives. For example, if the natural monopolist succeeds in reducing costs by 10 per cent, the regulator may be expected to respond by insisting that prices also be reduced by 10 per cent. Indeed, the natural monopolist in this environment has no obvious reason not to allow costs to actually increase. In practice, average cost pricing is often adapted so as to encourage cost reducing innovations by allowing scope for some 'excess' profits. This type of regulation, adjusted average cost pricing is referred to as rate of return regulation. More recently, regulators have adopted the so called CPI-X approach, where CPI represents the inflation rate as measured by the consumer price index and X represents the required decrease in real prices within the relevant market. For example, if X was 3 per cent and inflation was also 3 per cent, there would be no change in nominal prices but a 3 per cent decrease in real prices. In the UK, where this approach was first adopted, X was fixed for a certain period of time, say, five years. During this five year period, cost reductions beyond X per cent, in real terms, would not have to be passed on to the consumers, i.e. they could be retained by the firm as 'excess' profits. Of course, large reductions in costs would tend to be 'punished' by the bar (i.e. X) being set higher in subsequent periods. In addition, very large reductions in costs during the period would place significant pressure on the relevant regulator to renege on the agreement.

Franchise Bidding

Rather than regulating the natural monopolist on an ongoing basis, it may be preferable to auction the (franchise) right to be the natural monopolist in the first place. If the auction is done on the basis of the highest bid winning, the outcome is likely to be equivalent to the standard monopoly outcome. However, the monopoly profits are transferred to the state as a result of the bidding process, as the bidders would find themselves forced to bid higher and higher amounts until almost no net excess profits could be expected. A possible alternative is for the auction to be done on the basis of bidders committing to charging a certain price and providing a particular quality of service to customers in the future. The results of this process are likely to be close to the results obtained by average cost pricing regulation, as bidders would find themselves forced to offer lower and lower (quality adjusted) prices until almost no net excess profits could be expected. A further possibility is for the 'auction' to be done on the basis of a number of criteria; 'bidders' would then compete on the basis of quality as well as price and other considerations. This latter possibility is often referred to as a 'beauty contest'. With a certain set of criteria, a beauty contest and an auction could be equivalent in terms of results.

Public Enterprise and Privatisation

Rather than the state attempting to regulate the natural monopolist, many governments, particularly within Europe, have in the past elected to be the natural monopolist. Within an Irish context, airport management, airline ownership, electricity, natural gas and transportation provide examples of state ownership of enterprise. The distinctive feature (and advantage or disadvantage depending on one's political, social as well as economic, perspective) of this approach is that the objective of the natural monopolist is no longer necessarily the maximisation of profits. Management of a public enterprise may be somewhat accountable to voters, usually indirectly via the relevant Minister's responsibility for the public enterprise, and, as such, it is possible that the management's goal will be the maximisation of public welfare, however defined. Opponents of state ownership of enterprises generally point to the so called soft budget constraint, with management and workers, it is claimed, being united in their efforts to extract public funds for 'their' enterprises. However, EU restrictions on state aids to public-owned enterprises have removed at least some of the force of this argument.

Regulation and Natural Monopoly: Policy and Practice

A movement away from public ownership and enterprise and towards privatisation began in the early 1980s. Within a European context, the UK government led by Margaret Thatcher was at the forefront of this movement; the privatisation of British Telecom (1984) and British Gas (1986) represented very significant economic and political events. The experience in the USA in the late 1970s and early 1980s was one of market liberalisation or deregulation, as opposed to denationalisation, with the aviation, telecommunications and trucking markets providing high profile examples. However, and perhaps not surprisingly, many of the large privatisations within the UK were subsequently followed up by the setting up of specialist independent regulatory agencies (e.g. Oftel and Ofgas), as the process of competition failed to take off in what were industries still characterised by tendencies towards, or elements of, natural monopolies. The lesson from the UK privatisation experience appears to be that the creation of market conditions suitable for facilitating the process of competition or the continued/renewed regulation of a natural monopoly is at least as important as the formal ownership structure (i.e. public or private enterprise). In this regard, specific regulatory agencies have certain advantages over the use of the courts or other state agencies in regulating the day to day activities of firms in these naturally monopolistic markets. The regulatory agencies, encouraged by the experience of collecting and analysing specialised market information on demand and cost conditions over time, can act proactively, particularly in comparison to the courts, e.g. in the context of natural monopolies, stopping an abuse before it has occurred is generally easier and superior to trying to unravel the effects of an abuse after it has occurred. In addition, by placing some degree of separation between macro management, by the relevant politicians of the regulatory agencies and micro management of the markets, by members of the relevant agencies, politicians are placed at arm's length from micro decisions.

Ireland appears to have somewhat reluctantly accepted the proposition that monopoly and/or a lack of competition is inefficient and EU Directives with respect to liberalisation of major public utilities (e.g. telecommunications, postal services, electricity and natural gas) were eventually implemented or are in the process of being implemented. Perhaps one advantage of this general policy reluctance in the past was the ability to learn from the UK experience and establish the relevant regulatory agencies (e.g. the Office of the Director of Telecommunications Regulation (ODTR), later renamed the Commission for Communications Regulation (ComReg), which regulates telecommunications and postal services markets, and the Commission for Energy Regulation (CER), which regulates electricity and natural gas markets), prior to or along with, as opposed to after, market liberalisation.

When decisions of the regulatory agencies are appealed, the various regulatory agencies in Ireland, as well as the courts, have ongoing important decisions to make with respect to pricing and investment decisions within markets, or within the particular elements of markets, that are naturally monopolistic.[9] In the context of a downstream natural monopoly (e.g. fixed line telecommunications), the level of the resulting consumer price is highly visible, while in the context of an upstream natural monopoly (e.g. transportation of natural gas), the level of the access price charged to downstream firms may be less politically sensitive, but still of crucial importance, particularly so if the upstream firm itself also operates in various downstream markets. Politicians also have choices to make with respect to the political as well as the economic desirability, or otherwise, of different degrees of vertical separation (e.g. accounts separation or complete vertical separation), e.g. eircom or Bord Gáis Éireann.

Ireland only relatively recently started the process of privatisation. After successfully selling its stake in Irish Life, the state privatised Telecom Eireann (later eircom). Initially, the privatisation proved to be a political success as eircom's share price increased by over 20 per cent above its floatation price. However, eircom's share price then fell, and remained, for the rest of its relatively brief (initial) existence as a public limited company, considerably below its floatation price. From a political perspective, the evolution of eircom's share price still has repercussions for future privatisations in Ireland, e.g. Aer Lingus and Voluntary Health Insurance, where alternatives to an initial public offering are being considered (e.g. a management buy out or a partial sale to another firm).[10] Nevertheless, it does appear that the battleground for future debates in the public ownership versus private ownership arena lies in the details of the privatisations (e.g. the particulars of employee share options) as opposed to any serious divergences in underlying political philosophies.

5 POLITICAL ECONOMY: COMPETITION POLICY CASES

Traditionally, economists interested in public policy issues adopted a public finance or public interest approach, which viewed the government and/or the bureaucracy as attempting to maximise societal welfare, however this concept was defined. In the early 1980s, the alternative public choice perspective became increasingly influential, particularly in the USA. The key insight offered by the public choice perspective, at least at a theoretical level, is to view, or model, all (economic and/or political) agents as pursuing their own self interests in all political economy settings. As such, politics, and more specifically public policy, is viewed as an ongoing struggle between politicians, bureaucrats and the electorate, as well as many other players, e.g. employer and employee groups, regulators, the judiciary, other interest groups and the media. Whereas the public interest perspective views government involvement in the economy as an attempt to correct for some market failure (e.g. externalities, including perhaps market failures with respect to distribution and equity which require a coordinated response), the public choice perspective views government involvement in the economy as the outcome of a struggle between the aforementioned agents or groups; the market failure explanation is not entirely ruled out in this framework, merely widened to incorporated rent seeking actions by the relevant vested interests.[11] For example, it may be in the interests of various representatives to highlight the existence of some claimed market failure and then to champion a specific remedy, one that may also, perhaps coincidently, be in the particular interests of its own members.

In the context of competition and regulatory policy, the public choice perspective offers some potential insights. Competition authorities and regulatory agencies should be at least somewhat suspicious of claims from representative bodies that their proposed restrictions on competition, which may well be in response to some at least perceived market failure, are inevitably in the public interest. Visions of completely uncontrolled competition between, say, competing refuse collecting trucks in the one small housing estate, competing bus operators (be they public, or private, owned) racing towards the same bus stop, competing hospitals chasing down perspective clients and competing NCT operators offering to approve your vehicle, despite your vehicle's best efforts, only highlight the need for a rational policy to, and specific framework for, competition, and does not imply the more general and inevitable failure of competition in those specific markets. Within the specific context of the regulatory arena, the public choice perspective also highlights the issue of regulatory capture. Ongoing interactions between one dominant firm and the relevant regulatory agency runs the risk of so called regulatory capture, where the agency ends up, perhaps despite its best efforts, representing the issues of the dominant firm. In particular, for newly created, but under funded, regulatory agencies, it would be difficult for the regulators not to be overly influenced by the highly informed incumbents, although the, at least somewhat informed, potential entrants, should they exist, may provide a partial counterweight.

Non-Internationally Traded Services Sector

Given the importance of the non-internationally traded services sector for the Irish economy (see Section 2), the general ability of Irish policymakers to influence the development of the sector and the availability of a framework for examining the effects of implementing a suitably designed competition and regulatory policy, it is at least potentially instructive to examine a number of specific case studies.

Groceries Order

To economists interested in competition policy, perhaps the most controversial provision of the Restrictive Practices (Groceries) Order, 1987 is the prohibition on retailers selling many grocery products (e.g. bread and milk) below the relevant suppliers' net invoice price. Fears of predatory pricing by the large retail multiples, where price wars which would eliminate the smaller competitors, would be followed by price 'gorging', are used to defend this provision. However, two counter arguments present themselves. First, the Competition Authority could take actions against predatory actions by any of the retail multiples, albeit perhaps after the event. Second, and more substantially, off-invoice discounts cannot be taken into account, i.e. retailers are forced to impose a mark up that is at least equal in size to off-invoice discounts. Crucially, sizeable off-invoice discounts appear to be widespread in the grocery trade. The Office of the Director of Consumer Affairs is charged with prosecuting breaches of the Groceries Order. In January 2004, Dunne's Stores and Tesco were each fined over €2,000 for selling baby food products below cost; even more recently (May 2004), Dunne's Stores was fined €1,000 for selling frozen foods below cost. Perhaps somewhat ironically, the Groceries Order has arguably facilitated some non-Irish discount retailers (e.g. Lidl and Aldi) in increasing their market shares, as they source a significant portion of their produce from foreign suppliers, and thereby, in effect, avoid the Groceries Order.

Professions Study

The Authority is currently in the midst of a professions study, which aims to detail and examine the possible pro-competitive and anti-competitive motivations behind, and effects of, restrictions in the supply of various construction, legal and medical services in Ireland. At a general level, the public choice perspective encourages one to view with at least some suspicion the principle or practice of self-regulation. The Opticians Board in Ireland (Bord na Radharcmhastóirí) provides a possible example, as the majority of its members appear to be optometrists or opticians, giving rise to a threat of regulatory capture. An obvious policy response to the possibility of regulatory capture would appear to be to ensure that practitioners never constitute a majority on the relevant regulatory body. Of course, some practitioners should be included, so that the regulatory board can avail of their experience and specialised knowledge. Particular attention appears to being paid by the Authority to the barristers, medical practitioners and solicitors professions with respect to restrictions in advertising, entry and organisational formats. In addition, demarcation issues in the barristers and solicitors professions appear to be under review from a competition policy perspective.

Retail Pharmacy

The retail pharmacy sector is highly regulated in Ireland, although probably much less so than in many other countries. From a competition policy perspective, apparently excessive restrictions on competition, and arguably unjustified from a public interest perspective, come in a number of forms. Barriers to entry in terms of access to the relevant profession have existed for many years in terms of the highly restricted access to the required third level degree course, although this have been relaxed somewhat recently with the setting up of some new third level degree courses. Barriers to entry with respect to pharmacy ownership remain in that foreign trained graduates cannot own a pharmacy that is less than three years old. In addition, there is also an arguably justifiable comprehensive ban on mail order and Internet sales. In January 2002, following a High Court challenge, rather severe location restrictions were revoked. Among the location restrictions was a requirement that any new pharmacy had to locate at least 250 metres (5km in rural areas) from the nearest competitor and demonstrate that setting up would not have an adverse effect on the viability of competitors. In addition, given that the state is by far the largest purchaser of medicines, it is not surprising that the state is involved in a process that fixes certain prices in retail pharmacies. However, the extent of the mark ups agreed between the state and representatives of retail pharmacists appears excessive (e.g. in the Drug Payment Scheme).

Banking

The Authority is currently involved in a study of the non-investment banking sector, which directly accounts for approximately 4 per cent of GNP in Ireland. From a competition policy perspective, a number of plausible markets appear to be both highly concentrated and contain significant regulatory barriers to entry. Particular attention appears to be focused on the ownership and administrative structures of the various payment clearing systems and on the markets for personal current accounts and loans to small and medium sized enterprises. The general non-availability of interest bearing current accounts in combination with the non-imposition of charges on many users of current accounts appears to suggest the presence of a significant level of cross-subsidisation, which, in turn, suggests the presence of market rigidities and perhaps the absence of a suitably competitive environment.

Conclusion

The public choice perspective would also have much to say with respect to many other existing Irish regulations that impact on the competitive process, e.g. retail planning guidelines/laws (e.g. with respect to the location and scale of out of town shopping centres and specific types of outlets) and restrictions on off-licences (e.g. the very high cost of obtaining a licence). It is crucial to note, however, that competition policy enthusiasts are not claiming or even suggesting that all such guidelines, regulations and laws are anti-competitive, merely highlighting the need for a considered approach to the enacting of such rules, i.e. some form of competition proofing.

6 FUTURE ISSUES

As previously mentioned, there is general recognition of the increased importance of microeconomic policymaking at the national level. However, there is also growing recognition of the importance of microeconomic policymaking at the international level. Tax competition and tax harmonization provide standard examples in the area of international tax policy, most often in the context of corporation tax or deposit interest retention tax (DIRT) but also in the context of expenditure taxes, while state aids have provided the standard example in the context of interstate industrial policy, most often, at least in the past, in the context of some version of the 'national champion' argument. However, increasing attention in the international arena is likely to be focused on issues that are even more closely associated with competition policy. There has been an increasing level of cooperation between the USA and the EU in terms of the application of competition laws. This is particularly evident in the treatment of global mergers, where it is generally in the merging parties' interests to waive some of their confidentiality rights. Cooperation is less evident, and perhaps less feasible, in cases not involving mergers (e.g. abuse of dominance), where one authority may only learn of another authority's investigation when it becomes public information. Given confidentiality requirements, outside of merger cases, it is possible that increasing cooperation will have to come through the utilisation of formal comity procedures. Under a traditional comity procedure, each authority undertakes to take into account the important interests of the other authority or country. Under a more proactive positive comity procedure, one authority can request another authority to address (alleged) anticompetitive activities that are harming the interests of the former authority, but taking place in the territory of the latter authority. From a global economics perspective, comity procedures have the attraction of allowing 'foreign' surplus to be given at least weight by the 'domestic' authority (and vice versa) and are, therefore, to be encouraged.

From an international perspective, the related issues of parallel imports and price discrimination are also likely to increase in importance, particularly in the context of increasing globalisation. Imports, other than through the authorised distribution channels, of genuine products that have been legally marketed in another country are known as parallel imports.[12] Common examples of parallel imports include certain brands of jeans, children toys and CDs/DVDs that are

211

sourced from parts of Eastern Europe and/or the Far East. Whether or not parallel imports are legal, in cases where the brand owner has trade mark rights in the country of importation, depends on the importing country's trademark regime. The European Economic Area (EEA) retains a policy of regional exhaustion, where parallel imports into the region (e.g. from Hong Kong) are illegal but parallel imports from countries within the region are legal. This policy, which is to at least some extent out of step with international practice, protects EEA based (and other) producers but penalises EEA consumers, as EU prices tend to be much higher than the prices charged elsewhere for identical products. More generally, the international pricing of pharmaceuticals, at least some of which would be regarded as essentials (e.g. AIDs drugs), provides a more important example of the issue of the appropriate public policy towards price discrimination. Arguably, pharmaceutical companies should be allowed to practice at least some degree of price discrimination in order to recoup their initial investments. Indeed, the practice of richer countries paying a relatively high price while poorer countries pay a much lower price may not have any detrimental effects on overall societal welfare, as the alternative may be that the product is only sold at the higher price in the richer countries or that it is not produced at all. However, it is also possible that societal welfare declines as a result of price discrimination, as the total output of the product often falls under price discrimination. In summary, a more informed policy towards international price discrimination and, more specifically, parallel imports is required.

From a national policy perspective, a number of issues are likely to increase in importance in the near future. As previously indicated, the desirability or otherwise of various levels of vertical separation within dominant firms operating in markets that contain at least some elements of a natural monopoly will have to be further confronted. For example, complete vertical separation would require the splitting up of a firm. This will be particularly important in markets containing commercial state-sponsored bodies, e.g. Bord Gáis Éireann, the Electricity Supply Board and Radio Telefís Éireann. In addition, the boundaries of the responsibilities of the various agencies that affect competition policy and regulation are likely to become increasingly blurred in the next few years. For example, the Competition Authority has recently increased its consumer advocacy efforts, a responsibility linked in the past to the Office of the Director of Consumer Affairs. Indeed, a merger of the two offices could be possible (as is already the case within the Office of Fair Trading (OFT) in the UK), notwithstanding apparently conflicting roles and responsibilities with respect to the Groceries Order. In addition, there could be pressure for a merging of the network regulatory agencies in energy (natural gas and electricity), communications and perhaps even broadcasting (currently regulated by the Broadcasting Commission of Ireland).

It is clear that at both the national and international level, there is increasing recognition of the importance of microeconomic policymaking. This is particularly true in the area of competition policy and regulation, where the growth in interest has come to some extent at the expense of industrial policy. Particularly in Ireland, competition policy has come a long way in a very short period of time, as may be witnessed by the continued evolution in the size and importance of the Competition Authority and the other relevant regulatory agencies.

Indeed, the increased importance of competition policy, regulation and their associated agencies in Ireland has probably occurred as a result of the increased general recognition of the crucial importance of the non-internationally traded services sector of the economy.

Endnotes

* The author gratefully acknowledges helpful comments and suggestions by Carol Newman and John O'Hagan; unfortunately the usual disclaimer applies, i.e. any remaining errors and all views expressed remain the responsibility of the author. This Chapter draws upon some material previously published by the author in G. Turley and M. Maloney (editors), 'Microeconomic Policy Issues in Ireland', *Principles of Economics: An Irish Textbook*, Gill and Macmillan, Dublin 2001, pp. 266-84, and N. Economides, 'Comment on the Microsoft Antitrust Policy Case,' *Journal of Industry, Competition and Trade*, March 2001.

1 For an accessible introduction to, and overview of, Irish competition policy and regulation from both an economic and legal perspective, see P. Massey and D. Daly, *Competition and Regulation in Ireland: The Law and Economics*, Oak Tree Press, Dublin 2003. For a more formal treatment of the microeconomic aspects of competition policy, see S. Bishop and M. Walker, *The Economics of EC Competition Law: Concepts, Application and Measurement*, Sweet & Maxwell, London 2002. In addition, the interested reader should maintain regular contact with a number of online sources for up to date information on competition policy and regulatory matters; the Competition Authority's website (www.tca.ie) contains links to many of the relevant regulatory bodies' websites.

2 See PricewaterhouseCoopers LLP, *Consumer Pricing Report 2003: A PricewaterhouseCoopers Report to Forfás*, Forfás, Dublin 2003.

3 This claimed non-minimisation of costs by monopolists, which was first highlighted by H. Liebenstein, 'Allocative Efficiency vs 'X-Efficiency'', *American Economic Review*, June 1966, sits rather uncomfortably with the standard neo-classical economics assumption of profit maximisation, i.e. how could profit be maximised if costs are not minimised? However, J. Vickers, 'Concepts of Competition' (An Inaugural Lecture delivered before the University of Oxford on 2 November 1993), and others have highlighted the underlying lack of performance comparisons, or 'yardstick' competition, in a monopoly environment as being the source of the cost inefficiency.

4 The earliest reference to the issue of rent seeking appears to be G. Tullock, 'The Welfare Cost of Tariffs, Monopolies and Theft', *Western Economic Journal*, June 1967.

5 The reduction in demand caused by these increased prices comes from two sources – demand substitution by consumers and supply substitution by new competitors. Demand substitution represents the reduction in consumer demand caused by the increased prices, while supply substitution by new competitors represents the response of new competitors in terms of producing new (relatively close substitute) products in response to the increased prices.

6 The interested reader is directed towards the Competition Authority's, 'Notice in Respect of Guidelines for Merger Analysis', *N/02/004*, Dublin 2002, available at www.tca.ie, for further details of the practical application of the HHI.

7 For the Chicago School approach, see G. Stigler, *The Organisation of Industry*, University of Chicago Press, Chicago 1968. For the Harvard School approach, see J. Bain, *Barriers to New*

Competition: Their Character and Consequences in Manufacturing Industries, Harvard University Press, Cambridge MA 1956.

8   See S. Dalkir and F. Warren-Boulton, 'Prices, Market Definition and the Effects of Merger: Staples-Office Depot (1997)', in J. Kwoka and L. White (editors), *The Antitrust Revolution: Economics, Competition and Policy* (Third Edition), Oxford University Press, Oxford 1999, Case 6.

9   Regulation of prices may also be required in markets that are naturally oligopolistic, particularly if the number of firms is very low; the regulation of mobile telephony charges by ComReg provides a pertinent example.

10 From a narrower economics perspective, the success, or otherwise, of the privatisation of Eircom should be judged primarily by the effect of the privatisation on the process of competition within the Irish telecommunications market(s).

11 See J. Farrell, 'Information and the Coase Theorem', *Journal of Economic Perspectives*, Fall 1987, for an extended discussion of the relative merits of a pure market led approach, based on property rights, and an approach based upon the market supported by a benevolent, but somewhat bumbling, bureaucrat.

12 For more details, see F. O'Toole and C. Treanor, 'The European Union's Trade Mark Exhaustion Regime', *World Competition: Law and Economics Review*, September 2002.

CHAPTER 9

Agriculture, Rural Development and Food Safety

Alan Matthews

1 INTRODUCTION

Agricultural and food policy remains a prominent aspect of economic policy debate in Ireland. This is despite the shrinking economic importance of the sector in GDP and employment. Agriculture no longer has the dominant role in economic activity which it once had, although when the contribution of the food industry is factored in, the agri-food sector remains a significant player. In 2003, it accounted for almost 9 per cent of Irish GDP and 9 per cent of employment. The agricultural sector remains important in other ways. Together with forestry, it occupies over 70 per cent of the land area of the country and it thus has a significant impact on the physical environment. It remains the single most substantial contributor to the economic and social viability of rural areas. It is also the largest contributor to greenhouse gas emissions accounting for 29 per cent of Ireland's total in 2003. Finally, agri-food exports contributed over 8 per cent of total merchandise exports in 2003 and food and drink expenditures accounted for 22 per cent of household consumption expenditure. Thus agricultural and food policy is intimately linked to debates on economic competitiveness, rural development, the environment and food safety and quality.

Another reason for the interest in agricultural and food policy is the decisive influence of government interventions on the fortunes of the industry. This dependence can be highlighted in a single statistic: the income accruing to farmers from agricultural activity arises entirely from public policy transfers from both EU and Irish consumers and taxpayers. Agricultural activity within the EU is highly protected from world market competition. EU tariff levels on agricultural and food imports average around 33 per cent, compared to 2 per cent for industrial goods, and for some agricultural products exceed 200 per cent. This massive government intervention in favour of a particular industry raises a series of questions. What objectives is it designed to achieve? Are these objectives justified? Is the support provided achieving these objectives? Is the support being provided efficiently? These are particularly pertinent questions at present because agricultural and food policy faces challenges on a number of fronts. These include the likelihood of further trade liberalisation emerging from WTO agricultural trade negotiations, the challenge of assimilating farmers in the accession countries of central and eastern Europe, the need to promote more sustainable agriculture in environmental terms, as well as to assure consumers of the safety and quality of food being produced.

The purpose of this chapter is to describe these challenges in more detail and to discuss the appropriate policy responses. Section 2 provides a brief overview of some salient characteristics of the Irish agricultural sector and describes the main features of recent structural change in the industry. Section 3 discusses the changing policy environment at EU and international levels. Section 4 looks at the rationale for rural development policies and at the policy framework, which has been put in place to encourage balanced regional and rural development. Section 5 highlights the role of the food industry and examines the growing emphasis given to food safety regulation. Section 6 concludes the chapter by summarising some of the conflicting tendencies at work as the agriculture and food sector faces into a more market oriented and competitive environment.

2 CHARACTERISTICS OF THE AGRICULTURAL SECTOR

Production

The agricultural industry produced food products and raw materials valued at €4.9 billion at producer prices in 2003. Its share of GDP at factor cost was an estimated 2.7 per cent in that year (down from 5.6 per cent in 1997). According to the CSO's Labour Force Survey, around 110,600 persons worked in agriculture in 2003, accounting for 6 per cent of total employment. Because the Labour Force Survey measures employment on the basis of principal economic status it excludes many, if not all, of those who work part time in agriculture. Other data from the CSO's Agricultural Labour Input surveys which gives the total number who work for some period in agriculture show that the total number in 2002 was 240,100 equivalent to 158,100 full time jobs. The discrepancy between the share of the labour force in agriculture and its share of GDP is a first indication that labour productivity and thus farm income might be relatively lower in the sector than in the economy at large.

Climatically, Ireland is better suited to grassland than crop production. Of the total agricultural area of 4.4 million hectares in 2003, over 90 per cent was devoted to grass and rough grazing. Livestock and livestock products accounted for just 63 per cent of total output at producers' prices in 2002 (Table 9.1). These figures exclude the direct payments, which farmers also receive from the production of these commodities. This explains the fall in the relative importance of cattle production over this period as successive rounds of CAP

216

reform have reduced the producer price of cattle (see Section 3). The table also highlights the growing share of material and service inputs as a proportion of gross agricultural output. As well as the fall in the value of output arising from CAP reform, this reflects the increasing intensification of agricultural production, a phenomenon which has given rise to concern about agriculture's impact on the environment.

Table 9.1

Composition of Agricultural Outputs and Inputs, Selected Years
(per cent of gross agricultural output by value)

Total Outputs	1990	1996	2002
Cattle	34.8	29.9	25.5
Milk	29.1	30.8	30.9
Crops	21.1	21.5	24.2
Pigs	5.2	7.2	6.5
Sheep	4.2	4.9	4.4
Other	5.5	5.7	8.5
Gross agricultural output at producer prices	100.0	100.0	100.0
Total Inputs	*50.3*	*55.9*	*68.0*
Feed, fertiliser and seed	22.3	25.2	29.6
Other current inputs	28.0	30.7	38.3

Source: Department of Agriculture and Food, *Compendium of Agricultural Statistics*, Economics and Planning Division, Dublin 2004.

An important characteristic of Irish agriculture is its export orientation. The export market absorbs more than 80 per cent of dairy and beef output. Around 40 per cent of Irish agri-food exports go to the UK, around 35 per cent to the rest of the EU and 25 per cent are exported outside of the EU. The importance of sales to third country markets outside the EU, which are only possible with the aid of export subsidies, leaves Ireland vulnerable to any changes in agricultural support arrangements which would target these subsidies. The continued use of export subsidies is under challenge from other trading countries in the WTO negotiations on agricultural trade liberalisation (see Section 3).

Price Developments

Agricultural output and input prices increased rapidly in nominal terms between 1980 and 1990. Since then, agricultural input prices have continued to increase, albeit more slowly, while output prices have fallen in nominal terms. The real price of agricultural output, measured as the ratio of output prices to the consumer price index, is a good indicator of the purchasing power of farm products relative to consumer goods and services. This ratio has more than halved over the period 1980 to 2002. This fall in the relative price of food over time, which is not unique to Ireland but is a general phenomenon in all industrialised economies, is crucially important in understanding the adjustment pressures on agriculture and hence the reasons for government intervention in the sector.

The fall in relative food prices reflects the interplay of the supply and demand for farm products. On the one hand, the supply potential of the farm sector has dramatically increased as the scientific revolution gathered pace, making available to farmers a range of productive new inputs such as improved seed varieties, better fertilisers, more powerful machinery, and more effective chemicals and pesticides. As a result of this technological innovation, the supply of agricultural products has increased rapidly. However, the market for this increased output has not grown to the same extent. Growth in demand is dependent on growth in population and in per capita incomes. But the rate of population growth in industrialised countries has slowed down and in some cases has virtually ceased. While per capita incomes continue to grow, a smaller and smaller proportion of this increase is spent on food. The consequence has been a downward pressure on the aggregate price level for agricultural products relative to other commodities.

This in turn puts a downward pressure on farm incomes and has encouraged farm family members to take up non-farm job opportunities. In all industrialised countries, the share of the farm workforce in total employment has fallen significantly. In Ireland, the numbers at work in agriculture fell from 330,000 in 1960 to 110,600 in 2003. If this adjustment process proceeds smoothly, the reduction in the numbers engaged in agriculture should ensure that farm incomes, on average, stay in line with average non-farm incomes. For various reasons, however, some farmers may find it difficult to leave farming in the face of this downward pressure on farm incomes. Unemployment may be high in the non-farm sector, or their age and skill profile can make it difficult for them to find off farm employment. Many farmers appear trapped in agriculture with low incomes. Government transfers to agriculture have been justified in the past as a response to this perceived problem of low average farm incomes relative to the rest of society.

The process of adjustment to falling real farm prices is reflected in ongoing structural change in agriculture. In 2002, there were around 136,000 individual farms. Their average size in terms of land area is 32 hectares although there is considerable diversity around this average. This average area farmed is large in EU terms, but because of the relatively low intensity of land use the average size of farm business in Ireland is at the smaller end of the EU spectrum. There is an important regional dimension to differences in farm size, with a predominance of smaller farms in the West and the North-West, and a greater proportion of larger farms in the South and East. Small farm size is frequently associated with a low margin farming system (mainly drystock) and a predominance of older farmers, many of whom are unmarried. The number of farms is falling over time, at a rate of about 2 per cent per annum. A more disaggregated analysis shows that all of the decline is concentrated among smaller farms (less than 20 hectares) whose number fell from 85,000 to 59,000 between 1992 and 2002, while the number of larger farms is stable at around 77,000.

Farm Incomes

The changing composition of income sources in farm households can be tracked over time using data from the Household Budget Surveys conducted by the CSO. Whereas in 1973, 70 per cent of farm household income was derived from farming, this had fallen to 41 per cent in the 1999/2000 Survey (Table 9.2). Income from farming in this table includes the direct payments which farmers receive under EU agricultural policy (discussed in Section 3). Income from farming compares unfavourably with average industrial earnings, although comparisons are difficult for statistical and conceptual reasons.[1] For example, the average family farm income estimated in 2002 by the Teagasc National Farm Survey was €14,925, compared to the average annual industrial wage in December 2002 of €27,180. However, this comparison is not comparing like with like. The average family farm income on the 40 per cent of full time farms in the Teagasc Survey was €27,758 (bear in mind, however, that this figure must remunerate the capital invested in the farm and that there is more than one labour unit engaged on full time farms, so it is not directly comparable to the industrial earnings figure either). Conversely, the average income from farming of the remaining 60 per cent of part time farms in the Teagasc Survey in 2002 was only €6,951. However, on around 48 per cent of all farms, either the holder and/or the spouse have an off farm job. The increasing importance of off farm income means that average farm *household* incomes are now close to average incomes in the non-farm economy.

Table 9.2
Percentage of Total Farm Household Income from All Sources, 1973 - 1999

	1973	1980	1987	1994	1999/2000
Farming	70.1	58.3	54.2	51.3	39.0
Other direct income	19.1	26.3	17.6	37.0	50.3
Transfer payments	10.8	15.2	28.3	11.7	10.6
Gross income	100.0	100.0	100.0	100.0	100.0

Source: CSO, *Household Budget Survey,* Stationery Office, Dublin, various issues.

Table 9.3 compares the average incomes of farm households with those of urban households, other rural households, and the state average. It indicates that farm households, on average, had a slightly lower gross income (€32,951) than the average household, but a higher disposable income (€29,514) due to lower direct taxes. Average household income is a good measure of living standards, although it does not take account of differences in the effort or resources required to generate this income. Also, farm households are slightly larger than households in general. Taking the larger size of farm households into account, both gross and disposable income per farm household member was lower than for households on average. The fact that average farm household income is now on a par with average non-farm household income does not mean that there is no longer a problem of low farm incomes. Because farm incomes, like incomes in general, are not equally distributed, many farm households continue to live in poverty. But even here, the most recent data show that poverty levels among farm households are not that different to non-farm households. In 2001, 21.3 per cent of farm households fell below the 50 per cent relative poverty line, compared to 31.6 per cent of non-farm rural households and 18.7 per cent of urban households.[2]

Table 9.3

Average Annual Household Income, 1999/2000, (€)

Income Source	Farm households	Other rural households	Urban households	State average
Farming income	12,866	252	14	1,011
Non farm employment	14,270	20,924	29,506	25,949
Other direct income	2,315	2,818	4,986	3,413
Total state transfers	3,501	4,537	4,158	4,219
Gross income	*32,951*	*28,531*	*38,665*	*34,592*
less total direct taxation	3,437	4,116	7,088	5,974
Disposable Income	*29,514*	*24,415*	*30,456*	*28,618*
Persons per household	3.56	3.16	3.00	3.08
Gross income per person in household	*8,290*	*7,726*	*10,152*	*9,292*
Disposable income per person in household	*2,329*	*2,445*	*3,384*	*3,017*

Source: CSO, *Household Budget Survey Preliminary Results 1999/2000*, Stationery Office, Dublin 2001.

3 THE POLICY ENVIRONMENT

Common Agricultural Policy (CAP)

At the heart of the original Common Market was an economic deal between France and Germany under which France obtained access to the German market for its agricultural exports in return for opening the French market to German industrial goods. Thus a common agricultural policy had to be included in the Treaty of Rome, which established the European Economic Community in 1958.

The objectives of this common agricultural policy were spelled out in Article 39 of the Treaty and are worth quoting in full:

The objectives of the common agricultural policy shall be:

– To increase agricultural productivity by promoting technical progress and by ensuring the rational development of agricultural production and the optimum utilisation of all factors of production, in particular labour;

– Thus, to ensure a fair standard of living for the agricultural community, in particular by increasing the individual earnings of persons engaged in agriculture;

- To stabilise markets;
- To provide certainty of supplies;
- To ensure that supplies reach consumers at reasonable prices.

These five objectives of efficient agricultural production: fair incomes for farmers, stable markets, food security and reasonable consumer prices would be broadly acceptable to most people, though the sharp eyed will note the ambiguity of the wording (What is a fair standard of living for farmers? What is a reasonable price for consumers?) and the potential for conflict between different objectives. However, the mechanisms put in place to achieve these objectives have prioritised the farm income objective at considerable cost to the EU budget and consumers.

These mechanisms have changed over time. We first describe the original mechanisms whose legacy still determines the basic architecture of the CAP despite the reforms which have taken place. For each of the main commodities produced in the EU, each year the Council of Agricultural Ministers establishes a *target price* (or its equivalent). This is the price Ministers would ideally like producers to receive over the coming year. To maintain the market price around this target level the EU has at its disposal a number of policy instruments, including import controls, market intervention and export subsidies. The most important form of import barrier in the past was the *variable levy*. By setting this levy equal to the difference between the EU target price and the world price, the EU ensured that no produce could be imported into the Union below the target price and so undermine the market price received by EU producers. Variable levies have been replaced by fixed import tariffs since 1995 under the terms of the WTO Agreement on Agriculture. Price support to producers was further strengthened in the event of excess EU supplies by a guarantee that producers could sell farm produce to a government agency at a price (called the *intervention price*) usually set some 10-30 per cent below the target price. Intervention was intended to deal with temporary surpluses of supply. Once the market had recovered and prices had risen, intervention stocks could be sold. Today, intervention functions more as a safety net measure to be used only as a last resort. As the EU became more than self sufficient in many temperate zone foods, greater reliance was placed on *export subsidies or refunds*. These export refunds bridge the gap between the high internal market prices and the lower world prices in most years and make possible the export of higher priced foodstuffs out of the EU. High import tariffs, intervention purchases and export refunds are the principal means of supporting prices to farmers under the CAP. In addition, farm incomes are supported by means of direct payments whose importance has grown with successive reforms of the CAP.

The CAP has its own budget instrument, called the European Agricultural Guarantee and Guidance Fund (usually referred to as FEOGA, after its French initials). Price and income support is funded by the FEOGA Guarantee Section. The Guidance Section is used to fund policies to modernise farming structures. It was originally intended, that up to one third of total CAP funding would be spent through the Guidance Section, but for years the Guarantee Section absorbed the lion's share (up to 95 per cent) of the budget. Only in recent years has the share of spending through the Guidance Section been increased as the EU gives greater weight to its rural development policy (see Section 4).

MacSharry and Agenda 2000 CAP Reforms

The operation of the CAP price support policy ensured a greater degree of internal price stability than in other countries and meant higher per capita incomes for a greater number of farmers than would otherwise have been the case. However, these achievements were bought at a price. The resulting increase in output could not be absorbed by the natural growth in demand, leading to the accumulation of stocks and to dumping on international markets. Thus the EU, which was initially a deficit producer of many agricultural products, became a major net exporter. An obvious consequence of this was the escalating budget cost of purchasing surplus production for intervention storage and of financing export refunds.

The distribution of support payments was also questioned. Because support is proportional to production, most of the support goes to the largest farmers who need it least. The European Commission calculated that 70 per cent of arable aids and livestock premia went to the largest 17 per cent of farmers in 2000. Furthermore, the costs of the policy are borne disproportionately by low income consumers who spend relatively larger amounts of their household income on food. Price support also encouraged the intensification of agriculture which has been damaging to the environment. Because land for agricultural use in the EU is in fixed supply, any increase in production requires the more intensive use of non-land inputs such as chemicals and fertilisers. The support policy led to increasing tension with the EU's trading partners who objected to the loss of their markets to EU subsidised exports. The policy was also inefficient as an increasing proportion of the transfers from taxpayers and consumers failed to be reflected in improved farm incomes.

During the 1980s a number of half hearted attempts had been made to limit the budgetary cost of the CAP. However, the 1993 reforms introduced by Agriculture Commissioner Ray MacSharry, albeit still incomplete, went much further in that they initiated a significant reduction in support prices for the first time, at least for cereals and beef. Supply control measures were extended (particularly through the introduction of 'set aside' for cereals and oilseeds) and the role of intervention support, particularly in the beef sector, was greatly reduced. Compensation for these price reductions and intensified supply controls was provided by means of arable aid and livestock premia payments. These market regime reforms were accompanied by new agri-environment, forestry and early retirement schemes for farmers.

A further round of CAP reform was agreed in March 1999 as part of the negotiations on the Agenda 2000 agreement to prepare the EU for eastern enlargement. This pursued the same model of reductions in support prices while compensating farmers by increasing direct payments. For the first time, the dairy sector was included in the reform although implementation was postponed until

2005. As a result of these reforms, the share of direct payments in farm incomes increased. In 1992, the year before the MacSharry reform, direct payments accounted for 22 per cent of Irish farm income. By 2002, direct payments accounted for up to 70 per cent of farm income. For beef, sheep and cereal farms, in many cases they amounted to more than 100 per cent of farm income, implying that farmers are not covering their costs even when selling at protected EU prices. At world prices, most production of these commodities given the scale and production technologies currently used by farmers would be uneconomic.

Mid Term Review of the Agenda 2000 Reforms

The MacSharry and Agenda 2000 direct payments required that a farmer must plant sufficient arable land (in the case of cereals, oilseeds and protein crops) or keep a sufficient number of animals in order to draw down these payments. Such payments are called coupled payments because they are linked to the amount each farmer produces. Because the rules differed for each payments scheme (with respect to payment dates, inspection requirements, etc.), claiming these payments involved farmers (or their advisors) in a great deal of paperwork and administration. A second criticism, as demonstrated by the fact that on many farms the value of income from farming is less than the direct payments received, was that many farmers were keeping livestock or growing crops simply to collect the subsidies, rather than responding to market demand.

The Mid Term Review (MTR) of the CAP was agreed on 26 June 2003 at the Luxembourg meeting of the Agricultural Council (hence it is sometimes referred to as the Luxembourg Agreement). It proposed three main changes to the CAP support mechanisms. The most important change was to replace all premia and arable aid payments by a single farm payment to each farmer. This single farm payment is based on the level of assistance received by each farm in the reference period 2000-2002. Farmers are entitled to receive this payment, so far without time limit, regardless of changes in the area planted to crops or the number of livestock on their farm, or indeed regardless of whether they produce on their farm at all (subject to the conditions specified below). This *decoupling* of the payment from production means that, in future, farmers will make their production decisions based on the relative market returns from each enterprise rather than the size of the subsidy available. The new payment system enters into force in 2005. The single farm payment is linked to respect for standards in the areas of the environment, food safety, plant health and animal welfare, as well as a requirement to keep all farmland in good agricultural and environmental condition, so called 'cross compliance' (see Section 4).

Second, the MTR introduced the *modulation* of direct payments. This means that the single farm payment is reduced by 3 per cent in 2005, 4 per cent in 2006 and 5 per cent from 2007 onwards, subject to the exemption of the first €5,000 of direct payments per farm. These funds are transferred for use in financing rural development programmes, with rules ensuring that the bulk of the funds will be returned to the Member States which contribute them.

Third, the MTR continued the *reform of the market regimes* by lowering support prices and increasing direct payments in compensation. For Ireland, the most important market reform concerns the milk regime where a further reduction in support prices, on top of those agreed in the Agenda 2000 package from 2005, will be undertaken. Other sectors affected include cereals and rice and (in separate proposals agreed in April 2004) cotton, tobacco and olive oil. Proposals to reform the sugar sector along similar lines were made by the Commission in July 2004.

Central and East European Enlargement 2004
Yet another shock to be absorbed by EU agricultural markets is the elimination of all barriers to trade in agricultural products between the EU-15 and the accession countries of central and eastern Europe (CEECs) from May 2004 and the extension of CAP price and income supports to farmers in these countries. There were two main concerns during the negotiations. The first was that EU-15 agricultural prices were much higher than those prevailing in the CEECs. It was feared this would encourage a significant increase in CEEC production after accession, which would exacerbate the over production problem in the enlarged EU. Second, agriculture is much more important in both output and employment terms in all of the accession countries. Many commentators feared that extending CAP support to accession country farmers would require such a big increase in budget expenditure as to call into question the continued survival of the CAP without further radical reform. In fact, in purely agricultural terms, enlargement has been a much smoother process than many envisaged.

Considerable price convergence had already taken place in the years prior to accession as the applicant countries adopted agricultural policies more akin to the CAP, so the incentive to increase production when membership occurred was much smaller than previously forecast. Also, relative price levels are only one factor which determine agricultural output. Production levels in the CEECs will be held back for years to come because of structural weaknesses in management, technology, marketing, input services and food processing. In the longer run, however, these countries do have considerable unexploited yield potential and should be in a position to increase their production significantly. However, the 2003 Mid Term Review, which decoupled CAP payments from production, will reduce the incentive for farmers in the accession countries to increase production simply to gain access to higher levels of subsidy.

Given the dominant role which direct payments now play in the CAP budget, the budget debate revolved around the issue of whether, and how, these payments should also be made to farmers in the accession countries. The EU's financial perspective for the 2000-2006 period agreed in the Agenda 2000 negotiations assumed that this would not happen. It argued that farmers in the accession countries had not experienced a reduction in support prices and thus had not earned the right to compensation payments. This proved an impossible argument to sustain. The applicant countries argued, with some justification, that these payments were now an integral part of the CAP and to exclude their farmers would result in a two tier system with very unequal conditions of competition. The compromise agreed in October 2003, and incorporated into the accession agreements in December 2003, was to gradually phase in these payments over a ten year period, so that their full impact on the EU budget is not felt until 2013. Unless there is a radical downward revision in the volume of the EU's own resources in the next financial perspective covering the 2007-2013 period, it now appears that the CEEC-10 enlargement can be financed within the current budgetary ceiling. However, budgetary restrictions will continue to be a factor influencing the future shape of the CAP. The impending accession of Bulgaria and Romania, both countries with large agricultural sectors, as well as the need to finance compensation to EU dairy and sugar farmers for reductions in price support, will keep the EU agricultural budget under pressure for some years to come. The MTR regulation provides for direct payments to be cut if expenditure threatens to overshoot the CAP market expenditure ceiling.

WTO Disciplines on Agricultural Support
The WTO Agreement on Agriculture which came into force in 1995 establishes rules on the manner and amount of government support to agriculture. All border restrictions, including the EU's variable levies, were converted into fixed tariffs which are bound at a maximum rate. Furthermore, these bound tariffs were reduced by 36 per cent on average compared to their levels in 1986-90 over a six year period beginning in 1995. There is also an obligation to ensure that a minimum of 5 per cent of the domestic market is open to foreign competition which is achieved through the use of tariff rate quotas. These allow imports from third countries at a preferential duty rate but only for the quota determined quantity. For countries which use export subsidies, these subsidies had to be reduced by 36 per cent in value and 21 per cent in volume relative to the average for the period 1986-90; no new export subsidies can be introduced. With regard to domestic support to agriculture, the Agreement distinguishes between permitted and non-permitted forms of support. Support that does not influence, or only minimally influences farmers' incentives to produce is permitted and there are no disciplines applied (support of this kind is considered decoupled from production and therefore not to cause distortions to trade). Trade distorting support, such as market price support, is capped and had to be reduced by 20 per cent compared to the base period 1986-88.

A new round of negotiations to liberalise agricultural trade began in March 2000 as foreseen in the WTO Agreement on Agriculture. In November 2001, these negotiations were folded into the general round of trade negotiations launched by the WTO Ministerial Council at its meeting in Doha, Qatar, with a target date for completion of 1 January 2005 and a mid term review at Cancún, Mexico, in September 2003. The negotiations have proved difficult, not least because of disagreements between developed and developing countries over agricultural subsidies. The Cancún meeting, which was supposed to reach agreement on the overall targets for cuts in tariff and subsidies, collapsed without an agreed outcome. Negotiations continued, and there was an important breakthrough in May 2004 when, for the first time, the EU indicated that it was prepared to negotiate an end date for the elimination of export subsidies provided all other forms of export support used by other countries were eliminated in parallel and provided there was a satisfactory agreement reached in the other areas of the negotiations. In July 2004 at Geneva, WTO members agreed a framework document for the next stage of the negotiations. It foresees substantial cuts in tariffs and domestic support based on the principle that the highest levels of support should be cut the most, while allowing that countries can nominate sensitive commodities where smaller tariff reductions will be permitted. The July 2004 agreement only sets out the principles of a final agreement; the actual extent of the reductions remains to be negotiated. It is thus too early to evaluate the extent to which a new agreement will require further changes to the CAP beyond those already agreed in the Mid Term Review in 2003. Irish beef and dairy exports currently are quite dependent on export subsidies, and their phasing out even over a lengthy transition period is bound to have a negative effect on the prices farmers receive.

WTO disciplines, along with CAP reform, are slowly changing the focus of government support, from supporting production to supporting the producer, and from paying for surplus food production to paying farmers for the provision of other services which the public values. In the EU, this changing emphasis on the objectives of public support for farming is reflected in the growth of the 'second pillar' of the CAP concerned with rural development which is described in the following section.

4 RURAL DEVELOPMENT

Second Pillar of CAP

Mention was made earlier of the fact that the price and market support component of the CAP was, from the outset, accompanied by a policy to encourage the modernisation of agriculture through structural improvement. This structural policy initially consisted of measures to promote greater efficiency in agricultural production, processing and marketing. In 1975, a new instrument was added to make payments to farmers in less favoured farming areas to try to stop the exodus of farmers which was threatening the social stability and the survival of the natural environment in these areas. Although still focused on agriculture, it was the first example of a territorial or area based measure rather than a purely sectoral measure. Rural policy gained momentum as a specifically European issue in 1988 when the Commission presented its communication *The Future of Rural Society* which explicitly linked cutbacks in farm support with the need to encourage rural diversification.[3] It recognised for the first time that sustainable development in rural areas could not be based on agriculture alone but depended to an even greater extent on the successful growth of non-agricultural enterprises. It also highlighted the diversity of rural areas both in terms of their geographical features and the challenges they face.

Thus, in the reform of the EU Structural Funds in 1988 a specific objective to support rural development and to encourage the adaptation and diversification of agricultural production was introduced. In 1992, the MacSharry CAP reform saw the introduction of three further accompanying measures incorporating an agri-environment programme, an early retirement scheme and the afforestation of agricultural land to join the existing less favoured areas scheme. The growing emphasis on rural development was also reflected at this time in the launch of the LEADER programme in 1991 (see below). However, these various measures and programmes remained uncoordinated and poorly funded compared to the price and market support element of the CAP.

In March 1999, as part of the Agenda 2000 CAP reform strategy, EU leaders decided to reinforce rural development policy in several ways. Much preparation had preceded the Agenda 2000 strategy, including an important rural development conference in Cork in 1996. The reform resulted in a clearer statement of the objectives of rural development policy. It aimed to complement reforms in the agricultural market sectors in promoting a competitive, multifunctional agricultural sector, and sought to encourage alternative sources of income in rural areas, while supporting agri-environment measures. The reform also produced a unified system of rural development measures in a single Rural Development Regulation which has become known as the 'second pillar' of the CAP. Member States can choose from a 'menu' of 22 measures that respond best to the needs of their rural areas. They include measures to support investments in farm businesses, to improve the human resource structure of farming (installation aids for young farmers, early retirement scheme, training), compensation for farming in less favoured areas and areas subject to environmental constraints such as nature reserves, aids to processing and marketing of agricultural products, and forestry. While most of the measures remained directed at farmers, a special article (Article 33 of the Regulation) aims to promote the wider economic development of rural areas throughout the EU. Member states submit rural development programmes covering the period 2000-2006 for approval by the Commission which then authorises the funding. Over €50 billion was made available to co-finance these rural development programmes in the period 2000-2006 (€7.1 billion per year), allocated between Member States on the basis of objective criteria. A complicating factor is that the funding for these plans is split between the FEOGA Guarantee and Guidance Funds, so that the overall level of funding for rural development is less than transparent.

Rural development was further strengthened in the June 2003 reform of the CAP. A number of measures were added to the 22 already in place, including support for farmers' participation in schemes to improve food quality, animal welfare and environmental protection. At the same time, as we have seen, the reform introduced the concept of modulation designed to transfer funds from the first pillar (market price and income support) to the second pillar. In July 2004 the

Commission proposed to introduce a single programming and funding instrument, the European Agriculture Rural Development Fund. This Fund would have three objectives: improving the competitiveness of farming and forestry; supporting measures to improve the environment and land management; and wider rural development. The Commission also proposed to increase the level of funding to €13.7 billion per year for the next financial perspective period 2007-2013, although this level of funding has yet to be agreed by the European Council and the European Parliament.

This section asks what are the implications for Ireland's rural areas of this increased priority for rural development at EU level. It discusses the meaning of rural development and the justification for rural development measures before describing the current policy framework for Irish rural development. It also addresses the role of agri-environment policies which are now seen as an important component of overall rural development strategy.

Definition of Rural Development

Rural development as an *objective* may be defined as seeking to sustain vibrant rural communities with a balanced structure of age, income and occupational groups, capable of adapting to ongoing economic, social and cultural change, enjoying a high standard of living and an attractive quality of life and with sufficient income and employment opportunities to allow individuals and families to live with dignity.[4] Two issues are raised by this definition. The first is what is meant by rural. In Census terms, rural areas are defined as those areas outside towns and villages with a population of more than 1,500. However, it is now understood that there is a key link between settlement and urban patterns and the well being of the surrounding hinterland and communities. Counties with strong urban centres retain population while those with the lowest urbanisation rates experience persistent population decline.[5] It is artificial to distinguish between rural areas and their immediate urban centres. Thus the 1999 White Paper on Rural Development defines rural areas as all areas outside the five major urban areas. The second issue raised by the definition is the geographical scale against which success should be measured. For example, is it sufficient to achieve balanced economic growth at regional level, or is the objective to be achieved for each county or even each Rural District? Recognition of the intimate link between rural areas and their urban centres suggests that it would be useful to define targets and indicators in terms of 'urban catchments' but there is currently no administrative structure to define or represent these areas.

Rural development can also be defined to mean the *strategy* used to achieve this objective. Here its key characteristic is that it should be multisectoral and multidimensional. Rural development is not confined to a single sector, such as agriculture, but embraces initiatives across a range of natural resource sectors (marine, forestry, mining), the promotion of enterprise, infrastructure, human resources and tourism. Rural development also implies more than economic development, and extends to providing access by rural people to social services, ensuring effective organisational structures and systems of governance to meet collective needs, protection of the physical environment, and strengthening local and regional cultures. As the 1999 White Paper on Rural Development puts it, 'the rural development policy agenda constitutes all Government policies and interventions which are directed towards improving the physical, economic and social conditions of people living ... outside of the five major urban centres'.[6] Of course, this very wide definition of rural development interventions could turn out to be a source of confusion because of the multiplicity of agencies involved in delivering these programmes. To overcome this, the government operates a policy of 'rural proofing' of all national policies to ensure that policy makers are aware of the likely impact of policy proposals on the well being of rural communities. Rural proofing stands alongside the existing mechanisms of poverty proofing and equality proofing by which policies are assessed at design and review stages for their impact on the areas of concern.

Another way to limit the scope of rural development is to focus on rural development as a *process*. In this sense, rural development is not only concerned with achieving a particular set of outcomes, such as the creation of viable employment opportunities in rural areas, but is also identified with a particular *style* of development characterised by a 'bottom up' rather than 'top down' approach. Top down approaches are associated with mainstream programmes designed and delivered by central agencies and provided uniformly across the country. Bottom up approaches (also referred to as area based approaches) are characterised by an emphasis on local participation in the formulation and implementation of development objectives for an area, by a preference for exploiting indigenous skills and resources rather than relying on 'imported' expertise and capital, by the attempt to integrate social as well as economic development and, for some at least, by a concern that development should benefit the more marginal and disadvantaged groups. A key issue here concerns the structures which are put in place to facilitate the coordination of the top down and bottom up approaches.

Rationale for Rural Development Policies

It is a relevant question to ask what is the rationale for government support for rural development measures. If people wish to live and work in Dublin or one of the other major cities, why should the government intervene to try to prevent this? As noted above, an important recent justification for rural development measures has been to compensate for cutbacks in farm support. The hope is that it is easier to gain acceptance for reduced agricultural support if offsetting measures to benefit those who might lose out from this process are put in place, but this narrow rationale clearly cannot explain the adoption of the wide ranging rural development objectives set out in the 1999 White Paper. An important argument is that those who seek to live and work in Dublin are not necessarily doing so from choice and would prefer to remain in a rural area if sufficient employment opportunities were available. In terms of the typology of policy objectives outlined in Chapter 1, this is clearly an equity argument. The implication is that resources should be used to compensate for the competitive disadvantages of rural areas (for example, to provide higher grant aid levels to assist enterprise startups in rural areas) in order to achieve the socially desired objectives of balanced population and economic growth. This can be complemented by an efficiency argument in terms of market failure. This is often couched in terms of the hidden costs – diseconomies – of urban congestion while rural resources remain under utilised. Long distance commuting and residential development located at greater and greater distance from where people work resulting from unbalanced development is simply not sustainable in the longer term. There is also an argument that individuals, who might be unwilling to commit to living in rural Ireland if asked to make the decision in isolation, might be very willing to do so if they were aware that there was a concerted plan to build up and support rural communities. Here government policy can provide an important element of credibility by underlining its commitment to a rural development strategy, for example, through its decisions on infrastructure investment and the location of public services and public administration offices. In these cases, rural policy is justified over and above any argument based on concepts of equity and balanced distribution of opportunities across geographical areas.

The growing importance of rural development policy at EU level has been reflected in increased funding for and the introduction of new rural development agencies and measures in Ireland. While the rhetoric of rural development is relatively new, there is a long history of rural development initiatives which can be traced back to the establishment of the Congested Districts Board by the British administration in 1898. In the context of the country's poor overall economic performance until the 1960s, these measures failed to stem the fall in the Irish rural population, taking place since the 1840s. With improved economic growth, however, this fall was reversed in Leinster in the late 1960s, and the population recovery spread to all provinces during the 1970s. Between 1971 and 1981, the population of aggregate rural areas grew by 10 per cent, and by a further 3 per cent between 1981 and 1986. This recovery in rural population numbers halted in the period 1986-91 when all regions apart from the East region experienced a fall in rural population. With the more buoyant economy in the 1990s, there was again an increase in the aggregate rural population between 1991 and 1996 and even more so between 1996 and 2002. Over the 1971-2002 period, the rural population increased by 11 per cent, while the urban population increased by 50 per cent.

A simple headcount does not tell the whole story. The recovery in the rural population has not been uniform across all districts. About half of all Rural Districts experienced population decline during the 1991-96 intercensal period, with the highest proportionate decrease being recorded in the western part of the country and the Midlands, and one fifth continued to show a decline in the period 1996-2002. Rural areas also have higher than average dependency levels, particularly in the western and border counties where those over 65 years comprise a very high proportion of the population. Many rural areas also have a weak economic structure, with a high dependence on agriculture, the lack of a diversified employment base and the continued out migration of those with higher levels of education. The low population density and unbalanced demographic structure of many rural areas creates difficulties for both public and private service provision (health, transport, shops) and leads to increasing isolation and social exclusion. But it would be wrong to associate all rural areas with problems arising from remoteness and deprivation. Rural areas today are very heterogeneous, and the problems facing those areas contiguous to urban centres are more often the problems of managing the overspill of urban growth.

Rural Development Policy Framework
In 1999, the Government issued a White Paper on Rural Development which, as we noted earlier, set down a clear objective for rural development as well as a set of principles as the basis for strategy. These principles are implemented through the National Development Plan (NDP) 2000-06. The largest single element is the CAP Rural Development Plan, which comprises the four CAP accompanying measures. This is complemented by the Agriculture and Rural Development Priority (Sub-Programme) in the two Regional Operational Programmes administered by the Border, Midland and Western (BMW) Region and the Southern and Eastern (S&E) Region, respectively. The Plan identifies 17 per cent out of the total expenditure which will be spent to promote rural development. Although this allocation seems high, the expenditure is hugely biased towards the agricultural sector and, within that, to income support measures.

A key promise of the NDP 2000-06 was the completion within two years of a National Spatial Strategy (NSS) to plan the country's spatial development. Ireland's economic success in recent years has been accompanied by spatial patterns of development which have seen employment opportunities becoming more concentrated in some areas, while economic weaknesses remain in others. The ESS, which was published in 2002 is a twenty year planning framework designed to deliver more balanced social, economic and physical development between regions, supported by more effective planning. The key concept behind the ESS is that, in order to drive development in the regions, areas of sufficient scale and critical mass must be built up through a network of gateways and hubs. The NDP identified Dublin, Cork, Limerick/Shannon, Galway and Waterford as existing gateways. The NSS added four new national level gateways, including Dundalk and Sligo, as well as Letterkenny/(Derry) and Athlone/Tullamore/ Mullingar acting as linked gateways. The NSS identifies nine, strategically located, medium sized hubs to support and be supported by the gateways and to link out to wider rural areas. The hubs identified are Cavan, Ennis, Kilkenny, Mallow, Monaghan, Tuam and Wexford, as well as Ballina/Castlebar and Tralee/Killarney acting as linked hubs, to promote regional development in their areas. The NSS also identifies an important need to support the role of smaller towns, villages and rural areas at the local level.

The NSS will be implemented through planning guidelines at regional level linked to county and city plans based on its principles, as well as through influencing the spatial aspects of national infrastructure investment including transport, energy and communications. The regional planning guidelines are under preparation. Guidelines have already been published on rural housing. It remains to be seen whether the new spatial strategy will be more successful in prioritising investment in a few favoured locations than earlier attempts at a spatial strategy in the 1960s (the Buchanan Report) or the 1970s (the IDA's regional industrial plans). The NDP itself attempts to defuse criticism by arguing that the development agencies will endeavour to spread the location of enterprise 'across a wide spread of locations in both Regions'. How this 'dispersal' approach to the location of enterprise can be made consistent with the proposed gateway approach with its implied concentration of resources is unclear. The government's decentralisation programme for the civil service announced in the 2004 Budget also appeared to ignore the NSS guidelines, scattering the 10,000 civil servants to be moved over 53 different locations.

In addition to public spending through the National Development Plan, there are a number of other programmes which directly target rural communities as envisaged in the White Paper on Rural Development. One of the more innovative of these is the LEADER programme launched as an EU funded initiative. LEADER is a bottom up process with area based, local action groups implementing local development programmes. Under this programme, groups covering defined geographical areas are invited to tender for support on the basis of a development plan each prepares for its area. Activities which can be funded include vocational training, rural tourism, small firms, craft enterprises, local services and the marketing of local products. LEADER I ran from 1991 through 1994 in selected rural areas, while LEADER II operated on a nation wide basis during the period from 1994 through 1999. Currently, 22 local action groups are funded under the LEADER+ initiative for the period 2000-2006; while there is a complementary LEADER National Rural Development Programme operated by 13 local groups in areas of the country not covered by LEADER+. Other local development programmes include the CLÁR programme launched in 2001 to provide funding to targeted regions which suffered the most depopulation between 1926 and 1966 and the rural development aspects of the cross border programmes PEACE and INTERREG. The Department of Community, Rural and Gaelthacht Affairs was established in 2002 with the remit, *inter alia*, of promoting economic and social development in rural communities and is responsible for administering these programmes.

Agri-Environmental Issues
In addition to support for agricultural restructuring and rural enterprise development, the other main objective of EU rural development policy is to protect the rural environment. Agriculture plays both a negative and a positive role in environmental protection and in the preservation of rural landscapes. On the one hand, intensive agriculture is associated with a range of environmental risks

including water pollution and the loss of biodiversity and valued amenities. Thus, agricultural production is increasingly influenced by environmental regulations designed to minimise these risks. Planning permission is now required for large intensive livestock units. The Nitrates Directive, designed to improve water quality, limits the number of livestock farmers can carry, as well as requiring investment in storage facilities for animal manure to ensure that it is spread only in the months when the land can absorb it. Livestock production is a major contributor to Ireland's greenhouse gas emissions, and reduced livestock numbers may be sought as a way of meeting Ireland's obligations under the Kyoto Protocol. On the other hand, it is increasingly accepted that farmers are managers of natural resources and provide environmental services as well as foodstuffs, in what is now characterised as a multifunctional agriculture. Farmers are not normally paid by the market to provide such services. Where these services are valued by society, there is a case for public support.

The EU took a big step to integrate environmental considerations into the CAP with the launch of an agri-environment scheme in 1994 as one of the accompanying measures of CAP reform. This is implemented in Ireland as the Rural Environment Protection Scheme (REPS), under which farmers follow environmentally friendly farming practices in return for additional payments. Forty four thousand farmers, accounting for 1.5 million hectares of farmland, were participating in REPS 1 by 1999. As part of the CAP Rural Development Plan, the number of participants is expected to increase to around 70,000 by 2006 in REPS 2, which would imply that over half of all farmers would be enrolled in the scheme by that date. However, by the end of 2002, the number of farmers participating in REPS 2 had actually fallen slightly as compared to the end of REPS 1. Only 61 per cent of REPS 1 participants had re-enrolled in REPS 2 by that date. Farmers have criticised the relatively high cost of drawing up the necessary farm plans, the failure of the payments to keep pace with inflation and the perceived high degree of bureaucracy associated with implementation and compliance. The Department of Agriculture and Food is seeking to make changes to the scheme in order to enhance its attractiveness to farmers for the remainder of the plan period.

An important concept introduced as part of the June 2003 CAP reform is cross compliance. Cross compliance means that farmers must be in compliance with EU and statutory standards in the field of environmental protection, public health, animal and plant health and animal welfare and are required to keep land in good agricultural and environmental condition to be eligible to receive the single farm payment. Whereas insistence on cross compliance was optional following the Agenda 2000 CAP reform, member states are now required to ensure that land or production in receipt of direct payments is farmed with appropriate respect for the environment and the other mandatory standards. Payments can be reduced or withheld in the event of non-compliance.

Cross compliance is now the baseline for payments under the first pillar of the CAP. This will lead to a rethinking of the role of REPS in the future. REPS until now, has functioned largely as an extensification scheme. In return for accepting restrictions on fertiliser use, farmers were eligible to receive additional payments under the scheme. Many REPS participants already used less fertiliser than the recommended limits; for these farmers the scheme operated as an income enhancement scheme rather than producing additional environmental benefits. Others would argue that the REPS philosophy flies in the face of good environmental policy, where the guiding principle is that the polluter pays. If excessive use of fertiliser or high stocking densities by farmers causes environmental damage, the public should not have to pay to prevent this damage. In any case, under the principle of cross compliance, farmers can only receive CAP payments if they restrict stocking densities and fertiliser use to the point where environmental damage is avoided. It does not make sense to offer farmers more money to reduce stocking densities and fertiliser use further if there is no further environmental benefit to be gained. In future, the REPS scheme should revert to its original intention to pay farmers for the additional costs in supplying additional environmental benefits which are valued by the public at large, such as the provision of habitats, or the maintenance of hedgerows or stone walls, over and above good environmental practice.

5 FOOD PROCESSING AND FOOD SAFETY

Food Industry
Very few agricultural products are sold directly to the consumer – vegetables, fruit and eggs in farmers' markets being the main examples. Most agricultural products are purchased by food processors who prepare food for final consumption for either the domestic or export markets. Output of the Irish food industry (including drinks) in 2002 amounted to about €16.9 billion or more than three times that of primary agriculture. Net output (which subtracts the value of raw materials purchased by the industry and gives a better idea of its contribution to the overall economy) was valued at €7.1 billion in 2002 and amounted to over 8 per cent of GDP at market prices. The industry provides direct employment for up to 51,000 people or 19 per cent of the total industrial workforce. While there are over 800 individual plants in the industry, the 40 largest firms with over 250 employees account for around 40 per cent of the employment and almost 60 per cent of the output.

The market for food is changing rapidly due to changing consumer demands and market structures. Changing consumer lifestyles are having a decisive influence on food demand. Increased numbers of working women, reduced leisure time and the decline in the traditional family unit are changing eating habits and increasing the demand for convenience foods. Thus important growth areas for the food industry are the food ingredients business (such as dairy ingredients, meat and by products such as pizza toppings and meat flavourings, and other ingredients such as colourings, flavourings and malt) which produce ingredients for pre-prepared foods, as well as the food service sector (embracing all forms of catering and eating out). Eating out now accounts for 20 per cent of food expenditure in Ireland, while the equivalent figure in the USA is over 50 per cent. The other important trend is the growing importance of retail concentration which is shifting market power to the giant retailers. Just 25 retailers in Europe now account for 45 per cent of food sales. In Ireland, three multiples account for over 50 per cent of retail sales. This concentration of buying power gives the large retailers substantial power to dictate terms to their suppliers, including not only price but also quality and safety characteristics.

The Irish food industry has a number of strengths and weaknesses in meeting these market challenges. Production facilities are modern, in part because of generous EU investment aids in the past, and Irish food benefits from a good marketing image abroad. However, the relatively small scale of the industry inhibits cost competitiveness and access to markets. It also makes product and process innovation more difficult. The industry remains reliant on commodity products with limited penetration of value-added markets. Certain sectors, such as meat processing, are characterised by over capacity. A specific support programme for the food industry was included in both the 1994-99 and the 2000-2006 National Development Plans. These initiatives are designed to enhance the industry's competitiveness and innovative capabilities, while ensuring that development is underpinned by attention to food safety and consumer demands. Food safety issues are considered in more detail in the remainder of this section.

Growing Concern over Food Safety

From earliest times food has been particularly susceptible to exploitation, and there is a long history of food legislation with the purpose of preventing consumers being either cheated or poisoned! Measures for the protection of the consumer against the adulteration of food and drink are among the earliest examples of social legislation. Since then the scope of food law has been greatly widened. Examples of some of the matters now covered by legislation include the produce of diseased animals posing a threat to human health; sanitary conditions in food preparation, packaging and handling; pesticide and hormone residues in food; packaging materials which may pose a threat to health; food additives; the labelling requirements for food products; and weights and measures legislation.

Despite the undoubted improvement in food purity and in merchandising practices brought about by this legislation consumers are increasingly uneasy about the safety and quality of the modern food supply. Issues of recent concern include agrochemical residues in food, the increasing number and diversity of food additives, the use of illegal substances in livestock production, the existence of nitrates in drinking water and genetically engineered foods. There have been sharp falls in the consumption of particular foods caused by publicity given, for example, to Bovine Spongiform Encethalopathy (BSE) in cattle, listeria in soft cheeses or salmonella in eggs. Consumer concerns also extend beyond the safety of food products to their production methods including genetic modification, animal welfare and environmental and ethical concerns.

The risk of food borne diseases has increased for a number of reasons. Best hygiene practices are not always followed in commercial and domestic kitchens. Fewer people are preparing their own food and more eating outside the home means a higher proportion of people at risk in outbreaks. The increasing demand for ready to go foods has resulted in food being served in a growing number of non-traditional outlets such as garage forecourts. The global distribution of food has lengthened the food chain. The increased competition and price constraints on food producers has led the food sector to seek cost reductions through ever more complex food processing and may sometimes encourage producers to adopt practices which have adverse health effects. Nutrition is another area of concern. While consumers are preoccupied with food safety at present, food quality issues and the nutritional value of food may re-emerge as a more important policy issue in future.

Fortunately, in Ireland, food problems have not emerged to the dramatic extent reached elsewhere. However, the increase in food poisoning notifications (E-coli, for instance) suggests that vigilance is essential. Food production and tourism are major elements in the economy, and both depend crucially on a favourable international perception of the safety of Irish food. So along with the issue of the health and lives of its own citizens, Ireland has a vital economic interest in becoming a centre of excellence in food safety.

Economic Considerations

In economic terms, the need for governments to regulate for food safety is the result of a market failure. This arises because consumers are not necessarily in a position to determine the safety characteristics of food they consume on the basis of visual inspection alone. There is thus an asymmetry of information between the producer and consumer of food. In this, the market for food safety is like the market for used cars. Sellers have more information about the quality of the car than buyers. Because buyers often cannot tell the difference between a good and a bad used car, both good and bad cars must sell at the same price and the seller of a good car is unable to extract a premium for quality. In the same way, there is a tendency for food safety to be undersupplied by the market because consumers are not always able to distinguish between high and low food standards.

Of course, if we go to a restaurant and subsequently experience illness due to food poisoning, we are unlikely to patronise that restaurant again. Where there is the likelihood of repeat purchases, food businesses have an incentive to maintain high standards in order to maximise the likelihood of retaining our custom. The development of brand names, or supermarkets who monitor quality on our behalf, are other ways in which market institutions can respond to the asymmetry of information. However, sometimes firms themselves may be unaware of, say, the carcinogenic risk associated with a particular additive or production process. There may also be strong externalities that justify government intervention, either on the production side (one rogue producer who fails to meet adequate food standards can put the reputation of an entire national food industry at risk) or on the consumption side (an infectious food borne illness imposes wider costs on society that transcend those incurred by the individual consumer). This is the economic case for governments to step in to ensure that minimum food standards are maintained.

While the failure to observe adequate food standards can impose economic costs both on individuals and society at large, maintaining and enforcing these standards is also a costly exercise. For economists, this raises the question whether the benefits from a particular food regulation (in terms of the avoided cost of food illnesses or, for an exporting country, the loss of market reputation in export markets) exceed its costs. The idea that we should try to balance benefits and costs in setting food regulations suggests that trying to achieve zero risk is not the optimal strategy. Removing all risk from eating food is likely to be hugely expensive, and the economic benefit from lowering risk from a minimal to a zero risk of contracting an illness may not justify taking this extra step. There may also be an alternative and more efficient instrument available to achieve the same degree of risk reduction. Governments, of course, should not take such decisions on the basis of cost benefit studies alone; moral and ethical criteria must also be taken into account. However, the economist's framework of balancing the expected benefits from risk reduction against the costs of achieving such reductions should be an important adjunct to the decision making process in food safety regulation.

European Union Food Safety Framework

These growing concerns prompted the incoming European Commission in October 1999 to make food safety a top priority. In January 2000, the Irish Commissioner for Health and Consumer Protection, David Byrne, produced a White Paper on Food Safety which outlined a comprehensive strategy to restore consumers' confidence in their food supply.[7] There were three elements to the strategy: new legislation on the safety of food and animal feed; a new agency to offer scientific advice on food borne threats; and more stringent control and enforcement.

A new General Food Law, which brings together the general principles of food and animal feed safety was agreed in 2002. Up until then, EU food law had been motivated mainly by the desire to facilitate the free movement of foodstuffs throughout the internal market, by removing technical barriers such as differences in standards. The new law made food safety and consumer protection the cornerstone of the regulatory regime. Including animal feed in its provisions was a major advance as animal feed has been the source of many food scares in the past decade. The general principles which now underlie food safety policy emphasise a whole food chain approach (food safety must be ensured at all stages of the food chain, from the producer through to the consumer), risk analysis (meaning that the policy is based on a scientific understanding of risk with due account for the need for precaution when scientific opinion is not yet clear), operator liability (all food sector operators are now responsible for ensuring the safety of the products which they import, produce, process or sell), traceability (from 1 January 2005 all foodstuffs, animal feeds and feed ingredients must be traceable right through the food chain) and openness (citizens have the right to clear and accurate information on food and health risks from public authorities). This General Food Law is supplemented by a large number of targeted regulations addressing specific food safety issues, such as the use of pesticides, food supplements, colouring, antibiotics and hormones in food production; rules on hygiene; and legislation setting down procedures for the release, marketing, labelling and traceability of crops and foodstuffs containing genetically modified organisms.

The second Commission initiative was the creation of the European Food Safety Authority (EFSA) in 2002 to provide a source of independent, objective scientific advice on food related risks. The new Authority has responsibility for the EU Rapid Alert System for food which links EU countries in cases of food borne threats. It will take time to establish the credibility of the new Agency among consumers. The Commission explicitly rejected the option of modelling it on the US Food and Drugs Administration which has responsibility not only for risk assessment (i.e. quantifying the risk associated with a potential food hazard) but also risk management (i.e. taking the necessary decisions to respond to a perceived food borne risk such as strengthening existing regulations). The Authority's role is limited to giving its opinion, and it will be up to the Commission (in conjunction with the Council and the Parliament) to initiate the required action.

The third initiative was to improve the EU framework for control and enforcement of food safety legislation. Enforcement of food regulations is the responsibility of national governments albeit under the oversight of the EU. An EU framework directive lays down norms and procedures relating to inspection and enforcement, and the Food and Veterinary Office of the European Commission, which is based in Grange, County Meath, controls the performance of national authorities and makes recommendations aimed at improving national control and inspection systems. The Commission's powers to ensure enforcement in Member States have been criticised in the past as slow and unwieldy. An important enforcement change is the extension during 2000 of the EU Product Liability Directive to primary agricultural products such as beef, milk, fruit and vegetables. This will make farmers liable for damages if consumers take legal proceedings against them and if there is proof that they are responsible for putting unsafe food into the food chain.

The EU legislation regulating the release and marketing of genetically modified (GM) organisms and foods is particularly controversial. The legislation has the twin objectives of ensuring that GM food poses no risk to public health, the health of animals or to the environment, and that consumers are fully informed about genetic modification through labelling. GM organisms or foods are those in which genetic material has been altered in a way that does not occur naturally by mating or natural recombination. The EU had approved a number of GM products until late 1998 under the Novel Foods regulation, but growing public concern over their supposed environmental and health risks led several EU countries to demand a moratorium on new approvals. New EU regulations in 2001 and 2003 were designed to permit the moratorium to be lifted. They put in place a new set of procedures for the approval of all food and feed derived from GM ingredients, as well as requiring all products containing GM ingredients to be labelled as such, and those ingredients traceable to their source.

The EFSA first conducts a risk assessment based on available scientific evidence. The Commission drafts a proposal to either grant or refuse authorisation based on that opinion which is then approved or not by representatives of the member states on the basis of qualified majority voting. If the member states, and subsequently the Council of Ministers, fail to reach a decision, then the Commission has the authority to authorise approval if the risk assessment is positive. The regulation on labelling and traceability provides that all foods which contain more than 0.9 per cent of an approved GM product must carry a label stating 'This product contains genetically modified organisms' or 'produced from genetically modified (name of organism)'. Business operators must transmit and retain information about products that contain or are produced from GM ingredients at each marketing stage.

In May 2004, the EU approved a GM variety of sweet corn for import and sale (but not for cultivation) thus ending the moratorium in place since 1998. However, this and subsequent approvals were decided by the Commission itself, as there was not a qualified majority among the member states to reach a decision. Whether this will be sufficient to support the EU's case in a complaint brought by the USA, Argentina and Canada that the EU's moratorium on approvals was illegal under WTO rules will be clear when the WTO issues its judgement on the dispute in late 2004. Approval per se may mean little if European food manufacturers and retailers fear they will lose customers by putting GM ingredients in their products. However, with a small but rapidly growing proportion of the world's crops planted to GM varieties, consumer attitudes may change if they are asked in future to pay a big premium for GM free products, and if future GM varieties have more obvious benefits for consumers than those which have been released to date.

Irish Responses
In Ireland, the Food Safety Authority was set up in 1999 to ensure that food produced, distributed or marketed in the State meets the highest standards of food safety and hygiene and to coordinate food safety activities 'from farm to fork'. The Authority has functions in relation to research, advice, coordination of services and certification of food. It operates the national food safety compliance programme by means of service contracts with the agencies involved in the enforcement of food legislation (including Government Departments, Health Boards, local authorities, and the Radiological Protection Institute). Around 1,800 persons in total are involved in the inspection and control of food. In addition, the Authority works with industry and training bodies to improve, harmonise and

coordinate food safety and hygiene training through the country. The Authority is required to operate on the basis of scientific principles and with the primacy of consumer interests in mind.

Initiatives such as the National Beef Assurance Scheme and the National Sheep Identification System have been launched to ensure the identification and traceability of animals/meat. Controls on BSE remain in place to ensure that meat from confirmed cases and from herds in which cases have been located does not enter the food or feed chains. Another priority area concerns residue testing which is particularly focused on detecting illegal growth promoters in cattle and antibiotic residues in pigs. A new cross border Food Safety Promotion Board known as Safefood has been established under the Good Friday Agreement to contribute to the improved coordination of food safety activities on the island as a whole. Its functions include food safety promotion; research into food safety; communication of food alerts; surveillance of food borne diseases; and the promotion of scientific cooperation and linkages between laboratories.

The growing demand for food safety and improved animal welfare will increasingly impact on farmers. Even in the absence of government regulation, the private sector and particularly the large retail chains are insisting that their suppliers meet stringent hygiene and safety standards. These demands will require farmers to undertake additional investments and will accelerate the process of structural change in the industry. However, they also open up additional marketing opportunities. Instead of selling beef as a commodity product, for example, it becomes possible to produce beef for particular niche markets and to guarantee consumers that their particular requirements have been met. One fast growing market is for organic produce. Organic production in Ireland is relatively limited, with 1,000 registered producers and 30,000 hectares, or 0.5 per cent of the agricultural land area, in organic production or in conversion in 2002. The 2002 report of the Organic Development Committee estimated that a target of 3 per cent of agricultural land under organic farming by 2006 was a feasible goal. A national steering group has been established to promote marketing and research, and financial assistance for farmers wishing to convert to organic production is available under the REPS agri-environment scheme. The decoupling of direct payments should also give a boost to organic production in future.

6 CONCLUSIONS

The agri-food sector is one of the key sectors of the Irish economy, accounting for around 9 per cent of both GDP and employment. This chapter has emphasised the way in which the sector is heavily influenced by government policies promoting specific objectives. The substantial protection provided to EU agriculture means that almost all the income generated by agricultural production arises because of transfers either from consumers or taxpayers resulting from the operation of the

Common Agricultural Policy. The share of budget transfers from taxpayers, which now accounts for 70 per cent of Irish farm income, is particularly striking.

This system of transfers is threatened by further WTO trade commitments, by the need to accommodate EU enlargement and by an increasingly powerful environmental lobby concerned about the negative impact of intensive agricultural production on the environment. It is, in any case, costly and inefficient from an EU perspective; inequitable in its effects as most of the support goes to the larger farmers who need it least; and ineffective in meeting its objectives as structural change in the industry leading to out migration and a reduction in the number of farms continues apace. How competitive Irish agriculture would be in a more liberal trade environment, competing with third countries at world market prices, has not been explicitly addressed in this chapter but is a very live topic when farmers meet to discuss the future. Many farmers will have difficulty surviving at their present levels of scale and productivity. Irish agriculture has many strengths, but these have often been neglected during the era of protection. Over the next decade, more emphasis must be put on strengthening the competitiveness of farm production while ensuring that it lives up to ever higher consumer demands for safety and environmental sustainability.

The relative decline in the importance of food production, given its central importance in the past in rural areas, has stimulated the search for an alternative basis for rural development. In principle, with the publication of the 1999 White Paper on Rural Development and the follow up expenditure in the National Development Plan 2000-2006, there now exists a coherent and coordinated strategy to this end. Considerable attention has been given to the partnership or 'bottom up' approach to rural development, as practised by the LEADER groups, area partnerships and County Enterprise Boards. Advances in our understanding of the dynamics of rural growth have highlighted the importance of dynamic urban centres, or gateways, in underpinning growth in their surrounding rural areas. Hence the importance of the national spatial strategy announced in 2002. The National Plan contains a commitment to balanced regional development, with the implicit objective of encouraging more rapid growth in the less favoured BMW region as compared to the better endowed S&E region. However, as we noted above, there is a danger that the rhetoric is not yet matched by appropriate resource allocations. In particular, as long as the bulk of rural development funds are allocated to the agricultural sector, rural development programmes will be inhibited in the contribution they can make to the development of rural areas.

The paradox should be noted that, at a time when government intervention in agricultural markets is being reduced, the demand for greater regulation of food markets has never been greater. While the rationale for continued agricultural support becomes less and less persuasive as farm incomes approach equality with incomes in the non-farm sector, the growing complexity of the food chain and fear of the consequences of new technological advances is fuelling consumer demands for greater food regulation. While a perfectly sound case for regulation can be made, it is important to bear in mind that all regulation imposes costs as well as benefits and that the task of the regulator is to find the appropriate balance. Economists are particularly well trained to assist in finding this balance through assessing the costs and benefits of alternative regulatory policies.

Endnotes

1   A. Matthews, *Farm Incomes: Myths and Reality*, Cork University Press, Cork 2000, contains a discussion of these difficulties.

2   Department of Agriculture and Food, *Annual Review and Outlook 2003-04*, Economics and Planning Division, Dublin 2004.

3   Commission of the European Communities, *The Future of Rural Society: Commission Communication to Parliament and the Council*, Office for Official Publications of the European Communities (OOPEC), Luxembourg 1998.

4   Department of Agriculture and Food, *Ensuring the Future – A Strategy for Rural Development in Ireland: A White Paper on Rural Development*, Stationery Office, Dublin 1999, p. 19.

5   National Economic and Social Council, *Population Distribution and Economic Development: Trends and Policy Implications*, Stationery Office, Dublin 1997.

6   Department of Agriculture and Food, *op. cit.*, p. 20.

7   European Commission, *White Paper on Food Safety*, OOPEC, Brussels 2000.

PERFORMANCE AND POLICY ISSUES: PREDOMINANTLY PUBLICLY FUNDED SECTORS

CHAPTER 10

Health: Funding, Access and Efficiency

Anne Nolan[*]

1 INTRODUCTION

This chapter examines the health sector, a key component of Irish economic activity and the subject of much recent policy discussion. In terms of its economic impact, expenditure on the health services accounted for 8.1 per cent of GDP and 9.1 per cent of total employment in 2002.[1] After years of expenditure growth barely in line with inflation during the 1980s and early 1990s, expenditure on the health service in Ireland has increased dramatically since 1997, increasing by nearly 80 per cent in real terms from 1997 to 2002. While Irish health expenditure as a proportion of GNP has increased from 7.3 per cent in 1991 to 8.2 per cent in 2001, health expenditure as a proportion of GNP has also risen across the EU and OECD, with the result that Ireland still ranks among the low spenders on health, in terms of health expenditure as a proportion of GNP (see Table 10.1).[2]

The challenges facing the Irish health service today are therefore very different to those of the 1980s and early 1990s. While much discussion in Ireland during that period focussed on the under funding of the health services (public expenditure on the health services decreased in real terms in some years during the 1980s), the emphasis has shifted now to consider issues such as the efficiency and effectiveness of such increased investment, concerns shared by many other countries. In light of increasing expenditure, cost containment measures that aim to make patients and providers more aware of the resource implications of their decisions are becoming increasingly common. While ensuring that increased expenditure delivers services efficiently and with sufficient effectiveness in terms of health outcomes are important concerns, the extent to which access to health services is distributed equitably across the population is a much discussed issue in Ireland and elsewhere. Of crucial concern in Ireland, is the extent to which coverage by private health insurance confers faster access to hospital services.

244

Table 10.1
Health Expenditure as a % of GNP[1] (Selected OECD countries, 1991 and 2001)

	1991	2001	% of population over 65
Austria	7.2	7.8	15.5
Denmark	8.6	8.8	14.8
Finland	9.3	7.0	15.1
France	8.8	9.4	16.2
Germany[2]	7.2	10.8	16.9
Ireland	*7.3*	*8.2*	*11.2*
Netherlands	8.2	8.6	13.6
UK	6.0	7.6	15.9
USA	12.5	13.8	12.4

Sources: OECD, *Health Data,* OECD, Paris 2004 and European Commission, *AMECO Macro Economic Database 2004*, www.europa.eu.int 2004.
[1]While health expenditure is usually expressed as a proportion of GDP, the large divergence between Irish GDP and GNP figures means that, for comparative purposes, it is more appropriate to express health expenditure as a proportion of GNP (see also A. Nolan, and B. Nolan, 'Ireland's Health Care System: Some Issues and Challenges' (Proceedings of ESRI/FFS Budget Perspectives Conference 2004), ESRI, Dublin 2004).
[2]Data refer to 1990.

An additional issue, which receives much attention in discussions about the Irish health sector, is the complex relationship between the public and private sectors in both the financing and delivery of health services. While the government intervenes to a large degree in the regulation and financing of health care in Ireland, and to a lesser degree in the provision of public health services, the private sector also has a significant role to play in the financing and delivery of health services. While the majority of expenditure is funded from general taxation, private insurance and out of pocket expenses by individuals comprise an important element of health sector financing in Ireland. In addition, many health services are provided by private practitioners, such as general practitioner (GP) and dental services, and the majority of hospitals are privately owned institutions which receive most of their funding from the state. This complex interaction between the public and private sectors has important implications for equity and efficiency, particularly in the hospitals sector.

The remainder of this chapter focuses on these themes of access, efficiency, effectiveness and cost control in the context of discussions on key issues with regard to the health services in Ireland. Section 2 briefly outlines the structure of the Irish health service, concentrating on the organisation of eligibility for free health services to ensure equity of access to health care as well as the interactions between the public and private sectors in both the financing and delivery of health services in Ireland. This section also briefly describes the recent *Health Service Reform Programme*, announced by the government in mid 2003. Section 3 discusses the rationale for government intervention in the financing and delivery of health services (see also Chapter 2 on the role of the state), outlining the various efficiency and equity justifications for government intervention in the sector. Section 4 discusses the four sources of finance in the health sector, concentrating on private insurance, which plays such a significant role in the financing of health care. It also discusses the equity and efficiency concerns surrounding this complex intermix between public and private health care, in particular in the hospitals sector. Section 5 outlines trends in health expenditure in Ireland, comparisons with other OECD countries and discusses the problem of measuring output from the health sector and making international comparisons at an aggregated level, or at a disaggregated level between different interventions/ treatments. This section also discusses initiatives to support cost control in terms of health sector expenditure, concentrating on measures at the micro level that attempt to influence the behaviour of patients and providers alike. Section 6 concludes the chapter.

2 STRUCTURE OF IRISH HEALTH SERVICE

The Government, the Minister for Health and Children and the Department of Health and Children have overall responsibility for the provision of health services in Ireland. The department's primary role is to support the Minister in the formulation and evaluation of policies for the health service, as well as the strategic planning of the health services in consultation with the health boards, other government departments, the voluntary sector and other interested parties.

The health boards, which were established in 1970, are responsible for the actual delivery of health services in their area of influence. The Department takes account of a range of factors in determining what proportion of total funding should be allocated to each health board. These factors include the cost of providing services in the previous year, pay costs, health service developments and funding for agreed specific items. The boards provide many of the services directly (e.g. district nurses, public nursing homes) and they arrange for the provision of other services by health professionals, private health service providers, voluntary hospitals and voluntary/community organisations. There are currently ten health boards: three area health boards located in the eastern region under the guidance of the Eastern Regional Health Authority (ERHA) and seven regional health boards covering the rest of the country.

Eligibility for Free Public Health Services
All individuals who are ordinarily resident in Ireland are granted either full or limited eligibility for public health care services. Individuals with full eligibility, termed 'medical cardholders' or 'public patients', are entitled to receive all health services free of charge, including GP services, prescribed medicines, all dental, ophthalmic and aural services, maternity services, in-patient services in public

hospitals and specialist treatment in out-patient clinics of public hospitals. At present just under 30 per cent of the population are medical cardholders.

The remainder of the population, those with limited eligibility ('non-medical cardholders' or 'private patients'), are entitled to free maternity services, in-patient services in public hospitals (subject to a €45 charge per day), specialist services in out-patient clinics (again, subject to a €45 charge per day), assistance towards the cost of prescribed medicines over a monthly limit (under the Drugs Payment Scheme) and assistance towards the cost of prescribed medicines for certain chronic conditions (under the Long Term Illness Scheme) or high cost treatments (under the High Tech Drugs Scheme). They must, however, pay for all GP consultations and all dental, ophthalmic and aural treatments. Ireland is unique within the EU-15 in the extent to which individuals must pay for GP services: only the Netherlands also excludes a significant proportion of the population from eligibility to free GP care.

Eligibility for a medical card is dependent upon income and is decided on the basis of a means test with the income thresholds set nationally and updated annually. The intention is that the decision to seek medical care should not be dependent on economic resources/ability to pay. Currently, the weekly income thresholds are €142.50 for a single person living alone, €200 for a married couple and €250 for a married couple with two children. The limits increase for those aged 66 years and over (e.g. for a married couple the limit increases to €224).[3] From 1 July 2001, all individuals aged 70 years and over are also entitled to a medical card, regardless of income. In special circumstances such as a cancer diagnosis, an individual who is otherwise ineligible on the basis of income or age may be granted a medical card.

Table 10.2 shows the change in medical card coverage and private health insurance coverage since 1980. As discussed in further detail in Section 4, private health insurance in Ireland is primarily taken out by non-medical cardholders to cover the costs of private or semi-private hospital care in public and private hospitals. At present, just under 50 per cent of the population are covered. Medical card coverage stayed relatively stable at approximately 37 per cent over the 1980s but fell every year during the 1990s as income guidelines failed to increase in line with increases in average incomes. The growth of private insurance cover in Ireland is often seen as surprising as private health insurance is primarily taken out to cover hospital costs and yet all individuals are entitled to free public hospital services (although non-medical cardholders must pay a modest daily charge). In addition, up to very recently, primary care services such as GP or dental visits were not covered by private health insurance, except where large deductibles were exceeded.

Recent studies have confirmed that a primary reason for taking out private health insurance is to ensure speedy access to hospital rather than superior accommodation; as public waiting lists increased in the 1980s and household incomes increased in the 1990s, the demand for insurance grew. The private health insurance market in Ireland is further discussed in Section 4. In 2002, approximately 21 per cent of the population did not have a medical card or private health insurance; data from the 2001 Quarterly National Household Survey Health Module shows that over three quarters of the those aged over 18 years without a medical card or private health insurance were aged under 35 years. While these individuals are entitled to receive free public hospital services (subject to the small charges described above), they must pay in full for any primary care consultations or private hospital services. Medical cardholders may take out private health insurance if they wish; however in 2001 only 2 per cent of those over 18 years had both a medical card and private health insurance.[4]

Table 10.2

Medical Card and Private Health Insurance Coverage
(Percentage of the Population, 1980-2002)

Year	Medical card	Private health insurance
1980	35.0	26.1
1985	36.7	31.2
1990	36.7	34.4
1995	35.2	37.9
1996	34.5	38.4
1997	33.6	39.2
1998	32.0	40.5
1999	31.1	41.8
2000	30.3	45.0
2001	31.2[1]	48.5
2002	29.8	49.4

Sources: Department of Health and Children, *Health Statistics,* Stationery Office, Dublin, various issues; Department of Health and Children, *White Paper: Private Health Insurance*, Stationery Office, Dublin 1999; General Medical Services Payments Board (GMSPB), *Annual Report and Financial Statements 2002*, GMSPB, Dublin 2003; Health Insurance Authority, *Annual Report and Accounts 2002*, Health Insurance Authority, Dublin 2003; D. Watson, and J. Williams, 'Perceptions of the Quality of Health Care in the Public and Private Sectors in Ireland' (Report to the Centre for Insurance Studies, Graduate Business School, University College Dublin), Dublin 2001.
[1]The increase in medical card coverage from 2000 to 2001 is accounted for by the extension of eligibility to all over 70s in July 2001.

Delivery of Health Services
While the state is heavily involved in the financing of health services in Ireland (see Section 4), it mainly leaves the delivery of health services to the private sector, with the hospital and primary care sectors providing particularly good examples of the intermix between the public and private sectors in the financing and delivery of health services in Ireland. There are three different types of hospital in Ireland: voluntary hospitals, which are run on a not for profit basis by private organisations (usually religious institutions) but which receive most of their funding from the state; health board hospitals which are owned and operated

by the health boards and the final category comprises entirely privately owned, operated and funded hospitals. Public hospital services are provided in voluntary and health board hospitals and most of these hospitals also provide private health care but they must clearly distinguish between public and private beds. In 2000, there were 60 publicly funded acute hospitals, 23 of which were voluntary hospitals located mainly in the Eastern Regional Health Authority area and 35 hospitals were entirely privately owned and operated.

Primary care services are mainly provided by independent professionals (e.g. GPs, pharmacists, dentists etc.) who may be contracted to provide services in the public sector, in addition to services provided to private patients (approximately two thirds of GPs also have contracts to provide services to medical cardholder patients). The General Medical Services Payments Board (GMSPB) undertakes the reimbursement of providers for GP, dental, optical and pharmaceutical services supplied to medical cardholders as well as the reimbursement of pharmacists for services provided to non-medical cardholders under the various drugs schemes. Section 5 discusses in more detail the equity and efficiency implications of differing methods of doctor reimbursement.

The Irish healthcare system therefore has a mixture of a universal public health service and a fee based private system. Some services are publicly funded and delivered (e.g. treatment as a public patient in a public hospital), some are publicly funded but privately delivered (e.g. GP consultations by medical cardholders), some are privately funded and delivered (e.g. GP consultations by non-medical cardholders, treatment as a private patient in a private hospital) while some are privately funded but publicly delivered (e.g. non-medical cardholders must pay a modest charge for treatment in public hospitals).[5] This complex mixture has implications for the allocation of resources both between the public and the private sector and between different types of care (see Section 4 for further discussion of the equity and efficiency implications of the public private mix in Irish health care, in particular the implications for the hospitals sector).

Health Service Reform Programme
While the structure as outlined above still governs the operation of the health services, in June 2003 the government announced its commitment to a major reform of the health service. The *Health Service Reform Programme* aims to implement the recommendations contained in three recent reports on the health system: the *Report of the National Task Force on Medical Staffing* (the Hanly report), the *Report of the Commission on Financial Management and Control Systems in the Health Service* (the Brennan report) and the *Audit of Structures and Functions in the Health System* (the Prospectus report). Issues highlighted for reform included the coordination and division of functions between the different agencies involved in planning, managing and delivering health services in Ireland and the degree of financial accountability exercised by those making most resource using decisions in the health service, in particular hospital consultants.

By far the most contentious aspect of the reforms is that relating to the regional organisation of hospital services contained in the Hanly report. As a result of the European Working Time Directive, the hours worked by non-consultant hospital doctors (NCHDs) must be reduced to 48 hours per week by 2009 with the first phased reduction to 58 hours due on 1 August 2004 (at present NCHDs work an average of 75 hours per week). In response to this directive, the Hanly report recommends a movement away from the current consultant led service towards a consultant provided service, with health professionals working in multidisciplinary specialist teams. To this end, the report recommends, for the two pilot areas examined (the East Coast Area Health Board and the Mid Western Health Board), a reconfiguration of hospital services in each region into a system with one major hospital and a network of local hospitals with certain services still provided on a national (e.g. liver transplant) or supra-regional (e.g. radiation therapy) basis. The most controversial aspects of the report concerned the stipulation that emergency services should be based in major hospitals only. Other aspects of the reform programme include the reduction in the number of health service agencies to reduce fragmentation and facilitate enhanced policy coordination, and the establishment of a Health Services Executive which will undertake the management of the health service on a national level, leaving the Department of Health and Children free to concentrate on policy formation and issues of strategic development.

3 WHY GOVERNMENT INTERVENTION?

Despite the fact that the private sector accounts for approximately 20 per cent of expenditure on the health services (see Section 4) and is heavily involved in the provision of health services in Ireland, the public sector remains the main agent responsible for the finance and delivery of health services in Ireland. Chapter 2 discussed the rationale for government intervention in the economy in general. In terms of the health services, efficiency concerns relating to asymmetric information, uncertainty and the existence of externalities, as well as equity or distributional concerns, motivate government involvement in health care. Where the government does not directly involve itself in the provision of health care services, it may have a role in terms of financing, regulation, pricing (taxation and subsidies) and information provision.

While asymmetric information, uncertainty and externalities are the most readily identifiable indicators of market failure in the health sector, health care markets also suffer from imperfect competition in the sense that many of the conditions for perfectly competitive markets are absent or deficient. Many services, e.g. hospital services, are subject to economies of scale, producers can often influence the level of demand and/or price, and price signals are often absent, particularly where third party reimbursement systems are in operation. Most importantly however, the assumptions of perfectly informed consumers, the absence of uncertainty and the absence of externalities are violated in health care markets.

Asymmetric Information

The nature of the relationship between producers and consumers in health care is distorted by asymmetric information. Patients are essentially buying the doctor's knowledge and/or information when they visit. In comparison with other goods and services, information acquisition on the part of the consumer in health care markets is made more difficult by the nature of the product. Learning by experience is complicated by the fact that every illness episode is heterogeneous and the consumer cannot sample the product before purchase or is unlikely to have had prior experience of the same product. In addition, the information is often technically complex, involving many years of study.

The relationship has often been characterised as a principal agent one; due to the high costs of acquiring such technical information, the patient relies on the doctor to act in their best interests in terms of diagnosis and treatment decisions. While asymmetric information justifies a role for government in regulating the behaviour of doctors and other health care professionals through licensing, regulating the pharmaceuticals that can be prescribed to patients and improving consumers' information, it does not follow that government intervention in either the financing or provision of health care is necessary.

Uncertainty

Health care markets are also characterised by uncertainty, i.e. lack of information about the future. This necessitates a role for insurance in offering the consumer protection against uncertainty. Ill health is inherently unpredictable, both in terms of financial costs and physical and emotional suffering. However, the problems of adverse selection, moral hazard and cream skimming may arise in a private health insurance market, leading to efficiency and equity failings. Adverse selection arises when the insurer cannot distinguish between low and high risks, because individuals purchasing insurance have better information about their risk status than the insurer. Insurers must therefore base the premium on the risk pool that includes both low and high risks. Low risk individuals will not purchase insurance because the premium does not reflect their risk status leaving only high risk individuals in the risk pool. This can make the fund unsustainable. The solution is to have compulsory insurance or differential premiums. However, due to concerns that certain high risk individuals would be denied access to health care under a private system with differential premiums on the basis of age and health status, most governments intervene to provide compulsory health insurance for most basic health services.

Moral hazard behaviour, where an individual's behaviour is affected by their insurance status, may arise in the form of excessive utilisation of resources on the part of the patient and also providers (as they know that their patients do not bear the full costs). Cost sharing initiatives, which aim to make both patients and providers more aware of the resource implications of their decisions are becoming increasingly common and will be discussed further in Section 5. However, to some extent the professional relationship between doctor and patient should limit moral hazard behaviours.[6]

A final problem associated with a private insurance market is that of cream skimming. Insurers will obviously try and encourage low risk persons to insure with their company. Once again, due to equity concerns about certain sections being denied medical treatment, governments intervene to either offer compulsory insurance or to regulate the sector. In Ireland, the government strictly regulates the behaviour of the two major private insurers in the Irish market in an attempt to prevent cream skimming through the principles of open enrolment (no one can be refused cover), community rating (all individuals face the same premium) and lifetime cover (once insured, an individual's policy cannot be terminated). However, as private insurance in Ireland essentially provides cover for services already available free of charge (or heavily subsidised) in the public sector, the rationale for these restrictions on behaviour, in particular community rating, has been questioned.

Due to concerns over the ability of the private market to deliver insurance efficiently and equitably (in particular adverse selection, moral hazard and cream skimming behaviours must be absent), governments in Europe have tended to intervene by providing compulsory insurance for most basic health services (e.g. in France and Germany all individuals are compulsorily insured for most health services and the system is funded through the social insurance scheme with the contributions of those on low incomes or that are economically inactive paid by the state). In Ireland, the state intervenes by providing compulsory insurance for certain services (mainly hospital services) to the full population, providing compulsory insurance for all services to certain vulnerable sections of the population (medical cardholders) and strictly regulating conduct in the private insurance market.

Externalities

The health care sector may also be characterised by the presence of externalities when private costs or benefits are out of line with social costs or benefits. For a positive/negative externality, private benefits/costs are less than social benefits/costs, meaning that output is below/above the socially optimal level. The standard solution to an externality is to levy a Pigouvian tax in the case of goods or services that produce negative externalities or to offer a subsidy in the case of goods or services that produce positive externalities. Free childhood vaccinations against infectious diseases and excise taxes on cigarettes are the most obvious examples of government intervention in the health sector due to the presence of externalities. A vaccinated population confers a positive externality on society while second hand cigarette smoke confers a negative externality on society; in the absence of government intervention vaccination levels would be less than the socially optimal level due to higher social benefits than private benefits while smoking levels would be greater than the socially optimal level due to higher social costs than private costs. Of course, the efficacy of taxes in changing behaviour to reflect the socially optimal level depends on the price elasticity of demand for the good/service, the availability of substitutes, its budget share etc. (see also Chapter 3).

A related concept is that which regards health care as a merit good. While it is commonly assumed that the individual is the best judge of his own interests, with merit goods such as education, healthcare or cultural facilities (e.g. museums) this assumption does not necessarily hold. In the absence of government intervention, too little of the good in question will be consumed as individuals are unaware of the long term benefits. The government therefore intervenes to ensure that all citizens receive free or heavily subsidised basic health services, even if private professionals provide many of these services.

Equity

Apart from efficiency concerns, the desire to ensure that health care should be distributed equitably across the population motivates government intervention in the sector. However, there is much discussion over what is meant by equity in the context of the health services (see also Chapter 6). Is the objective equality of opportunity (i.e. access to health care) or equality of outcome (i.e. health status)? Many governments intervene to smooth out differences in health outcomes that are not related to need factors such as age, gender or health status, but rather to socioeconomic characteristics such as income, area of residence, level of education etc. For example, a recent study found that women in Ireland from the unskilled manual and unemployed social classes were significantly more likely to give birth to low birth weight babies than those in the other social classes.[7] However, most governments also subscribe to the notion of equality of opportunity in the sense that access to health care should be distributed on the basis of need for care, not on the basis of non health related attributes, such as ability to pay (which is the case for many other commodities). But definitional problems also arise here. How do we define access? Most studies proxy access by utilisation, arguing that access to health services is equitable if utilisation rates are similar, even after controlling for need factors such as age, gender and health status. However, it is obvious that even if everyone enjoys the same access to health care, persons in equal need may end up consuming different amounts of care (and types of care) due to differing tastes and preferences.[8]

An additional issue concerns the progressivity of funding sources, i.e. most governments subscribe to the view that health services should be financed in relation to ability to pay (those on higher incomes should pay a higher proportion of their incomes in taxation, social insurance contributions etc.). Such thinking motivates government involvement in the financing of health care services, offering free services to those on low incomes or in particularly vulnerable situations.

In practice, the government uses a variety of instruments to intervene in the health sector. While the government intervenes heavily in terms of regulation, pricing, information provision and financing in Ireland, it mainly leaves the provision of health services to private operators, who consequently receive much of their funding from public sources (e.g. GP services and voluntary hospital services). While government intervention to correct market failures is an accepted feature of modern economies, government failure may itself lead to efficiency or equity failings. In particular, government intervention in terms of provision may lead to inefficiency, as government owned and operated facilities face a loose budget constraint. In addition, regulatory capture by vested interests may result in regulations that lead to an inefficient level of output, e.g. the restrictions on pharmacy locations which existed prior to the revocation of the 1996 Health Regulations Act in 2001. Ensuring that public funding sources are progressive in their impact is also an important concern (see the following section).

4 HEALTH SECTOR FINANCE

Overall Position

Health care is generally financed from four main sources, with different countries assigning different levels of importance to each source. Table 10.3 presents the sources of finance for selected OECD countries for 2001. In terms of public sources of finance, countries such as France and Germany rely much more heavily on social insurance contributions than general government sources, i.e. taxation, for their revenue. Social insurance contributions, which are compulsory and generally shared between the employer and employee, tend to be earmarked for specific purposes; in Ireland the 'health levy' amounts to 2 per cent of taxable income (those earning less than €356 per week in 2004 are exempt). However, it is not a major source of health sector finance in Ireland, amounting to only 1 per cent of total revenue in 2001. As in other countries, revenue from general taxation in Ireland is not earmarked specifically for the health services, which means that it must compete with other areas of public expenditure for attention.

Due to universal eligibility for free public health services in many countries, the share of total expenditure funded through private sources (out of pocket payments by individuals and households, private insurance payments and other sources of finance, e.g. voluntary donations) is much smaller than that accounted for by public sources. The exception is the USA, which provides free health care only for the old and those on low incomes (through the Medicare and Medicaid schemes respectively) and consequently relies more heavily on private sources of finance, particularly insurance.

The prevalence of universal entitlement to free public health services across Europe results in monetary costs for health care consultations that are effectively zero, meaning that there is little incentive to control utilisation. As discussed further in Section 5, cost sharing, either through co-payments, co-insurance or deductibles, can help to control utilisation, although there are concerns that such initiatives may reduce necessary as well as unnecessary utilisation. Nonetheless, most countries levy minimal charges on consumers in an attempt to make them more aware of the resource implications of their behaviour. For example, in Ireland, a charge of €45 per day applies to individuals without medical cards for treatment as an in-patient in the public hospital sector. As Table 10.3 illustrates, out of pocket payments are now more important than private insurance as a source of finance for all the countries examined except France, the Netherlands and the USA. However, there are concerns that as governments come under increasing pressure to fund public health programmes and out of pocket payments become more important as a source of revenue, a greater share of the funding burden falls on those in ill health.[9]

Table 10.3
Sources of Finance for Total Health Expenditure for Selected EU-15 and OECD
Countries (Percentage of Total Health Expenditure, 2001)

Country	General government	Social insurance	Out of pocket payments	Private insurance	Other private sources
Austria	28	41	18	7	6
Denmark	83	0	16	2	0
Finland	60	16	20	3	2
France	3	73	10	13	1
Germany	10	69	11	8	2
Ireland	*75*	*1*	*12*	*6*	*6*
Netherlands[1]	5	82	10	17	9
USA	30	15	14	36	5

Source: OECD, *Health Data,* op. cit. and OECD, *Health Data*, OECD, Paris 2003.
Note: Data for the UK are unavailable.
[1]Data for Netherlands refer to 2000.

A crucial issue concerning taxation and social insurance contributions as well as out of pocket payments and insurance is the extent to which they are a progressive source of revenue, i.e. whether those on higher incomes pay a higher proportion of their income in tax, social insurance contributions, out of pocket payments and insurance. A recent study which examined the progressivity of different sources of finance for a number of OECD countries, found tax and social insurance contributions to be progressive sources of finance in Ireland, with taxation a particularly progressive source. However, Ireland performed poorly when out of pocket payments and private insurance payments were examined, with both found to be regressive sources of finance.[10]

Private Health Insurance
It is useful to examine the private health insurance system in Ireland in more detail, principally because it is unusual in an international context in the extent to which the system interacts with the public system, particularly in the hospitals sector. Much recent discussion has also focussed on regulatory reform in the light of EU regulations regarding competitive behaviour between private insurers. There are two main private health insurance companies in Ireland, VHI and BUPA.

As a result of the Third EU Directive on Non-Life Insurance, BUPA entered the market to compete with the VHI in 1996, although both are subject to strict state regulation on their conduct. There are also a number of smaller employer provided health insurance schemes such as the St. Paul's Garda Medical Aid Society, the Prison Officer's Medical Aid Society and the ESB Medical Provident Fund. However, VHI and BUPA accounted for 82 per cent and 13 per cent respectively of the private health insurance market in 2003, with the restricted membership schemes accounting for the remaining 5 per cent.[11]

The VHI, a state-owned non profit making company, was originally established in 1957 to provide insurance against hospital expenses for the then 15 per cent of the population who were not entitled to free public hospital services. Despite the extension of entitlement of cover for free public hospital services to the remainder of the population in 1991, the reduction in tax relief from the marginal rate of tax to the standard rate of tax in 1996 and increasing premiums, private insurance coverage in Ireland has grown steadily since 1957 to reach nearly 50 per cent of the population by 2002. As stated above, the expansion in private health insurance cover is all the more striking given that private insurance cover does not generally cover the cost of primary care consultations, except where large deductibles are exceeded (although recently the two insurers have introduced additional plans with partial cover for primary care services). However, factors such as differing waiting times for admission to hospital between those with and without insurance, improved economic conditions and increased incomes, continued policy support for private coverage (principally through the tax code) and an expanding role for employer provided private health insurance are all important in explaining the growth in coverage.

The profile of those covered by private health insurance is also worth mentioning. There is a strong relationship between private insurance cover and socioeconomic characteristics such as income, educational attainment and health status. Interestingly however, there is no evidence of adverse selection in the market for private health insurance in Ireland with 53 per cent of those in very good health having private health insurance in comparison with only 15 per cent of those in bad or very bad health.[12]

A number of recent surveys have attempted to explain the appeal of private health insurance in Ireland, in the context of universal entitlement to free or heavily subsidised public hospital care. A survey of a random sample of the population in 2000 found that, among both the insured and the not insured, the most commonly cited reasons for having private health insurance were, in order of importance, to avoid large medical bills, to ensure quick treatment and to ensure good hospital treatment (see Table 10.4). Issues such as being able to have a private bed or a private room were perceived as much less important by both sets of respondents. Similarly, when those that were insured were asked what would concern them most about having to give up private health insurance and relying on the public sector, 72 per cent cited the length of wait with only 20 per cent citing the quality of care, 5 per cent the choice of consultant and 3 per cent non-medical amenities. Among the uninsured, the main reasons for seriously considering private insurance would be the length of wait (74 per cent) and the quality of care (19 per cent) with choice of consultant and non-medical amenities being cited by only 5 per cent and 2 per cent of respondents respectively.

Table 10.4
Reasons for having Private Health Insurance (Percentage of Respondents citing Reason as 'Very Important')

	Insured	Not insured
Avoid large bills	88	75
Ensure quick treatment	85	71
Ensure good hospital treatment	73	61
Ensure consultant care	59	41
Arrange time of treatment	57	39
Choose consultant	43	23
Private bed	25	10
Private room	22	8

Source: Watson and Williams, *op. cit.,* Tables 6.2 and 6.13.

Access to Hospital Services

These responses highlight public concern with waiting times and the perception that patients with private insurance have shorter waiting times and are guaranteed consultant care, in comparison with those that must rely on the public system. The Quarterly National Household Survey, in its 2001 health module, found that these concerns were to some extent justified. It found that 25.2 per cent of medical cardholders had waited for 12 months or longer for in-patient admission to a public hospital while only 12.4 per cent of those with private insurance cover had been waiting for 12 months or longer. For out-patient consultations and day care procedures or investigations, the corresponding figures were 8.3 per cent and 9.8 per cent (medical cardholders) and 4.7 per cent and 2.6 per cent (private insurance cover).[13] While there are obviously differences in age and health status across the two groups which may impact on the types and duration of treatments, the results do indicate that public patients face substantially longer waiting times than those with private health insurance.

Statistics for bed occupancy in public hospitals also lead to concerns that access to hospital for elective procedures in Ireland is not distributed by need. Public hospitals in Ireland must allocate a proportion of their beds for private or semi-private use; currently the designations are approximately 20 per cent for in-patient beds and approximately 30 per cent for day beds. However, research on patient discharges shows that for elective in-patient admissions in 2000, private patients accounted for 29.8 per cent of discharges while for emergency in-patient admissions, private patients accounted for 21.4 per cent of discharges. Only for day procedures were discharges distributed in favour of public patients with 23.1 per cent of discharges for day procedures classified as private in 2000. However, in all cases (elective and emergency in-patient services and day procedures), the increase in private discharges from 1999 to 2000 was much greater than that for public patients.[14] There are therefore very real concerns that access to hospital for elective procedures in particular is not distributed according to need, but rather by private insurance cover (and by extension, ability to pay since those with private insurance cover are concentrated in the top levels of the income distribution).

However, quite apart from concerns surrounding access to hospital services as a result of this public private mix, there are also efficiency concerns. Private patients in public hospitals are not charged the full economic cost of their care and treatment; this therefore gives insurers an incentive to encourage the treatment of private patients in public rather than private hospitals and public hospital managers an incentive to encourage the treatment of private patients as they represent an additional income stream for the hospital. This goes against an often cited rationale for the private insurance system in Ireland – that it relieves pressure on the public hospital system. It is also an inefficient use of resources as it reduces the revenue available to the public sector from this source. While not directly linked to the insurance system, the fact that hospital consultants are remunerated in different ways for public and private patients (capitation and fee for service respectively) may distort their incentives and lead them to devote more time towards private care (see also Section 5). There are therefore concerns that, while private insurance is an important component of health sector financing in Ireland, its intermingling with the public system leads to serious equity and efficiency failings.

The Department of Health and Children on the other hand, argue that the public private mix in the hospital sector in Ireland has a number of advantages: it ensures that staff continue to be attracted to the public sector, consultants' time is used more efficiently as public and private patients are on the same site, it facilitates linkage in terms of medical knowledge and facilities and probably most importantly represents an additional income stream for the public hospital system.

Regulation of the Private Health Insurance Market
The operation of the private health insurance market in Ireland is strictly regulated by the government, despite the opening of the market to competition as a result of the 1994 Third EU Directive on Non-Life Insurance. The Health Insurance Authority was established in 2001 to act as regulator of the sector. The Irish government obtained permission from the EU to continue to ensure that all insurers abide by the principles of open enrolment, lifetime cover and community rating, and these principles are enshrined in the 1994 Health Insurance Act. Open enrolment means that no one can be refused insurance

(subject to a maximum age limit of 65 years and a waiting period before a claim can be made), lifetime cover implies that once an individual is insured, the insurer cannot terminate their contract on the basis of age, risk status or claims history while community rating effectively means that the young and healthy subsidise the old and sick as premiums cannot be differentiated on the basis of age, gender or health status.

The continued stability of the community rating system means that a risk equalisation scheme must be implemented. Risk equalisation aims to remove differences in insurers' costs that result from differing risk profiles among their members; in Ireland, the risk profile of BUPA members is younger than that of VHI members. Risk equalisation involves a transfer of funds from one insurer to the other in order to spread the claims of high cost members between both insurers (in proportion to their market share). However, this has proven contentious, particularly on competition grounds, and to date, no transfer of funds has taken place.

5 HEALTH SECTOR EXPENDITURE

Irish Health Care Expenditure

Public expenditure on the health services has increased greatly since the mid 1980s, from €1.7 billion in 1986 to €8.4 billion in 2002. In real terms, public expenditure has increased by 217 per cent since 1986, with most of this increase occurring since 1997. This is in contrast to the experience during some years of the 1980s when public health expenditures fell in real terms (e.g. between 1987 and 1988 public health expenditure decreased by 2.6 per cent in real terms). However, given the large proportion of health expenditure accounted for by labour costs (see below), when public expenditure is deflated by average earnings, the increase since 1986 is more modest at 139 per cent (see Figure 10.1). While both non-capital and capital public expenditure increased substantially in the late 1990s, capital expenditure increased at a faster pace, thus explaining the increasing share of total public expenditure accounted for by capital expenditure (which increased from 4.5 per cent of total public expenditure in 1986 to 6.0 per cent in 2002).

Of the non-capital public health expenditure programme, by far the largest component comprises expenditure on the general hospitals service (which comprised 48 per cent of total non-capital public health expenditure in 2002). The remaining components of non-capital public health expenditure are, in order of importance, the community health services programme (which mainly includes expenditure on the provision of primary care services to those on low incomes, i.e. GP services, pharmaceuticals, dental, ophthalmic and aural services), the programme for the handicapped, the community welfare programme (which mainly includes cash grants to those incapacitated for work), the psychiatric programme, the general support programme and the community protection programme (which mainly includes expenditure on the prevention of infectious diseases, food hygiene standards and health promotion).

Figure 10.1

Health Expenditure in Ireland: 1986-2002[1]

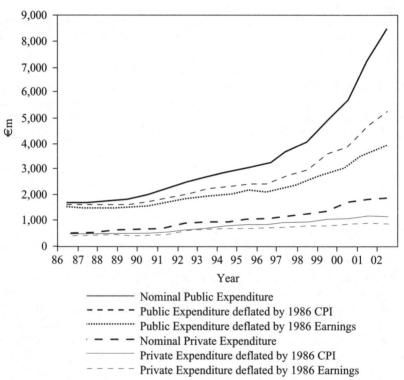

Year

———————— Nominal Public Expenditure

– – – – – Public Expenditure deflated by 1986 CPI

··················· Public Expenditure deflated by 1986 Earnings

· – – – – Nominal Private Expenditure

———————— Private Expenditure deflated by 1986 CPI

– – – – – Private Expenditure deflated by 1986 Earnings

Sources: For expenditure data see, Department of Health and Children, *Health Statistics 2002*, Stationery Office, Dublin 2003; for consumer price index data see, CSO, *Consumer Price Index*, Stationery Office, Dublin, various issues, and for average weekly industrial earnings see, CSO, *Industrial Earnings and Hours Worked*, Stationery Office, Dublin, various issues, and CSO, *Statistical Bulletin*, Stationery Office, Dublin, various issues.
[1]While the CSO publish data on public sector earnings, the data exclude the health sector and are only available back to 1995.

While no programme has seen its level of expenditure decrease, the proportions allocated to different programmes have changed considerably over the last number of years (see Table 10.5). For example, while the community health services and general hospital programmes accounted for 15 and 50 per cent of total non-capital public health expenditure in 1990, the respective allocations had changed to 17 and 48 per cent by 2002. In part, this reflects the aspirations of the most recent Health Strategy published in 2001, which envisaged more emphasis on health promotion and prevention rather than on the traditional roles of diagnosis and treatment, in particular through an expanded role for general practitioner (GP) and other primary care services as the first point of call for most individuals' contact with the health services.

Table 10.5

Components of Non-Capital Public Expenditure
(Percentage of Total, 1990-2002)

Programme	1990	1994	1998	2002
Community protection	2	2	3	3
Community health services	15	16	17	17
Community welfare	9	10	7	9
Psychiatric	11	9	9	7
Handicapped	10	10	11	12
General hospital	50	49	49	48
General support	5	4	5	4

Sources: Department of Health and Children, *Health Statistics,* Stationery Office, Dublin, various issues.

While the government is heavily involved in the financing, and to a lesser extent in the delivery, of health services in Ireland, the private sector plays an important role in both areas. Indeed, when the substantial involvement by the private sector in the financing and provision of health services in Ireland is included, total health expenditure (both public and private) amounted to over €10 billion in 2002. The proportion of total health expenditure accounted for by the private sector has declined slightly over the last decade, from 24.8 per cent in 1990 to 18.5 per cent in 2002, reflecting a proportionately larger increase in public sector expenditure rather than any decrease in private sector expenditure.

Comparative Perspective
Despite large increases in Irish health expenditure over the 1990s, Ireland still ranks below many other OECD countries in terms of health expenditure per head of population. Data from the OECD for 1997, presented in Table 10.6, indicate that Ireland was ranked sixteenth out of 20 in terms of per capita total health expenditure, expressed in US dollar purchasing power terms. The USA, Germany and France topped the table, spending $3,939, $2,416 and $2,163 per capita respectively while New Zealand, Spain and Portugal spent the least ($1,357, $1,287 and $1,219 per capita respectively). Among the EU-15, Ireland's total health expenditure was ranked in twelfth place (spending $1,417 per capita), with only Portugal, Greece and Spain spending less per capita in 1997. By 2000, Ireland had moved up one place in the rankings among the EU-15 countries

(spending $1,774 per capita), with Finland joining Greece, Portugal and Spain in spending less per capita on health than Ireland in 2000.

Effectiveness of Health Sector Expenditure

However, levels of expenditure per head of population provide no guidance as to whether this expenditure is efficiently and effectively spent or distributed equitably across different sectors of the population. In terms of the effectiveness of health sector expenditure, it is useful to examine where countries rank in terms of health outcomes and whether there is any correlation between such measures and health expenditure. For example, OECD data for 1997 show that Ireland is ranked nineteenth, nineteenth and sixteenth out of 20 OECD countries in terms of male life expectancy, female life expectancy and infant mortality respectively. Among the EU-15 countries, Ireland is placed in fourteenth, fourteenth and thirteenth place on these indicators respectively. However, a study by the OECD found that aggregate measures of health sector output (such as life expectancy, infant and perinatal mortality etc.) were only weakly related to health sector expenditures in OECD countries.[15]

The weak association between health spending and health outcome indicators highlights the fact that social, environmental and cultural factors such as diet, exercise, genetic inheritance, lifestyle, education, social status, income distribution, social support and housing, and their complex interactions, may be more important in determining the level and distribution of health outcomes than simple health expenditure. The recent increases in resources devoted to health promotion and prevention (e.g. through the smoking in the workplace ban, breast cancer screening, promotion of healthy eating etc.) reflects this realisation that lifestyle factors are also crucial in influencing population health outcomes.

A related strand of research concentrates on the pitfalls involved in using crude measures of health status to assess health sector performance. In its 2000 report (*Health Systems: Improving Performance*) the World Health Organisation (WHO) took a much broader approach to assessing performance than simply examining improvements in life expectancy or infant mortality to include the responsiveness of the system (ascertained through questionnaires) and fairness of financial contribution.[16] In terms of overall health systems performance of the countries of the EU-15 and Australia, Canada, Japan, New Zealand and the USA (see Table 10.6), the top three performing countries were Japan, Sweden and Luxembourg while their rankings in terms of expenditure were thirteenth, tenth and fourth respectively. While there are countries (such as Canada and Luxembourg) who spend a lot and consequently rank highly in terms of health sector performance, there are also exceptions to this trend, namely, Denmark, Germany and the USA whose high levels of expenditure are not reflected in health sector performance and on the other hand, countries such as Japan and Sweden whose spending is in the middle range of countries yet who perform very well.

Table 10.6

Total Health Expenditure Per Capita and Health Outcome Rankings
(EU-15 and Selected OECD Countries, 1997)

Country	Expenditure	Male life expectancy	Female life expectancy	Infant mortality	World Health Organisation (WHO)
Australia	8	5	6	11	10
Austria	11	13	10	6	8
Belgium	7	12	9	15	11
Canada	5	3	7	12	5
Denmark	6	17	20	10	15
Finland	14	18	11	3	16
France	3	11	2	5	4
Germany	2	15	13	7	12
Greece	17	6	8	17	17
Ireland	*16*	*19*	*19*	*16*	*18*
Italy	12	4	5	13	9
Japan	13	1	1	2	1
Luxembourg	4	14	15	4	3
Netherlands	9	7	12	8	6
New Zealand	18	9	14	19	19
Portugal	20	20	18	18	20
Spain	19	8	3	9	14
Sweden	10	2	4	1	2
UK	15	10	16	14	7
USA	1	16	17	20	13

Source: For data on expenditure (total health expenditure per capita expressed in USA $ PPP), male and female life expectancy (at birth) and infant mortality (per 1,000 live births) see, OECD, *Health Data,* op. cit. For data on World Health Organisation (WHO) ranking of countries on overall health system attainment, see WHO, *World Health Report 2000: Health Systems: Improving Performance*, WHO, Washington D.C. 2000, Annex Table 9.

Measuring the Output of the Health Sector

The above highlights the fact that any assessment of health sector performance is beset with the problem of how to measure the output of the health sector. Cross country comparisons of performance tend to rely on aggregate indicators such as life expectancy and mortality rates, but at more disaggregated levels (e.g. hospital, GP practice) easily available indicators of output such as hospital admissions, in-patient days, discharges, number of procedures undertaken, number of consultations etc. are employed. However, these are essentially throughput measures and, in certain cases, they can provide misleading information on the performance of health service providers. For example, an increase in hospital discharges year on year for the same amount of inputs could be construed as an increase in productivity but it could simply be because the hospital is discharging patients 'quicker but sicker'.[17]

Casemix

In the context of hospital services, the need to account for the variety and intensity of treatments undertaken has resulted in the increasing use of the casemix adjustment to monitor output. The casemix measure assigns all in-patient cases exclusively to one category – there are approximately – 500 in total – called a diagnosis related group (DRG). Each DRG represents a class or category of cases which may be expected to have the same clinical characteristics, receive similar treatment and use the same amount of hospital resources, i.e. doctor and nursing input, theatre, laboratory, pharmacy, catering and cleaning costs. A casemix adjusted cost is then estimated for each hospital and hospital group (teaching vs. non-teaching). Hospitals performing poorly relative to others in the group lose funding whereas those performing better receive extra funding; in Ireland, the casemix adjustment to hospital budgets is therefore budget neutral and aims to increase hospital efficiency. In 1993, the casemix adjustment was applied on a pilot basis to fifteen acute public hospitals and was initially used to make adjustments to 5 per cent of the in-patient budget; the remaining 95 per cent was based on the hospital's historical allocation. The rate of adjustment to hospital budgets (known as the blend rate) has increased over time to 20 per cent of the in-patient budget and to 10 per cent for day cases, with all acute public hospitals discharging more than 5,000 patients per annum subject to some degree of casemix adjustment by 2002.

Economic Evaluation of Treatments

Much recent research has concentrated on assessing the efficacy of different treatments. Essentially, there are three different, but related, approaches to assessing efficacy in this context: cost benefit analysis, cost effectiveness analysis and cost utility analysis. In all cases, costs are measured in terms of monetary units. The measurement of benefits or outputs proves more problematic. Cost benefit analysis is rarely employed as benefits must be converted into monetary units. Cost effectiveness analysis goes one step further by measuring output in terms of natural units of outcome for the programme being evaluated, e.g. life years gained. It is then possible to calculate a cost effectiveness ratio, which represents the additional cost per additional unit of outcome.

Cost utility analysis attempts to overcome the failing of cost effectiveness analysis by accounting for the quality of the additional life years gained. Once again, costs are measured in monetary units but outputs are measured in terms of quality adjusted life years (QALYs), which reflect both the quality and quantity of additional life years gained. Results are presented in terms of a cost per QALY achieved; unlike with cost effectiveness analysis, cross programme comparisons are possible. Much recent literature has therefore centred on the use of the QALY as a generic measure of output, with the construction of league tables of health care interventions, ranking them by cost per QALY achieved. However, the adjustment for quality relies on the subjective evaluations of patients or survey respondents. This inevitably leads to problems: different respondents may place different values on outcomes depending on their own situation (e.g. a patient suffering from a certain condition may value a treatment more highly than a healthy individual surveyed as part of a random sample of the population). Despite the advances in such research in recent years, no approach can deal with the thorny question of what is the appropriate level of resources to devote to certain interventions, i.e. what is the appropriate threshold of resources, beyond which the costs are too large relative to the expected benefits.[18]

Why is Health Expenditure Increasing?

For the EU-15, per capita total health expenditure (expressed in US dollar purchasing power parities) increased by 5.3 per cent annually on average between 1990 and 2000, ranging from 1.8 per cent in Finland to 8.4 per cent in Ireland. For OECD countries (excluding Hungary and the Slovak Republic for which data are missing), the average annual increase was 5.7 per cent with, once again, no country experiencing a decrease in total per capita health expenditure.[19]

What are the factors driving this increase in health expenditure, both in Ireland and across the OECD? On the demand side, such factors include changing demographic structures (particularly ageing populations), increasing incomes, increasing access to free public health services, increasing insurance cover and rising consumer expectations (see the discussion on Wagner's Law in Chapter 2). Cross sectional studies attempting to explain the factors driving health sector expenditure increases across countries typically find that aggregate income is the most important factor with an elasticity of one or greater. While there has been some debate over the accuracy of such estimates (in particular, micro studies of individual behaviour typically find little or no influence for income on health services utilisation), recent discussion has centred on the role of supply side factors in influencing spending. Attention has now focused on factors such as rising medical prices, technological change, increasing capital stock and labour costs, the regulatory regime governing behaviour in the health sector and the incentive structure facing health care providers. Given the labour intensity of the sector, the impact of labour costs on health expenditures cannot be underestimated. In Ireland, labour costs account for approximately two thirds of health expenditure; therefore changes in the level and type of employees has implications for spending on the health services.[20] Related to this is the concept of Baumol's disease (see also Chapter 2) whereby public sector employees demand wage increases in line with those of their private sector counterparts. However, while in the private sector (the 'progressive' sector), such wage increases are accompanied by improvements in productivity, in labour intensive sectors such as health, education and public administration (the 'non-progressive' sectors), productivity improvements are harder to implement. However, productivity improvements in the health sector are not impossible; for example, increased use of IT in the operation and management of the health service was recommended by the Brennan report as an aid to increasing productivity in the health service.

Attempts to control the growth in spending across the OECD initially concentrated on macro reforms such as caps on spending or employment freezes. However, 'with little attention paid to the underlying structure of incentives, there is growing doubt about the capacity of purely macroeconomic approaches to sustain overall spending control.'[21] In terms of microeconomic reforms, measures such as promoting the use of the GP as a gatekeeper to hospital services, remunerating doctors on a capitation (rather than fee for service) basis for services provided in the public sector, funding hospitals on a casemix (i.e. adjusting for the nature and intensity of treatments undertaken) or prospective budget basis with rewards and sanctions for cost savings/over runs rather than on a simple retrospective budget basis, encouraging day surgery over in-patient stays and encouraging the prescribing of generic drugs are all seen as increasingly important in containing costs. On the demand side, implementing some form of cost sharing to make consumers more aware of the resource implications of their behaviour is common.

Cost Sharing
As stated in Section 2, cost sharing initiatives take one of three forms. Co-payments are a fixed charge (e.g. in Ireland, non-medical cardholders pay €45 if they visit accident and emergency without a referral from their GP), co-insurance is a fixed percentage and deductibles are charges that apply after a certain threshold has been reached (e.g. in Ireland, non-medical cardholders are entitled to free prescription drugs once their monthly drug bill exceeds €78). There has been much criticism of cost sharing initiatives however. There are concerns that while they seek to make patients more aware of the resource implications of their health care consultations, they may reduce 'necessary' as well as 'unnecessary' consultations, thus increasing the tendency to incur higher costs at a later stage of illness. However, most concern concentrates on the equity consequences with fixed charges being seen as particularly regressive.

In the light of the possible trade off between cost sharing and equity of access, most countries in practice, attempt to protect lower income groups or those who are chronically sick. In implementing cost sharing, most now recognise that the most equitable method is to use a deductible, which has to be reached before the public subsidy is introduced. Even if cost sharing regimes are carefully designed to ensure that low income or vulnerable sections of the population are not disproportionately affected, cost sharing may have a limited impact given that doctors, rather than patients, make most utilisation decisions. In practice, most countries attempt to levy some form of modest charge on consumers, while simultaneously ensuring that the incentives that doctors face do not encourage excessive utilisation.

Doctor Reimbursement
The way in which doctors are reimbursed for the services that they provide has important implications for health care spending. Fee for service and capitation

payments are the dominant methods of reimbursing doctors for their services. In a fee for service regime, doctors receive a fee for each consultation while in a capitation regime, they receive an annual payment per patient that is weighted for characteristics such as the age and gender of the patient. A study of a cross section of 19 OECD countries in 1987 found that health care expenditure was 11 per cent higher in countries where fee for service was the dominant form of remuneration for out-patient care in comparison with countries with capitation systems.[22]

In Ireland in the 1980s, much discussion centred on the reimbursement system for GPs. Prior to 1989, GPs received a fee for service payment from both their public and private patients (for the former group, this was paid by the state). However, due to concerns that such a payment system encouraged GPs to engage in 'demand inducement', i.e. to recommend unnecessary follow up visits, the system was changed in 1989 for medical cardholder patients. Now, the state reimburses GPs for services provided to medical cardholder patients on a capitation basis (a payment that is weighted for the age, gender and distance from the doctor's surgery of the patient) while GPs continue to receive a fee for service payment from their non-medical cardholder patients. Capitation payments remove the incentive to arrange unnecessary follow up visits but may encourage the GP to discourage necessary as well as unnecessary follow up visits, to shorten consultation periods and to refer patients to secondary care as early as possible. This distinction between patients is mirrored in the hospital system where consultants receive a fee for service payment from their private patients (often reimbursed by private insurance) and a capitation payment from the state for their public patients. The Brennan report on financial accountability in the health services in Ireland (see earlier) was extremely critical of this practice, arguing that it encourages consultants to minimise the time spent with public patients in favour of private patients. In Ireland therefore, the debate over the role of different payment regimes in controlling spending has been overshadowed by concerns that different regimes for different categories of patient results in inequitable treatment.

6 CONCLUDING COMMENTS

In this chapter, an overview of the financing and delivery of health services in Ireland, as well as key policy issues, was provided. The challenges facing the Irish health service today are very different to the concerns of the 1980s when the issue of how to provide services in a climate of real expenditure decreases was paramount. Irish health expenditures have increased dramatically since the latter years of the 1990s; the key issues now facing the Irish health services are how to ensure that access to services is distributed according to need rather than non-need factors such as ability to pay, to ensure that increasing levels of expenditure are spent efficiently and effectively and to ensure that costs are contained.

The discussion on the private health insurance system in Ireland highlighted the distributional issues surrounding the complex intermix between the public and private sectors in the Irish health sector, particularly in terms of hospital care. The increasing popularity of private health insurance cover was seen to be in part a response to concerns about access to services and treatment quality between those with and without private insurance cover. Data from a recent household survey supported these fears with those with private insurance having shorter waiting times than those without. However, there are concerns that any attempt to adopt a common waiting list would remove the incentive to take out private health insurance and could result in a significant fall in membership, which would increase further the pressure on the public system. In addition, the practice whereby medical consultants treat private patients, and junior doctors treat public patients implies differing standards of hospital care between the two groups. On the regulatory side, despite EU regulations on competition between insurers, there has been limited competition between the two insurers in the market, with only one new entrant since the market was opened to competition in 1994.

While access concerns dominate much discussion about the health services in Ireland, the steady growth in health expenditure in recent years has generated increasing concerns as to whether this increased investment is being efficiently and effectively spent. Despite the increases in expenditure in recent years, Ireland still spends less per capita on health than many other OECD countries and performs poorly in terms of aggregate health outcomes such as life expectancy and mortality rates. However, there seems to be little relationship between health expenditure and such aggregate measures of performance; such exercises highlight the difficulties involved in proxying health sector performance with such crude measures of output. Measuring the output of the health sector is notoriously difficult; throughput measures such as number of consultations may lead to misleading conclusions while concepts such as quality adjusted life years (QALYs) rely heavily on subjective assessments of health care benefits. The development of the casemix method in the context of hospital services however represents an opportunity to explicitly account for the nature and intensity of treatments undertaken, rather than relying on simplistic measures of throughput. In response to ever increasing health expenditures, cost containment measures, which initially concentrated on macro approaches, such as employment freezes, have increasingly considered more micro measures. Measures such as the reimbursement system for doctors and cost sharing initiatives aim to make both providers and patients more aware of the resource using implications of their behaviour.

In terms of the overall structure of the public health services in Ireland, there has been much discussion that profound structural change, rather than piecemeal measures to improve access or efficiency, is necessary. At the heart of this discussion in Ireland is the view that the current structure of the health services, in terms of such issues as staffing, organisation and strategic planning is ill equipped to deal with the challenges of providing health services in Ireland in the twenty first century. As mentioned earlier, three major reports commissioned by the government dealing with respectively, staffing (the Hanly report), financial management (the Brennan report) and structures and functions (the Prospectus report) have consequently recommended wide ranging reform of the health services, particularly in the areas of the concentration of hospital services, medical staffing in hospitals and the number of agencies undertaking the coordination of public health services in Ireland. Whether their findings and recommendations will be implemented, and to what extent they will radically change the structure and operation of the Irish health system, remains to be seen.

Endnotes

*   I would like to thank Carol Newman and John O'Hagan for comments on an earlier draft of the chapter and Joe Cullen, ESRI, for assistance with some of the data. All views expressed are those of the author and are not necessarily shared by the Economic and Social Research Institute (ESRI).

1   See Department of Health and Children, *Health Statistics 2002*, Stationery Office, Dublin 2003, Table L6, and CSO, *Quarterly National Household Survey* (First Quarter 2004), Stationery Office, Dublin 2004, Table 2b.

2   While the proportion of the population aged 65 years and over differs considerably across the countries presented in Table 10.1, there is little relationship between expenditure and age distribution. This is supported by international studies, which find that the age structure of the population is a largely insignificant determinant of health expenditure. More important factors are GDP per capita and institutional arrangements (see for example, U. Gerdtham, J. Sogaard, F. Andersson, and B. Jonsson, 'An Econometric Analysis of Health Care Expenditure: A Cross-Section Study of OECD Countries', *Journal of Health Economics*, May 1992, and OECD, 'Health Care Reform: Controlling Spending and Increasing Efficiency' (Working Paper No. 149), OECD, Paris 1994, Annex).

3   The average weekly industrial wage in Ireland in December 2003 was €558.69 (CSO, *Industrial Earnings and Hours Worked*, Stationery Office, Dublin 2004).

4   See CSO, *Quarterly National Household Survey: Health* (Third Quarter 2001), Stationery Office, Dublin 2002, Table 1.

5   L. Kurunmaki, 'The Irish Health Care System: Cost Containment Measures during the 1980s and 1990s' (LSE Health Discussion Paper No. 11), LSE, London 1999.

6   K. Arrow, 'Uncertainty and the Welfare Economics of Medical Care', *American Economic Review*, December 1963.

7   J. Barry, H. Sinclair, A. Kelly, R. O'Loughlin, D. Handy, and T. O'Dowd, *Inequalities in Health in Ireland – Hard Facts*, Department of Community Health and General Practice, Trinity College, Dublin 2001.

9   See A. Culyer, E. Van Doorslaer, and A. Wagstaff, 'Comment on Utilisation as a Measure of Equity', *Journal of Health Economics*, 1992.

9   E. Mossialos, A. Dixon, J. Figueras, and J. Kutzin (editors.), *Funding Health Care: Options for Europe*, Open University Press, Buckingham 2002.

10   A. Wagstaff, and E. Van Doorslaer, 'Equity in Health Care Finance and Delivery', in A Culyer, and J Newhouse (editors), *Handbook of Health Economics*, Volume 1B, Elsevier, Oxford 2000. The data upon which this study was based for Ireland relate to 1987. All individuals are now eligible for free public hospital services with non-medical cardholders paying a small daily charge (in 1987, approximately 15 per cent of the population, on high incomes, were ineligible for free public hospital services while the remainder received free public hospital services with no charge) and tax relief on health insurance premiums is now only available at the taxpayer's standard rate of tax (prior to 1996, tax relief was available at the taxpayer's marginal rate of tax).

11 Health Insurance Authority, *The Private Health Insurance Market in Ireland*, Health Insurance Authority, Dublin 2003.

12 While there is also a strong relationship between income and health status, a study using 1994 data showed that, even after controlling for income, the probability of having private health insurance was significantly lower for those in poor health. See C. Harmon and B. Nolan, 'Health Insurance and Health Services Utilization in Ireland', *Health Economics*, 2001, pp. 135-45.

13 See CSO, *Quarterly National Household Survey: Health* (Third Quarter 2001), Stationery Office, Dublin 2002, Tables 3, 4 and 5.

14 M. Wiley, 'Reform and Renewal of the Irish Health Care System: Policy and Practice' (Proceedings of ESRI/FFS Budget Perspectives Conference 2001), ESRI, Dublin 2001.

15 See OECD, 'Health Care Reform: Controlling Spending and Increasing Efficiency' (Working Papers No. 149), OECD, Paris 1994, Table 12.

16 World Health Organisation (WHO), *World Health Report 2000: Health Systems: Improving Performance*, WHO, Washington D.C. 2000, and for a critique of the choice of indicators, see Institute for Health Sector Development (IHSD), *Improving Health Systems by Measuring Health Status: Is WHO Serious?*, IHSD, London 2000.

17 B. Nolan, 'Affordability versus Quality, Effectiveness and Equity: Is there a Trade-Off?', in OECD, *Health Care Reform: The Will to Change*, OECD Health Policy Studies, OECD, Paris 1996.

18 *Ibid.*

19 OECD, *Health Data,* First Edition, OECD, Paris 2004.

20 Wiley, *op. cit.*

22 OECD, *Health Care Reform: Controlling Spending and Increasing Efficiency*, op. cit., p. 7.

22 Gerdtham *et al, op. cit.*

CHAPTER 11

Education: Market Failure and Government Interventions

*Carol Newman**

1 INTRODUCTION

The primary function of the education system is to equip individuals with the knowledge and skills necessary to participate in the economy at both an economic and social level. An educated labour force will produce more efficiently leading to faster economic growth; access to a quality education system enhances economic opportunities; and an educated population will be more politically aware and personally fulfilled. However, as discussed in Chapter 2, the market often fails to optimally provide certain goods and services equally to all. Education is one such non-market service, like health (discussed in Chapter 10), that requires some form of government intervention in order to be optimally provided. As with any good or service characterised by market failure the role of government is to ensure that its provision occurs in an efficient and equitable way. The government may achieve this either through the direct provision of the service or the regulation of some aspects of its provision.

Education is an important component of any economy not only in terms of the extent to which the government is involved in the sector and the interesting policy issues that this raises, but also in terms of the numbers of people directly involved in education, both those employed in providing the service and those attending full-time education. In Ireland, education is largely publicly provided with a small private component. In 2002 education accounted for 13.8 per cent of total public sector expenditure and in the first quarter of 2004 contributed 6.5 per cent to total employment.

There are three layers to the Irish education system: primary, second level and third level or the tertiary sector. The responsibility for the government's role in the provision of education at primary and second level rests with the Department of Education and Science, while the Higher Education Authority (HEA), an independent statutory body, largely manages provision at third level. In 2001/2002 there were 3,282 primary schools and 750 second level schools aided by the

Department and 34 third level institutions including seven Universities and fourteen Institutes of Technology (ITs). In total there were just over 900,000 students enrolled in full-time education, 23 per cent of the total population. As illustrated in Figure 11.1, while the total number of students at primary level has declined since the early 1990s due to the changing demographic profile of the population (see Chapter 4), the total number at second level has remained relatively stable illustrating the increase in numbers staying on in school at this level. In addition, overall participation in the tertiary sector has increased over the last decade as a result of various government initiatives over the 1990s aimed at increasing third level participation.

Figure 11.1
Numbers Enrolled in Full-time Education by Level in Ireland, 1990 to 2002

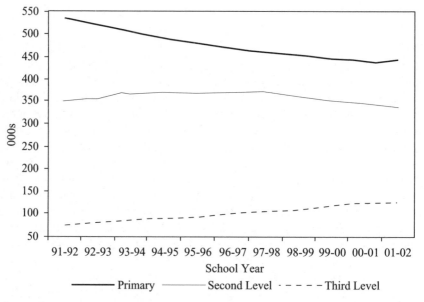

Source: Department of Education and Science, *Key Education Statistics 1991/92-2001/02,* Stationery Office, Dublin 2003.

The aim of this chapter is to present an analysis of the role and performance of the Irish government in delivering an efficient and equitable education service and to outline some of the interesting economic policy issues relating to its provision. In Section 2 the economic justifications for government intervention in the provision of education are outlined. Section 3 examines government educational policy in an Irish context focussing on recent policies aimed at promoting growth, through various education initiatives, and equity, both within the system and as an end goal in the wider distributional context. Before concluding, Section 4 examines the effectiveness of government in delivering an efficient and equitable education service covering issues relating to the efficiency of the system in an Irish context and relative to other OECD countries, the allocation of funds across different levels of education, the individual returns to education and the extent to which inequities exist within the system.

2 RATIONALE FOR STATE INTERVENTION

A minimal level of education is essential for the normal functioning of a market economy. In the absence of an education system citizens will lack the basic skills necessary to participate in the economy: for example, an illiterate individual may be unable to follow basic rules and regulations imposed by government such as reading road signals. A properly functioning education system performs an important social engineering function by facilitating the transfer of common values and morals in the absence of which anarchy may result. For these most basic reasons, government intervention in the provision of basic education services is justified. In most developed economies the government requires that all individuals remain in education up to some minimum age: in Ireland education is compulsory up to the age of 16. As such, the state plays a very direct role in the provision and funding of compulsory education.

In this section, the extent to which the government has a necessary role in the provision of education beyond this basic level is examined. Government intervention in any market can be justified where the market fails to optimally provide the good or service (see Chapter 2). In this section, the extent to which the market may fail to provide education is explored and the arguments for state involvement set out. These arguments differ depending on the level of education, a factor also considered here.

Private vs. Social Return
Education is an investment in human capital yielding both private and social returns. The decision to invest in human capital accumulation, like any other investment, will depend on the investor's evaluation of the expected present value of the stream of costs and benefits flowing from that investment. At an aggregate level, the government, in making a decision on whether and how much to invest in the education system, will weigh up the cost of the investment (including the actual cash outlay, the opportunity cost of people not contributing to production while in full-time education and any efficiency losses associated with the financing of education through the tax system) with the aggregate returns to the economy of having a well educated workforce (such as the extent to which it will contribute to the more productive use of resources, higher levels of output and faster economic growth). Other social returns might also be considered such as greater equality in terms of opportunities, social inclusion and improved cultural and political participation. A firm making a decision to invest in training courses to improve the human capital of its workers will undertake the investment if the

present value of the expected future returns to that investment, in the form of higher productivity and reduced costs, is greater than the cost of the investment. Of course, in the firm's case the possibility that this investment may lead to its employees demanding higher wages or being headhunted by competitors must also be factored into this evaluation. An individual's decision to invest in personal human capital, such as a third level degree for example, will involve a comparison of the costs such as tuition fees, books, and foregone earnings and the personal benefits accruing from that investment such as greater employability, higher earnings, greater job satisfaction and social inclusion.

However, investment in education confers *positive externalities* on the rest of society that will not be taken into account by individuals or firms. These can take the form of productivity improvements which will contribute to economic growth above and beyond those for which an individual/firm is remunerated through higher wages/profits; improvements in the quality of services, for example, the health or legal professions; or other social benefits such as reduced crime rates, increased political participation and a healthy democratic system. By ignoring these social returns individuals and firms will underinvest in education and training (i.e. education will be provided below the socially optimal level), thus providing justification for government involvement in its provision. Of course it could also be argued that education confers some negative effects on society through the creation of divides between different social classes but it is unlikely that these will outweigh the positive external effects.

Empirical Evidence

Theoretically the decision for an individual, firm or government to invest in the education system appears quite straightforward. However, in reality an exercise like this is severely hampered by the difficulties faced in quantifying the returns to education. At an aggregate level it is well documented that the accumulation of human capital plays a key role in the growth process (see Chapter 5). Human capital can be considered an input into the production process and its accumulation will lead to faster growth rates and ultimately convergence to some steady-state level of output growth. Others have postulated that human capital accumulation contributes even more to growth in the way it facilitates the development and diffusion of new technologies. The OECD estimates that public and private expenditure on educational institutions amounts to about $1,300 billion dollars per annum, 6 per cent of the collective GDP of OECD member states. In actual fact, it is likely that this figure understates the extent of this investment as it does not take into account earnings foregone by individuals engaged in full-time education. With such a substantial outlay involved the importance of understanding and attaining some quantification of the returns to this investment is obvious. Recent studies by the OECD have found empirical evidence of the positive link between human capital accumulation and output growth.[1] In Ireland's case human capital accumulation is often cited as being one of the most important contributing factors to Irish economic growth in the 1990s (see also Chapter 5). The OECD estimates that human capital accumulation accounted for more than half a percentage point acceleration in growth in Ireland in the 1990s. The extent to which government involvement in the provision of education is justified on these grounds depends on whether these returns are in excess of those privately yielded by the individuals and firms engaged in human capital accumulation. However, the social returns to education have rarely been incorporated into empirical studies of this kind.

An alternative approach has been to analyse the returns to education at a more microeconomic level. An extensive literature exists on quantifying the private individual returns to education and the contribution of educational attainment to productivity. While findings suggest that education leads to higher private returns in the form of higher wages, the link between educational attainment and productivity has been more difficult to quantify.

An alternative view to the human capital view is the screening theory of education. This theory suggests that there is no link between individual educational attainment and productivity improvements but that the only purpose of education is to serve as a signalling device to employers as to who the most productive employees are likely to be. This argument is based on the observation that those with the greatest ability, which is determined by unobservable factors such as family background, opportunities, access to quality schools etc., are more likely to be educated and more likely to be productive. Employers will opt to recruit and pay higher salaries to well educated individuals who through attaining an education have signalled their productive ability.

From an empirical point of view, no consensus has been reached on the link between educational attainment and productivity. In any case, where there are private returns to education, be they a reward for productivity improvements or otherwise (for example, personal fulfilment or satisfaction), the investment should be undertaken by the individual themselves with no justification for government intervention on these grounds. In particular, the private returns to education are higher for third level compared with compulsory education making government involvement in the former more difficult to justify in the absence of some quantification of a social return to the investment. As established earlier, the social returns to a minimal level of education are very significant with the economy left unable to function in its absence. However, the extent and scale of the social returns to third level education remains unresolved.[2] If they exist and are significant then some government involvement may be justified.

Much less documented but equally significant is establishing the extent to which investment in ongoing training and education by firms or individuals yields benefits to society in excess of those that firms are rewarded for in terms of productivity improvements, lower costs and higher profits or individuals are rewarded for in terms of higher earnings or better employment prospects. For example, continuous education and training (CET) will prevent skills shortages, create a more adaptable labour force with greater innovative ability and make the economy more attractive to outside investors all of which will facilitate economic growth. In addition, CET may create a happier more personally fulfilled society. The OECD have acknowledged that improving the skills of the workforce on an ongoing basis (an area where the Nordic countries perform particularly well) will be important for economic growth by facilitating the development of an adaptable and flexible labour force (see Chapter 4).[3] They find a positive link between CET and workers' performance in terms of productivity, employment opportunities and earnings. In addition to these private returns they acknowledge the existence of social returns to CET justifying a role for state involvement in promoting lifelong learning activities (see Section 3).

Overall, studies of the kind outlined in this section do not take into account the additional positive welfare effects associated with education, such as a healthier population, reduced crime, a healthy democratic system and higher levels of political participation, which can lead to an underestimation of the returns to human capital accumulation from a societal welfare point of view. As such, education is, and will remain, an important aspect of government economic policy.

Other Market Failures

In addition to justifying state involvement in the provision of education on the grounds that the social rate of return exceeds the private rate of return, other market failures may prevent education from being optimally provided in the absence of government intervention. This is particularly the case for non-compulsory education for which further discussion of the rationale for state involvement is warranted.

Credit Market Failure

Education would be, for the most part, unaffordable if privately provided and most people would rely on credit markets to finance their schooling. Credit markets will fail to operate efficiently in this environment for two reasons. First, most students applying for loans to pay for their studies will lack collateral of any kind to guarantee the loan, and second, the benefits of education will vary substantially across individuals with no guarantee of success and hence no guarantee that the student will be able to repay the loan in the future. In the absence of collateral and a means of repayment, banks will be unwilling to finance individuals to pay for private education. This failure of credit markets to finance private education warrants government intervention in the provision of education services, especially at third level: government involvement usually comes in the form of direct financial assistance to students (for example, free tuition fees, government guaranteed loan schemes etc.).

Imperfect Information

Aside from credit market failure, the provision of education itself is characterised by imperfect information at many different levels resulting in sub-optimal outcomes in the absence of government intervention. First, it can be argued that individuals do not have full information on the merits of schooling and will underinvest in education in a free market. Furthermore, the extent of this knowledge gap may be unevenly distributed across the population, depending on factors like social class and family background, exacerbating the problem. To overcome this, the government can provide incentives to encourage individuals to participate in education, particularly beyond the compulsory level of schooling (for example, maintenance grants for those participating in third level education who qualify).

Second, individuals lack information regarding the quality of the education service being provided. If operating in a private market setting, the fee charged, as in any other market, would provide some indication of quality. In the case of primary and second level education where parents can afford to pay fees for their children to attend private schools, market forces will operate in the standard way with higher fees signalling better quality institutions. However, in most cases parents cannot afford to pay for their children to receive a private education and so the choice of school becomes limited to that which is available in the local vicinity. In the absence of government intervention to ensure certain quality standards are met there will be no incentive for schools to deliver an efficient service. It is difficult to justify the extension of this argument to third level institutions where students can live away from home or even travel abroad to study and so competition among third level institutions to attract students can ensure that quality standards are met. With more choice the role of government is to ensure that all students have equal access to the system (discussed later), are informed of the options that are available to them and that this information is transparent, accurate and readily available.

An alternative to the regulation of quality standards is to allow schools to be privately run and for the government to regulate the credit markets used to finance education. One possibility is for the government to grant vouchers to all individuals which they can spend as they please, allowing them to choose schools which suit their preferences and meet their standards. A second possibility is for the government to guarantee loans to students which they must repay once their studies have been completed. Of course, this can lead to similar problems to those outlined at the start of this section as there is no guarantee that students will be in a position to repay these loans at a later stage. Many OECD countries operate publicly secured student loans to finance tuition fees or living costs associated with third level education. In fact, in Australia, Iceland, New Zealand, Norway and Sweden student loans amount to 0.2 per cent of GDP or more.[4] A similar Graduate Contribution Scheme is currently being proposed for the UK and if implemented will take effect in 2006. The OECD has recently made similar recommendations for funding third level education in Ireland. This issue will be returned to in Section 4.

Equity

Government intervention in the provision of education is also justified on equity grounds. As argued earlier, education is a key determinant of earnings and employment prospects. As such, education plays an important role in determining not only the level of income in society but also the distribution of that income. A key role for government is therefore to promote *equality of opportunity* by attempting to ensure equal access to education for all of its citizens. The Irish government attempts to achieve this through various policy initiatives discussed in Section 3 below such as free compulsory education up to a certain age and free fees in third level institutions. The government also attempts to ensure that discrimination on gender, race, ethnic, disability or any other grounds does not take place within the education system by ensuring equal access to all groups in society.

However, since individuals' *a priori* educational prospects and, as already highlighted, information on the merits of education are unevenly distributed across the population, it is more likely that specific socioeconomic groups, usually those at the lower end of the income distribution, will underachieve in relation to educational attainment. Therefore, on *horizontal equity* grounds it is justified for the government to target education expenditure and programmes at potentially educationally disadvantaged socioeconomic groups. In fact, this is also justifiable on efficiency grounds if the extent of the information problems outlined above are greater among these groups, justifying targeted higher levels of expenditure. Intervention on these grounds will also satisfy the principle of *vertical equity*. Since education determines future earnings, by redistributing tax revenues to poorer socioeconomic groups in the form of education investments a more equal outcome will result once the returns to these investments have been realised.

3 EDUCATION POLICY IN IRELAND

Irish education policy was slower to evolve than many other OECD countries. The most significant development in Irish education policy took place in 1967 with the introduction of free second level education for all. Since the 1960s, education expenditure as a percentage of national income has doubled and since the early 1990s, the Irish government has recognised the importance of education for economic, social and cultural development demonstrating a real commitment to investment in education and training.

Education policy in Ireland can be divided into two strands, each of which attempt to achieve different objectives for the economy. On the one hand, education policy aims to facilitate the accumulation of human capital in the economy with the aim of fuelling economic growth. On the other hand, education policy aims to aid the government's policy objective of equity by ensuring equal access to, and opportunities within, the system. The OECD has clearly identified the role of education policy in fulfilling these objectives. The OECD's current mandate for education and skills is 'making learning a reality for all' while at the same time promoting educational equity. In fact, many of the developments in education policy over the last decade have been motivated by OECD reviews and findings. In addition, there is much cooperation at an EU level in the development of education and training policies, for example by offering opportunities to learn abroad through various exchange programmes, developing networks of academic excellence and expertise etc.[5] In this section the focus is on specific Irish policy initiatives but the fact that most are motivated by recommendations made at higher levels of governance should be borne in mind.

Policies Aimed at Promoting Economic Growth

The main role of education is to produce a well educated workforce that can meet the demands of an expanding economy. A more skilled and productive labour force will produce more output, facilitate the development and diffusion of new technologies further fuelling growth, and will make the economy a more attractive place to invest, particularly if the skills of the labour force match labour demand. The OECD recognises the particular prevalence of this role for education with the acknowledgement that modern day economies are both 'knowledge based' and 'knowledge driven' where the ability to innovate is the key to successful economic development.

Acknowledging the fact that a well educated and skilled labour force is a key determinant of competitiveness, in 1997 the Irish government established an Expert Group on Future Skills Needs to assist in the development of national strategies to tackle the issue. In October 2003 the Expert Group produced its fourth report amid serious concerns about slowing growth of the Irish economy and an erosion of Ireland's competitive position. The key challenge facing the Irish economy over the coming years is to maintain competitiveness by improving labour productivity and minimising unemployment. In addition, they recognise that this can only be achieved through the development of a labour force that can support high value, knowledge based industries such as the ICT sector, the biotechnology sector, engineering, the construction industry, the food processing sector, the logistics sector and the financial services sector. This can be achieved by increasing the proportion of highly skilled workers in the labour force through initiatives aimed at upskilling, reskilling, improving the quality of vocational systems, increasing the proportion of third level science and engineering graduates, improving the take up of further education for disadvantaged groups and establishing a more targeted immigration policy.[6] One such strategy, resulting from OECD recommendations, was the acknowledgement of the role adult education can play in this regard as set out in a government White Paper on Adult Education issued in 2000 marking 'lifelong learning' as the underlying principle of educational policy. Policies aimed at achieving these goals are implemented at all levels of the education system.

Initiatives at Primary and Second Level

The decline in the number of students pursuing scientific subjects at second level in the 1990s sparked concern about the ability of the Irish labour force to meet its future skills needs. In 2001 only 12 per cent of Leaving Certificate students were enrolled in chemistry and 16 per cent in physics compared with 16 per cent and 20 per cent respectively in 1990.[7] In addition, there is a gender bias in the take up of these subjects with males much more likely to pursue physical science subjects than females. The problem is exacerbated by the fact that the demographic structure of the Irish economy is changing with the overall school going population in decline (see Figure 11.1 for the decline in the numbers attending primary level schooling over the last decade). Given the current and future importance of scientific and technically focussed jobs in knowledge based industries in the Irish labour market, if these trends continue they will have serious implications for Ireland's future economic development. The declining numbers taking part in the physical sciences at second level will inevitably follow through to lower third level participation in these fields, resulting in fewer graduates skilled in these areas.

In response to this growing concern the Department of Education and Science established a Task Force on the Physical Sciences to explore the problem and offer potential solutions. The Task Force found that the problem is both real and significant and set out a six point action strategy to address the situation at all levels of the Irish education system covering areas such as equity of access (see below), the reform of the school curriculum and modes of assessment, the promotion of science in career development and science education at third level (see below).

Recognising the need to facilitate the matching of skills to the needs of the labour force, in 2000 the OECD conducted a review, endorsed by the Education Committee and the Employment, Labour and Social Affairs Committee, assessing the role of career information, guidance and counselling services in integrating choices made within the education system and labour market prospects of graduates. While this report found that Ireland has a well developed career guidance service, actions such as developing a better balance of services within schools, better coordination across different agencies offering career guidance information, better development of skills and qualifications of those providing the guidance and integrating career guidance into the lifelong learning framework by providing for better access to services both within the education system and the labour force, were recommended.[8]

Initiatives at Third Level
Higher education in particular plays a crucial role in developing and sustaining an advanced society. The HEA in its Strategy Statement 2004-2007 identifies the vital role that the higher education sector has to play not only in educating and training the labour force required for the development and expansion of knowledge based industry, but also in being the central resource for research, development and innovation. The 2001 report of the Expert Group on Future Skills Needs further highlighted the need for Ireland to attract and retain researchers recommending the need for the higher education system to achieve

substantial increases in the output of doctorates particularly in science, engineering and technology, to facilitate undergraduate students to progress into postgraduate research and to attract international researchers to Ireland.

The ability of the higher education system to perform this role depends on its ability to engage in quality research. The Irish research environment has changed significantly in recent years as a result of a number of key developments in the provision of funding for third level research. The most significant development was the establishment of Science Foundation Ireland (SFI) in 2000. The role of SFI is to support research in strategic areas that advance the country's technological and economic success and reputation. By doing so the aim of SFI is to 'enhance Irish science, engineering and economic growth and bring Ireland distinction for its sustained research excellence'.[9] In addition to this, in 1998 the Programme for Research in Third level Institutions (PRTLI) provided a new general source of research funding and in 1999 and 2001, respectively, the Irish Research Council for Humanities and Social Sciences and the Irish Research Council for Science, Engineering and Technology were established providing new and significant sources of funding for individual researchers and research projects in these fields. The HEA in its most recent report recognises the need to sustain the current level of investment in research infrastructure in Ireland along with other measures aimed at improving the career structure of professional researchers, attracting overseas researchers and assuring that the quality of research training is sustained.[10] Incorporating developments of this kind into educational policy will be crucial in assuring the Irish economy is adequately equipped to compete in a more knowledge-based global economy.

In 2004 the Irish Minister for Education and Science invited the OECD to carry out a review of higher education in Ireland to evaluate the extent to which the Irish higher education system is achieving its strategic objectives of placing itself in the top rank of the OECD in terms of quality and levels of participation, and the wider EU objective of becoming the world's most competitive and dynamic knowledge based economy and society. The Review found that the Irish third level education system compares well to other OECD countries (see Section 4) but there is a need for higher levels of investment if Ireland is to meet these objectives in the future. The Review Report also called for significant structural changes in areas like the strategic management of research and innovation, the management of third level institutions and issues relating to access and participation, among others. However, the Review acknowledges the fact that state funding alone will not be sufficient and recommend that private contributions from students be considered. This issue is discussed further in Section 4.

Policies Aimed at Promoting Equity

While participation rates in education have increased significantly in Ireland over the last number of decades, up to the 1990s education policy in Ireland focussed on increasing the overall level of participation in education with little attempts to promote equity in access to the system. Inequalities in education can manifest themselves in two ways, either through inequalities in educational achievement or the level of education attainment across different groups. These inequities are not confined to educational divides on the basis of social class but could manifest themselves as inequities across ethnic divides, people with disabilities, gender or race.

With the introduction of free second level schooling in the 1960s and compulsory education up to the age of 16, participation in schooling is almost universal across all groups in society. However, the problem lies in the extent to which all individuals realise their true potential within the schooling system regardless of circumstances or social background. Increased levels of funding can go some way to alleviating these inequalities in the education system; however, targeting expenditure at the most vulnerable groups will be more effective. This has been recognised within Irish education policy since 1995 when the Irish government issued a White Paper on Education recognising the need to design education policies to directly combat educational disadvantage. Subsequently, in 1998, the Education Act defined educational disadvantage as the 'impediments to education arising from social or economic disadvantage which prevent students from deriving appropriate benefit from education in schools'. The Act provided for the establishment of an Educational Disadvantage Committee to advise the Minister for Education on policy issues specifically relating to targeting disadvantage within the education system. In addition, combating educational disadvantage is incorporated into the government's National Anti-Poverty Strategy which includes as an overall objective the need to ensure that those living in poverty can participate in and benefit from education in a way that will allow them move out of poverty and prevent others from becoming poor.

Other inequities are also covered by government policy. In June 2001, the Gender Equality Unit was established in the Department of Education and Science under the Equal Opportunities Promotion and Monitoring measure of the National Development Plan. This unit aims to ensure that 'the Department of Education and Science is enabled to integrate a gender dimension into all its services, actions, programmes and measures for children and adults at all levels'. In addition, more recently the Educational Disadvantage Committee have proposed developing a Traveller Education Strategy aimed at ensuring equality of outcomes from education for members of the Travelling community.

Initiatives at Primary and Second Level
Specific policy initiatives aimed at promoting equity within the education system have largely targeted compulsory education since the main determinants of post-compulsory educational achievement are educational background and the foundations laid at an early stage of educational development. Two types of policy initiatives have been introduced via the Educational Disadvantage Committee to tackle the inequities apparent in both access and achievement within the Irish education system. First, the school curriculum has been reformed offering alternative less academic educational routes allowing less academically

minded students the opportunity to attain a successful education in areas better suited to them, for example, the Junior Certificate School Programme, the Leaving Certificate Applied Programme and the Leaving Certificate Vocational Programme. Second, expenditure has been targeted at disadvantaged schools or communities focussing on school inclusion and promoting achievement in education. Such initiatives include, among others, 'Breaking the Cycle', 'Early Start' programmes and the 'Home School Community Liaison Scheme'.[11] In addition, the government specifically allocates resources to pupils with special educational needs in primary schools. More recently, the contribution that adult education can make to tackling education disadvantage has also been highlighted.

Initiatives at Third Level
By far the most significant development in higher education policy aimed at promoting equality of access to third level education was the introduction of free tuition fees for full-time, third level undergraduate EU students in 1996. Over the last number of years the increase in the number of places at third level institutions has also served to improve access to third level education. The government also provides specific financial incentives to individuals participating in third level education such as the Higher Education Grants Scheme and The Vocational Education Committee's Scholarship Scheme (which provide maintenance grants on a means tested basis), special rates of maintenance grant for disadvantaged students, funds for students with disabilities etc.[12] In addition, third level institutions themselves operate programmes to encourage participation by all groups in society (for example, the Trinity Access Programme which facilitates access for students from disadvantaged backgrounds or the presence of disabilities offices to ensure equal treatment of students with disabilities).

The promotion of equal opportunities in third level falls under the remit of the HEA. The HEA recognises the promotion of social inclusion as a key national policy objective. In a recent submission to the OECD they stated in particular that expanding opportunities in higher education to promote lifelong learning will play an important role in future government policy. In May 2003, a report to government on supporting equity in higher education called for further policy reforms in this regard including increases in the level and coverage of maintenance grants, an extension of the income threshold at which students are required to pay service charges, and specific changes to student supports for repeat year students, part time students, mature students and those in receipt of 'special' maintenance grants. They also called for a review of means testing procedures, the administration of student supports and the free fees initiatives amidst a gradual move internationally away from a reliance on taxpayers to fund third level participation toward an increasing role for parents and students in this regard. The importance of these proposed reforms is further strengthened by the recommendation made by the OECD Education Committee in their review of higher education in Ireland in 2004 calling for private contributions from students for third level education coupled with a significant reform of the means-tested and special needs grant systems. This issue is discussed further in Section 4.

4 DELIVERY OF EDUCATION SERVICES

Having provided an outline of the specific objectives of various educational policy initiatives in Ireland over the last decade, in this section the effectiveness of government in its delivery of education services is evaluated. Evaluating the performance of government in the provision of a service like education is complicated by the fact that many of the returns to education are intangible. This makes traditional cost benefit analysis very difficult as often the benefits are impossible to quantify. Instead, government involvement in the sector can be evaluated in relation to its delivery of an efficient and equitable service.

From an efficiency point of view the government will attempt to achieve both productive efficiency, in terms of achieving value for money and efficient outcomes, and allocative efficiency, in terms of allocating funding efficiently across different levels of education. The education system in Ireland is therefore first evaluated at an aggregate level in terms of its overall contribution to the economy and how this performance relates to other OECD countries to determine how productively efficient the government is in its delivery of the service. Following this the allocation of funding across different levels of education is outlined and critiqued to establish the extent to which the Irish government achieves allocative efficiency. In addition, it is also important to identify the individual returns to education, to establish the extent to which incentives to invest in further education are realised. Finally, from an equity point of view, the extent to which the system offers equal opportunities or improves the distribution of income by leading to more equal outcomes is examined.

Productive Efficiency: Delivering a Quality Education Service
Public Expenditure on Education
Table 11.1 presents statistics on the proportion of education expenditure in GDP (GNP for Ireland), both public and private, for a selection of OECD countries in 1995 and 2000. In 2000, public expenditure on education as a percentage of GNP in Ireland was 5.7 per cent down from 5.9 per cent in 1995. A decline was also experienced in most other countries presented with the exception of Denmark where there was a slight increase.

With a declining birth rate and a reduction in the proportion of the population of school going age the demand for education expenditure will fall over time. As a result, across most OECD countries a stabilisation or even a fall in spending on education is expected. Also illustrated in Table 11.1 is the relatively small level of private expenditure on educational institutions. The proportion of private expenditure in total expenditure on education remained quite stable over time with only the Netherlands experiencing a significant increase (from 3.8 per cent to 7.7

per cent). In 2000, this proportion is highest for the USA, Germany and the UK at 30.5, 18.2 and 12.7 per cent respectively, while for Ireland it is much lower at 8.8 per cent, but high in comparison with some of the other countries presented (for example Finland or France).

Table 11.1
Expenditure on Education as a Percentage of GDP, 1995 and 2000

	1995			2000		
	Public	Private	Total	Public	Private	Total
Austria[1]	6.2	0.3	6.5	5.8	0.3	6.1
Denmark[1]	7.4	0.2	7.6	8.4	0.3	8.7
Finland	7.0	n/a	7.0	6.0	0.1	6.1
France	6.0	0.4	6.4	5.8	0.4	6.2
Germany	4.6	1.0	5.6	4.5	1.0	5.5
Ireland [2]	*5.4*	*0.5*	*5.9*	*5.2*	*0.5*	*5.7*
Netherlands	5.0	0.2	5.2	4.8	0.4	5.2
UK	5.1	0.9	6.0	4.8	0.7	5.5
USA	n/a	n/a	n/a	5.0	2.2	7.2

Source: OECD, *Education at a Glance, OECD Indicators 2003*, OECD, Paris 2003.
Note: Public expenditure includes public expenditure on educational institutions plus public subsidies to households. Private expenditure includes expenditure on educational institutions from private sources. 'n/a' indicates that data are not available.
[1]For Austria and Denmark, public subsidies to households are not included in public expenditure but in private expenditure.
[2]Education expenditure in Ireland is expressed as a percentage of GNP due to the large divergence in GDP and GNP in Ireland (see Chapter 2).

Education expenditure in Ireland in 2002 accounted for 13.8 per cent of total government expenditure, up from 12.2 per cent in 1995 and makes up a greater proportion of total government expenditure in Ireland compared with many other OECD countries. In Table 11.2 the level of expenditure on educational institutions by student for Ireland and a selection of OECD countries is presented for 2000. In all countries spending per student increases across education level with the highest spending per student at third level. In Ireland, spending per student is lower than in all of the other countries for both primary and second level at $3,385 and $4,638 respectively, and higher than all but three of the countries presented for tertiary education at $11,083. These figures suggest that while Ireland spends more on education in terms of its proportion of total government expenditure it spends less per unit when compared with other countries, particularly for compulsory education.

It is difficult to draw conclusions on the performance of the sector on the basis of the level of government expenditure alone as higher levels of government expenditure do not automatically imply a higher quality service. This is particularly the case for Ireland with a large proportion of the education budget swallowed up by inflationary cost increases. In particular, since education is such a labour intensive service the majority of the budget is absorbed by salaries and wages. In Ireland, in 2002 salaries and wages accounted for 69 per cent of total education expenditure and Irish teachers are some of the highest paid in the OECD ranking seventh after 10 years of experience.

Table 11.2
Expenditure on Educational Institutions per Student by Level of Education, 2000 (expressed in equivalent US dollars converted using PPPs)

	Primary level	Second level	Third level
Austria	6,560	8,578	10,851
Denmark	7,074	7,726	11,981
Finland	4,317	6.094	8,244
France	4,486	7,636	8,373
Germany	4,198	6,826	10,898
Ireland	*3,385*	*4,638*	*11,083*
Netherlands	4,325	5,912	11,934
UK	3,877	5,991	9,657
USA[1]	6,995	8,855	20,358

Source: As for Table 11.1.
Note: Figures include expenditure on both public and private institutions.
[1]Figures for the USA include expenditure on public and independent private institutions only.

Benchmarking Education Performance
Despite the fact that Ireland invests less in education compared with other OECD countries, investment levels have increased over time and there is evidence to suggest that Ireland has yielded significant returns to this investment. Given the importance of education to the economy's future prosperity, the European Commission has recognised the need for countries not only to understand how they are performing at a national level but also how they compare with other countries, particularly those that they may compete with for investment in high-value, knowledge-based sectors. The performance benchmarks agreed at an EU level are that by 2010; the percentage of early school leavers should not exceed 10 per cent, the percentage of 15 year olds with low achievement in reading literacy should have decreased by at least 20 per cent compared to their 2000 levels, the percentage of 22 year olds having completed upper secondary education should be no lower than 85 per cent, the total number of graduates in mathematics, science and technology should increase by at least 15 per cent, and the average level of participation in lifelong learning should be at least 12.5 per cent of the adult working-age population. The need to establish a process for benchmarking Ireland's performance in relation to these criteria has since been acknowledged by the Expert Group on Future Skills Needs. In July 2003 a report by the Group

evaluated Ireland's performance in each of these areas and made recommendations as to how policy should proceed in the future to achieve the targets set out by the EU. The following discussion draws on the results and recommendations presented in this report.[13]

Ireland performs well in relation to the first criterion with the proportion of early school leavers (15 to 19 year old age group) falling from 9.4 per cent of the population to 8.2 per cent of the population between 1996 and 2002. In terms of the second criterion, the OECD rank literacy levels of 15 year olds for Ireland and a range of other OECD countries on the basis of the OECD's PISA combined reading literacy scale.[14] Ireland ranks fifth in the OECD in terms of reading literacy, second in the EU-15 after Finland. Ireland does not perform so well in relation to numeracy for which it is ranked fifteenth in the OECD but performs better in relation to scientific literacy for which it is ranked ninth. In terms of low achievers on the reading literacy scale Ireland also performs well ranking fifth out of 27 developed countries.

The third criterion on which to benchmark Ireland's performance relates to the proportion of the young population that have attained at least upper second level education. As already discussed Ireland was late to make any substantial investments in the education sector compared with other OECD countries with free second level education only introduced in the 1960s. The extent and timing of this investment has had a significant impact on the education profile of the population. In Table 11.3 the proportion of the population with at least upper second level education for Ireland and a selection of OECD countries are presented for 2001. Ireland has the lowest proportion of its population with at least upper second level education of the countries presented at 58 per cent. This does not compare well to countries like Denmark, Germany and the USA where this proportion is over 80 per cent. In Ireland's case, this poor education performance is due to a low level of education attainment in the older age groups. There has been a marked improvement in education attainment over time with 73 per cent of the youngest age group (25-34) having at least an upper second level education. However, while this figure is comparable to some countries it is lower than most and lower than the EU's target of 80 per cent. A key issue for future policy is to increase retention and success rates at second level to ensure that the labour force is equipped with the necessary training to serve the future demand for skilled labour.

The fourth criterion calls for an increase in the number of science, mathematics and technology graduates at third level. Overall, third level participation rates have increased over the last decade from 74,449 students in 1991/92 to 124,589 students in 2001/02 (see Figure 11.1). This can be attributed to the broadening of college places and types of courses on offer. Of more significance, however, is the proportion of third level graduates by field of study. In Ireland's case, while the total number of students enrolled in science courses more than doubled between 1980 and 1998, the proportion of all students opting for science courses fell from 14 to 12 per cent.

Table 11.3

Population that has Attained at Least Upper Secondary Education
by Age Group, 2001

	25-64	25-34	35-44	45-54	55-64
Austria[1]	77	84	81	73	65
Denmark	80	86	80	80	72
Finland	74	87	84	70	51
France	64	78	67	58	46
Germany	83	85	86	83	76
Ireland	*58*	*73*	*62*	*48*	*35*
Netherlands[1]	65	75	69	61	50
UK	63	68	65	61	55
USA	88	88	89	89	83

Source: As for Table 11.1.
[1]For Austria and the Netherlands figures refer to 2000.

In technology courses, while the numbers enrolled increased from 3,364 to 8,497 between 1980 and 1998 the proportion of total students opting for technology courses only increased by one percentage point. This is a worrying trend given the importance of producing graduates in these fields for Ireland's future economic prosperity.

However, since these statistics relate to university courses only they may overestimate the extent of the problem given that ITs have played an important role in increasing the numbers participating in third level particularly in more vocational subject areas. In fact, the proportion of Irish graduates in the physical sciences was above the OECD average and at the average for mathematics and statistics in 2000.

In addition, in 2000 Ireland ranked first out of 11 of the EU-15 countries in terms of the proportion of graduates in science and technology per 1,000 inhabitants aged 20 to 29. Despite the fact that Ireland performs well in relation to science and technology graduates compared to other countries, the decline in the take up of science subjects at third level is a worrying trend that will need to be further addressed by government in the future.

The final criterion on which Ireland's performance in relation to education and training can be evaluated is in terms of the proportion of the working age population in lifelong learning. Ireland performs poorly in relation to this criterion with only 22 per cent of the adult population taking part in education and training, ranking thirteenth out of 15 OECD countries. However, there is some evidence to suggest an increase in the number of adults engaged in third level education on the basis of a substantial increase in the number of students in part-time third level courses between 1995 and 2001. Nevertheless, the government's (2000) White Paper on Adult Education (see Section 3) is a step toward encouraging participation in lifelong learning, which will be crucial in enhancing the skills of the Irish labour force into the future.

Allocative Efficiency: Distribution of Funds Across Levels

A further issue in evaluating the performance of government in delivering an efficient education service is determining the extent to which the government efficiently allocates funds across different levels of the education system. Most of the developments in education policy over the last decade have been funded under the National Development Plan which aims to increase employability, encourage entrepreneurship and promote equal opportunities.

As illustrated in Table 11.4, the proportion of total education spending in Ireland is greatest for primary level and second level compared with third level education even though education spending per student is highest in the tertiary sector (see Table 11.2). Aside from Denmark and Finland, Ireland spends a greater proportion of its education budget on third level compared with the other countries presented. Furthermore, the proportion of total expenditure allocated to third level increased between 1992 and 2002 with a corresponding decline in the proportion allocated to primary level (see Figure 11.2).

Table 11.4

Proportion of Public Expenditure on Education by Level of Education, 2000

	Primary, secondary and post-secondary non-tertiary	Tertiary
Austria	72.5	27.5
Denmark	65.8	34.2
Finland	63.9	36.1
France	79.9	20.1
Germany	73.3	26.7
Ireland	*69.3*	*30.7*
Netherlands	71.0	29.0
UK	76.9	23.1
USA	75.7	24.3

Source: As for Table 11.1.

[1]For Denmark, post-secondary non-tertiary is included in tertiary education and excluded from primary, secondary and post-secondary non-tertiary education.

[2]For the USA, post-secondary non-tertiary is included in both tertiary education and primary, secondary and post-secondary non-tertiary education.

Allocation of Funds at Primary and Second Level

The government adopts a centralised approach to allocating resources to primary level and second level schools with some variation across different types of schools such as vocational, community and comprehensive schools. Private feepaying schools are only allocated resources to cover teachers' salaries. Of greater significance at this level of education is the allocation of teachers to schools. This is largely decided on the basis of student enrolment. There may also be a number of ex-quota posts, such as guidance teachers, deputy principals or home-school liaison officers allocated on the basis of school size or need (for example, if the school is located in a disadvantaged area they may qualify for more ex-quota posts). In some cases there may also be larger student-teacher ratios linked to certain programmes aimed at tackling disadvantage. Overall, student-teacher ratios have been reduced at both primary level and second level over the 1990s.

Figure 11.2
Allocation of Expenditure Across Levels of Education in Ireland, 1995 to 2002

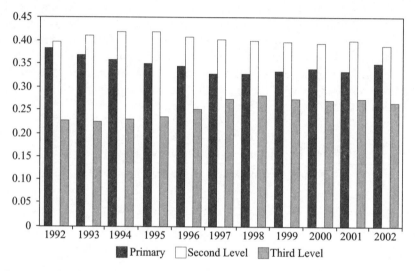

Source: As for Figure 11.1.

The most significant component of government expenditure on education at this level is wages and salaries. Capital expenditure also makes up a large proportion of the education spend at both primary level and second level at 11 and 9 per cent respectively in 2002. In addition to the allocation of resources to schools, some resources are allocated directly to students for primary level and second level education such as book grants, free school meals, 'Back to School Clothing Allowances' etc. However, these types of individual transfers play a much more significant role in the third level sector in the form of maintenance grants to third level students (discussed below).

Allocation of Funds at Third Level
The higher education system in Ireland is predominantly publicly funded. The HEA is responsible for the allocation of funding to universities and some other institutions while the Department of Education and Science is responsible for funding the ITs. In 2004 this responsibility will also be transferred to the HEA. As already mentioned, in 1996 free tuition fees were introduced for eligible full-time undergraduate EU students. These fees are paid to higher education

institutions by the state. Prior to the launch of the PRTLI (see above), state funding for research was low. This scheme is managed by the HEA and awards funding for research on a competitive basis across universities based on the quality and merit of the proposed research. Up to 2003, approximately €600 million had been allocated under the programme. Other capital funding is allocated on a case-by-case basis. In total, capital expenditure makes up a greater proportion of the overall budget compared with primary level and second level at 13 per cent. When all income is taken into account state funding as a percentage of total funding amounts to 80 per cent for universities and 90 percent for ITs.[15]

By far the most contentious issue in relation to the allocation of third level funding, and the topic for the remainder of this discussion, are government expenditure on student transfers, both in the form of tuition fees and maintenance grants, which form a significant component of tertiary sector state expenditure compared with primary level and second level education. Twelve per cent of total government expenditure allocated to third level funding is in the form of student supports. Consensus has not been reached on the extent to which the government should be involved in directly funding individuals to attend third level education, either through free fees initiatives, grant schemes or other types of direct subsidies to private individuals/households.

The private returns to third level education are significant in terms of higher earnings, higher labour force participation rates and lower unemployment risk (see below). In addition, statistics show a high correlation between third level participation and social class of parents. It is therefore difficult to justify the use of taxation income, collected from the general public, to finance individual participation in the accumulation of human capital which may yield significant private returns in the future. In addition, the effectiveness of such schemes is questionable. Alternative mechanisms such as offering state guaranteed student loans, voucher systems etc. have been explored by the HEA in the 2002/03 review of third level tuition fees and student supports. However, in July 2003 it was decided that there would be no changes made to the current system. The issue was again addressed by the OECD Education Committee in their 2004 review of higher education in Ireland. The Review Report recommended that some form of private contributions from third level students are necessary in order for the third level education sector to achieve the investment levels required for it to develop an internationally competitive tertiary sector. The extent to which these recommendations are taken on board by the Irish government remains to be seen.

Individual Returns to Education
As outlined in Section 2, the main motivation for individuals investing in education is to increase their human capital and therefore their earnings potential. The earnings return to education has been well documented in the Irish context with evidence not only suggesting a positive relationship between earnings and educational attainment but also suggesting that this earnings advantage increases with the length of time spent in the labour market.[16] Higher levels of education

are not only associated with higher earnings but also higher levels of labour force participation and lower unemployment risk. Table 11.5 presents these rates by gender for Ireland and a selection of OECD countries for 2001.

Table 11.5
Labour Force Participation Rates and Unemployment Rates by Level of Educational Attainment and Gender, 2001

		Below upper secondary		Upper secondary and post secondary non-tertiary		Tertiary	
		LF	UE	LF	UE	LF	UE
Austria	Males	70	7.2	84	2.9	91	1.4
	Females	49	5.7	69	3.3	84	1.8
Denmark	Males	75	4.0	87	2.7	94	3.4
	Females	57	6.2	79	4.0	89	3.1
Finland	Males	70	10.5	86	7.9	91	3.8
	Females	61	12.7	79	9.2	87	4.7
France	Males	76	9.7	88	5.1	92	4.2
	Females	57	14.4	76	9.3	85	5.3
Germany	Males	77	15.6	84	8.1	90	3.9
	Females	50	11.5	70	8.4	82	5.1
Ireland	*Males*	*79*	*5.5*	*93*	*2.3*	*95*	*1.5*
	Females	*40*	*5.1*	*64*	*2.8*	*80*	*1.7*
Netherlands	Males	77	2.5	89	1.1	90	0.4
	Females	47	3.5	73	2.3	83	1.7
UK	Males	67	9.4	88	4.1	93	2.4
	Females	51	5.7	77	3.7	86	1.8
USA	Males	75	7.5	86	4.2	91	2.2
	Females	52	8.9	73	3.4	81	2.2

Source: As for Table 11.1.
Note: Figures for Tertiary are taken as an unweighted average of Tertiary Type B education and Tertiary Type A education and Advanced Research Programmes as classified by the OECD. LF refers to Labour Force Participation Rate. UE refers to Unemployment Rate.

For all countries, labour force participation rates are higher and unemployment rates lower the higher the level of education attainment. Evidence from the ESRI's Living in Ireland Panel Survey supports these results highlighting the implications of a low level of education attainment on long-term labour market integration.[17] Equally across all countries participation rates are lower and unemployment rates higher for females compared with males at all levels of education, but particularly for those with lower than upper second level education. However, since no adjustment has been made for the fact that overall female labour force participation rates are lower than for males (see Chapter 4) it is difficult to ascertain the extent to which this difference can be attributed to gender differences in educational achievements and subsequent job prospects. Nevertheless, of particular note in the Irish case is that the participation rates of females with less than upper secondary education is one of the lowest of all countries presented while rates are comparable with other countries for the other education levels. Also of interest in the Irish case are the high participation rates of males with upper second level education or more compared with the other countries. Furthermore, unemployment rates for males with higher levels of educational attainment are among the lowest of all countries. However, the fact that Ireland was near full employment at this time must be taken into account before drawing conclusions about the extent to which investment in education determines labour force participation rates. Nevertheless, the evidence suggests that in the Irish case, like many other OECD countries, the individual returns to education are significant in terms of earnings, labour market participation and unemployment risk.

Equity

Since earnings are a key determinant of wellbeing, a lower probability of participating in the labour force, a higher probability of unemployment and lower average earnings of those with lower levels of education attainment, together imply that inequalities in educational opportunities will have serious implications for the distribution of income in the economy. This does not take into account the other negative welfare effects associated with education failure such as social exclusion or crime, for example, which exacerbate the need for government education policies which target such inequities.

Across countries, evidence suggests that those who fail to complete upper second level education are more likely to come from disadvantaged backgrounds.[18] For example, in France in the late 1990s 62 per cent of 15 year olds coming from the poorest two income deciles had to repeat at least one year in school compared with 17 per cent in the richest two deciles. In the US in 1999, over three quarters of high school dropouts came from below median income families while only 8 per cent came from the highest income quartile. In the UK in the late 1990s, young people from households headed by a professional and a managerial worker were twice as likely to remain in full-time education at the age of 18 compared with those headed by an unskilled manual worker. In an Irish context research has shown that those from working class and unemployed families are more likely to underperform in Junior and Leaving Certificate examinations relative to their initial ability compared with other social groups. In addition, participation in tertiary education is highly correlated with the educational attainment and social background of parents (see below) with those from unskilled, manual backgrounds less likely to stay on in full-time education compared with those from professional backgrounds.[19]

At primary level and second level government policy has focussed on the retention and achievement of students from disadvantaged backgrounds.[20] At primary level, between 1996 and 2002 the overall student-teacher ratio in national schools was reduced to 18.4 from 22.3 and the number of students enrolled in special needs programmes increased from 13,534 to 16,358. At second level, the proportion of students in the junior cycle taking part in the special Junior Certificate School Programme increased from 1,051 to 4,267. In addition, there were substantial increases in the number taking the Applied Leaving Certificate Programme (3,595 to 7,495) and the Vocational Leaving Certificate Programme (16,511 to 41,917). These figures highlight the extent to which government resources have been targeted at achieving equal access to primary level and second level education for all, particularly those from disadvantaged backgrounds. Between 1996 and 1999, the proportion of school leavers with no qualification level declined from 4.0 to 3.2 per cent. In addition, between 1997 and 1999 the proportion of school leavers in work increased from 41.1 per cent to 48.4 per cent. These figures provide some evidence of improvements in overall retention and achievement within the system.

Of more significance, however, is the extent to which this follows through to equality of access and achievement at third level. In May 2003, a report to the Minister for Education and Science on Supporting Equity in Higher Education provided an analysis of the extent to which equality of access at third level has improved in Ireland over the last number of years. Between 1980 and 1998, participation in third level education by students whose fathers are semi-skilled workers and unskilled workers increased from 9 per cent and 3 per cent to 23 and 21 per cent respectively. However, overall participation rates of this age cohort increased from 20 per cent to 44 per cent over this period. The majority of the increase was accounted for by increased participation by students whose fathers are in higher socioeconomic groupings. For example, participation rates of students whose fathers are higher professionals increased from 59 per cent to 97 percent. Similar increases in participation rates were observed for students whose fathers are employers and managers or farmers. Despite some evidence of an increase in participation rates by lower socioeconomic groups, they continue to be under represented at third level (bottom three groupings accounted for 20 per cent of all participants compared with 43 per cent by the top three groupings). In addition, students from higher socioeconomic backgrounds are highly represented in universities while students from lower socioeconomic backgrounds have higher representation in the non-university, third-level sector. Furthermore, the rate of non-completion in the non-university sector is more than twice that found in universities. These trends highlight the need for continued government efforts to promote equity at all levels of the education system.

5 CONCLUSION

Education plays a vitally important role in the economic, social and cultural development of all economies. Not only is education the key to economic development in the contribution it makes to enhancing the skill level, productivity and competitiveness of the economy, but it plays a vital role in determining the income level and social status of individuals and as such will directly impact on the distribution of income in an economy. Due to the failure of private markets to optimally provide education, the government has a crucial role to play in ensuring education services are provided in such a way as to optimally meet these objectives.

In an Irish context, educational policy attempts to ensure the delivery of an efficient and equitable service. Evidence suggests that Ireland performs well in achieving desired educational outcomes such as high achievement in terms of reading literacy, or high education participation and attainment rates (see Section 4). However, the government has a long way to go in its delivery of an equitable service which ensures that individuals from all groups in society realise their true potential within the system. However, the outcome of the government's bottom up approach to tackling educational disadvantage may not be realised for a number of years.

Looking to the future, educational policy will continue to focus on initiatives aimed at improving Ireland's competitiveness primarily through the promotion of lifelong learning and reform of the tertiary sector. Higher education is now an internationally traded service providing both teaching and research services nationally and internationally. In order for Irish higher education institutions to be in a position to compete internationally it is well recognised that change and reform is both necessary and inevitable. The 2004 OECD review of higher education in Ireland has called for significant changes to the structure, management and financing of Irish higher education institutions. A willingness to make these changes in a timely manner will be crucial to delivering on the national and EU objective of becoming the worlds most competitive and dynamic knowledge based economy and society.

Endnotes

* I would like to thank John O'Hagan for his helpful comments on an earlier draft of this chapter.

1 See OECD, 'Does Human Capital Matter for Growth in OECD Countries? Evidence from Pooled Mean-grouped Estimates' (Economics Department Working Papers No. 282), OECD, Paris 2002 (available at http://www.oecd.org), and OECD, 'Links Between Policy and Growth: Cross-country Evidence', *OECD Economic Outlook*, OECD, Paris 2000.

2 See OECD, 'Growth Effects of Education and Social Capital in the OECD Countries' (Economics Department Working Papers No. 263), OECD, Paris 2000 (available at http://www.oecd.org), for an overview of recent literature in this area.

3 OECD, *Improving Workers' Skills: Analytical Evidence and the Role of the Social Partners*, OECD, Paris 2003.

4 OECD, *OECD Economic Survey of the United Kingdom: Graduate Contributions for Higher Education*, OECD, Paris 2004.

5 See http://europa.eu.int for further details.

6 Expert Group on Future Skills Needs, *Responding to Ireland's Skills Need: The Fourth Report of the Expert Group on Future Skills Needs*, Forfás, Dublin 2003.

7 See Department of Education and Science, *Task Force on the Physical Sciences: Report and Recommendations*, Department of Education and Science, Dublin 2002.

8   See OECD, *Review of Career Guidance Policies: Ireland, Country Note*, OECD, Paris 2002.

9   Science Foundation Ireland, *Vision 2003-2007: People, Ideas and Partnerships for a Globally Competitive Irish Research System*, Science Foundation Ireland, Dublin 2003.

10 Higher Education Authority, *Creating Ireland's Innovation Society: The Next Strategic Step*, Higher Education Authority, Dublin 2003.

11 See http://www.education.ie for details of these programmes.

12 See http://www.education.ie for a full list of financial incentives available.

13 Expert Group on Future Skills Needs, *Benchmarking Education and Training for Economic Development*, Forfás, Dublin 2003.

14 See *ibid*.

15 See Higher Education Authority, *Financial Management in Irish Institutions of Higher Education*, Higher Education Authority, Dublin 2003, for more detail on the allocation of funding to third level institutions.

16 For examples, see A. Barrett, J. FitzGerald and A. Nolan, 'Earnings Inequality, Returns to Education and Immigration into Ireland', *Labour Economics*, ESRI, Dublin 2002, and OECD, 'Investment in Human Capital through Upper-secondary and Tertiary Education', *OECD Economic Studies*, OECD, Paris 2002.

17 See S. McCoy, and S. Smyth, 'Educational Expenditure: Implications for Equality', *Budget Perspectives 2004*, ESRI, Dublin 2004, for an overview of literature in this area.

18 Examples taken from: OECD, 'Investment in Human Capital through Upper-secondary and Tertiary Education', *OECD Economic Studies*, OECD, Paris 2002.

19 McCoy and Smyth, *op. cit.*

20 Statistics presented in this section are taken from The National Economic and Social Forum, *Early School Leavers,* Forum Report No. 24, National Economic and Social Forum, Dublin 2002, and The Department of Education and Science, *Statistical Report*, Stationery Office, Dublin, various years.

Subject Index